Joseph Pegale

Blacks in the New World
Edited by August Meier and John H. Bracey

hist ┌→ tragic story
     └→ unsung Heroes

what if → portukrem project make students an
"unung hero"
          my wown & google eg

A list of books in the series appears at the end of this volume.

Lynching in the New South

Lynching in the New South

Georgia and Virginia,

1880–1930

W. Fitzhugh Brundage

University of Illinois Press
Urbana and Chicago

Publication of this work is made possible in part by grants from the National
Endowment for the Humanities, an independent federal agency, and the
Department of History, Queen's University, Kingston, Ontario.

First paperback edition, 1993

Library of Congress Cataloging-in-Publication Data
Brundage, W. Fitzhugh (William Fitzhugh), 1959
    Lynching in the New South : Georgia and Virginia,
  1880–1930 / W. Fitzhugh Brundage.
      p.   cm. — (Blacks in the New World)
    Includes bibliographical references to (p.   ) and index.
    ISBN 0-252-01987-3 (cl : alk. paper). ISBN 0-252-06345-7 (pbk : alk. paper).
    ISBN 978-0-252-01987-6 (cl : alk. paper). ISBN 978-0-252-06345-9 (pbk : alk. paper).
    1. Lynching—Georgia—History. 2. Lynching—
  Virginia—History. 3. Georgia—Race relations.
  4. Virginia—Race relations. I. Title. II. Series.
  HV6465.G4B78 1993
  364.1'34—dc20   92-26034
                    CIP

*Dedicated to my mother
and the memory of my father.*

Contents

Acknowledgments

During the course of writing this book I have accumulated a wealth of personal debts. Librarians at the Georgia Historical Society, the Georgia Department of Archives and History, the Atlanta Historical Society, Emory University, the University of Georgia, the University of Virginia, Virginia Polytechnic Institute and State University, Hampton University, the University of Richmond, Virginia Historical Society, Virginia Union University, Virginia State Library, National Archives, and Library of Congress were generous with their knowledge and time. In particular, Virginia Shadron and Dale Couch at the Georgia Department of Archives and History were far more supportive than I had any right to expect. Jan Ertzberger of the Photocopying Center at the University of Georgia kept her good humor despite the literally thousands of microfilm copies I requested.

I am also indebted to John A. Washington and Letitia Grant of the Society of Lees of Virginia for generous financial assistance during graduate school and for ensuring that filiopietism does not prevent the family from looking forward. The Charles Warren Center for the Study of American History and the Advisory Research Council at Queen's University also provided much needed summer research grants.

Several friends opened their homes to me during my wanderings. Tina Groover of Chapel Hill, North Carolina, and Mary McKeegan of Alexandria, Virginia, both gave me sanctuary from summer heat. Kelly and Betty Garges of Atlanta generously provided me with a lovely home for two summers.

Friends and scholars have contributed greatly to this project. Robert W. Malcolmson, chair of the History Department at Queen's University, took an interest in this book and secured timely financial support. Alan Brinkley worked with me since the book's inception as an essay in one of his courses. His compassion during trying times and his generous and incisive criticism greatly enriched my graduate education. At the University of Georgia, I took unscrupulous advantage of several of my colleagues, including Numan V. Bartley, William F. Holmes, Randy Sparks, Mart Stewart, and Bennett Wall. A special word of thanks is in order for Will Holmes, who sharpened my ideas about southern violence and history more than he perhaps recognized. George Rawlyk, my colleague at Queen's, has been a handy thesaurus and a valuable sounding board. Barton Shaw and Roberta Senechal generously read the book in manuscript form and offered valuable suggestions. At the University of Illinois Press, Richard L. Wentworth and Karen Hewitt gently guided a novice author through the process of producing a book. And Mary Giles expertly pruned unneeded pronouns and clauses from the thicket of my prose.

I owe my deepest gratitude to August Meier and David Herbert Donald. August Meier prodded me to dig deeper in the archives, to think harder, and to explain my ideas more clearly. David Herbert Donald's trenchant criticisms of the various drafts of my dissertation, his classroom brilliance, and his dedication to excellence have been a continuous inspiration.

Heidi Wulczyn, my wife, has retained her good spirits and put up with me despite my obsession with one of the most grisly chapters in American history. Finally, this book is dedicated to Elizabeth Brundage, and to the memory of Robert Brundage. It is with great sorrow that I cannot offer this token acknowledgment of my appreciation to my father in person.

Introduction

Of the various forms of lawlessness prevalent in the United States during the past two centuries, lynching remains one of the most disturbing and least understood. In 1905, the sociologist James Cutler observed, "it has been said that our country's national crime is lynching." [1] So commonplace were lynchings that Mark Twain, with his characteristic sarcasm, renamed the country the "United States of Lyncherdom." But for many modern-day white Americans, lynch mobs conjure up images of cowboys, cattle rustlers, and a generally wholesome tradition of frontier justice. Lynching, it seems, represents for many a stage in the conquest and settlement of the West; it was a lamentable but necessary form of justice that persisted until formal institutions could take its place. As with many historical myths, there is a small kernel of truth in this view of frontier vigilante justice. The full tragedy of lynching has little to do with frontier justice, or the western United States, however. If lynching was a national crime, it also was a southern obsession. Few images of the travail of white-black relations in the South are more compelling than those of baying hounds and armed whites chasing black men across moonlit swamps, of frenzied mobs torturing and mutilating their victims, and of festive crowds gathering to gawk at the dangling or charred bodies of lynching victims.

Buried in the columns of the *Richmond Daily Enquirer* on Friday, March 30, 1900, was an arresting story that reveals how deeply embedded mob violence had become in the turn-of-the-century South. "The boys of the East End of Richmond," the newspaper explained, "who had been having trouble with the negroes of that section, became so enraged that on last Tuesday they decided to take the matter at once in hand and lynch the offenders." Stumbling upon a twelve-year-old black boy in the neighborhood, the white youths drove him from the area with stones. The black child, fearing for his life, sought protection in a white woman's house. A mob of white boys assembled around the front gate of the home, shouted abuse, pelted the house with stones, and demanded the boy. When the white woman refused "to give up the dark [*sic*]," the boys yelled back that "they would get him if they had to die." Recognizing the dangers of the worsening situation, the woman sent a servant to bring the police. With their arrival and the arrest of four of the white children, all of whom were younger than thirteen, the crowd of children finally dispersed. The boys were promptly fined and sternly warned against future violence. Black and white newspaper editors alike commented on the sad state of affairs when mere children were contemplating lynching other children. But as long as lynchings were frequent in the South, the editor of the *Richmond Planet,* a black weekly, feared, children would learn by example. The newspaper concluded tragically, "Yes, lynching is demoralizing to young and old."[2]

Against a background of the hundreds of lynchings of blacks each year in the South, the violent escapades of white children in Richmond appear almost comic. And yet such behavior reveals much about the place of lynching in the New South. However hollow the threats of the white boys to lynch their black victim may have been, the event itself represented nothing so much as an initiation or a rite of passage in which the young white boys assumed for themselves the role of defenders of the white community. The boys, however, failed to understand that, because of their youth, they could not properly shoulder the role of men. Their mistakes, at least in the eyes of whites, were to resort to excessive measures to punish a minor transgression and, more important, to usurp the responsibility of white men at too young an age. But, as the newspaper editors recognized, the children's behavior demonstrated the extent to which southern culture was saturated with the ethic of mob violence.

Lynching in the American South during the late nineteenth and early twentieth century was but one manifestation of the strenuous and bloody campaign by whites to elaborate and impose a racial hierarchy upon people of color throughout the globe. Across the globe, as W. E. B. Du Bois observed in 1903, "the problem of the twentieth century is the problem of the color line."[3] The combined weight of imperialism, industrial capitalism, and racism pressed Europeans and their descendants in the Western Hemisphere, Africa, and Asia to search for solutions to the vexing "color problem." From French West Africa and the Belgian Congo to the American South, elaborate and ruthless systems of coercive labor harnessed the labor of blacks. And in such far-flung locations as South Africa, Papua New Guinea, and the American South, whites experimented with complex systems of racial segregation. But when viewed in a comparative perspective, the exceptional history of lynching in the United States becomes apparent. Even as white Europeans and North Americans drew the color line with greater and greater precision, lynching remained a peculiarly American—and increasingly southern—phenomenon.

The culture that sustained the practice of mob violence in the South in the late nineteenth and early twentieth centuries also moved the region out of the mainstream of Western practices of criminal punishment. Under the banner of progress the antiseptic justice of the penitentiary replaced the older tradition of public vengeance throughout most of the Western world. At a time when punishment elsewhere was increasingly hidden from the glare of public observation, lynching in the South seemed to be a throwback to the brutal rituals of executions at Tyburn in eighteenth-century London. The South, in short, seemed to be moving against the current of the nineteenth century.

To a degree unmatched elsewhere in the nation, mob violence became a pervasive and semiofficial institution in the South. Drawing upon traditions of lawlessness rooted in slavery and the turmoil of Reconstruction, lynch mobs in the South continued to execute alleged wrongdoers long after lynching had become a rarity elsewhere in the nation. By the late nineteenth century, mob violence had become a characteristic feature of race relations in the South that would symbolize black oppression for as long as the practice continued. Lynching, like slavery and segregation, was not unique to the South, but it assumed proportions and a significance there that were without parallel elsewhere. Lynching came to define southern distinctiveness every bit as much as the Mason-Dixon line marked the boundary of the region.

With obscure origins traced to seventeenth-century Ireland and by others to eighteenth-century America, the practice of organized mobs punishing alleged wrongdoers in a summary fashion was an established custom by the end of the colonial period. During the bitter struggle of the American Revolution, mobs of zealous patriots whipped, and less often hanged, Loyalists and British sympathizers. After the Revolution, lynching expanded across the frontier, as mobs used whipping, rituals of humiliation, and occasionally hangings to impose social order.[4]

During the antebellum period, mob violence became a truly national phenomenon. In the North, where public disorder became incorporated into the rhythm of urban life, mobs threatened—and in several instances murdered—abolitionists, Mormons, Catholics, immigrants, and blacks. And with the discovery of gold in California, vigilante justice invaded mining camps and boomtowns, reaching a climax in the San Francisco vigilance committees of the 1850s. As lynching spread across the nation, two ominous trends emerged. Increasingly, mobs ignored existing legal institutions and meted out extralegal punishment. The blood lust of lynch mobs also seemed to grow over the years, with lethal punishments replacing many of the older penalties such as tarring and feathering and whipping.[5]

In the slave states of the South, mob violence became intimately tied to the defense of slavery. Organized vigilance committees kept a watchful eye for suspect slave behavior, inflammatory abolitionist literature, and unorthodox attitudes. When conditions warranted, mobs silenced both real and imaginary abolitionists and savagely suppressed slave uprisings. By the close of the antebellum era, the tradition of mob violence had evolved into an integral part of southern culture.[6]

The exigencies of the institution of slavery fostered violence, including a powerful extralegal undercurrent. Violence, if sometimes only the threat of it, became a customary way to compel deference and acceptable behavior in slaves. Slaveholders, to whom the state had conferred the widest possible powers over their slaves, judged the seriousness of offenses and fixed the kind and amount of punishment to be administered. Although planters generally struggled to maintain authority without inflicting arbitrary violence on their chattels, even the most successful could not contain the violence inherent in slavery. In turn, this thread of violence reinforced a fatalism about the inevitability of conflict in human relations, especially relations between blacks and whites.[7]

Slavery also contributed to the weak legal institutions that increasingly distinguished the South from the rest of the nation. In the North, the accelerating pace of economic development and the growth of cities required the permanent and dependable exercise of state authority on behalf of capital and property. Consequently, courts and law enforcement agencies, including recently created urban police forces, assumed a greater role in preserving social order. In the South, planters were wary of the establishment of any powerful legal institutions that might challenge their autonomy. White southerners, Wilbur J. Cash observed in an often-quoted passage, developed "an intense distrust of, and, indeed, downright aversion to, any actual exercise of authority beyond the barest minimum essential to the existence of the social organism." They preferred to rely on a code of honor and such traditional, extralegal methods of punishment as whipping and ostracism to safeguard community morals and virtues.[8]

Central to the sanctioned extralegal violence in the South was the peculiar southern code of honor that the institution of slavery simultaneously perpetuated and strengthened. While Americans elsewhere turned to judging self-worth according to notions of dignity and decorum, southerners steadfastly retained a code of honor, with its corollaries of the glorification of motherhood and feminine virtue, as a gauge for measuring a man's worth. In a culture where skin color determined status, white women, regardless of class, were enshrined on the pedestal of ladyhood and became the symbol and repository of white racial purity. The defense of white feminine virtue, especially against sexual aggression by black men, was at the heart of southern honor. While historians debate whether the code of southern honor preceded the development of slavery or was an outgrowth of it, the important point is that an elaborate code of behavior that required white men to respond to challenges to their honor by acting outside of the law had become custom by the antebellum period.[9]

The obverse side of white honor was the pervasive racist stereotypes of blacks as degraded and dishonorable. Defenders of slavery portrayed blacks in Africa (a convenient metaphor for blacks freed from the civilizing influences of slavery) as heathens and brutal savages. Their supposed mental and physical inferiority prevented them from rising above their violent passions, passions that erupted unpredictably and with staggering brutality. The deadened sensibilities of blacks, whites endlessly repeated, responded only to swift and harsh physical punishment. The dogma of black inferiority gave whites license to punish blacks ruthlessly without suffering attacks of conscience.[10]

The tradition of mob violence that had taken root in the antebellum South differed both in character and frequency from the later practice of lynching. Before the Civil War, whites, not blacks, were the preferred victims of mobs. Whites who deviated from community standards of behavior, whether by abusing their spouses and children or by holding unorthodox moral, political, or social beliefs, often suffered at the hands of mobs. And communal punishments of deviant whites were complete with many of the trappings of ritual scapegoating that later in the century would be virtually reserved for blacks.[11]

The lynching of blacks during the antebellum era usually occurred only in exceptional circumstances. The interests of slaveholders ran counter to eruptions of mob violence. As the historian Eugene Genovese has pointed out, white planters were loath to allow their slaves to be executed summarily because mob violence endangered slave property, weakened the power of planters, and threatened to "open the way for initiatives by the white lower classes that might not remain within racial bounds." Furthermore, planters preferred to hand the execution of criminal slaves over to the state, in no small part because the state compensated planters for executed slaves. In the day-to-day reality of the antebellum South, whites had little reason to fear coordinated attempts by blacks to challenge white dominance. Only the exceptional slave rebellion or the periodic frenzy of whites to reassert their supremacy in the face of some perceived imbalance produced mob violence against blacks.[12]

With the outbreak of the Civil War, the practice of lynching in the South began to assume its postwar character. As long as the combat lasted, lynching became intertwined with the far more deadly violence of the war itself. Throughout the conflict, spasms of mob violence were experienced in southern communities where whites feared imminent slave insurrections. Large numbers of slaves were executed in gruesome spectacles aimed at intimidating the slave community into submission and loyalty. In the backcountry, where allegiances often were divided between the Union and the Confederacy, partisans on many occasions summarily executed their opponents in a manner that cannot easily be distinguished from lynching.[13]

The conclusion of the war and the subsequent abolition of slavery unleashed an unprecedented wave of extralegal violence. Many white southerners, embittered by defeat and unsettled by the turmoil of Reconstruction, responded by expanding antebellum customs of communal violence to meet new conditions. Thus, the events of the postbellum era served both to perpetuate and to expand the role of extralegal violence in southern culture. At the root of the postwar bloodshed was the refusal of most whites to accept the emancipated slaves' quest for economic and political power. Freed from the restraints of planter domination, the black man seemed to pose a new and greater threat to whites. During a period when blacks seemed to mock the social order and commonly understood rules of conduct, whites turned to violence to restore their supremacy.

Mob violence, to a much greater degree than ever before, became a tool for enforcing conformity to prevailing racial roles. The dismantling of slavery left a void in the enforcement of white supremacy, threatening to deprive planters of their traditional prerogative of disciplining blacks as they chose. Planters, unable or unwilling to renounce the free-handed discipline of the antebellum plantation, whipped, shot, and killed thousands of blacks for arguing over crop settlements, wages, labor contracts, or simply for failing to display sufficient deference.[14] White violence also verged on systematic political terrorism. The Ku Klux Klan, paramilitary groups, and other whites united by frustration and anger ruthlessly defended the interests of the Democratic party, the avowed party of white supremacy. The magnitude of extralegal violence during election campaigns reached epidemic proportions, leading the historian William Gillette to label it guerilla warfare.[15]

If the extralegal violence of Reconstruction presaged the epidemic of violence of the late nineteenth and early twentieth centuries, it also differed significantly. Much of Reconstruction violence was a direct attack on Republican state governments and ruling political parties. Lynch mobs later in the century, in contrast, rarely had overt political motives. They would pose a de facto challenge to the authority of the state, but they would have no intention of overthrowing legally constituted authority. Rather, their aim would be to impose punishments that they were more able or more willing to inflict than the state.[16]

The response of legal authorities to the extralegal violence during Reconstruction also differed in important ways from the response to mob violence later in the century. Reconstruction violence provoked federal authorities to attempt to prosecute and punish perpetrators of racial and political violence. Recognizing that the success of Reconstruction depended on the suppression of organized campaigns of coercion, Congress passed sweeping measures to enable the federal government to restore order in the region. Vigorous campaigns against Klan violence in several states, particularly North and South Carolina, produced a dramatic decline in organized violence. Admittedly, elsewhere federal officers labored against enormous obstacles and endured repeated frustrations in their struggle to curb white violence. But as modest as the accomplishments of these efforts were, they had no subsequent counterpart during the late nineteenth and early twentieth centuries.[17]

The abandonment of federal intervention in southern affairs and the withering of the Republican party's commitment to protect black rights during the 1870s go far to explain the diminishing protection against extralegal violence that blacks received in the New South. The restoration of white supremacy remained incomplete—a task finally accomplished during the 1890s—but the return of "home rule" to the region meant that southerners had a free hand to restrict the fundamental rights of blacks. The collapse of Reconstruction altered the balance of power that had existed between whites and blacks. New and stringent laws redefined laborers' rights and property laws to favor planters; law enforcement agencies pointedly excluded blacks; and elaborate election laws whittled away at black voting rights. As the combined weight of the social, economic, and political oppression bore down on blacks, whites seemed less compelled to resort to organized extralegal violence to regulate black behavior. Increasingly, whites preferred to use the courts and the convict lease system to discipline blacks. But the tranquility that appeared in race relations during the 1880s was only relative; whites continued to employ brutal force to control laborers, intimidate black politicians, and silence militant blacks.[18]

The epidemic of lynching that swept the South in the late nineteenth century was not simply a persistence of Reconstruction violence. Not until the late 1880s did the number of lynchings in the South begin to climb. The new wave of racial violence climaxed in 1892, when mobs executed an estimated 71 whites and 155 blacks, the largest number of lynchings in the history of both the South and the nation. By 1893, the lynching of blacks in the South had become such an everyday event that Atticus G. Haygood, a prominent white Methodist bishop and a concerned observer of southern race relations, complained that the killing of blacks "is not so extraordinary an occurrence to need explanation; it has become so common that it no longer surprises." [19]

With each succeeding decade, the proportion of lynchings that occurred in the South rose, increasing from 82 percent of all lynchings in the nation during the 1880s to more than 95 percent during the 1920s. In the Northeast, where lynchings occurred rarely, mobs killed only two whites and seven blacks between 1880 and 1930. The Midwest proved more fertile soil for lynch mobs; there 181 white and 79 black victims died. And in the Far West, where vigilantism continued to flourish throughout the late nineteenth century, mobs lynched 447 whites and 38 blacks. The toll of mob violence outside the South, however shocking, is overshadowed by the estimated 723 whites and 3,220 blacks lynched in the South between 1880 and 1930. Casualties of mob violence in some lynch-prone states in the South equalled or exceeded the totals of entire regions outside the South. For example, the 492 victims killed by mobs in Texas surpassed the number of lynchings in the thirteen states that comprised the Far West.[20]

The blatant connection between lynching and race in the South also became starker over time. Outside the South and border states, 83 percent of mob victims were white. In the South and the border states, in contrast, the overwhelming majority of victims—85 percent—were black. Between 1880 and 1930, the proportion of lynching victims in the South who were white decreased from 32 percent to 9 percent. Thus, although mob violence had deep roots throughout the nation, and its victims included whites, Native Americans, Chicanos, and Asians, by the late nineteenth century lynching had become primarily a southern and racial phenomena.

Although the sheer horror of lynching has stirred many artists and writers to probe deeply for the roots of the practice, the scholarship on lynching has only recently moved beyond its infancy. The study of lynching, like that of many other forms of popular violence, is made difficult by manifold obstacles to traditional methods of historical research and interpretation. "For historians," Richard Hofstader once observed, "violence is a difficult subject, diffuse and hard to cope with." [21] Few forms of American violence are more obscure in their origins and unfolding than mob violence. Consequently, many of the most important attempts to unravel the history of lynching have been made by sociologists, psychologists, and other social scientists who have used social science models to find patterns in the apparent chaos of lynching.

For the early scholars of lynching, writing during the 1920s and 1930s, mob violence seemed to represent the periodic explosion of primordial racism. At a time when accounts of mob violence still regularly filled the columns of newspapers, the existence and perpetuation of racism itself was taken for granted; the question that attracted interest was why racism found an outlet in violent attacks on blacks. The answer, according to many observers, especially southern sociologists, could be found in the failure of southern institutions to provide adequate controls to stifle mob violence. Weak educational, religious, and civic institutions, poverty, and ineffective law enforcement agencies failed to instill sufficient respect for the rule of law or human dignity. Only when the mechanisms for social control became strong enough would mob violence and the values that sustained it subside. Thus, for these observers, lynchings marked a phase in the economic and social maturation of the South; as the South became increasingly urbanized and industrialized, lynching would no longer be condoned and the practice finally would be suppressed.[22]

The major shortcoming of this interpretation of lynching was that it rested on the assumption that the existence of racism need not be explained by anything more than ignorance, backwardness, and poverty. In an era when white racism had a palpable intensity that seemed unchanging, and when concerned individuals were intent on both arousing opposition and finding practical means to battle mobs, it is not surprising that the origins of racism itself often attracted little attention. Furthermore, the emphasis upon lynching as a symbol of southern backwardness predictably became intertwined with an explicit championing of "progress" and modernization. There was little appreciation of the contradictory effects of "progress" on the South, effects that could exacerbate no less than ameliorate racial tensions.

By asking a simple question of why people "needed" race prejudice, John Dollard, a psychologist, redirected the study of southern race relations in general and lynching in particular. Dollard suggested that one answer could be found in the socially accepted channels for aggression in the South. Because day-to-day life generates continual frustrations, Dollard argued, each individual must either turn aggression inward and release it at some future time, or direct it toward some acceptable target. In the South, social conventions welcomed the release of white frustrations on blacks, a defenseless group who were associated with whites' repressed fears and desires. The apparent irrationality of much white violence against blacks, Dollard suggested, reflected the combination of "direct aggression"—rational aggression against the individual or group responsible for frustration—as well as previously repressed aggression, which added an irrational element. The violent tone of southern race relations, then, was the culmination of "free-floating" aggression seeking an outlet.[23]

Other scholars located a variety of sources for the frustrations that so often bred violence. Several sociologists traced the rise and fall in the frequency of lynchings to the economic conditions of whites. When cotton, the most important crop in the overwhelmingly rural South, was in demand and prices high, whites were content and unlikely to vent their frustration through systematic violence against blacks. When cotton prices declined, however, blacks became convenient scapegoats for mobs of whites frustrated by economic reversal. The frequency of lynching, in short, was a barometer of the economic frustration of white southerners.[24]

Dollard also stressed the role that lynching and violence played in maintaining a caste system in the South. Because all whites shared benefits both from the exploitation of blacks and from the caste system, they were united in their devotion to preserving white supremacy. Subsequent work by scholars influenced by Dollard argued that custom alone was not enough to keep blacks in their place; only continual vigilance by whites maintained white superiority. Lynching was just one tool, if the most brutally effective tool, to perpetuate white dominance. By resorting to mob violence, whites drew caste boundaries and reaffirmed their superiority, both to themselves and to blacks. Along these lines, the historian James McGovern recently has suggested that "whites were conscious of their unlimited power over blacks and were willing to administer it through lynchings because they knew they could do so with impunity." [25]

The "frustration-aggression" theory has a common-sense plausibility, which in part explains why it remains, either implicitly or explicitly, an element in many explanations of lynching. The theory has been subjected to considerable revision in the past half-century in an effort to explain why frustration should inherently produce aggression. The only explanation possible is that there is some inherent aggressive tendency in human nature waiting to be provoked by frustrating experiences. Given that aggression is the inherent product of human frustration, then lynching is simply a southern variation of the human condition. Even when carefully stated, the theory threatens to become a tautology. Finally, the application of the theory to the study of lynching has tended to focus attention on some specific, primal cause. As a result, the complexities of mob behavior and the variations in the causes of mob violence have often been obscured.[26]

Alternatively, since the 1920s some scholars have found the inspiration of lynching to lie in deeply rooted psychological tensions among whites about gender and sexuality. Whites, one early student of mob violence has argued, projected forbidden fantasies onto blacks and then vented their anger on the creature of their own creation, the black rapist. In *Light in August,* William Faulkner foreshadowed much of what would later be written about white southerners' twin obsessions with race and sex. When Joanna Burden, who is white, is killed under confused circumstances by Joe Christmas, a deeply disturbed man of unclear racial ancestry, the local community responds with obvious relish. At the climax of the novel, Christmas becomes the scapegoat for the repressed sexual longings of Percy Grimm, the leader of the mob that murders and mutilates him. Perhaps with Grimm's twisted psyche in mind, the historian Joel Williamson has suggested that "black men were lynched for having achieved, seemingly, a sexual liberation that white men wanted but could not achieve without great feelings of guilt." Tortured by their frustration, white men projected their thoughts upon black men "and symbolically killed those thoughts by lynching a hapless black man. . . . In effect, the black man lynched was the worst part of themselves."[27]

Recently, other scholars have suggested another cultural explanation for lynching. Mob violence was one of the most hideous manifestations of ingrained cultural attitudes of the patriarchal, honor-bound South. The central peculiarity of southern culture, the persistence of the notion of honor long after it had withered elsewhere in the nation, created a climate particularly prone to ritualized affirmations of traditional values. Lynchings, in one fell swoop, confirmed inherited, inflexible attitudes toward blacks, women, and patriarchal rule.[28]

For all of the valuable insights offered by these interpretations of lynching, much about mob violence remains unclear or even unexplored. Some interpretations of lynching are fundamentally ahistorical. For example, early attempts to discover the socioeconomic causes of lynching, such as Arthur Raper's *The Tragedy of Lynching,* outlined the conditions that produced contemporary mob violence, with the assumption that the same conditions could be traced throughout the history of lynching. Raper argued that mobs flourished in isolated, backward communities like the ones that dotted the vast expanse of south Georgia. And yet, mob violence had been chronic when the same region had been undergoing rapid development and could not, in any real sense, be described as stagnant or backward. Similarly, the existence of a time-honored regional code of honor does help explain the peculiar southern proclivity to lynch, but many questions cannot be resolved by reference to the code of honor. Honor did not exist synchronically outside of history anymore than did other southern cultural traits. Across the late nineteenth and early twentieth centuries, honor exerted a loosening grip on the South. Moreover, honor is a very blunt interpretative instrument with which to explain the significant geographical variations in the propensity of southerners to lynch.

Psychohistorical interpretations of lynching have all too often been flawed by the tendency to explain away the complex and contradictory phenomena of lynching as simple reflections of individual psychology. Psychological interpretations have failed to provide any convincing explanation for regional variations in lynching or to chart its frequency over time.[29] Until the literature on the postbellum South addresses many fundamental questions about family life, the transition from childhood to adulthood, and sexuality in the white or black communities during the postbellum period, only the flimsiest foundation for a sophisticated psychohistorical interpretation of mob violence will exist. Finally, as David Stannard has pointed out, historians should be cautious about applying psychological methologies to mass phenomena in which, with few exceptions, so little can be learned about the participants.[30]

No explanation of the butchery of lynch mobs can be entirely satisfactory unless it is sensitive to the historical and regional variations in mob violence. The lethal racial prejudice evident in lynching cannot in itself serve as an explanation for the practice. More than four decades ago, the sociologist Oliver C. Cox, in his pioneering work, *Caste, Class, and Race,* rejected the notion that the origins of modern race prejudice could be traced back to "its genesis in some 'social instinct' or antipathy between peoples." Instead, he argued that the origins of racism could be found in the early modern era when Europe imposed its domination on "weaker. . . peoples with subtle theories of racial superiority and racial masterhood."[31] Hence, racial prejudice was a weapon in the economic exploitation of others rather than an expression of "primordial" racial superiority. Although Cox failed to detail the origins of racism adequately, he made the noteworthy contribution of insisting that the concept of racism was too often applied to a set of ideas and opinions, and too often the social context of those ideas was forgotten or ignored.[32]

Cox's observations about the nature of racism are especially appropriate to the topic of lynching in the late nineteenth and early twentieth century South. The motto of white supremacy and all of its attendant slogans have been elaborately analyzed, disclosing its nearly continuous grip on white southerners until the revolution wrought by the civil rights movement. But precisely because "white supremacy" was a vague folk concept used to describe varied patterns of behavior and belief, it is an inadequate explanation for such a multifarious and inconsistent phenomenon as southern mob violence.

Postbellum mob violence offers compelling evidence that white racism was not a continuous thread or uniform theme in southern history. As long as lynchings are interpreted as a ritualized expression of the values of united white communities, the task of explaining both the great variations in the form and the ebb and flow of lynching across space and time will remain incomplete. To answer these questions, an understanding of both variations in the salience of racist ideologies from era to era and the specific historical circumstances of racially inspired violence must be combined. Distinctive conditions, not some rigid notion of white supremacy, explain why mobs executed more blacks in central Georgia than in the low country of South Carolina. Specific circumstances explain why mob violence persisted in Mississippi years after the practice had declined in North Carolina. That lynch mobs victimized blacks most often was an outgrowth of much more than just some sweeping white desire to "keep blacks in their place." At work stirring up mobs and focusing their wrath upon certain targets were social, economic, and political concerns rooted in the dramatic changes that the South underwent between 1865 and 1930.

The regional variations in mob violence and in the responses of both black and white southerners to it affirm the degree of diversity that existed in race relations, even during a period disgraced by the most vicious white racism. The slogan of white supremacy was pervasive across the South—it was an article of faith for most white southerners—and yet political and economic forces and the conventions that emerged from them generated regional variations in race relations. Much existing literature on the late nineteenth and early twentieth centuries dwells upon the static character of white oppression of blacks. Apparently, the boundaries of racial behavior, once molded in the 1880s and hardened in the 1890s, varied little until the 1940s. However, the growing literature on blacks in specific states and localities has demonstrated (although it has not always stressed adequately) the important variations and significant changes that took place during these years.[33] Historians of race relations and of southern blacks have much work to do in answering Howard N. Rabinowitz's call to investigate the fluidity in racial contact that persisted across the era of segregation.[34] A fuller understanding of the history of mob violence during the New South is just one step toward a fuller understanding of the continuity and change that marked southern race relations from the Civil War until the black freedom struggle of the past half-century.

Of course, the history of lynching did not begin in 1880 or end in 1930, the dates that frame this book. Mob violence had scarred the nation and the South for at least a century before 1880, but the practice began to change significantly after Reconstruction. More and more the jurisdiction of the mob retreated to below the Mason-Dixon line, and increasingly blacks became the favored victims. And although the roots of the crisis in the late nineteenth century South can be traced partially to the turmoil of Reconstruction, mob violence peaked more than a decade after the uneasy conclusion of Reconstruction. The years from 1880 to 1930 mark a distinct period in the South's history. During the five decades following Reconstruction, segregation, sharecropping, white political hegemony, and, by no means least of all, lynching came to define the region. Industrialization, rapid expansion of the market economy, and sharecropping—the distinguishing features of the New South—are all central to the story of mob violence in the postbellum South.

With the onset of the Great Depression in 1930, changes in the South, which had typically occurred with glacial speed, accelerated rapidly. Southern agriculture underwent a decade or more of wrenching transformation, a process that had far-reaching implications for the traditions and conditions that had sustained mob violence. Although a combination of broad changes in the socioeconomic foundations and cultural attitudes of southern society began to deprive mob violence of the oxygen it needed to survive, it remained a lingering threat to blacks for decades after 1930. White southerners, particularly politicians, still lustily defended lynching, but their justifications could not give life to a dying tradition. This book, then, attempts to clarify and explain a distinct phase—the most southern and virulently racist phase—in the history of mob violence in the United States.

For several decades, historians have debated the question of whether the history of the South is better thought of in terms of continuities or discontinuities. Compelling arguments for both claims continue to be made.[35] This study of lynching makes no pretense to resolve the question. Rather, it rests in the middle ground of the debate. The history of lynching reveals the complex and often subtle combination of continuity and change that has characterized the history of modern southern race relations. Lynching in the late nineteenth and early twentieth centuries certainly owed something to the afterglow of antebellum traditions of collective violence. And yet, the persistence of lynching into the twentieth century was the result of conditions specific to the postbellum era. Even as lynchers in the New South drew on older traditions, their behavior differed both qualitatively and quantitatively from antebellum mob violence.

This contradiction extends as well to many of the characteristics of lynching and lynch mobs, some of which remained constant across the period while others changed noticeably. For example, lynchers who participated in the grisly rituals of execution during the 1880s would have detected few changes in the ceremonies of mob violence four decades later. And yet, there is clear evidence that there were changes in the attitudes toward the alleged crimes that merited summary punishment and to the merits of mob violence in general. In short, the history of lynching reveals a complex pattern of simultaneously fixed and evolving behavior and attitudes.

The continuity and change in the phenomenon of lynching in the New South, as well as its diffuse and episodic character, defy traditional historical narrative. Its settings are too diverse, its participants too anonymous, and its specifics too obscure to be charted like political elections or military campaigns. Some scholars have attempted to overcome the problems posed by contradictory and obscure forces behind mob violence by writing detailed case studies of notorious lynchings. With an eye for the setting, the historical context, and the consequences of specific lynchings, these historians have added a layer of texture and a level of precision to the history of lynching.[36] But few of the case studies have staked out new analytical tracks or have untangled the central questions about the historical evolution of lynching across the late nineteenth and early twentieth centuries.

By studying the broad sweep of mob violence, rather than a single lynching, it becomes possible to discern the variety of mob behavior. Not every lynching was an event laden with symbolism. To observe that some lynchings were literally banal is not to deny the obvious significance of the symbolism and ritual evident in other lynchings. Rather, it is to call for interpretations of mob violence that are broad enough to explain both the rituals of torture administered by huge mobs and the perfunctory murders carried out by secretive bands of whites.

The organization of this book is intended to reflect the varied and contradictory character of mob violence. The first five chapters are devoted to revealing the continuous and fluid characteristics of the behavior of lynch mobs. Although necessarily arbitrary, by separating the constituent elements of mob violence— the rituals, alleged causes, victims, and settings of lynching—patterns of behavior otherwise obscure or even invisible become apparent. The final three chapters offer a more conventional narrative of the evolving attitudes of black and white southerners toward lynching in Virginia and Georgia.

Throughout the book, Virginia and Georgia—states representative of the Upper South and Deep South respectively—are the focus of attention. The geographic subdivisions of the two states conveniently typify most of the important regions of the South. On the one hand, the history of mob violence in Virginia, the southern state with the fewest lynchings, offers insights into the conditions and circumstances that did not breed endemic extralegal violence. Georgia, on the other hand, is an obvious choice for a study of lynching: the character and harshness of white domination in the state, along with that of Mississippi, became the measure of race relations in the Deep South. As W. E. B. Du Bois observed in 1903, "Not only is Georgia. . . the geographical focus of our Negro population, but in many other respects, both now and yesterday, the Negro problems seem to have been centered in this state." [37] The sheer scale of mob violence in Georgia alone commands attention. In addition, the long history of mob violence in Georgia reveals fully the pathology of lynching in its various permutations over time and place.

By focusing upon these two states, this study offers an assessment of mob violence that addresses three important questions. First, how can the variation in mob violence over space and time be explained? Second, to what extent was lynching a social ritual that affirmed traditional values? And finally, what were the causes of the decline of lynching?

My approach is admittedly heuristic. The extant historical sources are so spotty and so riddled by racial bias that definitive studies of lynching almost certainly cannot be written. By borrowing freely from various methodologies and disciplines, I have attempted to combine broad theoretical discussions with illustrations drawn from individual lynchings. By drawing from anthropology and recent social and economic histories of the New South, I hope to convey the full complexity of mob violence and its place in everyday life. Few topics seem more appropriate to the application of some of the techniques of social anthropology than lynching. Because the richest details about incidents of mob violence usually relate directly to the act of execution by a mob, the significance and variations in the ritual of mob violence properly merit attention. In addition, the outpouring of excellent work on southern social and economic history makes it possible to speculate with greater sophistication about the socioeconomic context of postbellum mob violence. If this book accomplishes anything, I hope that it offers a portrait of lynching that is coherent and yet sensitive to those aspects of mob violence that remain beyond explanation or our ability to understand.

1
Mobs and Ritual

On December 11, 1940, a group of prominent antilynching leaders met to settle a debate that had raged among them over the definition of lynching. For years, the various organizations that chronicled mob violence disagreed over incidents of racial violence that might be labeled as lynchings. The recurring disputes were more than just idle hairsplitting: the controversy had both led to confusion over the actual toll of mob violence and provided ammunition to southern opponents of antilynching reform, who argued that proposed statutes against mob violence would open a Pandora's box of expansive judicial jurisdiction for a crime that eluded definition. The gathering finally agreed upon a definition, stipulating that "there must be legal evidence that a person has been killed, and that he met his death illegally at the hands of a group acting under the pretext of service to justice, race, or tradition." [1]

That such a meeting was ever necessary may strike us as extraordinary. Present-day scholars routinely refer to lynching as a "communal ritual," a "ritualistic affirmation of white unity," and a "scapegoat ritual" and seemingly have little doubt about just what constituted a lynching.[2] The ritual of lynching, the argument goes, both symbolized the social cohesion of white southerners and acted as a vehicle for bringing about that solidarity. Lynchings, rife as they were with symbolic representations, were like a text that white southerners read to themselves about themselves. Lynching, historians have suggested, summed up the values of the society that practiced it: participants in mobs not only enacted a ritual that affirmed their racial beliefs but also embodied their commitment to such values as white male dominance, personal honor, and the etiquette of chivalry. An endlessly repetitive ritual, performed again and again, year after year, lynchings celebrated and renewed fixed white southern social values and traditions.[3]

While this portrait of lynching has contributed valuable insights into the place of mob violence in the postbellum South, the sweeping assumptions upon which it rests threaten to obscure the complexities of southern mob violence. Attempts to interpret lynching as a ritualized event thick with the deepest values of white southerners may lead to undue emphasis on the unchanging, ritualized, and mass character of mob violence. Given the variety of forms that lynch mobs assumed, ranging from secretive small groups to enormous crowds, and given the prominence of improvisation in lynching, it is a mistake to conclude that mob violence was, to borrow a phrase from the anthropologist Clifford Geertz, a "metasocial commentary . . . [for] organizing collective existence." [4]

Virtually all lynchings shared important common elements. Mobs, on the pretext of punishing an alleged law-breaker or violator of local customs, summarily executed their victims with little if any regard for proof of guilt or evidence of innocence. Lynchings of blacks had a twofold nature: not only were they intended to enforce social conformity and to punish an individual, but they also were a means of racial repression. And a degree of community approval and complicity, whether expressed in popular acclaim for the mob's actions or in the failure of law officers either to prevent lynchings or to prosecute lynchers, was present in most lynchings. But for all of these common traits, the term *lynching* embraces a wide variety of mob actions and murders, some of which conform to a model of communal rituals but some of which emphatically do not. [5]

The starting point of a reconstruction of the role of lynching in the postbellum South is an examination of the form and content of lynchings themselves. There are methodological reasons to justify exploring mob violence as a performance before turning to the underlying causes that produced lynchings. No aspect of mob violence is more fully revealed by extant sources than the gruesome details of the actions of mobs. There also are substantive reasons to begin with the ceremonies of lynchings themselves. Mob violence, like other forms of collective action, was more than simply random and irrational violence. However much savagery and uncontrolled passion was vented by lynch mobs, there were predictable patterns to their actions, patterns that reveal much of the meaning of the pathology of lynching. Mobs, through their rituals and spontaneous behavior, communicated their aims, motivations, and own self-perception.

The great variations in form that mob violence could assume underscore the complex and contradictory character of lynching. No single model of lynching can describe adequately the great differences in size, organization, and motivation that distinguished mobs; there were small terrorist mobs intent on intimidating black sharecroppers, and huge mobs seeking vengeance against alleged criminals. Nevertheless, four general categories of mobs, based on size, organization, motivation, and the extent of ritual, may be identified. Although the level of violence associated with each type of mob varied from state to state, the traits that characterized each category of mob still remained consistent across the South. Small mobs, numbering fewer than fifty participants, may be separated into two types. They were either terrorist mobs that made no pretense of upholding the law or private mobs that exacted vengeance for a wide variety of alleged offenses. Posses, the third type, which ranged in size from a few to hundreds of participants, often overstepped their quasi-legal function and were themselves responsible for mob violence. Finally, mass mobs, numbering from more than fifty to hundreds and even thousands of members, punished alleged criminals with extraordinary ferocity and, on occasion, great ceremony.[6]

Careful attention to the variations in the forms of mobs reveals the significantly different patterns of violence in Georgia and Virginia. Virtually every form of mob violence occurred in Georgia. Mass mobs and private mobs executed the largest number of victims, but terrorist mobs and posses also claimed a substantial number of lives; in fact, they executed more victims than the total of all mobs in Virginia. In Virginia, mass mobs and private mobs were responsible for virtually all lynchings, and posses and terrorist mobs were inconsequential. Not only was mob violence more frequent in Georgia than in Virginia, but it also erupted in more diverse ways.

A taxonomy of mob violence that properly recognizes the variety and complexity of the phenomena of lynching exposes the diverse aims and targets of mobs. There can be little question that lynchings were inherently "conservative," directed as they were against blacks and other subordinate groups, and that the mere threat of mob violence became a form of coercion that sustained the status quo in the South. But it is a mistake to interpret all lynchings as a dramatization of the values and consensus of close-knit communities. The ideology of white supremacy gave license to violence of all kinds against blacks, but, because white southerners attached varied and contradictory meanings to the slogan of white supremacy, white violence against blacks necessarily took myriad forms. Even if most whites were committed to defending white power and maintaining the subordinate status of blacks, they advocated a wide range of strategies, including conflicting methods, to accomplish that end. Lynchings necessarily reflected these differing notions of white supremacy and consequently were much more than a simple ritualistic affirmation of white unity.

Terrorist mobs, who commonly bore such evocative labels as "whitecappers," "Ku Kluxers," "night riders," or "regulators," were responsible for fifty-nine of the four hundred and sixty lynchings in Georgia and only three of the eighty-six lynchings in Virginia from 1880 to 1930. Because they typically operated with great secrecy, attempts to determine the grand total of their victims or to chart the full extent of their activities are doomed to failure. Terrorist violence cannot easily be distinguished from other forms of extralegal violence prevalent in the South. On the continuum that extended from intimidation and whipping to the almost limitless savagery of the largest lynch mobs, terrorist violence was closest to traditions of communal justice that fell short of murder. Terrorist mobs, unlike other, more ephemeral lynch mobs, were often distinguished by enduring, even elaborate, organization. With a broad range of motives ranging from defense of traditional codes of morality to campaigns to intimidate black farmers, terrorist mobs are particularly suggestive of the diverse, even contradictory, aims of lynchers as well as the equivocal legitimacy that some types of mob violence enjoyed in the postbellum South.

The scarcity of terrorist violence in Virginia is just one indication of the extent to which the pattern of extralegal violence in the state differed from patterns elsewhere in the South. Although the violent regulation of community standards was an established practice in Virginia, as it was throughout the South, lethal forms of moral regulation were not. Furthermore, organized campaigns of terrorist violence did not lead to any lynchings in the state. It is tempting to trace the absence of lethal terrorist violence in Virginia to a tradition of lower levels of extralegal violence in the border states, but, in fact, many border states, including Missouri, Indiana, and Kentucky, suffered from serious and enduring forms of terrorist violence.[7] Instead, the rarity of terrorist violence in Virginia is indicative of the much more constricted role of all forms of extralegal violence in the state.

In Georgia, by contrast, a tenacious tradition of extralegal violence combined with volatile social conditions to fuel terrorist violence throughout the late nineteenth and early twentieth centuries. Because the various pressures that typically generated terrorist violence were enduring in Georgia—moonshiners intent on defending their craft, planters on controlling their laborers, and moral regulators on punishing lapses of conduct—it erupted sporadically and claimed a steady toll of victims until declining in the 1920s. And while the number of murders by terrorist mobs declined in the 1920s and 1930s, whippings and violent intimidation by self-proclaimed vigilantes remained frequent occurrences in the region at least until the 1940s. If the pattern of terrorist violence in Virginia departed from regional norms, the pattern in Georgia epitomized the enduring place of terrorist violence in southern life (Figure 1).

The traditional role of terrorist violence is most evident in the actions of mobs that drew inspiration from folk justice and punished individuals whose behavior

Figure 1. Lynchings by Mob Type, 1880–1930

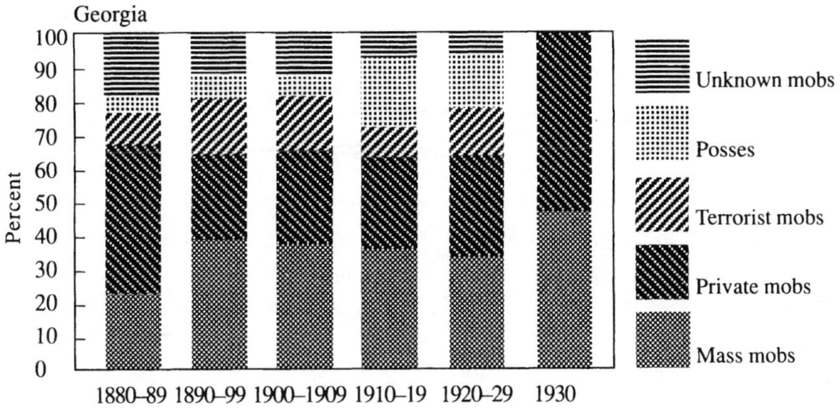

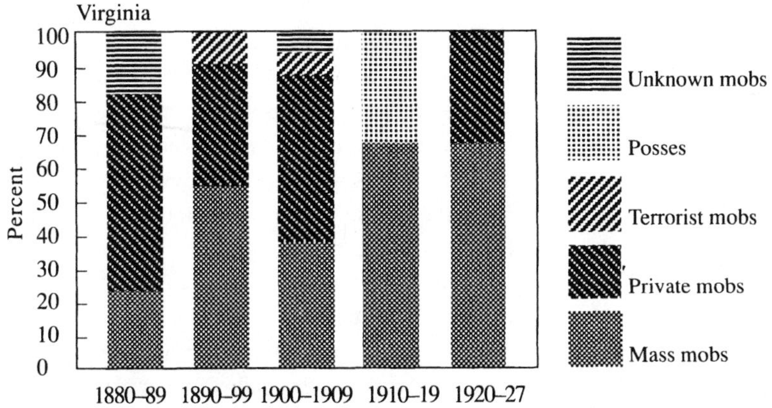

Georgia

Virginia

violated local standards of proper conduct. Outraged whites and blacks alike em-braced violence as a weapon of moral regulation and disciplined offenses such as drunkenness, public indecency, prostitution, wife-abuse, and laziness with whip-pings. Usually regulators did not intend to kill their victims, but only to drive them from the community. However, victims who either refused to comply with their demands or attempted to protect themselves often were shot or whipped to death. Accounts of near-lethal attacks prompted by moral transgressions filled the columns of small-town and county newspapers throughout the postbellum era. In 1907, for example, when R. H. Milam, a white farmer in Colquitt County, Georgia, failed to provide for his family despite opportunities for work, a group of white men flogged him and promised worse unless he reformed his behavior. In 1883, a cavalier regard for moral standards, including the taboo against incest, by Bully Roberson, a black farmer in Decatur County, Georgia, provoked a mob of blacks to mete out justice by flogging him to the point of death.[8]

The participants in mobs that punished moral lapses (according to local wisdom reported in news accounts) most often included family and neighbors of the offended individuals. Immediate and extended family could be counted on to punish husbands who beat their wives, peeping toms, or women who strayed from accepted codes of behavior. In January 1899, for instance, a young white woman in Miller County, Georgia, swore out a warrant against a young white man named Coot Phillips for "wronging" her. After being released on bond, Phillips organized a mob comprised of his father, two brothers, four cousins, and a neighbor and set out to punish the woman for "swearing damned lies." In the fracas that followed, the small mob gunned down the woman's father and brother when they attempted to protect her.[9]

During the 1920s, many defenders of morality were drawn to the revived Ku Klux Klan. Unlike other moral regulators who punished wrongs against their family or friends, Klansmen struck out violently against any moral transgression that caught their attention. As best as can be determined, the Klan drew much of its membership in the South from middle-class whites who longed for a return to traditional standards of moral conformity. United by their veneration of the traditional ethics of hard work, family devotion, and clean living, they adopted violent tactics to vent their frustration over the inability of law officers to deal effectively with moral offenses. Although the Klan's complex hierarchical national structure gave it the appearance of a tightly controlled organization, each Klan chapter had its own program addressed to local needs. Klansmen pilloried Jews, Catholics, and blacks in their publications and speeches, but in the South they reserved most of their violence for whites accused of sexual indiscretions, bootlegging, divorce, and other perceived moral failings. Between 1922 and 1924, for example, Klansmen in Macon, Georgia, whipped and beat several white men accused of adultery and bootlegging. Elsewhere in the state, Klansmen waylaid editors and lawyers who denounced or campaigned against the organization and its aims.[10]

Moral regulators usually stalked their victims under the cover of night and carried out their violent punishments with little if any conspicuous ritual. What little ceremony they staged was confined to their attire and the elaborate warnings they left—such as miniature coffins, threatening signs, or whips. Even the violence of the Ku Klux Klan, which missed few opportunities for symbolic gestures, was characterized by secretive late-night abductions and whippings on isolated byways. The whipping spree and campaign of intimidation by the Klan during the mid-twenties in Georgia, for example, consisted of clandestine late-night beatings.[11] For all the violence and turmoil created by the Klan and other moral regulators, the punishments they meted out only occasionally led to the death of their victims. By providing ample and graphic warning to all potentially disruptive elements that the vigilantes' moral codes would be upheld, extralegal sentences of whipping and expulsion often were sufficient to accomplish the mob's goal of moral regulation.

The economic distress of the rural South fueled a more lethal violence by organized groups who adopted terrorist violence as a weapon to defend their economic interests, whether as moonshiners or as dirt farmers. Motivated by a keen understanding of the threat federal taxation and law enforcement posed to their rural values, traditions, and economic security, moonshiners used violence to intimidate and punish people suspected of informing federal agents about illegal stills. The ensuing struggle divided communities, bred animosity among close-knit families, and provided ample fuel for violence. During the late nineteenth century, the coincidence of aggressive tactics by federal revenue agents and the social dislocations of economic depression sparked extensive violence, including whitecapping.[12]

Unlike moral regulators, moonshiners often set out to murder rather than merely to intimidate. United by ties of family and neighborhood, and further bound by shared economic concerns, they acted with surprising organization. Whitecapping organizations—moonshiners or people who the moonshine industry supported—in north Georgia, for example, marshalled members in counties throughout the region and at times managed to coordinate the activities of otherwise fiercely local groups of moonshiners.[13] Whitecapping in the defense of moonshining did on occasion expand beyond attacks on revenue informers and agents to include the punishment of both immoral whites and wayward blacks. In some communities, especially in the mountainous upcountry of northern Georgia, whitecapping expressed deep-seated fears about the status of blacks as well as economic change. In other areas, however, whitecapping seems to have been little more than a tactic to silence informers and impede revenue agents. Black moonshiners, especially in areas heavily populated by blacks, resorted to terrorist violence against black informers and in at least four instances murdered blacks for informing.[14] But if whitecapping was not solely a white activity, it is clear that important distinctions separated black whitecappers from their white counterparts. Although white terrorist mobs attacked victims on either side of the color line, black whitecappers never targeted whites. And white moonshining violence, given the proper local conditions, could expand into a militant moral crusade, whereas black moonshining violence appears to have had only the most limited aim of silencing informers.

Land-hungry white farmers also adopted terrorist methods as a means to shore up their increasingly vulnerable economic status. Worn down by falling cotton prices, which forced many whites to forfeit their mortgaged lands, and by the pressures that the growing population exerted on shrinking landholdings, some white farmers organized and waged prolonged campaigns of intimidation and violence against black sharecroppers and landowners. By driving away black tenants and ostracizing white farmers who rented to them, they hoped to create a labor shortage and force white landowners to employ only whites.

Scattered evidence suggests that whitecappers were not the poorest white farmers, but rather were those whites who bitterly resented their shrinking opportunities to move up the agricultural ladder from tenantry to landowning. That white landowners preferred to hire black tenants, who had a reputation of being more tractable, only exacerbated whitecappers' frustrations. With dwindling economic assets and little access to political power, whitecappers struck out against their black competitors and indirectly against white planters. Their attacks on blacks were not mere scapegoating; hard-pressed farmers had an acute sense of the tangible threat that black laborers posed to their access to land.[15]

The multifaceted motivations that lay behind violence by white terrorist mobs are evident in the lynching of Sterling Thompson in January 1901. Thompson, a modestly prosperous black farmer, lived in Campbellton, a small community on the outskirts of Atlanta.[16] His willingness to inform revenue agents of his neighbors' stills, coupled with his prominence in local Republican politics, provoked some whites to warn him to leave the community or risk harm. Several of his white neighbors also set their sights on gaining possession of his farm. When Thompson refused to sell, the frustrated whites laid plans to murder him and force his widow to sell. On the night of January 3, a small group of men organized and elected a Baptist minister "temporary captain." After trying unsuccessfully to lure Thompson outside so they could whip him, they fired a fusillade into his house. Thompson, like countless other whitecapping victims who attempted to protect themselves, returned the fire but finally was hit and killed.[17] No single provocation led to the mob attack. Instead the combination of Thompson's political activism, his religiously inspired crusade against moonshine, his independence, and his prosperity aroused the anger of his white neighbors.

Neither hard-pressed dirt farming whites nor moonshiners, of course, had a

monopoly on terrorist violence.[18] Well-to-do white farmers were active participants as well. Although planters seldom cloaked themselves in vivid attire or
created secret terrorist organizations, they did adopt terrorist methods to both
enhance their power and intimidate blacks whose behavior somehow threatened
their authority. Such mobs were comprised of a fluid group of neighboring landowners who shared a common belief that specific blacks were disrupting local
labor relations. "Wild talk" by a black, an offense that encompassed such infractions as proselytizing for African colonization, encouraging black laborers to
demand higher wages, enticing away tenants, or simply leaving a white employer
before the end of a contract, could stir whites into a violent frenzy.[19] With little if
any ceremony, white farmers inflicted as much violence as they deemed necessary
to create a terrorized, and hence more tractable, labor force.[20]

The mixed motives and varied targets of terrorist mobs reveal the heteroge-
neous and contradictory nature of some lynchings. However much participants in
terrorist violence perceived themselves as defenders of community values and conventions, their actions often had discordant consequences. Terrorist mobs at times
engaged in behavior that followed in the traditions of charavari and "rough-music"
in early modern Europe and punished individuals who had offended explicit communal traditions and social propriety. But at other times terrorist mobs pursued
goals that divided, sometimes deeply, the local white community and revealed
that not all residents of the local community shared the same understanding of
prevailing traditions and values.[21]

Both beleaguered, land-hungry, yeomen farmers, who drove black farmers
from their land through organized terror and murder, and white planters, who
silenced black employees who strayed from their proper place, believed that their
actions were traditional, orderly, and appropriate. But important distinctions separated the actions and beliefs of the two groups. The whitecappers who burned
black property and murdered blacks in Early and Miller counties, Georgia, in 1899
hoped that their campaign would produce entirely white counties. "The gang,"
a local newspaper explained, "has issued an order that no negro shall live in the
section in which the whitecappers are at work and the white people have been
notified that negroes shall not remain on their places under penalty of violence."
In contrast, the white planters in Talbot County in 1909 who set out to silence
Will Carreker, a "rabble-rouser," had no intention of purging the county of black
laborers; rather, they sought to expel from the community a troublesome black
who threatened their authority.[22] In both instances the white mob intended to intimidate, but did so for different reasons and with distinct aims. Whitecappers
who were embattled white farmers believed that they were defending the tradi-

tional economic status and rights of whites against the encroachment of a planter elite (measured by the advance of cheap black farm labor at the expense of white farmers). Planters who participated in terrorist violence believed that they were restoring and preserving their own economic domination. Because of these distinct, and sometimes competing, aims, whites often were sharply divided over the legitimacy of acts of terrorist violence. So deep were these divisions that, at a time when most lynchings went unpunished, many terrorist attacks were harshly condemned and terrorist mobs were even prosecuted.[23]

The terrorist violence that most often fostered division within white communities was attacks on revenue informers and other opponents of moonshiners. Newspaper editors thundered against moonshiners who adopted terrorist tactics and demanded that they be severely punished. The assault upon innocent and law-abiding citizens by moonshiners could not be tolerated, the *Savannah Morning News* explained in 1908, because it was both "criminal [and] cowardly in the extreme." The newspaper also challenged the legitimacy of the moral crusades that sometimes accompanied moonshining violence. While whitecappers committed the "most outrageous crimes" on the pretense of regulating the communities in which they lived, they soon began to revenge "all sorts of fancied wrongs."[24] More than a decade earlier, the editor of the *Valdosta Times* had scoffed at moonshiners' motives and actions: "In nine cases out of ten the 'regulation' act is prompted by some private envy or malice and in ninety-nine cases out of every hundred the object of the attack is superior in intelligence, in morals, and in veneration for the law to the regulators."[25]

Of greater immediate threat to the moonshiners than newspaper editorials were the efforts of state and federal authorities to suppress moonshining and the violence it spawned. Although the federal government willfully refused to exert any federal power to prevent most lynchings or to prosecute lynchers, it was active in the prosecution of moonshiners. Thus, southern whites who opposed moonshiners often had the vigorous support of the federal government and were able to prosecute them successfully.[26]

No similar federal intervention was forthcoming in the punishment of mobs who attacked black tenant farmers.[27] Local opposition to attempts to drive off black tenants, however, could be formidable. Campaigns against black farmhands, one editor warned, could not be tolerated because they posed "a menace to free government" and were "a deterrent to material prosperity."[28] The white employers of terrorized blacks sometimes took steps to suppress whitecapping either by protecting their black employees or by prosecuting whitecappers in local courts. Such efforts were bitter reminders to whitecappers that the slogan of white supremacy could not camouflage the contrasting interests of land-starved white farmers and planters.

The attack on Bill Brown, a black tenant, in Houston County, Georgia, in January 1893 suggests how terrorist violence by white farmers could pit white planters and their black farmhands against other whites. For several weeks in early 1893, whitecappers harassed and intimidated the black tenants on a plantation near the town of Fort Valley. During one of the attacks, the whitecappers shot and severely wounded one of the tenants. At the request of the county sheriff, the governor offered a $100 reward for the arrest of any of the whitecappers. Rather than intimidate the marauders, the announcement of the reward prompted them to give notice that they intended to "regulate" the tenants on the following Sunday night. When a small mob surrounded and began to shoot into Brown's home, he returned fire and killed one of his attackers. No lynch mob organized to kill Brown, however. Brown's employer, who had armed his tenants in preparation for the whitecappers' visit, rallied with many other local whites to support the black man. In an absurd turn of events that says much about the southern courts of the day, members of the mob threatened to bring charges against Brown for murder. Brown's supporters, including his employer, defended him and hired two white attorneys to represent him in court. To the gratification of many local whites, an all-white jury acquitted Brown of the charge of murder and ruled that the shooting of the whitecapper had been a justifiable homicide.[29] The verdict, the *Savannah Morning News* crowed, "vindicated the law, re-established confidence in the legal machinery and proclaimed to would-be 'regulators' that white capism will not be tolerated in Georgia." [30]

Whitecappers themselves sometimes became the targets of prosecution. Following the murder of Sterling Thompson in Campbell County, for example, seven men were tried and convicted of second-degree murder and received lengthy sentences in the state penitentiary.[31] Precisely because much whitecapping violence made no pretense of upholding the law and occasionally threatened the interests of white planters, whitecappers not only lacked the community protection enjoyed by other mobs, but they also faced steady condemnation in newspapers and the threat of prosecution when they attacked informers and black tenants.[32]

Of course, the suppression of terrorist violence was piecemeal and reflected the relative local power of whitecappers and their white opponents. While whitecappers who antagonized prominent whites risked prosecution, white planters continued to resort to violence against stubborn or unsubmissive black tenants with little fear of legal punishment until the 1930s. Virtually all terrorist mobs, whatever their motivation, shared the conviction that extralegal violence was the appropriate punishment for offenses that were either trivial crimes (at least in the eyes of the law) or were not crimes at all. But not all mobs enjoyed the same legitimacy in the eyes of officials or influential community members. Extralegal violence that followed in the traditions of rural moral regulation faced opposition within the white community only when it seemed to threaten anarchy. The whipping of a white man for adultery, the harassment of a black merchant by his black clients for an overly zealous pursuit of profit, or the beating of a drunken vagrant were likely to draw praise if they attracted any notice at all.[33] Only moral regulation that reached lethal proportions was likely to meet with any local opposition. But when terrorist violence either posed a direct challenge to the economic interests of white elites, or exposed and gave expression to the cleavage separating whites along social and economic lines, officials and white elites found ample inspiration to suppress it.

Lynchings by private mobs, like terrorist mob violence, can be described only with difficulty as communal "repressive justice" or as the equivalent of the Balinese cockfight that Geertz described. Rather than public events in which large numbers participated in a communal performance, lynchings by private mobs can best be understood as a form of private vengeance. The interesting question posed by the secretive character of such lynchings is not whether lynchings were a focal institution for deeply rooted values, but rather why some lynchings were central and inclusive rituals, or in the words of Marcel Mauss, "total social phenomenon" while others, such as lynchings by private mobs, were not.[34]

Private mobs accounted for 30 percent of all lynchings in Georgia and 46 percent of all lynchings in Virginia. Like terrorist mobs, private mobs were small, sometimes with as few as four or five participants but seldom with as many as fifty. They were closed groups, secretive in nature, and often concealed themselves with masks or disguises. Unlike terrorist mobs, however, they organized to punish alleged criminal offenses, including crimes of a serious nature.

The incidence of lynchings by private mobs is a barometer of both public attitudes toward mob violence and vigilance by law officers. In both Georgia and Virginia, private mobs accounted for the largest number of summary executions during the 1880s. But as racial and social tensions mounted in the 1890s and mob violence enjoyed broad support among white southerners, the percentage of lynchings by private mobs fell and the number of lynchings by mass mobs increased sharply. After 1900, the patterns in the two states diverge. In Virginia, the number of lynchings by private mobs rose significantly and accounted for the majority of lynchings between 1900 and 1920. In Georgia, however, the number of lynchings by private mobs did not increase substantially until the 1920s. Despite these differences, the trends of violence by private mobs in the two states are similar. The ebb and flow of private mob violence in Virginia foreshadowed similar patterns in Georgia and much of the rest of the South. As lynchings in Virginia attracted mounting scrutiny and the mob's legitimacy was challenged during the late 1890s, private mobs assumed a new prominence. As fewer and fewer lynchings occurred in the state, more and more of them were the work of private mobs. A similar evolution of attitudes and lynchings occurred in Georgia, although several decades later than in Virginia. Thus, rather than representing a new form of mob violence, the increasingly clandestine lynchings in Georgia and elsewhere in the South during the 1920s, 1930s, and 1940s demonstrated the resurgence of a form of mob violence that had always been present (Figure 1).

Private mobs punished crimes which, for reasons that are often difficult to discern, had failed to arouse communal passions. The most prominent were alleged crimes of violence, including murder, rape, and attempted rape.[35] That these alleged pretexts had failed to elicit swift communal response is evident in the long delays that often separated private lynchings from the precipitating offense; more than a quarter of the private lynchings in both Georgia and Virginia occurred more than three weeks after the alleged crimes had occurred. In some cases, as in the lynching of Horace Carter, a black tenant farmer, in King William County, Virginia, in October 1923, as much as a year lapsed between the provocation and the mob's revenge. Perhaps the most exceptional example of a lengthy interlude between a crime and its punishment by a private mob was the lynching of Jim Simmons, a black, near Cairo, Georgia, on November 18, 1890. Shortly after Simmons had completed a three-year sentence for attempted rape and returned to his home in Thomas County, a small mob of white men lynched him. For some observers, it was clear that members of the mob had not been satisfied with the sentence and had decided to punish Simmons themselves.[36]

Comprised of relatives, friends, and neighbors of the victim of the alleged crime, the members of private mobs were bound together by a shared sense of personal injury. This sense of personal loss provoked members of the Land family in Columbus, Georgia, to avenge the accidental shooting of their young brother in August 1912 by murdering T. E. Cotton, a black youth who already had been tried and sentenced for the crime of manslaughter. A similar collective desire for vengeance among the friends and fellow workers of a white yardman who had been assaulted by Jerry Lovelace, a black railroad hand in Merriwether County, Georgia, led to his killing in October 1911.[37]

In a few exceptional instances in Virginia and Georgia, aggrieved blacks resorted to private vengeance to punish other blacks for alleged crimes. Following the acquittal of Elmore Mosely on charges of shooting down a black neighbor in the presence of the man's wife and children in Prince George County, Virginia, in 1904, a small group of blacks murdered Mosely as he was returning from the trial. Similarly, with their patience exhausted after years of thievery, blacks in Glascock County, Georgia, turned to extralegal justice in 1897 and executed Josh Ruff, a black "desperado" they held responsible for the thefts. There may well have been other instances of private lynchings by blacks but, because whites only sporadically concerned themselves with such violence, the incidents went unrecorded.[38]

Private mobs, like their terrorist counterparts, devoted more attention to secrecy than to ceremony. Elaborate ritual served little purpose for private mobs, consumed by personal grievances and the lust for revenge. In 1913, a concern for secrecy led the mob in Calhoun County, Georgia, that murdered Robert Lovett, a black accused of murder, to don hoods and communicate with hand gestures derived from fraternal society ritual. So intent on stealth was the mob of roughly thirty masked men that executed Tom Ruffin, a black accused of attempted rape, in Dade County, Georgia, in March 1888, that they opened fire on curious whites who approached them. While private mobs sometimes carried their victims back to the scene of the alleged crime, or to the site of a previous lynching, they were just as likely to shoot or hang them in any convenient and inconspicuous spot. Few lynchings by private mobs involved the stereotypical immense, seething mobs. For instance, the mob of blacks that murdered Jack Johnson, a black charged with rape, in Carroll County, Georgia, in August 1884, laid in wait outside the ramshackle jail until he was allowed outside to relieve himself. They then shot him down with a salvo of rifle fire. Content simply to murder their victims, the mobs that executed Johnson and many others rarely mutilated corpses or left messages or warnings on the bodies.[39]

Private mobs, unlike terrorist mobs, usually murdered victims who were already in legal custody. In Georgia between 1880 and 1930, 80 percent of the victims of private mobs were taken from law officers, whereas in Virginia 94 percent of victims were taken from authorities. Despite their small size, private mobs in Georgia seized 42 percent of their victims from jails; in Virginia 60 percent of private mob victims were taken from jails. Without question, local law officers, whether through woeful incompetence or complicity, often aided the work of the mobs.

The lynching of General Williams, age fifteen, in Burke County, Georgia, on October 24, 1890, illustrates one law officer's complicity. The black youth allegedly murdered a young white boy who, coincidentally, was the nephew of the local constable. After arresting Williams, the constable used his own home as a jail rather than placing him in the county jail. Finally, after several days county officials ordered the constable to deliver Williams to the county jail. While the constable and his prisoner were in transit, a mob of ten men halted them and executed the black youth. News accounts left little doubt that the constable had intentionally turned Williams over to the waiting mob.[40]

Access to victims was gained by subterfuge as well as official complicity. A commonplace tactic was for men to pound on the jail doors late at night, claiming to have a prisoner to place in jail. Once inside, they seldom had difficulty compelling the jailer to hand over the keys to the cells. In the few instances in which the jailer or sheriff did refuse, threats to burn or dynamite the jail or execute all the prisoners usually overcame his inhibitions.[41]

Careful planning was evident in the lynching of Peter Bland, a young black farm tenant, in King William County, Virginia, on February 5, 1884. Several months before the lynching, Bland had severely beaten his white employer during an argument. On January 28, he was tried and sentenced to fourteen years in the state penitentiary for the assault. He then was returned to the local jail to await transport to prison. At about 2 o'clock on the morning of February 5, a man, claiming to be a policeman from a nearby town, woke the jailer and requested that he jail a prisoner in the policeman's custody. When the jailer left his home to cross the short distance to the jail, three men, armed with shotguns and pistols, held him up and took his jail keys. After locking the jailer in a room in the jail, the lynchers dragged Bland from his cell, shot him repeatedly, and finally hanged him outside the jail. The lynchers then politely freed the jailer, returned the keys, and disappeared. So well organized and quiet were the lynchers that the lynching passed unnoticed in the community until the following day.[42]

Sometimes denounced, more often ignored, private mobs lacked the legitimacy that broad local favor might have given them. In exercises of tortured logic, local newspaper editors and residents drew distinctions between those crimes that warranted lynching and those offenses that did not. Often, private mobs were perceived to have resorted to extralegal means to punish offenses that should have been left to the legal courts. Thus, in 1930, a jury in Thomas County, Georgia, convicted two white men of leading a small mob of whites that lynched a black man who had testified in court against them. The same jury refused to convict any of the members of a mass mob that had lynched a black charged with the attempted rape of a white child.[43]

Members of private mobs were among the first lynchers to suffer legal punishment for their crimes. On at least four occasions in Virginia between 1893 and 1901, members of private mobs were indicted and in two instances were tried and convicted of murder.[44] The first mob members convicted in Virginia were from a small private mob that had lynched an insane white man charged with rape in 1898.[45] In Georgia, however, private mobs became subject to local prosecution only after World War I. It was not until 1926 that the first members of a private mob were convicted in Georgia. And as in Virginia, the convicted lynchers were charged with the murder of a white man.[46] That the victims of both mobs were white is important, but so, too, is the fact that the mobs had offended local opinion by cavalierly resorting to summary justice to punish crimes widely perceived to be better left to the courts.

The typical response by whites to most lynchings by private mobs was a brief spasm of condemnation followed by silence. In a few cases, whites held public meetings, denounced the mob's actions, and pledged to ensure the safety of law-abiding blacks in the future.[47] Local newspaper editors often denounced extralegal murders by private mobs but seldom pressed the issue or persisted with their criticism beyond the immediate aftermath of the lynching. The timid criticism of newspaper editors was only the most conspicuous evidence of widespread acquiescence to violence by private mobs. Residents of communities in which private lynchings occurred were quick to announce that local opinion opposed the lawlessness and that they should not be condemned for an act in which they played no part and of which they claimed to know nothing. But such condemnation amounted to little more than hand-wringing followed by a desire to forget the entire episode. J. Loy Harrison, a resident of Walton County, Georgia, summed up the attitude that prevailed in most communities. After a mob of twenty-five men lynched four blacks in 1946, Harrison implored "Just bury them quick. Go ahead and bury them. That's the best thing to do." [48]

If private mobs were expressions of community will, they often voiced local white sentiment in only the most muted and ambiguous fashion. The diversity in lynch mobs highlights the care with which notions of ritual and of community should be used when analyzing mob violence. In more than 40 percent of the lynchings in Georgia and half of the lynchings in Virginia, small, secretive mobs were responsible. These lynchings could not, in any meaningful way, serve as vehicles to reaffirm widely held social values. The small mobs that carried out clandestine lynchings may have believed that they were acting in accordance with and were affirming the timeless prerogatives of whites to punish blacks, but their deeds hardly represented the expressed sentiment of the local white community. More likely, private mobs resorted to an improvised lynching in order to give their private grievances a patina of legitimacy that would have been absent had they simply murdered their victims in their jail cells or homes.

The transgressions that prompted private and terrorist mobs to resort to violence did not produce anything comparable to the "metasocial" events that Geertz described so evocatively. In contrast, the bloody work of posses came far closer to public events that had the power to fuse entire communities. If white southerners, even at the height of the mob frenzy in the 1890s, had reservations about the violence of private and terrorist mobs, they had few inhibitions about the violence of posses. The widespread participation in and glorification of posses by whites demonstrates that however much they disagreed about the legitimacy of some forms of extralegal violence, they could be drawn together in acts of mass violence.

The alleged purpose of posses was to capture rather than to lynch criminals, but in at least fifty-one reported instances, posses in Georgia completed their pursuit by murdering an unarmed or wounded suspect. In contrast, posses in Virginia apparently committed only one lynching. As in the medieval practice of hue and cry, southern posses usually formed immediately after the discovery of a crime. Sometimes legally deputized groups, but most often spontaneous gatherings comprised of neighbors, relatives, or witnesses to the crime, posses straddled a very thin line between being a legal and an extralegal arm of the law. They crossed that line when they murdered unarmed suspects or made no attempt to negotiate with armed suspects before resorting to violence.

Precisely why posses in Georgia were responsible for so many more lynchings than in Virginia is difficult to determine. In Georgia, and indeed in much of the South, the prevalence of posses and the violence for which they were responsible reflected the weakness of law enforcement in much of the South. Outside of the county seats and the immediate vicinity of towns, few communities had the resources to support law officers. Moreover, the handicap of poor transportation in rural areas limited the effectiveness of whatever law officers existed. Posses, which were cheap, quick, and ruthlessly effective, provided welcome assistance to law officers. Hence, posses and the violence they initiated endured in much of the South until at least the 1920s. Only gradually, with the expansion of law officers in rural regions and with the advent of state police in the South, did the role of posses diminish. Tradition also gave posses a prominence and legitimacy in Georgia that they did not enjoy in Virginia; law officers in Virginia did not rely on posses for assistance to nearly the extent that their counterparts in Georgia did. It is not clear whether Virginia officials did not trust posses to remain within the law or simply did not believe that they needed help from the citizenry, but it is apparent that law officers in Georgia, by routinely calling upon posses for support, contributed greatly to the carnage of mob violence.

The enduring place of posses in much of the South cannot be explained simply by feeble law enforcement that needed bolstering. Posses were much more than just cheap and expedient. They also combined the fellowship of a hunt with the honor of serving the alleged needs of the community. Ignoring the moonshine drinking and violence that accompanied most manhunts, newspapers often portrayed posses as protectors of home and hearth. In 1899, following the murder of Alfred Cranford and the alleged rape of his wife by Sam Hose, a black farmhand, near Palmetto, Georgia, posses began a manhunt that covered several counties and lasted more than a week. During the search, the newspaper reported, "women cheered them on while men waved their hats and gave vent to other demonstrations of sympathy as the party passed." The sensational crime even inspired white men from both neighboring and distant counties to volunteer. The *Atlanta Constitution* noted that Woodbury, a town near the scene of the murder, "is practically deserted. Every man and boy able to carry a gun and help in the chase has left home determined to assist in the capture. Business has been suspended and many of the stores have their shutters up awaiting the return of their owners."[49]

The swiftness of their summary justice set posses off from either terrorist or private mobs. Most victims were executed within a few days of their alleged offense. In Georgia, 48 percent never survived long enough to be placed in the hands of legal authorities. In the remaining instances, 28 percent of those turned over to authorities were taken by mobs and lynched before they reached a jail. In Virginia, where virtually all the "suspects" chased by posses were turned over to legal custody, 45 percent did not survive the trip to jail.

While whites perceived posses as legitimate extensions of the law, blacks saw them as nothing more than masquerades for lawless whites who relished the opportunity to flourish firearms and assume an air of responsibility. Consequently, when posses managed to corner alleged black criminals, they often fought desperately. In countless instances posses met black resistance with unconscionable and unrestrained violence. For example, the mob of law officers and citizens that fought a pitched gun battle with Walter Clark, a black accused of murder, in Danville, Virginia, in 1917 made no effort to seek a negotiated end to the standoff. Instead, they set fire to the house in which Clark had taken refuge and shot him as he tried to escape.[50] In other cases, posses set fire to swamps into which suspects had fled or hurled sticks of dynamite at fleeing suspects. Because of the broad latitude of violence that was condoned and the ease with which posses could disguise and justify their summary punishments, the full extent of their violence can only be conjectured.

With hounds and heavily armed whites racing on the trail of alleged criminals, manhunts often degenerated into indiscriminate violence against innocent blacks who found themselves in the paths of posses. Posses resorted to intimidation, and often torture, to compel blacks to divulge the whereabouts or escape route of fleeing suspects.[51] They shot down innocent blacks on the most flimsy pretexts, as in the case of Henry Jones, who was murdered in Colquitt County, Georgia, in 1918 because he ran from an approaching posse.[52] Perhaps the most extraordinary example of wanton slaughter was the manhunt that followed the murder of a planter in Lowndes County, Georgia, in May 1918. In addition to the death of the alleged criminal, ten innocent blacks also were slain.[53] That manhunts often deteriorated into mob violence hardly is surprising. Sensational crimes—murder, rape, or attempted rape—that typically incited the formation of posses were also those for which summary punishment was widely condoned by white southerners.[54]

Posses cared little about formality or ritual. They occasionally selected the site of execution with a symbolic aim in mind, as when the mob that lynched Bud Cosby, a black accused of kidnapping a baby in Fayette County, Georgia, in February 1918 carried out the execution at the spot where the kidnapped child had been found. Similarly, the posse that captured Tom Devert, a black charged with attempting to rape a white child in May 1918, in Ervin, Georgia, was not satisfied with simply murdering him. After riddling Devert with bullets, they carried his body to the black section of town and forced eighty blacks to witness the burning of his body. But just as often victims were simply shot down wherever they were captured. In keeping with their frenzied and disorganized character, posses carried out executions that were laden with little of the symbolism evident in some lynchings.[55]

Because posses were, in the eyes of whites, protecting law-abiding citizens and carrying out justice, they enjoyed popular blessing. Newspapers routinely applauded the heroism of posses and raised few questions about either their legitimacy or the bloodshed they caused. Only when posses got out of hand and recklessly abused blacks did they arouse tensions among whites, tensions reminiscent of those produced by overzealous slave patrols before the Civil War.[56] Excessive and arbitrary violence against trusted blacks sometimes infuriated white employers and led them to denounce posses.

In Brooks County, Georgia, in December 1894, a white posse, under the pretext of searching for a group of alleged black murderers, indiscriminately tortured and murdered five blacks. Whites took no meaningful steps to curb the mob until it terrorized blacks on the plantation of Mitchell Brice, one of the county's richest planters. Outraged in particular by the beating and disfigurement of an elderly black woman, Brice warned that any further violence would be suppressed ruthlessly and even intimated that he planned to prosecute members of the posse. The planter's intercession, in conjunction with the arrival of state militia and the arrest of the remaining black murder suspects, ended the slaughter. While compassion may have stirred Brice to intervene, of greater concern to him was the defense of his authority over his workers from the unruly actions of poor whites. Brice could think of no better way to condemn the posse than to point out that "it is composed of people who associate with negroes, eat at the same table with them, and drink out of the same bottle with them." He was not offended in principle either by the posse or extralegal punishment, but rather that the mob, without any justification, had mistreated his hard-working, well-behaved hands.[57]

As long as posses refrained from gross excesses of sadism, they operated without hindrance or threat of legal punishment. In only exceptional instances were members of a posse indicted or tried for killing a black suspect. And even when overwhelming evidence of extralegal violence existed, as, for example, was exposed during the trial of nine white men who had participated in the posse that murdered Jim Mitchell in Mitchell County, Georgia, in 1921, juries were quick to acquit.[58]

Mass mobs were the most spectacular type of mob and consequently have received the most scrutiny. Southerners usually had the mass mob in mind when they discussed and wrote about lynchings, whether on lecture tours, in novels, or in homespun letters to the editors of local rural newspapers. If observers and historians too often have treated mass mobs as "typical" mobs, they have not exaggerated their significance. Mass mobs were the most common type of mob in Georgia, accounting for more than 34 percent of all lynchings in the state. In Virginia, mass mobs were responsible for 40 percent of all lynchings. Often numbering in the hundreds, even thousands, and acting with widespread local approval, they could intimidate all but the most resolute sheriffs and could force their way into most jails. They wreaked vengeance for alleged crimes that often had attracted widespread local, and, in many instances regional, attention. Finally, ritual assumed a far greater significance in lynchings conducted by mass mobs than in those by any other type of mob.

The incidence of lynchings by mass mobs mirrored the trend of lynching in the South in general. In Georgia, they occurred infrequently in the 1880s, then rose sharply during the 1890s before declining gradually in each subsequent decade until the 1930s, when they became a rarity. In Virginia, a similar pattern also is apparent. Mass mobs claimed most of their victims during the 1890s. Then, the incidence of mass mob violence dropped sharply until the 1920s, when a temporary resurgence of such lynchings occurred. Although the dates of the rise and decline of extralegal violence in postbellum Georgia and Virginia differ markedly, it is clear that the ebb and flow of lynchings by mass mobs paralleled the general levels of lynching in the two states. The pattern of violence by mass mobs is a measure of the legitimacy of lynching in the South. As long as lynchings enjoyed broad popular support and faced little opposition from law officers or officials, mass mobs accounted for a substantial proportion of mob violence. As opposition to lynching mounted and support for extralegal violence eroded, lynchings by mass mobs occurred less often and the vengeance of private mobs claimed a larger proportion of mob victims (Figure 1).

The size of mass mobs, ranging from sixty to more than four thousand members, reflected the notoriety of the alleged crimes that had inspired the mobs. Predictably, heinous crimes stirred mass mobs into action; the more gruesome and widely reported the alleged crime, the larger the mob was likely to have been. Suspects charged with rape, attempted rape, or murder accounted for the vast majority of the victims of mass mobs.[59] Enraged by crimes perceived to be particularly abhorrent, the fury of mass mobs often could not be satisfied with a single victim and consequently multiple victims were likely. On several occasions mass mobs executed three victims at once, and a few bloodthirsty mobs lynched five and seven victims at a time.[60]

Mass mobs, despite their size, acted swiftly. In Georgia, they captured and executed more than 53 percent of their victims within a day of the alleged crime and more than 85 percent within a week. Similarly, in Virginia, mass mobs lynched 45 percent of their victims within a day and more than 75 percent within a week.

There is little conclusive evidence of who actually participated in mass mobs. Distinctions that some scholars have drawn between "proletariat" mobs, comprised of lower-class whites, and "Bourbon" mobs, which included prominent local residents, confuse the matter and are unconvincing.[61] Extant evidence suggests that the composition of a mob principally reflected the status of the victim of the alleged crime and local perceptions of the alleged crime. Mass mobs potentially included anyone willing to participate. As was true in other mobs, the family, friends and neighbors of an alleged criminal's victim often took part and assumed a prominent role.[62] Although mass mobs, like all other types of mobs, were male-dominated assemblies, women and even children, by inciting the crowd with cheers, providing fuel for the execution pyre and, scavenging for souvenirs after the lynchings, often figured prominently in the proceedings. This inclusiveness of all ages and both sexes gave the violence of mass mobs power to articulate and, in turn, help perpetuate time-honored cultural preoccupations to a far greater degree than any other form of mob violence.

The lynching of Reuben Hudson, a black vagrant charged with the rape of Mrs. James Bush, a young white woman, in 1887 is one example of the prominent role of the family of the alleged crime victim and the breadth of community participation in mass mobs. As news of the Hudson's crime spread in DeKalb County, Georgia, friends and neighbors organized a posse and began to search for the criminal. On the morning following the alleged assault, Hudson was arrested while trying to escape on the railroad. Crowds began to pour into the town of Decatur until several hundred had gathered; when the train carrying the suspect arrived, the crowd, to the cry, "Hang him, kill him, burn him!" easily overpowered the bailiff in charge of Hudson. Mrs. Bush, frail and traumatized, was brought before the prisoner. When asked if he was the "right negro," Mrs. Bush, shaking with fury, pointed to Hudson and answered, "That is him, before God!" Under the leadership of a young local doctor and Mr. Bush, the crowd immediately set off to find a tree on which to hang its prisoner. After locating an appropriate site, the mob repeatedly attempted to extract a confession from Hudson. Finally, they tired of his refusal to confess, and Mr. Bush and several other men pulled him up for good. Within minutes, Hudson died. Later, Mrs. Bush, along with crowds of men, women, and children, visited the scene of the lynching and praised the deed. A local newspaper concluded, "Every brute. . . who commits the crime Hudson committed, will find such a fate in store for him. Our wives, mothers, and daughters will be protected." [63]

As the participants in the lynching of Hudson suggest, mass mobs were not comprised of malcontents or backwoods hicks. Judge Samuel C. Goodwyn, a former judge and locally prominent politician, led the mob that executed a black man and a white man in Emporia, Virginia, in March 1900. Among the "solid citizens" in the mob that burned two blacks alive in Statesboro, Georgia, in August 1904, were a railroad auditor, a manager of the local ice company, and an accountant. The mob that lynched a black man on the outskirts of Macon, Georgia, in August 1922, followed the lead of the manager of a local hotel, the president of an insurance company, a local merchant, and a city firefighter. Of course, most mob members remain unknown. But there seems no reason to question contemporary news accounts that describe many mass mobs as including "the best citizens" of the community.[64]

Most mass mobs displayed considerable organization. At the very least, a certain degree of planning was necessary either to overpower law officers or to storm jails. In Georgia, mass mobs took 44 percent of their victims from jails and 72 percent from the hands of the law. In Virginia, they took 47 percent of their victims from jails, and all of their victims from the custody of law officers. Jails, if well-built, posed a challenge: planning and coordination were necessities when breaking into a building specifically designed to prevent inmates from breaking out. In 1908, the mob intent on lynching Alonzo Williams, a black charged with attempted rape, needed energy and ingenuity to take him from the jail in Lyons, Georgia. Members of the mob spent more than two hours climbing by ladder to the second story of the jail, cutting a hole in the wall, crawling through, and then finally ripping open the door of Williams's cell. The mob that lynched Sam Stephens, an alleged rapist, in Toccoa, Georgia, on June 14, 1915, needed even greater fortitude. After devoting more than five hours to breaking into the jail and being thwarted by the door of the black man's cell, the mob had to settle for firing hundreds of rounds through the cell door and into Stephens's body.[65] The mob that lynched William Lavender, a black accused of attempted rape in Roanoke, Virginia, in 1892, had to carry out a systematic block-by-block search throughout the city for hours before they discovered where the police had hidden him.[66]

Once a mass mob had captured its victim, the selection of the site of the execution, the act of execution, and the immediate aftermath of the lynching unfolded in a highly ritualized choreography. Mass mobs were not solely intent on murdering their victims; had they been they would have dispatched them with as little fanfare as did terrorist mobs and posses. Most mass mobs had didactic aims; their actions both conveyed the degradation that they believed their victim deserved and underscored the legitimacy of the extralegal execution. The ritual of execution, of course, was not codified and, like many other secular rituals, allowed ample opportunity for improvisation and variation. But, given that mass mobs were ephemeral and had a lifespan that ended with the life of their victim, it is striking how unvaried their rituals were.

Ritual provided a degree of order in mass lynchings, preventing disorder and bedlam from breaking out at any moment. Mundane considerations of safety for the mob members at least partially explain the concern for order. For example, the mob that lynched Jim Glover, a black charged with the rape of a thirteen-year-old white girl in Cedartown, Georgia, in 1904, demonstrated the hazards of too little organization. Following the capture of Glover, the mob of five hundred formed a circle and opened fire on him. Stray bullets killed one man and seriously wounded at least four other mob members. Similarly, the mob that captured Floyd

Carmichael, a black charged with attempted rape, near Atlanta on July 31, 1906, brought him before his alleged victim and opened fire on him moments after he had been identified. Despite frantic efforts to escape the fusillade, a white man who had been holding Carmichael was struck by several bullets.[67]

Mobs drew upon the rituals of public executions when they staged lynchings. Public executions, festive and long-remembered spectacles, were commonplace events in the South until the end of the nineteenth century. The ritual of confession and prayer before the execution, and even the collection of pieces of the rope used in the lynching, paralleled events at legal executions. Lynchings, of course, had far less pomp and ceremony than did legal executions, at least in part because many whites believed that legal executions failed to instill sufficient terror in criminals. Summary justice allowed for both popular participation in the punishment of miscreants and potentially unlimited violence and terror. Moreover, mass lynchings subjected the victim to humiliation and degradation far beyond anything approached by legal executions. The drama of mass lynchings, as the historian Bertram Wyatt-Brown has observed, replaced the antiseptic retribution of the gallows with the brutally explicit violence of the community.[68]

The order of ritualized mob violence had important symbolic significance as well. Rituals usually are not meant to express the emotions of individual participants in a direct, spontaneous way. Expressions of uncontrolled violence, as in the lynchings of Jim Glover and Floyd Carmichael, threatened to degenerate into chaos. "Ritual," the anthropologist Stanley Tambiah observes, "is not a free expression of emotions but a disciplined rehearsal of right attitudes."[69] By executing their victims in a ritualized manner, mass mobs harnessed furious passion and released it in stereotyped conventions. The ceremony of lynchings both established conventions and isolated them from commonplace usage. In common with all rituals, lynching drew a boundary between public and private, thereby "insulating public order from private vagaries."[70] Lynchings that made little pretense of supporting public order (most often lynchings by terrorist and private mobs) were precisely the ones that displayed little or no ritual. Mass lynchings, on the other hand, were rife with evocations of beliefs that were vital to the community.

Participation in mass mobs did not mean that all mob members shared the same beliefs in the efficacy or legitimacy of the lynching. Some spectators may have been shocked and disgusted by the violence they witnessed, but it was their visible, explicit, public act of participation and not their ambiguous, private sentiment that bound the lynchers both socially and morally. Communal participation in mob violence ensured that no single individual would be held responsible for the execution because mass lynchings became the expression of communal values of law and order, family honor, and white supremacy rather than personal vengeance. Mob members did not suffer wrenching guilt; rather, they rejoiced that they had punished a deserving victim.

Mass mobs chose execution sites for explicitly symbolic reasons. Usually, victims were carried back to the scene of the precipitating crime. For example, the mob that lynched Albert Aiken near Lincolnton, Georgia, on May 24, 1909, stormed the county jail, carried Aiken three miles away to the scene of his alleged crime, and hanged him. Newspapers easily perceived the mob's intent; "the place where the negro is said to have been lynched," the *Augusta Chronicle* explained, "is near the place where he committed the crime and it is supposed that the mob who took him there had it in view to let the many negroes in that neighborhood see that it is time that they quieted down and stopped their efforts to ride over the farmers in that section." [71] If the scene of the alleged crime was too distant, mobs chose other sites that conveyed their rage unambiguously. In several instances, they hanged their victims on the same trees that had been used in previous lynchings. [72] Less often, victims were executed near black churches or in black neighborhoods. [73] Whenever possible an easily accessible and highly visible location was chosen. The mob that murdered Henry Davis in Cuthbert, Georgia, on August 9, 1885, for example, selected a bridge over a railroad track to serve as the gallows so that the dangling body would attract the attention of passengers each time a train stopped to swing the body out of the way. [74]

Once the mob selected the scene of the lynching, final preparations were made. In most instances, a knotted rope was slipped around the victim's neck, and he was then given an opportunity to confess and, sometimes, to pray. In instances where blacks were charged with attempted murder or murder, whites often assumed that a conspiracy was involved, so confessions became pretexts to punish any alleged accomplices. That the confessions were made under extreme duress mattered little because mobs executed their victims whether or not they confessed. Confessions, however prompted, served to legitimize further the executions in the eyes of mobs. Thus, the mob that lynched Tom Ruffin in Trenton, Georgia, in 1888, sent a white-robed member into the office of the county treasurer on the day after the lynching to let it be known that the black man had confessed to having attempted to rape a white woman. [75]

After a satisfactory confession had been extracted and the victim's prayers were over, the execution began. In the overwhelming majority of instances, mobs simply hanged their victims. Once the bodies were fully suspended, the participants fired fusillades into the corpses. The honor of firing the first shot sometimes was reserved specifically for certain members of the mob. Mary Marmon, who allegedly had been raped by Page Wallace, a black, in Loudoun County, Virginia, in February 1880, readily accepted the offer to fire the first shots into his body.[76] Most often, husbands or relatives of the victim of the alleged crime began the fusillade.[77] Often the gun fire, rather than the noose, killed the victim. Because tradition demanded that all lynching participants fire into the corpse, large mobs sometimes riddled the bodies with hundreds or even thousands of rounds, leaving the mangled corpses almost unrecognizable.

Mass mobs, more than any other type of mob, were likely to torture or burn victims. The size and fervor of mass mobs and the anonymity offered by the vast crowds incited lynchers to acts of almost unlimited sadism. In Georgia, news accounts suggest that mass mobs tortured and mutilated nearly a quarter of their victims in grisly ceremonies. In Virginia, however, fewer than one in ten victims was mutilated.[78] The most frequent form of mutilation was the burning of the victim's body after he had been hanged. Only rarely did mobs forgo hanging their victims before burning them. Torture was usually reserved for victims accused of murder; the intention was to extend suffering beyond endurance rather than to extract a confession. James Irwin, who was tortured and burned for the murder of a white girl in Ocilla, Georgia, on January 31, 1930, suffered only some of the sadistic indignities devised by mass mobs before he expired. Members of the mob cut off his fingers and toes, pulled out his teeth with pliers, and repeatedly jabbed him in the mouth with a pointed pole. After castrating the black man and collecting yet more souvenirs, the mob burned its victim alive.[79]

With the completion of an execution, mobs often hung signs on the corpse. The signs sometimes displayed morbid humor—a sign placed on the body of John Bailey read "Please Do Not Wake Him"—or even advertised goods. An Alexandria, Virginia, tobacco merchant with an eye for free publicity hung an advertisement for his products on the lamppost from which the body of Joseph McCoy, a black charged with rape, was suspended.[80] Most often the signs warned that a similar punishment awaited any future criminal guilty of the same offense. The mob that lynched Magruder Fletcher, an alleged rapist in Virginia, left a typical sign that proclaimed "We protect our mothers, daughters, and sisters, The Committee." One especially verbose mob that lynched two black men charged with assault in Glynn County, Georgia, left a sign that explained "The enormity of crime in this county forces an outraged public to make a fearful example of those committing the crimes. Evil-doers take warning from what they see. Mase Sawyer [identified by the *Savannah Morning News* as 'the leader of the lower class Brunswick negroes'] take warning." The mob that hanged Thomas Israel for allegedly attempting to rape a white child near Sylvania, Georgia, assumed a more literary stance. "To all my race that passeth by," their sign read, "look on and take heed that I am justified for the cause of this crime, and have received the punishment that is due all violators of this act. Tom Israel. P.S. Blessed be those who leaves [*sic*] me alone, and damned be [he] who moves my bones."[81]

The spectacle of the dangling corpse, the charred remains of the body, and stern signs of warning invariably attracted spectators. Local authorities routinely allowed bodies to remain on display for at least several hours and sometimes for days. In some instances whites even took steps to preserve the lynching site. After John Henry Williams was burned in June 1921, residents of Colquitt County, fearing that pigs would destroy his charred remains, protected the smoldering pyre by building a fence around the site.[82] More often, spectators seeking souvenirs posed the greatest threat to the lynching site. They quickly collected pieces of the rope and splinters from the hanging tree, as well as links of chains used to secure burning victims. Following the lynching of Jim Rhodes near Charlottesville, Virginia, in October 1882, enterprising spectators sold pieces of the rope and tree limb used to hang the man.[83] Spectators sometimes gathered pieces of the lynching victim's body and, after burnings, pieces of bone.[84] In February 1923, following the lynching of two black men for murdering a member of a posse, a drug store in Milledgeville, Georgia, prominently displayed a finger and an ear in a large bottle with a sign reading "What's left of the niggers that shot a white man."[85] Just how often mobs mutilated the corpses of their victims is impossible to determine, but it is safe to assume, at the very least, that the bodies of those blacks charged with sensational crimes that attracted large mobs almost certainly did not remain intact.

In Virginia, the burial of the body of the mob's victim usually marked the conclusion of the violence of mass lynchings. Lynchings in Virginia seldom spawned extended campaigns of violence against blacks. In Georgia, however, the atmosphere of smoldering racial tension that lingered after mass lynchings sometimes flared into continued violence and indiscriminate attacks on blacks, especially in those regions of the state that were most plagued by mob violence. Whites searched out blacks that had been named in the lynching victim's confession, as well as blacks whose behavior had provoked resentment. At times, rampaging whites also attacked and burned black churches, schools, and fraternal lodges.[86]

A lynching could become the pretext for a reign of terror. In the aftermath of the lynching of two blacks for the rape of a white girl in Forsyth County, Georgia, for example, white tenant farmers used violence and intimidation to drive virtually every black, whether landowner or tenant farmer, from both Forsyth and Dawson counties.[87] Ray Stannard Baker, a northern journalist and the author of *Following the Color Line,* concluded from his study of lynchings, perhaps with some exaggeration, that "not one single mob stopped when the immediate work was done, unless under compulsion."[88] Baker's claim, however, obscures the important connection between mass lynchings and antiblack pogroms. Extended campaigns of violence typically followed mass lynchings but only rarely lynchings by either private mobs or posses. Although these episodes of ongoing terrorism were not the work of mass mobs, the whites who carried out the violence almost certainly believed that their deeds represented the continuation of the mass mobs' labor.

The meeting of coroners' juries to determine the cause of death was the concluding ritual of mass lynchings. The typical finding of these juries, that the victim came to his death at the hands of "unknown parties," was both predictable and puzzling. That juries confronted obstacles in investigating terrorist and private mobs is hardly surprising. But they faced few apparent difficulties in identifying participants in mass mobs, who made no pretense of camouflaging their identities and even gloried in their participation. What is paradoxical is that coroners' juries would adhere to the process of the law when they carried out bogus investigations of violence which, however much it violated the rule of law with impunity, they had no intention of condemning. In reports typically written out in crude longhand on any convenient piece of paper the most horrifying details of mass lynchings were recorded. The juries had little difficulty in finding witnesses who could describe events in detail. But even when the witnesses mentioned specific names, juries, which in many instances included men who had participated in the lynching, either exonerated the community of all involvement in the lynching or else openly applauded the mob violence.[89] The Early County, Georgia, coroner's jury, for example, met following the lynching of Aaron Coachman in 1884 and concluded that the black youth was killed by "citizens of Early County, who rose in mass and indignation." The jury proclaimed the lynching a justifiable homicide. Virtually the same words were parroted by a coroner's jury in Clay County, Georgia, that announced following the lynching of Dan Buck, a black youth, in 1891, "that Dan Buck having confessed the crime of an attempt to rape a respectable white girl, . . . the citizens rose up en masse and killed him." [90] The paradox is that coroners' juries would make any pretense at investigating the murders in the first place.[91] However token the process, in the eyes of white southerners the investigations by coroners' juries and grand juries were testimonials to the rule of law.

Lynching by mass mobs, and the massive retaliation it represented, shadowed all other forms of mob violence. Jacquelyn Dowd Hall, a historian, astutely observes that the extraordinary rituals and savagery of mass mobs "did not have to occur very often, or be witnessed directly, to be burned indelibly into the mind." [92] They helped to create a climate in which other lynchings, even when unaccompanied by ritual, could seem legitimate. Even though communities sometimes did not respond to all lynchings with the same approbation or tolerance with which they responded to mass lynchings, members of mass mobs undoubtedly congratulated themselves and were applauded for acting in the interests of their communities.

While white contemporaries were sensitive to some of the complexities of lynching and recognized differences between various types of mob violence, blacks understandably concentrated on the glaringly obvious fact that most mob violence was directed against them. For blacks in Georgia and Virginia, or anywhere else in the South, it no doubt would have been an exercise in academic hairsplitting to suggest that it made any difference whether they were lynched by a posse or a mass mob. Because mobs, whatever form they took, sent shudders throughout the black community, there was cold comfort in the fact that most lynchings were the actions of small numbers rather than swelling masses of whites.

That some blacks participated in or condoned mob violence suggests that under certain conditions, however rare, some did not view lynchings as an inherent expression of racial repression. As has been noted previously, terrorist and private mobs comprised of blacks murdered a small number of blacks in both Georgia and Virginia. In a few rare instances, lynch mobs were comprised of both blacks and whites. After years of enduring the unpredictable violence and extreme cruelty of Abe Redmond, a white farmer in Charlotte County, Virginia, a small number of blacks joined with their white neighbors in 1893 and lynched him. In one exceptional instance in Virginia, blacks even participated in a huge mass mob that lynched Walter Cotton, a black "desperado," and Brandt O'Grady, a white tramp suspected of aiding Cotton. On March 24, 1900, a mob ignored the timid protests of law officers and lynched Cotton in retaliation for the murder of several whites. Blacks who had witnessed the lynching (some accounts even suggest that they participated actively) demanded "You have lynched the negro; now lynch the white man." They led the mob that dragged O'Grady from his jail cell and lynched him near Cotton's dangling corpse.[93]

Even when the racial motivations in lynchings were explicit, blacks recognized that there were subtle distinctions among lynchings, and their response varied depending upon the nature of the violence they faced. Black tenants threatened by whitecappers understood that their white employers and assailants, for all of whites' talk of racial solidarity and white supremacy, had competing interests, and they tried to take advantage of divisions among whites for their own protection. Blacks looked to their employers to shield them from terrorist mobs, and sometimes that protection was forthcoming.

During the frenzy of mass mobs, however, blacks fully recognized the risks of appealing to whites for protection. Instead, they went into hiding and scrupulously avoided any act of provocation. For blacks who lacked (or refused to depend upon) white protectors, flight was one of the few responses to white violence that at once was independent of whites and yet typically did not inspire retaliation from them. In countless instances, news of mass mobs prompted blacks to flee their homes and hide. Whites, who interpreted flight in the wake of lynchings as a thinly veiled gesture of protest, often worried that the exodus of black farmhands posed a serious economic threat.[94] Whether flight should be judged a form of protest or common sense is open to debate. There is, however, reason to believe that flight was more than just a supine response. Sometimes, blacks congregated in large numbers and—more important—armed themselves. These actions, of course, did not prevent whites from storming jails or running down black victims, but they did ensure that large numbers of blacks gained at least temporary protection from indiscriminate violence.[95]

Even the funeral of a mob victim bore the marks of the kind of mob responsible for the lynching. Following private and terrorist lynchings, blacks held funerals for the mobs' victims with little interference from whites. But in the aftermath of mass lynchings, the families of victims often were unwilling even to accept the responsibility and cost of burial. The aunt of Joseph McCoy, a black lynched in Alexandria, Virginia, in 1897, voiced the bitterness of countless relatives when she remarked, "As the people killed him, they will have to bury him." The strained atmosphere in the wake of lynchings also constrained black ministers when they performed funeral services for the mob victims. Those so bold as to criticize whites who participated in lynchings risked retaliation. The Reverend William Gaines, who presided at the service for McCoy, angered whites by his sharp criticisms of the lynchers. Gaines suffered no apparent penalty in Alexandria, but in other instances whites were less forgiving and compelled black ministers whose funeral services and comments were judged incendiary to leave the community.[96] In March 1899, for example, following the lynching of at least four black men in Palmetto, Georgia, whites forced an outspoken black minister who claimed to have the names of some of the mob members to leave the community.[97]

Blacks, who seized upon any safe opportunity to protest against white violence, recognized that they could be outspoken after some lynchings, especially those by terrorist and private mobs. Aware that these types of mob violence were not uniformly condoned by whites, blacks took advantage of the opening and carefully released their pent-up frustration and anger. In 1894, for example, following the devastation wrought by the ruthless posse that murdered five blacks in Brooks County, Georgia, blacks held a mass meeting and issued a proclamation protesting the failure of law officers and the state to protect them. But any protest after a mass lynching required great tact because even token criticism might provoke additional white violence.[98]

During the tense aftermath of a mass lynching, intimidated blacks sometimes went to great lengths to divorce themselves from any appearance of protest. When George Bowen heard that he was accused of being in sympathy with Jesse Williams, a black lynched by a mass mob in Dodge County, Georgia, in 1892, he contacted the local white newspaper "to set himself right in public." He explained in a public, printed statement that he was "heartily in favor of the lynching and that all the negroes he had talked to are the same way." [99] Following the lynching of Obe Cox in Oglethorpe County, Georgia, in September 1919, a committee of blacks wrote a public letter applauding the mob. In a thinly veiled plea that the lynching not be used as a pretext to terrorize the black community, the letter announced "We certainly thank you for handling this case so nice, for it could have been worse for us. . . . Our white people fought no one but the brute, Obe Cox, which was right and we thank them for it." [100] Outraged that any blacks would endorse mob violence, the influential black *Chicago Defender* set out to discredit the letter writers. After an investigation, the paper concluded that blacks who endorsed the Cox lynchings "do not stand for much in the town and are excused for their utter ignorance in condoning crime [lynching]." [101] Given the cumulative effects of generations of terror and white violence, it is not surprising that a few blacks in Oglethorpe County or elsewhere would endorse the occasional lynching. But whites made a grave error when they took such endorsements on face value and failed to recognize the combination of fear, deception, and pragmatic deference that lay behind them.

Lynch mobs, with their explicit and brutal methods, sent a wide range of messages to blacks and whites alike. The small mob of whites who murdered Ben Teott, a black tenant in Echols County, Georgia, in 1897 aimed to alert blacks to the dangers of cattle theft and vandalism, but it also left a note explicitly warning Teott's employer to stop hiring "offensive" blacks and to alter his objectionable behavior (he apparently was the beneficiary of Teott's cattle rustling) or suffer the consequences.[102] To conclude that Teott's lynching exposed submerged class tensions among whites would risk reading too much into fragmentary sources. But it is clear that the lynching gave expression to tensions that divided the white community even as it united the mob participants. Moreover, if white racism gave license to racial violence in general, it did not extend equal prestige to all forms of mob violence.

There is an important difference between community approval for lynching in the form of open community participation and community acquiescence in the form of the refusal to investigate or prosecute lynchers. Although all lynchings were a means to defend the established order against unwelcome change or perceived threats, the variations in the form of communal participation have important implications for the degree to which lynchings could symbolically unite whites and reaffirm commonly held values. Terrorist and private mobs set boundaries for black (and white) behavior, but mass mobs, with their conventionalized rage, most fully exposed, strengthened, and preserved the social and racial foundations of southern society. The rituals of mass mobs, and to a lesser extent the less formalized behavior of posses, in which multitudes of whites participated, created a heightening of experience and moments of such exceptional and widely shared emotional intensity that they were quickly enshrined in local folk legend. Almost by definition, the furtive violence of private and terrorist mobs was not (at least in the eyes of whites) so clearly set off from other more mundane and quickly forgotten forms of violence. Moreover, the racist component of mob violence became more explicit in proportion to the degree of communal participation. Unlike the more secretive forms of mobs that struck out against the occasional white, mass mobs meted out extralegal justice to whites in only the rarest instances. In short, mass mobs, more than any other type of mob violence, gave vent to the most fulsome and virulent expressions of the racist pathology at the heart of southern mob violence.

As the antilynching crusade matured during the early twentieth century, reformers increasingly came to recognize the significance of the complexities and variations in mob violence. Despite law officers who became more conscientious about preventing extralegal violence, and despite national and regional movements against the values that justified and sustained lynching, some forms of mob violence persisted. Even as lynchings by mass mobs became rarities, the more secretive forms—terrorist and private mob violence—endured. And it was these tenacious but difficult to define types of violence that increasingly attracted the attention of reformers in the 1930s and 1940s. Not surprisingly, the antilynching crusaders who met in 1940 found it difficult to develop a comprehensive definition of such a multifarious phenomenon so deeply rooted in southern life.

2

"To Draw the Line": Crimes and Victims

As the number of lynchings rose steadily during the late nineteenth century, white southerners engaged in lengthy discussions among themselves over which crimes justified mob violence and which more properly should be left to the courts. In May 1893, the *Atlanta Constitution* called upon southerners to refrain from uncontrolled mob violence. "It may be hard to draw the line, but it must be done somewhere," the newspaper pleaded. "The stern justice administered by the people in their sovereign capacity must not be made too common." [1] Generations of southern whites, however, found it difficult to heed such advice. Most agreed that the crimes that posed the greatest menace to the racial hierarchy fell within the jurisdiction of the lynch mob, but they differed about the countless minor offenses that posed only the most modest threat to white authority. Because the notion of "a proper place" for blacks was inherently imprecise, the province of mob violence was necessarily ambiguous. Moreover, the simple truth that lynching, as a form of punishment, was susceptible to the personal whims of each lyncher ensured that the jurisdiction of the lynch mob was both expansive and capricious.

Despite appearances, the pathology of lynchings was neither random nor entirely irrational. A brutal logic underlay the violence. As a rule, lynchings were not spontaneous acts against convenient blacks. Whites almost always believed that mobs punished real transgressions and that the lust for vengeance played a prominent role in lynching. It was not essential to mob members that their victims be actually guilty of a crime, but it was important that some sort of infraction had taken place.

The ideology of white supremacy and the pervasive belief in black criminality among whites did not invest every black-white dispute with the full force of community outrage. Whites' perceptions of crimes and disputes varied, as did

*Focus on free
a (though being a
crime?)*

responses to them. Whites took into account not only the nature of the offense itself, but also who did what to whom. A seemingly trivial infraction of racial etiquette, such as a black man writing a letter to a white woman, was unlikely to incite the same response as a murder or an alleged rape. The ascending order to the seriousness with which whites viewed and responded to alleged offenses was demonstrated by the range of mobs, from private to mass mobs, that punished perceived transgressions. A complex link existed between the local perceptions of an alleged crime and the type of mob that punished that offense. The lowest order of offenses included minor infractions, such as theft and "wild talk," that could, but need not, incite mob vengeance. Such crimes seldom elicited the full force of ritualized communal violence and instead were the particular province of private and terrorist mobs. The second order, which included transgressions whites viewed as overt or implicit sexual crimes, often (but it should be stressed not always) called forth the full sadistic potential of southern mobs. Finally, the highest level included murder and murderous attacks which, more than any other crimes, incited large numbers of whites—indeed, even entire communities—to extralegal violence. Thus, the variations in mobs and the various degrees of legitimacy they enjoyed were intimately connected to prevailing attitudes toward and perceptions of crime (Figure 2).[2]

The escalating response to the perceived gravity of offenses, whether measured by the level of violence inflicted or the size and character of the mob, is, in part, a reflection of the persisting code of honor in the South. The ethic of honor imparted far more significance to certain crimes than to others and in turn demanded different responses, depending upon the seriousness of the offense. Raw human emotion also dictated the reactions to perceived transgressions; murder, to be sure, is a more provocative crime than theft and is more likely to inspire a passionate response. But the culture of honor played a crucial role in directing the release of spontaneous emotions and passions in certain time-honored customs.

*Good
ideas of
honor*

To aspire to honor in the South—and white men in all social classes coveted their honor—was to be vitally concerned about one's public reputation. Honor demanded that a person always see himself through the eyes of others because personal worth was determined not by self-appraisal but by the worth others conferred. The code demanded that each man be vigilant in guarding his honor against the persistent threat of slights, and that when his honor was violated he seek immediate personal vindication. All too often, the final defense of wounded honor lay in physical violence. Of course, a man might refrain from avenging a slight, but to do so risked tarnishing his honor and earning the reputation of a coward.[3]

Because the code of honor gave license to—indeed demanded—violence as a

Figure 2. Lynchings of Blacks by Category of Alleged Crime, 1880–1930

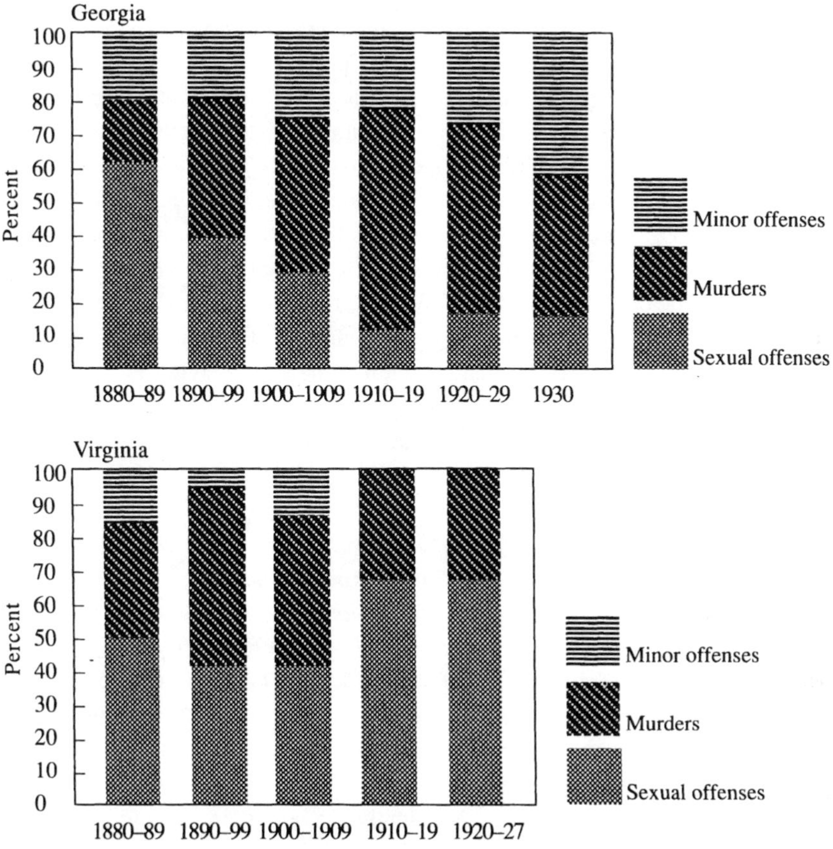

defense of honor, it bred all sorts of contests, ranging from street corner brawls to formalized feuds. In most circumstances, the code did not dictate a communal response. No one could take responsibility for an insult to another's honor because to do so was to imply that the slighted individual was unable or unwilling to defend his own honor and therefore was undeserving of community esteem in the first place. Violations of personal honor, however, could have broader repercussions. Because honor also bound together families, honor was more than a purely personal attribute. Each man committed his personal honor to the defense of his family's honor, and consequently only the finest line separated an affront against an individual and an insult to family honor. When that line was crossed, a man might respond by recruiting his immediate family to help him defend his reputation and, by extension, their honor as well.[4]

The ethic of honor also invested the community with collective honor. The defense of communal honor could take many forms, ranging from stoning boys from neighboring towns who courted local girls to banishing bootleggers. At the heart of community honor lay a defense of the traditions that preserved it, including a reverence of womanly virtue. While leaving the complexities of the place of southern women in the code of honor to later elaboration, it is enough to stress that just as a man's reputation could not be separated from the standing of the women in his family, so, too, a community's honor reflected the virtue of its women. The code of honor delegated purity and virtue to women, but it entrusted the defense of women's virtue to men. An attack upon a woman was an offense of such gravity that it demanded the fiercest retaliation and became a prominent motive for collective action. Serious offenses by blacks against prominent whites also menaced group honor and provoked a commensurate response. The primal bonds of community, obligation, and deference all came into play when, for example, a law officer was attacked.[5]

As important as honor was as an underpinning of southern culture and, more precisely, lynchings, it is important to recognize that the code could not escape untouched by the powerful changes in the South during the late nineteenth century. As the conditions that had protected southern honor from competing values of dignity and restraint changed, honor itself underwent changes.[6] A litany of toxic forces—emancipation, economic diversification, urbanization, and industrialization—during the late nineteenth century greatly weakened the culture of honor, and with each decade it became less formalized (witness the death of duelling) and its strictures bound day-to-day life less tightly. As honor eroded, the practice of lynching simultaneously underwent transformation. Over time, offenses that had demanded immediate vindication at the hands of the community did so with less and less frequency. In a process that varied in speed from region to region, the uneven erosion of honor bred disagreement among white southerners about both honor and the violence that it sanctioned. Contentious debates over "gun-toting" and all manner of violence were symptoms of honor's embattled status during the late nineteenth century.

It is not coincidental that in societies where honor is pronounced, dishonor is also conspicuous. In the South, dishonor became intimately intertwined with black inequality and subordination. During slavery, blacks by definition had been dishonored (in the eyes of whites at least), and even after emancipation whites continued to deny that blacks could posses honor.[7] Following emancipation, one of the most pernicious manifestations of the continuing dishonor of blacks was their depiction as habitual criminals, a portrait of the race that both shaped white attitudes toward lynching and legitimized violence that otherwise would have posed the most serious questions about civilization in the South.

During the late nineteenth century, most southern whites concluded that a transformation in the tone of race relations was underway. Their dread of social amalgamation with blacks, abhorrence of black education, and contempt for black efforts toward advancement became the fodder for the violent racial ideology of a new generation of white supremacists. Fired by the conviction that blacks, particularly those members of the new generation unschooled in appropriate behavior by slavery, were retrogressing into savagery, whites harbored growing fears of black criminality—especially fears of black rapists. A crime wave during the late nineteenth century contributed to the disturbed state of race relations. Mindful of prisons crowded with blacks, whites concluded that a new class of criminal blacks was responsible for the epidemic of crime that threatened to overwhelm the region.[8]

Like most myths, the myth of black criminality was (and indeed remains) resistant to change. Even while the practice of lynching changed significantly, whites clung to the notion that lynchings were the predictable consequence of black crime, particularly sexual assaults. Just as the myth obscured the reality of many of the causes of lynchings, it also smothered criticism and offered only the most pessimistic outlook for the future of extralegal violence. John Temple Graves, the Atlanta newspaper editor, astounded his Chautauqua audience in 1903 by baldly stating that "It [lynching] is here to stay." Lynchings, Graves and other whites speculated, might eventually cease to occur not because lynchers were criticized, but because blacks had adopted the values of whites. Only when blacks upheld the law and no longer posed a threat to whites, the argument went, would mob violence pass away. As Graves explained, "lynching will never hereafter be discontinued in this republic until the crime which provokes it is destroyed."[9]

Nothing more vividly conveys the impulsiveness of southern mobs than lynchings for seemingly trivial infractions. A black man's refusal to back down in an argument with a white, a reckless insult of a white, or a petty theft could all incite mob violence. The number of victims murdered for minor offenses, although neither so large as many critics and scholars of lynching have suggested nor so small as contemporary white southerners alleged, underscores the importance of mob violence as a means of systematic racial repression.

The crimes that provoked mob violence varied from region to region in the South. In Virginia, as in many states outside of the Deep South, the crimes were narrowly defined. Between 1880 and 1930, mobs in Virginia executed only seven victims for such minor offenses as arson, burglary, or horse theft. Mobs in Georgia and elsewhere in the Deep South, however, demonstrated a much broader conception of the crimes that justified extralegal punishment. In Georgia during the same period, slightly more than 25 percent of the black lynching victims were executed for minor transgressions or for breaching the color barrier, sometimes in seemingly insignificant ways. Not only did minor offenses provoke a sizable proportion of all lynchings in Georgia, but they also consistently incited mob violence during the five decades under discussion.[10]

The culture of racism and honor sanctioned lynchings for minor offenses, but it did not extend to them the symbolic significance of lynchings for more serious offenses. Lynchings for minor transgressions seldom were accompanied by any elaborate ritual. In Virginia, either private or terrorist mobs punished blacks charged with minor offenses, and in Georgia, where in rare instances posses and public mobs swung into action to punish minor offenses, terrorist and private mobs murdered the overwhelming percentage of blacks accused of trivial infractions (Figure 3).

Incidents that could escalate into mob violence were part of the normal workings of southern race relations. The elaborate codes of racial etiquette dictated even the most minute details of everyday conduct and determined how blacks addressed whites, how they comported themselves in the presence of whites, and even how they expressed humor, anger, or any other emotion. Blacks had to observe scrupulously the exacting standards of behavior lest they offend whites. Any behavior that departed from the local traditions of racial conduct might simultaneously offend whites' collective honor and threaten racial hierarchy.

In some instances, violations of the rules of racial etiquette led to an escalation of tensions between whites and blacks until whites resorted to extralegal violence. Bold talk was sufficient to initiate a chain of events that culminated in the lynching of Will Jones, a black tenant farmer in Schley County, Georgia. In February 1922, a black acquaintance of Jones had offered a ride in his car to a white woman. The offer, apparently perceived as a breach of racial etiquette, outraged neighboring whites. When Jones heard rumors that some whites planned to whip the car's owner, he angrily complained to the son of his employer, "it looked like that was damn poor business for folks to go off hunting a man that done something like that. That boy hadn't done anything except ask that woman to ride, and she didn't have to ride with him if she didn't want to. [Jones warned] that if anybody come to him that way, he would do his damndest to kill him."

Figure 3. Lynchings of Blacks for Alleged Minor Offenses, 1880–1930

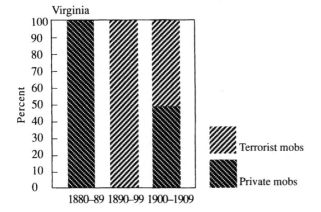

That whites would test the black man's boast was virtually certain, because his employer was related to the "outraged" white woman. Late on the night of February 13, a group of six men surrounded Jones's house and unsuccessfully tried to draw him out. When he attempted to escape through the back door, a gun battle ensued, and both Jones and his assailants were wounded. He survived the night, but on the following day another mob captured him and riddled his body with bullets.[11]

Blacks who showed insufficient subservience to racial protocol in myriad ways suffered at the hands of small mobs. Following the lynching of three blacks near Leesburg, Georgia, Enoch Daniels irritated some of his white neighbors by vociferously condemning the act. Despite threats and warnings to keep quiet, he persisted in his protests. On the night of April 27, 1899, a small group of whites dragged Daniels from his home and hanged him. In September 1919, a mob lynched Ernest Glenwood, a farmhand in Dooly County, Georgia, for circulating "propaganda." The black man, who had been trying to organize black workers to refuse to work for 60 cents a day, was overpowered by three white men. They tied his arms together, forced him to jump into a river, and then riddled his body with bullets as he struggled for air.[12]

Although arson and theft were long-established methods of anonymous black protest, and might therefore have been pretexts for mob violence, few lynchings were prompted by either crime. Yet, when arson and theft became pervasive problems and frustration with the difficulty of prosecuting suspected arsonists and thieves mounted, whites predictably advocated lynch law.[13] In 1899, after arsonists burned stables belonging to several prominent Terrell County, Georgia, farmers, the local editor concluded that "if these things [fires] continue, we will be forced to have a paid [police] department or a vigilante committee."[14] Whites typically resorted to whippings and beatings, rather than the noose, to punish arson and theft. When the punishment of alleged arsonists or thieves occasionally got out of hand, however, victims were killed.[15] In at least one instance, whites also justified lynching as punishment for an incorrigible thief who, despite previous punishment or warnings, persisted in committing crimes.[16]

Blacks guilty of nothing more than eccentric behavior could also become victims of mob violence. For example, in Jasper County, Georgia, in 1902, a mob murdered a black who apparently had terrified a little white girl when he offered to conjure for her. Even retarded or insane blacks who unintentionally committed crimes, and drunken blacks who offended whites, came to grief. Finally, blacks were lynched for such apparent trivialities as "frightening women," enticing a servant away, public indecency, and writing a letter to a white girl.[17]

Ambiguities and contradictions within the codes of racial etiquette and honor, which became more marked over time, gave rise to circumstances in which whites disagreed over the appropriateness of mob violence. Simply put, there were instances when the members of the local citizenry refused to accept that either the racial hierarchy or white honor were threatened by black behavior. White men who twisted mob violence to their personal ends could offend white sentiment by aping a dignity and standing they did not have. Explicit in many editorials against whitecappers and others who used trivial infractions by blacks as a pretext for mob violence were denials that the lynchers' actions could be justified as defenses of honor. Although the whites who punished Will Jones for his boastfulness believed that they were punishing a black for overstepping his place and laying claim to dignity beyond his status, the local newspaper and law officials saw their act as nothing but primitive brutality that deserved and received prosecution.

Far more often, the ambiguities of white supremacy and honor did not culminate in lynchings followed by prosecutions. Rather, whites accepted that a violation of white honor might demand extralegal punishment but felt no responsibility to administer the punishment as a community. The lynching of Tom Smith and John Coleman, two black sharecroppers, in Wilkes County, Georgia, in December 1888 sheds light on why minor infractions seldom mobilized whites to rise en masse. Although Smith and Coleman were charged with insulting a white woman and staging an insurrection, they, in fact, were caught in the middle of a controversy between their white employer, a Baptist minister and planter, and another white man who furnished them with supplies. When the black men tried to take their shares of cotton to the supplier, they provoked a bitter dispute between their employer and the supplier over who had first claims on the cotton. The planter swore out a warrant against the black men and retained the cotton. The supplier in turn provided the blacks with arms for protection, which they used when a small group of whites attempted to arrest them. Enraged by their resistance, the small mob captured the two blacks, tied rocks around their necks, and drowned them in a river. Their murders were more than just object lessons for the black community; the supplier himself was forced to leave the county out of fear for his life.[18]

The common thread that runs through the lynching of Smith and Coleman and many similar lynchings is that the alleged transgressions were interpreted to be grave insults to individual whites rather than as challenges either to the racial hierarchy or to communal honor. Seen in this light, the perception, at least according to contemporary accounts, that the white supplier was responsible for the dispute may help to explain why the larger white community played no role in the punishment of the black men.

The persistent scrutiny of black behavior for evidence of deceit and unacceptable aspirations, to be sure, threatened constantly to generate violent encounters. The averted look, the mumbled insubordination, or the momentary sneer by a black in the presence of a white might all be perceived to be grievous wrongs, but it was up to each white to make the intricate determinations of the magnitude of the insult. However explicit the rules that regulated black behavior, they were, except in the most obvious instances of intentional disrespect, open to the interpretation of each white. Consequently, just how whites perceived slights and what recourse they took varied. Whites might choose to ignore a slight, or they might violently punish it. The offended white had to determine if the perceived slight would injure his public standing, and whatever action he took, the actual punishment of the black who failed to demonstrate adequate deference was essentially a private matter. An offended white might draw upon support from his family and neighbors (who probably were kin also), all of whom had an immediate interest in the social reputation of the slighted individual. The larger community, however, had no similar obligation to participate in the punishment. Thus, the more trivial breeches of traditional codes of conduct typically did not fuel mass violence. Of course, even though whites may have taken into account the circumstances of minor infractions and recognized their equivocal threat to the fabric of race relations, the acceptance that disputes might be settled by violence opened the possibility for the use of mob violence (even if only of the most private forms) to punish even trivial slights.

The "unspeakable crime"—rape—gripped the imaginations of whites to a far greater extent than any other offense. Ignoring statistics that showed that sexual offenses did not spark most lynchings, white southerners maintained that rape was the key to lynching. Lynchings, as the Virginia author Thomas Nelson Page explained, expressed "the determination [of whites] to put an end to the ravishing of their women by an inferior race." [19] His patience tried by commonplace observations that rape was not the cause of most lynchings, Clarence H. Poe, a North Carolina farm journal editor, felt obliged to explain that "to say that men are lynched for other crimes than that against white women, and that therefore lynching cannot be attributed to it, is to be more plausible than accurate." The crime of lynching, he argued, began as a punishment for sexual assaults; "here and only here could the furious mob spirit break through the resisting wall of law and order." [20] Moreover, white southerners held a very broad conception of the behavior that posed a sexual threat. Methodist Bishop Warren A. Candler perhaps only slightly exaggerated widely held attitudes when he warned that "possible danger to women is inherent in every offense against white men." [21]

The shibboleth of rape in southern race relations played a vital role in legitimating mob violence. By raising the cry of protecting the "honor and sanctity of white womanhood," lynchers offered the most potent defense for their actions possible. As Ida B. Wells-Barnett, the outspoken black critic of lynching explained, "humanity abhors the assailant of womanhood, and this charge upon the Negro at once placed him beyond the pale of human sympathy." [22] Southerners, and even northerners, who condemned mob violence in principle tempered criticism by arguing that the awful provocation of rape overrode whites' usual reverence for law and order and that the mob must be pitied as well as condemned. [23]

The heightened fears of sexual assaults in the late nineteenth century bespoke profound and growing uneasiness among whites about the proper place for blacks in southern society and the apparent weakening of traditional methods for the social control of blacks. Philip Alexander Bruce, a historian from Virginia, spoke for many whites when he suggested that blacks committed rapes in proportion to the decline in their respect for whites. During slavery, when the racial and social order rested on a sturdy foundation, whites claimed that sexual assaults on white women by black men had been unknown. Only during the extraordinary atmosphere of Reconstruction, when blacks seemed to mock commonly understood rules of conduct, did black men begin to desire social equality and, even worse, sexual equality.[24]

The preoccupation with sexual attacks also was an expression of concern about the apparent weakening of conventional standards of sexual behavior and traditional gender roles. White southerners, who clung "with a vengeance" to a particularly potent blend of Victorian values, placed an inordinate stress on the dangers that uncontrolled sensuality posed not only to conventional morals but also to civilization itself. In an era of rapid social and economic change, when patriarchal rule faced trials from the nascent women's movement and the expanding economic role of women, polemics about the threat of sexual assault exposed the desperate efforts of white men to reaffirm their dedication to the idealization of male chivalry and shore up the traditional dependence of white women.[25]

The belief that black men posed a ubiquitous threat to white women, however irrational, rested on the assumption that the southern racial hierarchy depended on the prohibition of sexual access of black men to white women. At a time when white preachers and moralists insisted upon the paramount importance of retaining one's self-command, rationality, and freedom from self-indulgence, blacks came to symbolize life dominated by animal impulses and sexual immorality. Even more threatening, black men, driven by an uncontrollable attraction to white women, who personified a purity and civilization beyond either their experience or reach, were moved "to gratify their lust at any cost and in spite of every obstacle."[26] Because sexual relations, let alone sexual attacks on white women, could not be separated from contemporary attitudes that bound sexuality, gender, and power, violations of the racial barrier in sexual relations were blows against the very foundations of society and, in the eyes of whites, were the most abhorrent of all crimes.[27]

The alleged sexual crimes that mobs punished typically were portrayed as crimes of unspeakable brutality against defenseless women. A rape committed by a black man was the brutal subversion of civilization, of virtuous womanhood, by savagery. The black rapist demonstrated "a diabolical persistence and a malignant atrocity of detail that have no reflection in the whole extent of the natural history of the most bestial and ferocious animal. He is not content merely with the consummation of his purpose, but takes [a] fiendish delight in the degradation of his victim." [28] In what Jacquelyn Dowd Hall has aptly described as "a kind of acceptable folk pornography," the details of the physical and psychological suffering of frail rape victims stoked the passions of mobs.[29] Reports in 1888 that William Henry Smith, a black miner from Bluefield, Virginia, had raped a pregnant white woman, causing her to die while prematurely giving birth to a stillborn child, spurred on the mob that formed quickly and avenged the crime. And in 1884, when Mrs. Elijah Heard, a destitute widow in Troup County, Georgia, agonized because the rapist had not cut her throat and saved her a lifetime of shame, lynchers heard her lament as a clarion call for vengeance.[30]

In Georgia and Virginia, where more than half of the victims of alleged sexual offenses were young or adolescent girls, accounts of alleged rapes of children dwelled upon the brutishness of the blacks and the innocence of their victims. With an eye toward lurid detail, whites speculated about the lifetime of unimaginable physical and psychological suffering that the victims would endure. Rumor in 1897 had it that Joseph McCoy, a black laborer in Alexandria, Virginia, not only had repeatedly raped the six-year-old and nine-year-old daughters of his employer, but he also had infected them with syphilis. The mob that avenged the alleged rape of a fourteen-year-old white girl in Ware County, Georgia, in June 1908, was enraged by accounts that the girl had been raped repeatedly by at least three black men.[31]

Rather than constituting a distant or isolated threat, the menace of the black rapist might be found in any servants' quarters or sharecropper's cabin. Common wisdom held that neither white women in the comparative security of towns nor women on isolated rural farmsteads were free from the persistent menace posed by servants, farmhands, or roaming black rapists. Only constant care and vigilance could protect women from sexual attacks, which could occur at any time or any place. Even to ride in a vehicle driven by a black driver, a letter writer to the *Atlanta News* warned, was "a thousand times more dangerous than a rattlesnake" to white women because "personal contact often fires the hearts of these drivers with the lusts of hell." [32] The obsession with the threat of rape created a milieu of fear that sharply confined the day-to-day routines of women.[33] Observers blamed the threat of black rapists for a host of social ills, including the despondency of isolated farm women, the movement of white families off of the land, and even the ill-education of white children, whose parents kept them at home rather than expose them to possible risk while traveling to and from school.[34]

Even black servants, many whites cautioned, should not be trusted. In terms strikingly reminiscent of the laments of antebellum slaveholders about the ingratitude and treachery of slaves who turned on their masters, whites denounced servants who betrayed them by malicious intentions or actions against the women of the family. After the lynching of Ross Griffin, accused of the attempted rape of his employer's sister in 1887, the editor of the *Oglethorpe Echo* (and Griffin's employer) mused bitterly: "His was a peculiarly diabolical act. . . . In the family upon which he brought so much trouble he had been looked upon as a faithful servant. . . he abused the kindness which had been shown him; proved false to a solemn confidence." [35]

Defense of womanly virtue alone was sufficient justification for Griffin's execution, the sense of betrayal gave added incentive to the mob's vengeance. Precisely because of the horrible implications of alleged outrages committed by blacks upon their employers' wives and daughters, they aroused white fears far out of proportion to their statistical significance. Only twenty of the one hundred and twenty-four mob victims in Georgia and six of the thirty-three victims in Virginia were accused of such a crime. [36]

Given an atmosphere saturated with racial and sexual fears, it was tragically predictable that white men interpreted even trifling offenses by black men against white women as ample grounds for summary punishment. In the popular usage of white southerners, rape, at least when white women were involved, was an elastic concept that extended far beyond the contemporary legal definition of the crime to include attempted rape, aggravated assault, and even acts as apparently innocent as a nudge. On November 8, 1889, a mob lynched Orion Anderson in Loudoun County, Virginia, for an alleged attempted "assault" of a fifteen-year-old white girl. In fact, the black youth, a friend of the girl, had merely donned a sack on his head and frightened her while she walked to school. In 1906, a black man from Swainsboro, Georgia, was lynched after he was found hiding under a woman's bed in a white farmer's house. And in March 1917, Linton Clinton, a recently released former convict, apparently scared a little white girl when he asked her to read a letter to him. His "attempted outrage" prompted a lynch mob to track him down and murder him. [37] It is no more possible to determine the number of instances in which mob victims actually had committed rape than to know how many innocent black men were executed because of mistaken identity, or how many times whites used the charge of rape to camouflage murders inspired by aims other than the "protection" of white women.

Mob violence served as the ultimate sanction against willing sexual liaisons between white women and black men, a practice that defied the most fundamental notions of the southern racial hierarchy. For a white woman to have sexual relations with a black man was to encourage notions of equality in blacks, to challenge the belief that white women were the inaccessible property of white men, and to reject prevailing definitions of the social position of women. Most whites found it beyond belief that any sane white woman would stray so recklessly from conventional behavior. In those instances when white women did brazenly admit their relations with black men, the responses of the women's self-appointed protectors were entirely predictable, because a failure to punish such deviant behavior would expose the male relatives to certain censure. For Nathan Corder, a white farmer in Fauquier County, Virginia, there could be little doubt that his daughter's "unsound" mind explained why she had run off with and married Arthur Jordan, one of his black farmhands, in 1880. Corder had Jordan arrested in Washington, D.C., where the couple had been married, and returned to Fauquier County to stand trial on the charge of bigamy (allegedly Jordan already had a black wife). Four days after Jordan was placed in the county jail in Warrenton, a small group of masked men overpowered the jail guards, dragged him from his cell, and hanged him in the town's cemetery.[38]

The lynching of Peter Stamps on July 24, 1885, in Douglas County, Georgia, is another example of the severe consequences of defying the color line in sexual relationships. For almost a year, Stamps, a black tenant farmer, had been the lover of his employer's sixteen-year-old daughter without arousing suspicions. But when the white girl became pregnant the romance could no longer be kept secret. Stamps was promptly arrested for rape even though the girl adamantly refused to accuse him. While he was being transported to the county jail, a mob seized him and hanged him. The tragic affair ended when the young girl committed suicide by taking an overdose of sleeping pills. In this instance, as in untold others, the local newspaper editor extended his sympathy to the families of the white women, whose shame betrayed the most sacred notions of womanhood and family honor.[39]

Loose definitions of "sexual assault" provided a convenient pretext to lynch black men for offensive behavior that even white southerners could not construe as a sexual threat. Unquestionably, whites did accuse blacks of sexual offenses as a ruse to settle grudges. In March 1910, Albert Royal and Charlie Jackson, two farmhands in Turner County, Georgia, became embroiled in a dispute with several white planters over some debts. Shortly thereafter, one of the planters had Jackson arrested for an alleged assault on a white woman. The patent lie of the charges was exposed when the trial date arrived and no witnesses for the prosecution were present to testify against him. After his release, Jackson returned home, where, on April 14, a small group of white men captured him and his friend Royal, bound them to a tree, and shot them to death. It was common knowledge that the rape charges brought against Jackson were merely a pretense to drive him from the community. When that tactic failed, the white planters responded by executing the troublesome blacks.[40]

Occasionally, there were surprising instances in which the circumstances of a case were taken into account and summary punishment was not inflicted upon the accused criminal. The family and relatives of alleged rape victims might plead with mobs to allow the courts to punish the alleged assailant, and the public might take into account the age and repute of the parties involved as well as other mitigating conditions. One telling illustration of the importance of public perception is the near-lynching of Grant Bell in Polk County, Georgia, in 1899. Bell was accused of entering the home of Mrs. J. C. Lumpkin and assaulting the seventy-three-year-old widow while she slept. Shortly after Bell was taken into custody, a large crowd gathered around the county courthouse in Cedartown, and newspapers predicted that "the negro will be taken from the jail even if men have to tear the building to the ground brick by brick and [will be] put to death in a manner suiting the impulses of the outraged men." The newspaper's prophecies might have been fulfilled had several prominent local citizens, including the physician who had attended to Mrs. Lumpkin, not announced that there was strong possibility that the elderly woman's mind was "unbalanced" and that a trial for Bell would be scheduled within days. Whether because of doubts about Bell's guilt or because of satisfaction with the promise of a speedy trial, the crowd dispersed without threatening the jail.

Two days later when Bell's trial began, Cedartown was filled with spectators and expectant journalists, eager to witness the conclusion of the "blackest horror in the catalogue of crimes." Earlier suspicions about Mrs. Lumpkin's mental powers were borne out by her confused and rambling testimony, as well as her inability to describe her alleged assailant. In contrast, Bell's straightforward testimony impressed many observers and apparently swayed the jury, which acquitted him of all charges. The *Atlanta Constitution,* conveniently turning a blind eye to the role its own sensational stories almost certainly had played in the turmoil in Polk County, heralded Bell's acquittal as a "substantial victory for law and order."[41] Precisely why Bell escaped summary justice can only be conjectured. Probably, the efforts of a few prominent local citizens to uphold the machinery of justice played a role, as did Bell's appropriately deferential behavior and testimony. And not to be underestimated was Mrs. Lumpkin's widely known eccentric, even senile, behavior, which cast doubt on the charges.

In other instances, locally prominent whites corroborated the alibis of their black employees who were suspected of sexual crimes. And white women occasionally refused to be coerced into a hasty identification of their alleged assailants. For example, in 1922, when a mob of several hundred people in Johnson County, Georgia, brought Joe Drisdom before the white woman whom he had allegedly poured gasoline upon and burned, she refused to be pressured and was adamant in saying that he was not her attacker. Although disappointed, the mob returned Drisdom to the jail.[42] The near-lynching of Grant Bell and these other incidents do not demonstrate the evenhandedness of mobs so much as they do the role of public opinion. A concatenation of factors, ranging from doubts about the alleged assault to perceptions of the alleged victim, shaped neighborhood opinion and ensured that mob justice might not be inflicted following every alleged sexual transgression by a black.

Given that southern whites held that it was their "supreme duty" to prevent sexual relations between the races, and that the protection of southern womanhood was connected intimately with the domination of both white women and blacks, the lynchings of blacks charged with sexual offenses had the potential to enlist the broadest communal support and participation. And they often did. Mass mobs, with all of the accompanying ritual so often associated with them, frequently executed alleged sexual offenders in both Virginia and Georgia.

The lynching of Paul Jones on the outskirts of Macon, Georgia, in 1919 was in many regards archetypical of such an event. Jones, "a suspicious looking negro," was accused of raping a fifty-year-old widow as she made her way home from church. When news of the alleged assault began to circulate, large numbers of white men began searching frantically for suspicious blacks. Deputy sheriffs captured Jones in a nearby railroad yard, but a mob quickly formed and compelled the officers to take refuge in a railroad car. The county sheriff hurried to the scene and attempted to dissuade the mob from overpowering the law officers and lynching the prisoner. After extended negotiations he was permitted to take Jones to the home of his victim for identification. The bruised and battered woman, hysterical with fright, identified Jones as her assailant by blood marks that she claimed she had made upon his clothing. Roused by the victim's suffering and her "positive" identification, the mob, swelling to more than a thousand, seized Jones, shot him repeatedly, and then dragged him, still-living, several hundred yards before dousing him with gasoline and setting him ablaze. When the fire dwindled down without killing Jones, he was pulled from the pyre, resaturated with gasoline, and thrown back into the flames until only charred bones remained.[43]

The Jones lynching, like so many others, was set in motion by an allegedly frightful attack upon a virtuous woman, as attested by the fact that she was assaulted while returning from church. With the swift mobilization of white men intent upon both protecting women and dispensing justice, followed by the identification of the assailant by his victim, events moved inevitably toward their hideous conclusion when fire and gasoline were used to obliterate all but memories of the alleged assailant. The mutilation of Paul Jones was the culminating act of a ritual that imposed justice, restored order, purged villainy, and offered men an opportunity to act out their idealized role as protectors of sacred womanhood.

In the embellished prose of newspaper accounts and in the calculated lines of journal articles, white southerners exposed their fascination with the savagery of such lynch mobs. Mobs were supposed to be a bulwark against black violence, so when they strayed from this ideal and degenerated into revolting cruelty, they threatened precisely what they were intended to prevent. White southerners wanted to believe that mobs demonstrated tremendous self-control and restraint. Unable to accept the possibility that sadism nourished the destructive power of mobs, whites relied upon the excuse that the hideousness of the offense prompted the lynching. Thomas Nelson Page, whose attitudes about lynching are revealing because they were so thoroughly conventional, rationalized the brutality of mobs that punished alleged rapes: "For a time, a speedy execution by hanging was the only mode of retribution resorted to by lynchers; then, when this failed of its purpose, a more savage method was essayed, born of a savage fury at the failure of the first, and a stern resolve to strike a deeper terror into whom the other method had failed to awe." [44]

The rituals of mutilation, including both the castration of the lynching victim and the collection of gruesome souvenirs, sprang from deeper urges than Page recognized or was willing to admit. By mutilating the lynching victim, the mob simultaneously stripped his humanity and, not infrequently, his sexuality. Undoubtedly, the bloodthirsty fury of some mob members expressed the subconscious envy and sexual frustration that led both Percy Grimm, the white lyncher in William Faulkner's *Light in August,* and the anonymous knife-wielder in James Baldwin's *Going to Meet the Man* to find release by emasculating their victims.[45] The Georgia writer Lillian Smith untangled the barely submerged sexual impulses that surfaced in many lynchings when she observed that "the lynched negro becomes. . . a receptacle for every man's dammed-up hate, and a receptacle for every man's forbidden feelings. Sex and hate. . . pour out their progeny of cruelty on anything that can serve as a symbol of an unnamed relationship that in his heart each man wants to befoul." [46]

For all of the attention contemporaries (and subsequent historians) have devoted to the prominence of mutilation in lynchings for sexual crimes, most black victims accused of alleged sexual offenses in Georgia and Virginia do not *appear* to have been mutilated or, more specifically, castrated. Extant evidence, admittedly open to question, suggests that mass mobs mutilated one in three black victims lynched for alleged sexual offenses in Georgia and one in ten blacks lynched in Virginia. Almost certainly, we will never know how commonplace the practice was and therefore should be cautious in assuming that the ritual was a central, even defining, element of lynchings for rape. Even so, the most relevant measure of the importance of mutilation during lynchings for sexual crimes was never the percentage of black victims who were mutilated, but rather the lasting impression that each incident left upon observers.

A substantial number of the lynchings of alleged sexual offenders in the South differed markedly from the lynching of Paul Jones and the hundreds of other extralegal executions carried out by mass mobs. Nearly one-third of the lynchings for alleged sexual offenses in Georgia and more than half in Virginia lacked the broad popular participation, the elaborate ritual, or even the mutilation that would seem to have been justified by white attitudes toward crimes against white women. The mobs seeking vengeance for sexual transgressions sometimes were small, secretive private mobs that lacked many of the traits typically associated with extralegal executions for such offenses.

The lynching of George Towler in November 1889 in Pittsylvania County, Virginia, is but one example of a private mob's vengeance for an alleged sexual offense. Towler, a hired hand on the farm of William M. Mitchell, was discovered to be sexually intimate with the teenaged daughter of his employer. Although the Mitchell family later claimed that Towler had attempted to rape the girl, it was known locally that the two had been lovers for some time. Mitchell and his two sons, aided by two other white men, punished the black youth by hanging him without fanfare or ceremony a short distance from the Mitchell's home.[47] It is hard to determine precisely why the Mitchell family did not (or could not) recruit the larger white community to punish such an apparently heinous offense. But it seems likely that victims with little local standing or dubious reputations had greater difficulty in calling forth support. When the charge of rape could not camouflage a rumored or widely known liaison between a black man and a white woman, the male "protectors" of the woman may have preferred to punish the transgression privately in order to escape as much public humiliation as possible.

In some instances the circumstances, and not perceptions of the alleged offenses, may explain why private mobs rather than mass mobs punished alleged sexual miscreants. Passionate community outrage was the fuel that fed the violence of mass mobs, and anything that placed distance between the enraged community and the target of its wrath was likely to hinder ecstatic communal violence. Private mobs frequently executed alleged sexual offenders who had escaped to distant counties or who had been moved to county jails remote from the actual scene of the crime.[48]

A very small number of lynchings of blacks for sexual offenses were carried out by black mobs. It is hardly surprising that on rare occasions blacks would resort to lynch law in a region where extralegal violence was pervasive. Moreover, a counterpart to the patriarchal ethos that inspired white mob violence was prevalent among black men as well.[49] That blacks would apply extralegal punishments in a secretive fashion is predictable. Any threatened violence by a mass mob comprised of blacks, even if against another black, could not fail but to provoke whites' nightmares of black rebellion.[50] When black men turned to mob justice to protect or restore familial purity, they, unlike white lynchers, had no need for ritualized group dramas. The personal grievances that incited the rare black mob did not demand a ritual that affirmed sacred values or conveyed a warning. Murder was punishment enough. Thus, secrecy and an utter lack of concern for spectacle characterized the lynching of sexual offenders by blacks. The small mob of blacks, for example, that murdered Samuel Gibson, charged with raping his daughter in July 1884 in Troup County, Georgia, relied upon careful organization. But plans went awry when Gibson fought furiously with a razor and seriously wounded five assailants. Rather than incur further casualties, the mob gathered their wounded and simply shot Gibson to death in his cell.[51] Thus, partial answers to the question of why many perceived sexual offenses were punished without ceremony or communal participation can be found in local skepticism about the character of the alleged sexual transgression, the inaccesiblity of the victim, and the race of the victim of the assault.

While the southern rape complex is central to the history of lynching, there is a temptation to make it the central theme and to explain both too much and too little by dwelling upon the prevailing sexual mores in the South. If the bloodthirsty speeches of southern congressmen and editorials in southern newspapers from the 1890s through the 1930s are to serve as a measure, white southerners not only steadfastly defended mob violence well into the twentieth century but also remained mesmerized by the threat of the black rapist. Contemporaries such as Clarence Poe, Bishop Candler, and Benjamin Tillman of South Carolina were not entirely misguided in stressing the fervent and enduring devotion of white men to safeguarding racial purity. But however passionately the slogans of white supremacy were repeated and the image of the black rapist refined, the fact remains that the number of lynchings for alleged sexual offenses declined throughout the twentieth century.

If the various elements of white dogma about the black rapist underwent little apparent change, it still is possible to detect a decisive shift in its violent potential. There is a measure of truth in Clarence Poe's claim that the stimulus for lynching initially had been alleged sexual crimes. During the 1880s and 1890s, alleged "outrages" did prompt the majority of lynchings by all mobs. As the practice of mob justice persisted into the twentieth century, however, the number of lynchings for alleged outrages declined steadily, a trend particularly evident in Georgia. Between 1880 and 1889, alleged sexual infractions in Georgia led to more than 60 percent of all lynchings in the state. During the next two decades the percentage of lynchings for sexual transgressions declined to 27 percent. After 1910, "outrages" accounted for roughly one in six lynchings.[52]

In Virginia, the pattern of lynchings for sexual offenses differed from that in Georgia. Alleged sexual crimes prompted half of all lynchings (the largest percentage) during the 1880s. But during the 1890s, when the number of lynchings peaked in the state, the percentage of mob murders inspired by alleged sexual offenses fell to 36 percent. After 1900, when lynchings became a rarity in Virginia, alleged sexual crimes again provoked most of the instances of mob violence. Although the details of the trends in Georgia and Virginia differed, it is still clear that the overall decline in the number of lynchings for sexual offenses in both states suggests that the fear of the black rapist lost its power to mobilize mobs with each decade (Figure 4).

There are additional complexities to the ebb and flow of mob violence for sexual offenses. During the 1880s, lynchings for sexual offenses in both Georgia and Virginia were more likely to be punished by private rather than mass mobs. In Virginia, private mobs continued to be responsible for most such lynchings even as lynchings declined sharply. In the 1920s, the proportion of lynchings by mass mobs rose sharply and equaled that of lynchings by private mobs. In Georgia, by contrast, between 1890 and 1910 the number of lynchings for sexual crimes by mass mobs rose sharply and accounted for more than half of the total of lynchings for alleged outrages. But after 1910, the trajectory reversed, and sexual offenses became less likely to incite mass mobs and more likely to arouse private mobs to action.

This thicket of statistics suggests that contradictory trends were at work. Although fewer and fewer lynchings were precipitated by sexual offenses, a substantial number (particularly in Georgia between 1890 and 1910) were the work of

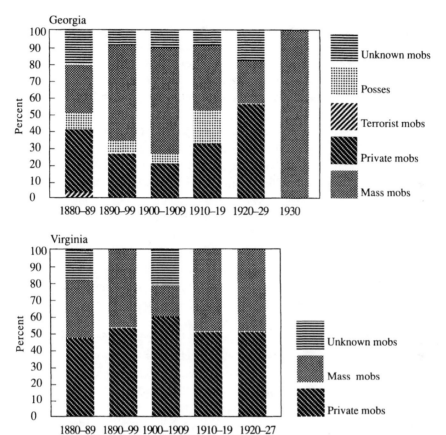

Figure 4. Lynchings of Blacks for Alleged Sexual Offenses, 1880–1930

precisely the type of mob—mass mobs—that riveted the attention of southerners. It comes as no surprise then that when Hooper Alexander, a lawyer, attempted to explain to the readers of *Outlook* magazine in 1907 why mob violence persisted in Georgia, he ignored the factual record and argued that "atrocious crimes committed by negroes upon helpless women and children. . . provoke with increasing frequency summary extra-legal punishments."[53] For Alexander and his contemporaries, it was the furious mass mobs that punished sexual transgressions, not the other mobs that punished a host of alleged infractions, that captivated their imaginations during the peak in lynching between 1890 and 1910.

Both the diminishing actual number and percentage of lynching victims accused of sexual transgressions are suggestive of the lessening fear of the black rapist and, more important, of the evolution of the southern code of honor. Of course, the marked decline in the incidence of lynchings for alleged sexual offenses cannot be separated easily from the incidence of lynching in general. Nor can effects of the changing attitudes about race relations and the power of the state on attitudes about mob violence be ignored. Even so, without some tentative and admittedly speculative observations about changes in the culture of honor, the pattern of lynching for alleged rape seems inexplicable.

Powerful solvents, in particular urbanization and industrialization, were at work on the code of honor during the late nineteenth century. Even though urban and industrial growth in the South lagged behind the rest of the nation, it fostered growing emphasis upon self-control and new conceptions of self-worth, all of which grated against the ideals of honor. In addition to the changes wrought by rhythms of industry and the exigencies of town life, the champions of the New South creed, including ministers, businessmen, and educators, extolled the virtues of discipline and personal dignity and implicitly denigrated the values of the Old South. The new values, of course, did not vanquish older southern values in one fell swoop. But with the construction of each new cotton mill and each new city block the survival of the code of honor was called into question.[54]

On first sight, the encroachments of new ideals of conduct may seem peripheral to the question of the place of women in southern society and the violent defense of "womanly honor." Yet, an important connection exists between the economic and social transformation of the New South and the changing status of women. Of fundamental importance was the challenge that nascent industrialization and urbanization posed to the household, that bulwark of male power, indeed of southern society itself. Before the Civil War, southern society had "consisted largely of a network of households that contained within themselves the decisive relations of production and reproduction."[55] The correlative of the household as the fundamental building block of southern society was an incontrovertible hierarchy based upon white male domination. The traditional conception of the household and of family could not escape powerful changes unleashed by the Civil War. The abolition of slavery, the continuing expansion of market-driven agriculture into the hinterland, and the advent of a new industrial order accelerated the redefinition of the household, and the redefinition of the status of women necessarily followed.[56]

Women themselves began to redefine their status. They staked out a larger and larger role in southern churches and by the late nineteenth century had become a powerful force within most church institutions. Their prominent role within voluntary associations of all kinds also attests to women's efforts to create new roles that were increasingly independent of male domination and indirectly challenged their traditional place. Finally, women activists in the South, despite the enormous obstacles posed by the prevailing racial and sexual hierarchy, voiced a muted critique of the traditional place of white women.[57]

The cumulative weight of these economic, social, and religious developments almost certainly tested the strength of the traditional codes of honor and gender roles. The transformation in attitudes toward women and male honor, however, was not a simple linear process. Instead, highly visible manifestations of traditional values seem to have carried over from earlier times and camouflaged important changes in those values. Thus, as the logic of economic and social change demanded, white men became less and less quick to perceive black behavior as either an insult to the honor of white women or an assault on the foundations of the traditional order.

Yet even as lynchings for the "unspeakable crime" declined, white men resorted to the ritual of mass mob violence with a desperation that, to all appearances, seemed to demonstrate the enduring vigor of the code of honor. Most southern whites only dimly perceived the evolution of attitudes toward sex roles and lynching. With so many beliefs and practices sustained and legitimized by honor and prevailing sex roles, whites predictably clung to traditional values. The seemingly contradictory pattern of lynching for alleged rape in the twentieth century perhaps offers a glimpse of the tensions released by the conflict between the dying code of honor and the vigorous rear-guard action to save white male dominance.

The erosion of honor picked up pace with the passage of each decade during the twentieth century. Reformers, including a growing number of white women, began to challenge the myth of the black rapist openly and to temper the propaganda that had justified extralegal violence in the past. That the fear of sexual assaults subsided even among women far removed from reform influences is suggested by an interview that the sociologist Margaret Jarman Hagood had with a white tenant farmer's wife in the 1930s. The woman, who still refused to allow her family to leave her alone either day or night, lamented that the threat of the "Big Black Nig" did not "work so well" as a means to control her granddaughter as it used to work in earlier times.[58] Punishment of alleged sexual transgressions by blacks increasingly became the province of the courts, which punished with a disregard for evidence and a ferocity only a step removed from the so-called justice imposed by mobs. Of course, the black rapist lived on as a rhetorical device used either to fend off northern attacks on southern traditions or to muzzle local nonconformists who struggled to redefine the region's racial and sexual attitudes. Although fear of the lurking black rapist never entirely left the region—as late as the 1950s the anxiety still paralyzed some white women and tormented white men—it exerted less and less power to foment mob violence.

Lynchings for sexual crimes were a part of the distinctive relations between the sexes. Social conventions and attitudes toward sexuality were set off from the national norms by the imperatives of the social and racial hierarchy of the South. The commitment of white men to maintain the structures of race and gender found expression in many conventions and rituals, not the least of which was lynching. The ability of whites to coerce blacks (and command white women) rested on values that many rape-inspired lynchings dramatized. Lynchings prompted by sensational alleged rapes displayed and reaffirmed rules of both black and white conduct to a far greater degree than did lynchings for minor offenses. Collectively, whites could not allow doubt about the constraints on black behavior to exist without weakening the whole structure of racial mastery. Thus, the circle of black transgression and white extralegal punishment was intended to lead back to the brutal confirmation of white, male power.

Homicides and attacks on whites by blacks, whether unprovoked or in self-defense, were the most common causes of mob violence. Moreover, in Georgia and the South as a whole, the proportion of lynchings prompted by murders and violent crimes (aside from alleged sexual offenses) increased over time. During the 1880s, alleged murders in Georgia provoked fewer than 20 percent of all lynchings. During the next four decades, 44 percent of lynchings were precipitated by murders, a number that peaked at 60 percent between 1910 and 1919. In Virginia, the pattern of extralegal violence against alleged murderers diverged from that of the rest of the South. Forty-three percent of lynchings were for murders during the 1880s, 57 percent during the 1890s. Following 1900, however, the percentage of lynchings prompted by murder fell until the 1920s, when they accounted for only a third of all incidents. If the patterns of mob violence inspired by alleged attacks by blacks on whites varied in Georgia and Virginia, the important point remains that in both states nearly half of all lynchings followed such crimes.[59]

Although killings of whites by blacks were rare; when they did occur the potential for mob violence all too often was realized. In keeping with the southern "culture of violence" identified by sociologists, few of the homicides involved unsuspecting victims of robbers or psychopaths. Most participants in cases of personal violence that led to lynchings knew each other and resorted to violence for reasons that both the killer and the victim understood.[60] While violent attacks often led to extralegal violence, the character of the lynchings varied substantially. Labor disputes and long-term disagreements that culminated in mob violence seldom stirred popular sentiment to a fever pitch, but attacks against law officers, officials, and white women provoked massive retribution.

Labor disputes between blacks and whites, which routinely bred frustration, suspicion, and anger on both sides of the color line, were sometimes fought out to bloody conclusions, thus weaving a thread of violence into southern labor relations. Clashes between white employers and black workers could have implications that extended beyond economic considerations. Because a defense of white authority, and conversely a challenge to that authority, were never far beneath the surface of any labor dispute involving whites and blacks, more than just economic motives could be at work in both the murder of a white planter by a tenant and the subsequent lynching of the tenant.

The black man who openly challenged his white employer was uncommon; had he not been, the racial hierarchy and the system of labor at its foundation would have been jeopardized. But some did challenge. Forty-nine of the two hundred and five blacks lynched for assault or murder in Georgia between 1880 and 1930 were charged with killing their employer or members of his family. In 1893, for example, Arthur Bennett, a black tenant farmer in Clayton County, Georgia, attempted to poison his white employer after failing to receive a satisfactory settlement for his cotton crop. In July 1901, Frank Earle, a black railroad cook, armed himself with a revolver and held up the railroad's payroll agent to get overdue wages that were owed to him. When John Ware, a tenant farmer in Franklin County, Georgia, refused to sell his cotton to the merchant of his landlord's choice in 1904, the two men began to fight and the black man killed the planter. In each of these cases, the black man's stand led to his swift execution by a mob. These lynchings drove home to blacks the peril of challenging their employers; as one white planter curtly explained, "when a nigger gets ideas, the best thing to do is to get him under ground as quick as possible." [61]

A proud black might vow that, regardless of the consequences, he would not permit a white man to "bulldoze" him. Many of the homicides that precipitated lynchings were the violent conclusions of long-simmering disputes. Blacks demonstrated a sensitivity to personal slights that was at least as developed as that of whites, but they had to use great caution when expressing their anger at perceived insults. In 1881, after months of arguments and threatened fights between William Allen, a black drayman in Warwick County, Virginia, and a white man he drove to work each morning, Allen challenged the man to a fight and, in the struggle that followed, killed him. In Amherst County, Virginia, wandering stock created mounting difficulties between James Carter and his white neighbor and climaxed in 1902 when the white accused Carter of setting fire to his outhouse. During the ensuing fight, Carter shot and wounded his assailant. Lynch mobs murdered both Allen and Carter within days of the episodes.[62]

The murder of a white man also provoked the ire of the white community because it had long-term repercussions on the family of the murder victim. To attack a white man, in the eyes of whites, was to attack the family that depended upon him for protection and support. The patriarchal ethos that suffused southern life ensured that white southerners understood exactly what Bishop Candler meant when he suggested that attacks on white men by extension were attacks on white women. By avenging the murder of a white man, a mob also avenged the desecration of the ideal of the patriarchal family. The lynching of the black murderer became a bloody drama in which the white community assumed the protection of the widow and fatherless family while at the same time it affirmed the tragic future and vulnerability that the family faced.

The mob that hanged Banjo Peavy, a black tenant farmer in Houston County, Georgia, in 1903 was infuriated that Peavy had murdered a young white man who was the "main dependence" of his widowed mother and three single sisters. As the newspaper accounts explained, he "had won the respect and esteem of the entire community, not only by his big heartedness, but by his constant attention and devotion to his widowed mother and sisters, who had learned to depend upon him entirely." Similar motivations incited a mob in Baker County, Georgia, a few weeks later to lynch three black men who had murdered F. S. Bullard, a white farmer. That the lynching occurred "was largely due to the fact that the Bullard family was left in a sad condition, his wife being a hopeless invalid and his several small children dependent."[63]

In those rare instances when white violence aroused black retaliation, whites responded in turn by dispensing summary punishment. In 1908 in Echols County, Georgia, for example, Jim Harris, a farm laborer, led a small group of other black men who severely beat a white doctor who had shot and killed a black man. But rather than providing a measure of justice for a crime white courts routinely overlooked, Harris's act led to his own lynching.[64] Uncontrolled explosions of anger enraged whites; when a violent fray did occur, as in the Allen, Carter, and Harris cases, mobs punished what they perceived as expressions of aggressive "insolence."

That violence erupted from labor disputes, intimidation, and frustration comes as no surprise in a violence-prone region where tradition demanded that all manner of conflicts be settled with force. What is notable is that beating a planter arguing

Figure 5. Lynchings of Blacks for Alleged Murders, 1880–1930

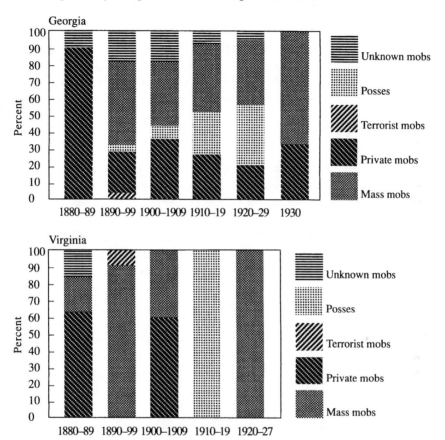

with a tenant, cutting a white in a gambling dispute with a black, or shooting a white neighbor over hunting privileges often failed to arouse a massive communal response.[65] Although mass mobs carried out nearly half of all lynchings for murder and violent attacks in Georgia, private mobs were responsible for one-third. In Virginia, private mobs punished more than one-quarter of the lynchings for murder (Figure 5).

For reasons that often can be perceived only dimly, whites did not interpret every attack by a black as an egregious assault on racial order. Certainly, assaults, attempted murders, and violence that fell short of murder seem to have been less likely to demand swift punishment or to arouse mass mobs to action. Extant accounts of lynchings rarely offer more than glimpses of why whites responded to the murders of some whites, such as those arising out of economic disputes, differently from the murders of other whites.

The explanation for the pattern of lynchings for murder almost certainly can be found in how the code of honor filtered whites' perceptions of conflicts between whites and blacks. That a substantial number of murders and attacks on whites did not produce anything comparable to mass, communal violence suggests that whites concluded that these transgressions, which may have impugned the personal and family honor of those immediately involved, posed only a limited threat to the collective honor of the white community.

It is a much less difficult matter to explain why whites interpreted certain murders or attacks as very serious blows to the racial order and to the collective honor of the community. Fifty-five mob victims in Georgia and two in Virginia were charged with violence against law officers, a crime that usually incited mass mobs to action in both states. Few crimes were more provocative in the eyes of whites than confrontations between law officers and blacks. An intricate web of family ties and local loyalties bound a good number of the citizenry in any rural community to law officers. In rural counties where the machinery of government was otherwise weak, sheriffs and other law officers enjoyed an unusual degree of prominence and prestige. With each passing year that a sheriff or town policeman served, the bonds of mutual obligation between him and the white citizenry grew stronger. Whites could not help but develop a sense of debt and obligation to the men responsible for much of the systematic pressure and violence that defined the place of blacks in any community. Few questioned law officers' interpretation of their mandate to maintain public order as a license to abuse blacks at will. In blacks, the cumulative effects of routine police brutality and systematic inequities in the courts simultaneously instilled a suspicion of and barely contained hostility toward police. Even trivial confrontations between white law officers and blacks were potentially volatile. And when a black challenged or attacked an abusive policeman—"the caretaker of the color line and defender of the caste system"—a furious response was unleashed from whites.[66]

Most of the violent encounters that led to lynchings occurred when law officers attempted to arrest criminals charged with such petty crimes as gambling, theft, or vagrancy. Ironically, the expansion of law enforcement agencies during the twentieth century may have contributed to the increase in violence between blacks and law officers. With each improvement in communications and transportation, local law officers could track down and arrest alleged offenders more easily. Previously, private citizens often had arrested accused criminals and transported them to jail, but, increasingly during the first decades of the twentieth century, local law officers assumed that duty. As the law became more intrusive, the likelihood of violent clashes between law officers and alleged black criminals rose.

The lynching of Willie Williams and two others on April 13, 1919, is but one of countless examples of a clash prompted by the highhanded tactics of law officers. The trouble began during a large picnic at a rural black church near Millen, Georgia. When a group of whites drove recklessly through the crowd that had overflowed into a nearby road, a church member became infuriated. Attracted by the commotion, a deputy sheriff and his assistant arrested the black man for drunkenness. During an ensuing argument between the officers and several blacks, the deputy sheriff began to pistol whip his prisoner. Several blacks attempted to stop the beating by seizing the officer's gun. In the struggle that followed, the two officers were shot. Within hours, a mob of more than a hundred enraged whites lynched the three blacks and roamed the county, burning black property, churches, and fraternal lodges and whipping blacks indiscriminately.[67]

The wounding or killing of a law officer, which whites perceived to be an unmistakable attack on the white community at large, called for elaborate, ritualized, and unambiguously public mob violence. Careful organization and orchestrated ritual were conspicuous in such lynchings. Accounts of the lynching of Gus Goodman, a black wanted for the murder of a black woman and, more important, the wounding of the sheriff of Decatur County, Georgia, in October 1905, reveal both how whites calculated the proper response to an attack on a white policeman and the deliberate effort to involve the entire white community. When the sheriff had attempted to arrest Goodman for the murder, Goodman shot him down. After Goodman's capture by the deputy sheriff, angry whites began to collect around the jail. Friends of the sheriff maintained a vigil in front of his house, waiting expectantly for news of the wounded man's condition. Sentries at the home relayed each update on the sheriff's condition to the crowd of several hundred that surrounded the jail. When it was announced that the sheriff would die, the mob at the jail "forced" the deputy sheriff to surrender his jail keys and then dragged Goodman from his cell. After hanging him to a tree near downtown Bainbridge, and after a photographer recorded the somber but proud faces gathered around the suspended corpse, the mob riddled the body with hundreds of rifle and shotgun blasts.[68]

Perhaps only the murder of a white woman by a black could match the power of attacks on white policemen to mobilize white communities to mob violence. In Virginia, both blacks lynched for the murder of white women between 1880 and

1930 were executed by mass mobs. Similarly, in Georgia fifteen of the twenty-one blacks lynched for such crimes were murdered by mass mobs. That violent attacks against white women prompted mass mobs to form is hardly surprising; such crimes gave rise to feverish speculation about the possibility of a sexual component to the crimes and stimulated powerful sexual fears. The mixture of macabre fascination and rage that such crimes aroused is captured by William Faulkner in *Light in August*. The crowds that gathered at the news of the murder of Joanna Burden, a white woman, "believed it aloud that it was an anonymous negro crime committed not by a negro but by Negro. . . and hoped that she had been ravished too: at least once before her throat was cut and at least once afterward." [69]

The punishment of blacks suspected of murdering white women called forth the full array of ritualized collective behavior. The lynching of Brown Washington in 1890 for the murder of a nine-year-old child, for example, was, in the fullest sense of the word, a community affair. The discovery of the body of Tommie West, with her throat slashed, threw Madison, Georgia, and the neighboring countryside into feverish excitement. A posse of a hundred deputized men, augmented by scores of unofficial participants, searched for suspects. Washington, a farm tenant who lived a short distance from the scene of the crime, was suspected, and the posse captured him with ease. After hours of "questioning" (undoubtedly a euphemism for the third-degree treatment), Washington broke down and admitted to the murder. Initially no threats were made to lynch him, but the jail was guarded by fifty men intent on preventing the sheriff from removing the prisoner for safekeeping.

The threat of mob violence mounted on the following day when Washington delivered his testimony before the coroner's jury. Although there was only the most circumstantial evidence against him, his confession was more than enough to convict him in the eyes of white listeners. When he described his frustrated attempts to rape the child and how he had murdered her with his dull pocket knife, members of the jury drew their knifes and had the foreman not managed to restore order they might have killed Washington on the spot. Outside the courthouse, a large crowd clamored for the black suspect to be delivered over to them. Pleas for law and order by the local circuit court judge and another prominent citizen, however, stilled the crowd. Out of deference to the men's request, the crowd dispersed without interfering with the prisoner's march to jail.

That evening, a large crowd of men "whose faces are seen on our streets daily and are among the best citizens," met at 8 o'clock promptly in the Madison town hall to decide on Washington's fate. A leading local businessman, after accepting the chairmanship of the meeting, proposed that a squad of ten men appointed by the meeting take Washington from the jail and deliver him to the waiting mob. The lynchers had little reason to fear strenuous efforts by the sheriff to protect the prisoner. Although the sheriff had wired Governor John B. Gordon requesting him to call out the militia, and the governor had ordered the Madison Home Guard to help the sheriff defend the jail, only three of the militiamen and none of the officers had reported for duty. Thus, the men entered the jail without difficulty and dragged Washington from his cell. To the yells of "Swing him up!" the mob hurriedly marched its prisoner outside of town. After suspending a noose from a convenient telegraph pole and slipping it over his neck, the mob compelled Washington to repeat his confession. Then, Washington was allowed to pray briefly before being jerked aloft and riddled with hundreds of gun shots. Before dispersing, the mob pinned to the pole a warning that "Our women and children will be protected." [70]

The open participation of men "of all ages and standing in life," the carefully organized public meeting that planned the mob's course of action, the obvious complicity of the militia, and the ritualized execution of Washington all highlight the degree to which the lynching was sanctioned by the community at large. Shared attitudes toward women, sexuality, and black criminality, combined with local bonds of community and family, focused the fears and rage of whites on Washington and guaranteed mass involvement in his execution.

The power of murders (and murderous assaults) to unleash the full destructive powers of mass mobs may be traced to several sources. First, violent attacks on whites were unambiguous and egregious challenges to white authority. Unlike instances of "bold talk" or inappropriate behavior in the presence of white women, the seriousness of which were open to interpretation, the killing of a sheriff while arresting a black suspect or the near-fatal attack on a white merchant by black robbers was conclusive evidence of a lethal lack of deference on the part of blacks. Because whites assumed that most murders were the work of groups of blacks intent on some deep and dark plot, they were chilling evidence of far-reaching threats to whites. [71]

The seriousness with which whites viewed black violence against white women and law officers also is evident in the heights of sadism reached during the punishment of crimes. Although mutilation and perverse degradation of the corpse were not unique to such lynchings, they were most commonplace following such crimes. The lynchings became explicitly devoted to the terrorization of the black community in a way that executions by other mobs seldom were. Among the litany of favored ceremonies were such public displays as dragging of corpses behind cars through town, riddling bodies to a point beyond recognition, severing ears and even the head from the victim's body, and burning victims alive. [72]

The lynching of blacks for violence against whites placed tight constraints on black behavior. In certain circumstances, where whites recognized that a dispute between a white man and a black man was a private matter, or a white's reputation or behavior failed to elicit sympathy, a black might get away with besting a white.[73] But few blacks could judge accurately how whites would respond to an outburst of violence. In a region where personal violence erupted frequently, blacks had to weigh carefully the possible consequences whenever they prepared to strike a blow to a white. By intimidating blacks through naked might, white lynchers endeavored to remove any inclination blacks might have had to resort to violence in their relations with whites. To strip blacks of violence, one of the traditional means of defending their personal honor, was to render them defenseless against indignities, slights, and scorn—in other words, dishonored. Thus, lynchings for murder and other violent attacks on whites were much more than just acts of vengeance. They also dramatized as few other rituals could the domination of whites and the degradation and dishonor of blacks.

So completely did stereotypes of black criminality shape white accounts of most lynchings that no entirely satisfactory portrait of the victims of mob violence is possible. White news accounts often warped the life histories of mob victims to fit conventional portraits of black criminals. In 1905, George Bernard Shaw observed contemptuously that "when a Negro is dipped in kerosene and set on fire in America at the present time, he is not a good man lynched by ruffians: he is a criminal lynched by crowds of respectable, charitable, and virtuously indignant, high-minded citizens."[74] Not surprisingly, lynchings, in part rituals of degradation, grew from and sustained notions of blacks as criminally disposed savages.

Despite the blatantly racist and thoroughly conventional terms in which newspaper accounts described most lynching victims, the historical record does allow for some generalizations. Mob victims were overwhelmingly male. Mobs murdered ten women in Georgia, but, apparently, none in Virginia.[75] Women lynching victims, with few exceptions, were accused of murder or complicity in other violent crimes and were lynched along with the men charged with committing the crimes. They also were most likely to be executed in the frenzy of violence of large mass mobs and posses rather than in the secretive manner of terrorist and private mobs.[76] That black women were rarely lynched reveals the different codes of racial etiquette that applied to black men and women. Obviously, black women did not pose the same threats to white women that whites believed black men did, and therefore whites tolerated blatant protests by black women that would have drawn very severe penalties had they been made by black men. Even during the tense atmosphere before and after lynchings, black women perhaps could voice their opinions and anger without suffering extralegal violence themselves.[77]

Many mob victims were young black men who may have shown insufficient caution in avoiding situations that older blacks might have perceived as dangerous. Often, black youths perhaps simply did not realize that their actions could be so easily misconstrued or that whites would mete out brutal punishment for seemingly trivial offenses. Sometimes, a simple childhood error provoked a lynching. In 1912, for example, a mob lynched a sixteen-year-old black boy for having killed a white playmate in a scuffle over a gun. Black youths who had not fully learned the importance of discretion when confronted with an awkward situation involving whites (especially white women) account for many of the victims of mob violence. When Sandy Reeves, a seventeen-year-old black boy in Pierce County, Georgia, in 1918 dropped a nickel on the ground and his employer's three-year-old daughter picked it up, he failed to understand how little leeway the southern code of racial etiquette allowed for youthful indiscretions. Without any signs of understanding the possible life-and-death situation he faced, Reeves snatched the coin away from the child and returned to work. The child, who was, in the words of the National Association for the Advancement of Colored People investigator, "a spoiled, arrogant offspring of southern white parentage of the prejudiced, Negro-hating type," flew into a hysterical rage, prompting her parents to conclude that she had been assaulted by the black youth. Later that night, a mob lynched Reeves.[78]

Any blacks who led a nomadic life as laborers in a rural industry—railroad workers, miners, lumber and turpentine hands, for example—kindled hostility even without committing any crime. Perhaps one in five mob victims in Georgia and one in three in Virginia were migrant laborers, or "floaters." The demand for unskilled migrant laborers undercut repeated legislative efforts to eliminate vagrancy by statute, ensuring that the threat of "floater criminality" continued to weigh on the minds of whites until at least the 1930s.[79] To the dismay of whites, the economic and social dislocations of the late nineteenth century seemed to have produced the "bad nigger" who "sneered at white pretensions, contemptuously challenged white authority, [and] assaulted white honor."[80] The editors of the *Savannah Morning News* captured the widespread antipathy toward floaters when they wrote: "They are worthless vagabonds who wander from place to place, and who do not hesitate to commit the most terrible crimes. They are the ones who commit murder and rape and they are the ones who are lynched. . . . These worthless black vagabonds haven't a single redeeming virtue. They are cruel and cowardly." [81] Whites feared that floaters, freed from the supervision of whites and the traditional controls of the black community, posed a continual threat to white women and children.

The crime committed by Reuben J. Hudson, in DeKalb County, Georgia, on July 27, 1887, epitomizes the threat that white southerners believed they faced from black floaters. Hudson, a vagrant "unknown in this place," stopped at an isolated home and asked a white woman for something to eat. While the woman prepared his food, he allegedly drew a revolver and overpowered her. After allegedly raping the woman and threatening her if she betrayed his crime, Hudson fled. On the following day, law officers captured him, only to surrender him to the mass mob that later hanged him.[82] Despite an appearance of harmless destitution, a black vagrant like Hudson might be a "social counterfeit" of the most dangerous kind. Through cunning he had exploited the unsuspecting charity of his victim, and only after accepting her generosity did he reveal his hidden character and intentions. Black vagrants provoked suspicion and in turn were vulnerable to the violence of mobs because their character was shrouded in mystery and their reputations were not part of local white memory.[83]

Whites seldom believed that previously submissive blacks committed serious crimes out of frustration. More often, whites claimed that the crimes resulted from a black's "bad disposition" rather than from a particular grievance. The transformation of the reputation of Sam Hose, a Georgian who killed his employer in self-defense, from a hard-working tenant to an embodiment of a "black beast rapist" exposes the power that stereotypical portraits of black criminals had over southern whites. Hose, or at least the portrait whites created of him, became an embodiment of all the southern blacks' alleged failings.

Before the spring of 1899, little distinguished Sam Hose from any other black laborer in rural Georgia. Despite having to provide for his family while still a youth—his mother was a near invalid and his brother an imbecile—Hose managed to learn how to read and write and gained the reputation of being a bright and capable man. After his sister married and his mother's health improved, he set out to find work in Atlanta, but various jobs kept him from reaching the city. Sometime in 1898 he arrived in Coweta County, located southwest of Atlanta, and began working for Alfred Cranford. Certainly nothing in his physical appearance fit the lurid image of a "burly black brute" that newspapers described; when lynched he weighed only 140 pounds and measured no more than five feet eight inches tall. If anything, he seemed bashful and reserved around whites.

Early in April of 1899, Hose asked his employer to allow him to return to his home to visit his ill mother. He also asked Cranford for money. The planter refused to advance him any money, and the two men exchanged harsh words. On the following afternoon, while Hose chopped wood at Cranford's home, his employer resumed the previous day's argument. The planter grew increasingly angry, drew his pistol, and threatened to kill Hose. In self-defense, the black man hurled his axe, which struck Cranford in the head and killed him instantly. Terror-stricken, Hose fled and began to make his way to his mother's home.[84]

After the killing of Cranford, whites seemed to be unable to imagine that Hose could be anything more than an inhuman fiend. Within two days of Cranford's death, newspapers reported the wildly sensational (and almost certainly fictional) story that on the evening of the crime, Cranford had been eating supper when Hose quietly crept up behind him and buried an axe in his skull. After delivering several more blows to the victim, Hose kicked Cranford repeatedly in the head. Then—so the accounts continued—the black man, as though demented, grabbed Mrs. Cranford and, with a pistol to her head, compelled her to accompany him while he robbed the house. He dragged her to the room where her husband lay dying, snatched the eight-month-old baby from Mrs. Cranford's arm, and threw it to the floor. (The baby, papers noted, probably would not survive its injuries.) "Within arm's reach of where the brains were oozing out of her husband's head," Hose raped Mrs. Cranford twice. Still unsatiated, he "carried her helpless body to another room, and there *stripped* her person of every thread and vestige of clothing, there keeping her till time enough had passed to permit him to accomplish his fiendish offense twice more and again." The ultimate indignity of Hose's rumored brutality was that "he was inflicted with loathsome 'Sxxxxxxs' [syphilis] for which *Mr. Cranford was having him treated.*" Before leaving the house, Hose is supposed to have announced, "Now I am through with my work, let them kill me if they can." [85]

Newspapers printed extra editions that blazoned the story of Hose's crimes across the country, with cumulative embellishments. Previously unexplained murders, rapes, and thefts from all corners of the state began to be identified as the work of Hose, and his inconspicuous life as a farmhand was recast as a life of brutal crimes and wandering. We only can speculate on how much the shocking descriptions of Hose's fictional crimes may have inspired, indeed justified, the brutality of the huge mob that tortured, mutilated, and burned him to death on April 25, 1899, in Coweta County. The dogma of white supremacy ensured that few white southerners who read about Hose had reason to question that he was a ravenous beast undeserving of human sympathy.

The distortion of Sam Hose's reputation suggests how little protection a black's local standing might provide against mob violence. A black's public reputation rested largely in the hands of the local white community. If some whites chose to defend a black threatened by a mob because of his previously "good character," they might prevent a lynching. But uprooted blacks like Hose or blacks who failed to maintain good relations with "good local white folk" were extremely vulnerable to mob violence. Even in those instances when a black's reputation, in conjunction with protection from a white patron, forestalled a lynching, the power of mob violence as a tool of intimidation was by no means weakened. By relying upon whites for protection, blacks were forced to accept the personal authority and guardianship of whites as the best possible guarantee of their rights. As the sociologist Oliver C. Cox explains, the black man "prostrates himself, as it were, before white men in recognition that Negroes may enjoy a degree of well-being only by the sufferance of their white neighbors." [86]

White notions of black criminality were linked inextricably to whites' justifications for, and understanding of, mob violence. Conventional portraits of black criminals emphasized ignorance, immorality, and savagery, all the while serving to deprive mob victims of any human sympathy. Few lynchings were complete without rumors of the mob victim's past depravities. Whites assured blacks that mobs lynched only "worthless" blacks and that industrious blacks need not fear mob violence, but long before a mob lynched Sam Hose and long after, blacks recognized that neither obsequiousness nor constant vigilance assured protection from the lynch mob.

Even in the most lynching-prone regions of the South, the pattern of mob violence defies simple categorization. Often, in the same community, two perceived offenses might occur but only one would provoke mob violence. Throughout the postbellum era, thousands of alleged criminals were executed legally for committing some of the same offenses that others were lynched for committing. Whites assessed the magnitude of alleged offenses by blacks and responded with the degree of severity they thought appropriate. These patterns help to reveal the deeper anxieties of whites that found release in mob violence. The diverse acts of perceived or real insubordination that may be cataloged under the heading of minor offenses, ranging from outright attacks on the economic order to offensive talk, called for violent sanctions, but the specific form of those sanctions varied. Offenses might be punished by whipping, beating, or lynching. The culminating act of white terror, the ritualized fury of the mass mob, was reserved for offenses that most threatened the moral and social order. The lynching of blacks accused of attacking white women and lawmen, deeds perceived as attacks on the respective moral repositories and defenders of the southern racial hierarchy, represented the most strenuous efforts of the white community to draw a final line of defense against the subversion of white supremacy and community honor. Despite the brutal capriciousness of mobs in the South, lynching represented an incremental form of terror.

Of course, the white editors of the *Atlanta Constitution* who warned lynchers not to allow lynching to become too commonplace failed to see the underlying roots of mob violence. They could not admit that all forms of violence, including mob violence, were a necessity for the preservation of the racial hierarchy. As Jesse Daniel Ames, a prominent leader of the antilynching movement, explained, "it is not good sales talk to advertise that white supremacy can be maintained in the South. . . only by force, coercion, and lynching." [87] As long as whites viewed violence as an expedient, even vital, tool to prop up the racial system, lynchings could not be conveniently restricted to only those crimes that whites perceived to be the most conspicuous challenges to the racial hierarchy.

3

"When White Men Merit Lynching"

In every southern state blacks accounted for the great majority of victims of mob violence, but some whites, almost proudly, boasted, "when white men merit lynching they are lynched." [1] Whites did, if only occasionally, become the targets of lynch mobs, and these occasions reveal that whites, in exceptional circumstances, could resort to lynching for reasons that were largely divorced from race. The same fervently held values of feminine purity, male chivalry, and family honor that fueled extralegal violence against blacks also played a role in the lynching of whites. For defenders of mob violence, each lynching of a white confirmed their belief that summary justice was not an expression of the base racial motivations of bloodthirsty whites, but rather the rightful action of good citizens provoked by fiendish crimes.

There were, of course, significant differences between the lynchings of whites and blacks, differences that white southerners routinely ignored. Whites displayed far greater tolerance of white criminality, and in turn the crimes that justified summary punishment were defined narrowly. Whereas mobs often lynched blacks for minor offenses, lynchers rarely punished whites for anything less than violent and sensational crimes. And the extralegal punishment of whites, to a much greater extent than the lynching of blacks, was likely to provoke local condemnation and relatives of the victims' dedicated efforts to punish or prosecute the lynchers. By ignoring the differences between the lynchings of whites and blacks, defenders of mob violence overlooked just how central race was to most lynchings. Instead, they convinced themselves that the lynching of whites was the consequence of the failings of the criminal justice system.

The significance of the lynching of whites far exceeds the small number of such occurrences because critics of the criminal justice system, with their cry for

speedier justice with fewer technicalities, swept aside most contrary arguments
that the courts already moved swiftly enough. Even many opponents of mob violence conceded that the punishment of criminals needed to be made swifter and
harsher, drawing the same conclusions from the lynching of whites that their opponents did: the great mass of southerners during the late nineteenth century had lost
faith in the courts.

The history of the lynching of whites in both Virginia and Georgia highlights
both striking similarities and differences. Between 1880 and 1930, mobs murdered
fifteen white men in Virginia and nineteen in Georgia. The lynchings of whites
in the two states represented the perpetuation of at least a century-old tradition of
punishing whites who deviated from community standards of behavior, whether
by abusing their spouses and children or by holding unorthodox moral, social, or
political beliefs. During the 1880s and 1890s, mobs in both Virginia and Georgia periodically claimed the lives of white victims. After the turn of the century,
however, the lynching of whites became highly unusual in both states, a fact that
mirrored patterns in the South as a whole. With each decade the blatant connection
between lynching and race in the South became starker. Precisely why the lynching of whites declined is difficult to determine, but it seems likely that with each
decade mob violence was increasingly reserved for blacks, thereby highlighting
the blatant connection between lynching and racial repression.

The patterns of mob violence against whites in Virginia and Georgia diverge
in one important regard; the total in Virginia comprises a significantly larger proportion (18 percent) of all of the lynchings in that state than does the total in
Georgia (4 percent). As the difference between Virginia and Georgia suggests,
whites comprised a larger proportion of the victims of mob violence in the Upper
South than in the Deep South.

In neither Virginia nor Georgia can the lynchings of whites be explained by
peculiar regional codes of justice. Mobs in Virginia claimed the lives of whites
in every region of the state, with the exception of the Shenandoah Valley, where
lynchings of blacks also were rare. Each region of Georgia, except the coastal
region, experienced at least three lynchings of whites. In short, the same communities that lynched blacks also lynched whites.[2]

The alleged crimes that provoked mobs to mete out punishment were similar
in both states. Nearly half of all victims in Georgia and nearly two-thirds of all
whites lynched in Virginia were accused of murder, and only a few were charged
with assault. Most of the remaining number were accused of rape. With the exception of two whites killed by whitecappers for informing revenue agents and one

white murdered for unknown reasons, all of the white mob victims were accused of committing serious violent crimes.[3]

The attitudes of whites toward crimes by whites help to explain why only certain crimes were likely to be punished by mob violence. Communities stirred to a frenzy by alleged crimes by blacks often remained tranquil in the face of similar crimes committed by whites. Few murders and assaults by whites aroused outrage among whites; instead, they were accepted in a matter-of-fact way and white murderers routinely escaped punishment or public censure. In 1880, Horace V. Redfield, a shrewd and perceptive observer of southern violence, concluded that "the moral sense of whole communities becomes so blunted that the man-slayer's status is not impaired."[4] Postbellum southerners, like their antebellum ancestors, "saw violence as unavoidable, as an essential fact of life somehow built in, profoundly, human relationships."[5] So routine was personal violence that one observer concluded in 1882 that homicide was "one of the probable contingencies of ordinary social life."[6] Consequently, given the proper set of circumstances, the white community viewed deaths that occurred during arguments and brawls between whites as excusable, if not entirely justifiable.

Violence by whites that diverged from these conventions could incite mob violence. Most of the murders and assaults that led to summary punishment were, if news accounts can be trusted, psychopathic behavior against unsuspecting and innocent victims. When in 1886 Frank Sanders, an itinerant farmhand employed in Franklin County, Georgia, murdered his employer and his employer's entire family, including three young children, and then burned their bodies to hide the crime, he committed a crime that fell far beyond the boundaries of acceptable violence. Similarly, Jim Rhodes's lifetime of crime in Virginia and Kentucky had led to numerous jail sentences, but only after Rhodes murdered a family of five in Albemarle County, Virginia, in 1882 did a mob lynch him.[7]

Extreme violence against white women also was an affront that the white community did not ignore. It is hardly a coincidence that more than half of the whites lynched in both Virginia and Georgia were charged with crimes against white women. Vigilante committees had long held jurisdiction over such violations of community standards. Voyeurs, old men who married young women, men guilty of public indecency, and those who engaged in adulterous relationships fell within the jurisdiction of the time-honored punishments of flogging, tarring and feathering, and banishment for deviating from community notions of domestic propriety.[8]

The mobs that lynched white men for crimes against women, however, were motivated by heinous offenses for which penalties like flogging were deemed inadequate.[9] The "vile nature" of Thomas Brantly's crimes, for example, stirred his neighbors in Decatur County, Georgia, to punish him summarily on July 29, 1885. Brantly, a good-looking and seemingly respectable bachelor of thirty, moved from Alabama to Decatur County in the fall of 1883. Shortly after his arrival, he married the widow of a rich and highly respected doctor. During the first year of their marriage, Brantly did little to attract notice, but his behavior deteriorated significantly during the winter of 1884, perhaps as a result of his alleged addiction to opium. Without any apparent provocation he would fly into a fury and beat his wife. Matters came to a head on July 21, when he allegedly beat her almost senseless with a horse whip, broke her ribs, and poured turpentine on the open wounds left by the beating. Despite her nearly fatal injuries, she escaped and sought the protection of her family. On the following day, the sheriff arrested Brantly and placed him in jail in the town of Bainbridge.[10]

Tales of Brantly's "licentious passion," "deviltries," and brutal conduct quickly spread around the town and county. Local indignation may have been high, but five days passed before a mob of fifty men appeared in front of the jail and demanded him. Despite the jailer's refusal to open either the jail or Brantly's cell, the mob had little difficulty in ripping open the doors with a crowbar. The mob dragged Brantly from his cell, marched him a short distance from town, and hanged him.

In the minds of most observers, the lynching was amply justified. The headline in the *Bainbridge Democrat* succinctly stated the newspaper's opinion: "An Outraged and Unprotected Society Protects Itself and Vindicates the Higher Law." The newspaper explained that the maximum sentence for wife abuse—a fine and twelve months' imprisonment—was entirely inadequate for Brantly's "outrages." "Hence it is that Judge Lynch interposed and supplied the insufficiency of the law as it is on the books." An *Atlanta Constitution* reporter concluded that "society has simply protected itself" against a gross violator of family and womanly honor.[11]

A crime against a woman also inspired the mob that punished Dock Posey on July 1, 1907. Only a week after moving to Whitfield County, Georgia, Posey brought his seriously injured stepdaughter to a doctor in Dalton, the county seat, and claimed that she had been raped. Several doctors managed to save the nine-year-old child, who, upon recovery, insisted that her stepfather had raped her. Posey at first denied her charges, but, when he was placed in jail, he broke down and admitted his guilt.

On the following day, twenty-five men marched to the jail and seized Posey. Weak with fear and begging for mercy, he was placed in a wagon and driven to a viaduct a short distance from the jail. After allowing the condemned man to pray, the mob hanged him. Before leaving, the unidentified "captain" of the mob ordered that no shots be fired into the body and that the corpse be allowed to hang until at least the following morning.[12]

Newspapers lost little time in explaining the moral of the Posey lynching. Posey's crime, "the more than beastly crime," condemned him. "Be the perpetrator white or black, . . . so long as Anglo-Saxon blood flows freely and purely," the *Dalton Citizen* proclaimed, "the result will be the same." [13] The *Chattanooga Times* pointed out that Posey "met the same speedy fate that would surely have overtaken him had he been a negro." [14] State Representative George O. Glenn of Whitfield County immediately endorsed the lynching. No punishment that could be inflicted could be too severe, he explained. An outlaw of the "deepest dye," Posey was not entitled to any protection. Nor should citizens be burdened with the expense of a trial for a "fiend" like Posey. "Call me what you will," Glenn concluded, "say about me what you please, but I stand for the protection, safety and virtue of the women of my native state." [15]

In addition to having committed serious crimes, white mob victims, in virtually all instances, stood out in some way in their communities. Rural southerners, as the historian Edward L. Ayers has noted, had "no notion of cultural pluralism or moral relativism—only right and wrong." [16] Neither a heinous crime nor an unsavory reputation for unruly and violent conduct was usually adequate to incite a group of local citizens to purge the community of the offending white. The combination of the two, however, could stir communal vengeance.

White mob victims typically had earned the enmity of their neighbors by being bullies, incorrigible adulterers, criminals, drunks, or opium addicts; they were, in short, people the community viewed not only as criminals but also as incurable deviants. Jim Rhodes, the man who murdered an entire family in Albemarle County, Virginia, in 1882, had exhausted the community's patience by his devotion to a life of unrepentant crime. Abe Redmond, a white farmer in Charlotte County, Virginia, for instance, gained a reputation as "the worst man that ever lived in Charlotte County" and a "notorious desperado." His unpredictable violence and unusual cruelty toward blacks and whites alike finally provoked a mob to lynch him in 1893. Similarly, newspapers portrayed William W. Watts, who was lynched for allegedly raping a white woman in Newport News, Virginia, in January 1900, as an ungrateful tramp, a morphine fiend, a petty thief, and an inveterate gambler.[17]

In addition to bearing the stigma of unsavory reputations, many of the whites lynched in Virginia and Georgia were vulnerable because they were recent arrivals in their communities.[18] Eight of the white men lynched in Georgia and seven in

Virginia were just such men. Although whites were particularly concerned about the threat posed by vagrant blacks, they also were suspicious of itinerant whites. Despite an acceptable appearance, a roving white man might not be what he appeared and could pose hidden dangers. Moreover, these whites, who were without relations or long-time friends, had few allies in the face of mob violence. Frank Sanders, who murdered an entire family in Franklin County, Georgia, exemplified the threat posed by the violent itinerant white. In October 1886, Sanders had been convicted of a misdemeanor and fined in the county court. Jonathan Swilling, a local white farmer, agreed to pay the youth's fine on the condition that Sanders work off the debt as a farmhand. It was only after Sanders murdered the Swilling family while they slept that his past misdeeds, including the murder of his wife in South Carolina, become known.[19]

Mob violence against whites drew heavily upon xenophobia, bigotry, and rural southerners' strong, indeed almost instinctual, urge to distinguish between full members of the community and interlopers.[20] With the important exception of Leo Frank, a Jewish industrialist lynched in Cobb County, Georgia, in 1915, none of the whites murdered by mobs in Georgia and Virginia appears to have been targeted because of ethnic origins or religious faith. Elsewhere in the South, however, members of ethnic and religious minorities, who were similarly without roots in southern society, occasionally encountered mob violence: Jewish and Chinese merchants, Mormon missionaries and Catholic priests, Italian sugarcane workers and Hispanic cowhands all fell prey to lynch mobs.[21] And the polyglot ethnic composition of the Southwest, especially Louisiana and Texas, spawned bitter ethnic hostilities that erupted sporadically in lynchings.

However great public outrage at the whites who committed sensational crimes often was, it is significant that, even with "extreme" provocation, the punishment of a white was left to the parties most interested in seeing "justice" fulfilled. The mobs that lynched whites were comprised typically of family, friends, and neighbors of the victim of the precipitating crime. These small groups, numbering fewer than fifty, and, in many instances, fewer than twenty-five members, often felt a deep sense of personal grief and injury that they directed toward the alleged culprit. The participants in such mobs, not surprisingly, were almost always white. While blacks on rare occasions resorted to extralegal measures against members of their own race, it was exceedingly rare for them to participate in the summary execution of a white man.[22] In Georgia and Virginia whites were only rarely lynched by large mass mobs.[23]

News accounts invariably described the mobs that lynched whites as "sober," "quiet," or "orderly." The lynchings of whites seldom became community rituals complete with the hysteria and carnival atmosphere that occurred during some lynchings of blacks. Although sometimes haphazardly organized, most mobs that lynched whites were tightly disciplined, even to the point of military precision, and dispatched their victims quickly. The mob that lynched James Moore in Macon, Georgia, on August 13, 1886, for example, included members of the Sandy Bottom Clippers—a baseball club that more closely resembled a gang—who marched double-time to the jail in precise columns.[24]

Lynch mobs seldom tortured or mutilated their white victims. Although many bodies were perforated with gunfire, an equal number were not. In some instances, a leader of a mob requested that his followers refrain from disturbing the body of a white victim in any way. In contrast, the bodies of most black victims were riddled by gunfire, if not mutilated in some more grisly manner. Moreover, the gruesome ritual of burning at the stake seems to have been reserved for blacks.

Such distinctions illustrate that, even in the act of lynching, whites drew a line separating the races. The private mob that lynched a white man for incest was as intent on expressing and affirming traditional values as the mob that lynched an alleged black rapist. Yet, the mobs, in the minds of their members, were responding to menaces of entirely different magnitudes. Whites viewed the crimes committed by Dock Posey and Thomas Brantly as the products of aberrant personalities rather than of criminality innate to their race. The mobs that lynched whites reconfirmed traditional boundaries of conduct, but they were content simply to purge the community of the offending individual. A modest group drama by a small mob, therefore, was a sufficient reminder that certain rules could not be broken without reprisals. In contrast, the (perceived) constant menace of black criminality, unlike the occasional threat that the white deviant posed, demanded that whites adopt far more conspicuous measures to maintain and reconfirm the boundaries of proper black conduct. Consequently, the lynchings of blacks, acts intended to intimidate all blacks, were much more likely to be public spectacles of mockery, humiliation, and torture than the lynchings of whites.

One of the most significant differences between the lynchings of whites and those of blacks was the white response to summary executions of whites. White responses to the lynchings of blacks, although varied, were predictable. But the reaction of the white community to the lynching of one of its members could neither be taken for granted nor cavalierly ignored. If there was any doubt about the guilt of a white mob victim, the white community often became seriously divided over the appropriateness of extralegal punishment, and mob members risked that the sting of gossip would expose their motives to public contempt. Even in cases when mobs lynched whites for offenses against white women, public support could quickly turn to hostility. Although the purity of a white woman who allegedly was raped by a black was beyond question, the lynching of a white man for rape could produce serious charges against the virtue of the very woman the lynching was intended to protect. The scrutiny of a white woman's morals that followed the lynching of a white man could, and often did, lead to a permanent stain on her reputation, and sometimes even led to her expulsion from the community.[25] Finally, whites who participated in the lynching of a white faced the real threat of prosecution or retaliation by their victim's family.

The lynching of William W. Watts on January 5, 1900, in Newport News, Virginia, offers one example of the ironic twists that often followed the lynching of a white for the rape of a white woman. On January 4, 1900, a city policeman discovered Mrs. Thomas N. Simpson screaming in her home. She alleged that Watts, a white tramp, had just raped her. The officer spread the news of the crime, and a search for Watts was begun. That afternoon, he was captured while on board a train bound for Lynchburg and was placed in jail. Although warned that a mob was being organized, the jailer felt sure that no effort would be made to lynch the prisoner and took no special precautions to protect him. Early the following morning, seven men surprised the napping jail guard and dragged Watts off. The mob first brought its victim before Mrs. Simpson so that she could identify him and then marched him a short distance away and hanged him.[26]

Initially, the newspaper accounts of the lynching were properly indignant about the alleged rape. While strongly condemning the lynching, the *Richmond Times* argued that the lynching demonstrated that southerners made no distinction with regard to race when punishing a man charged with rape. Watts was portrayed as a decrepit tramp, a morphine fiend, and a petty thief. So great was the stigma of his crime that neither his sister, a school teacher, nor his father, a police sergeant, would accept the body.

Within a few days, however, Mrs. Simpson's reputation, rather than her assailant's, came under suspicion. Rumors began to circulate that Watts may have been the victim of Mrs. Simpson's desire "to hide her shame." An innocent man, the *Richmond Times* complained, might have been sacrificed to protect an adulterous woman's reputation. The *Times* concluded, "the whole affair is most revolting" and was yet another "instance of the miserable effects of mob violence."[27]

A tragically similar sequence of events followed the lynching of James Moore in Macon, Georgia, on August 13, 1886. Moore, a former policeman fired for chronic drunkenness, allegedly assaulted sixteen-year-old Mamie Little shortly after she arrived in Macon in early August 1886. The first news accounts universally condemned Moore's crime and offered sympathy for his young and innocent victim. Public outrage, fanned by the *Macon Telegraph,* climaxed on August 13, when a mob stormed the city jail and lynched the alleged rapist.

Within days of the lynching, questions about the young woman's virtue began to be raised. Newspapers in Savannah and Millen, the two towns where she had lived previously, began to publish serious charges against her. Several former employers accused her of unbecoming behavior, including "stepping out" with a black boy, frequenting black brothels, and blackmailing her employer. With each new allegation, the number of her defenders shrank. Newspapers throughout the state began to take sides over the character of the young woman. The *Macon Telegraph* persisted in defending her to the last, at least in part because the editor of the newspaper was bent on stirring up popular sentiment to support a vigilante committee in Macon. The *Atlanta Constitution* lined up with the *Savannah Morning News* and led the attack on her rectitude. Almost daily, for two weeks, the two newspapers published recriminations against the woman, prompting even her defenders to have doubts. Finally, on August 21, she fled Macon in haste after a mob threatened to whip her. When she arrived in her hometown of Millen, she was met by a large and "not very cordial crowd." [28]

The aftermath of the Watt and Moore lynchings epitomized the savage turn that gossip could take. The two women, whose reputations and honor initially had justified the lynchings, were eventually publicly humiliated in their communities, and their moral lapses attracted far more comment than had the crimes that initially had awakened the mob. Mrs. Simpson and Mamie Little discovered the painful truth that their ostensible protectors—the white community—could also become their attackers. Suspicions about rape victims were never far below the surface; the unstated fear was that scheming, lying, vindictive women would entrap innocent men. Thus, although white women may have cried rape with ease, even recklessly, when frightened by a black man, they almost certainly were deeply reluctant to cry rape when attacked by white men because of the shame of public exposure, because of the conventional wisdom and double standard that implied that women were responsible for any sexual aggression committed against them, and because they understood that their charges might be received with harsh cynicism.

A modicum of local support for a lynching was vital to protect mob members from either prosecution or retaliation. Otherwise, friends and neighbors, and even local officials, might attempt to prosecute mob members. When a mob lynched a white there was always the potential that the white relatives and friends of the victim might be able to bring political influence to bear on phlegmatic local authorities and successfully prosecute the lynchers. Moreover, conscientious local authorities intent on prosecuting lynchers exploited cases of lynchings of whites to set legal precedents.

In a few instances, local authorities successfully prosecuted mob members. In fact, the first conviction of mob members for murder in Virginia followed the lynching of a white man. On July 12, 1898, a mob lynched Lee Pickett, a discharged mental patient charged with attempted rape in Patrick County, Virginia. Despite the vigorous efforts of a few prominent citizens to stifle any investigation, the Commonwealth's attorney brought charges against five white men and secured their convictions for second-degree murder. Although the sentences, which ranged from five to six years, now appear ludicrously mild, they were heralded by the *Richmond Dispatch* as "a new departure in Virginia justice" and "a great victory for law and order." The *Richmond Planet,* the state's preeminent black newspaper, used enormous type, as if to express its approval and amazement, in a headline announcing "The Lynchers Were Convicted." [29]

The successful prosecution can in part be explained by peculiar circumstances in Virginia. The changing attitudes of Virginians toward lynchings and the outspoken opposition of some public officials to mob violence made it more likely that lynchers would be prosecuted successfully. That mob members charged with lynching whites were prosecuted in other states, even if years after the conviction of Pickett's murderers, suggests that the distinctiveness of Virginia should not be overemphasized.[30] The first successful prosecution in Georgia also followed the lynching of a white man. Eleven white men were tried for the lynching of Dave Wright, forty, in Coffee County, Georgia, on August 30, 1926. Following a trial that attracted nationwide interest, the men received sentences ranging from four to twenty years in jail. The *Savannah Morning News* suggested many explanations for the first conviction of lynchers in Georgia but stressed the significance of the fact that the victim was white.[31]

Lynchers also faced the threat of retribution from the family or friends of white victims. Because many white mob victims apparently lacked friends or kin in the communities in which they came to grief, no one was likely to have made a concerted effort to revenge their murders. But in at least one instance in Georgia, outraged friends and family apparently avenged a lynching. Professor L. W. Perdue, a Yale-educated gentleman of "good family," moved to Montgomery County in southern Georgia in 1887. Being both educated and of vigorous intellect (in a region where both attributes attracted notice), Perdue established a school. Within several years it flourished to such an extent that he hired the daughter of one of the county's most prominent mill owners and turpentine manufacturers to work as his assistant.

Several months later, when the teaching assistant became pregnant, she accused Perdue of raping her. Her father and family friends "made it so hot" for the professor that he fled to Florida. Returning to Georgia several months later, he was arrested and placed in the county jail. Perdue claimed that he knew of several witnesses who would demonstrate both his innocence and the young woman's bad character. With only sparse and contradictory evidence of Perdue's wrongdoing, the county grand jury refused to indict him. Shortly thereafter, on November 23, 1895, twenty-three men broke into the jail and seized him. After carrying him several miles from town, in one of the rare instances of the mutilation of a white lynching victim, they stabbed him repeatedly, slit his throat, and riddled his body with shot until it was almost unrecognizable.

"There has been no more wanton or barbarous crime committed in Georgia," the *Macon Telegraph* fumed. The lynching was "an outrage so gross that all the powers of the government should be strained to their utmost in avenging it." Local authorities, however, made virtually no effort to prosecute the mob members. No doubt the influence of the young woman's father was more than sufficient to impede any investigation. His prominence, however, failed to protect him from the assassin's bullet that killed him late one night less than a week after the incident. Although the identity of the assassin remains a mystery, local wisdom explained the murder as revenge for the lynching.[32]

The potential notoriety and the threat of prosecution or retaliation that followed some lynchings were strong incentives for friends and families to turn to the courts to right a perceived wrong. Or, probably more frequently, whites resorted to ambush to settle a dispute.[33] If a white committed a sufficiently odious crime, neither prestige nor family influence assured safety from mob violence. But local sentiment seldom condoned the lynching of whites charged with commonplace crimes or crimes with extenuating circumstances, and mob members who overstepped these bounds might face indictments, community condemnation, and—in exceptional circumstances—trials or violence.

The lynching of Dr. William L. Ryder for murder on July 19, 1897, in Talbot County, Georgia, differed from most lynchings in almost every regard. For many contemporary editors, lawyers, and ministers, however, it vividly exposed southerners' seething discontent with the courts. From the spring of 1896 until the summer of 1897, Ryder's sensational crime, subsequent trials, and lynching attracted the close attention of newspapers throughout the state and provoked an extended discussion of public frustration with the legal system.

Ryder was born of "good family" on a plantation near Macon, Georgia, in

1865. After completing dentistry school in Philadelphia, he set up practice in Talbot County in 1894. Because both of his brothers had married into highly respected local families, he found easy acceptance in the community. Shortly after his arrival he became infatuated with a socially prominent young woman, Miss Sallie Emma Owen. Initially, he showed little apparent jealousy of the woman's other suitor, but Ryder's frustration mounted when she spurned his company. By early April 1896, he had begun to exhibit considerable mental distress. On Easter Sunday, April 5, 1896, he armed himself with a shotgun and marched to Miss Owen's home, where he found the young woman and her suitor in the parlor. He opened fire on the two, hitting the woman in the head with one bullet, killing her instantly and severely wounding her guest. In a mad frenzy, Ryder fled and attempted to commit suicide, but his furious efforts to poison and drown himself failed, and doctors managed to revive him.[34]

The murder aroused local emotions to a frenzy, prompting the sheriff to move Ryder to another jail for safekeeping. It also attracted the attention of the state's newspapers. The prominence of the criminal and his victims, the rage of a jilted suitor, and the slaughter of a paragon of southern womanhood called forth the most lurid prose that reporters could muster. Moreover, Ryder's trial, which would be conducted by several of the most prominent lawyers in the state, promised to develop into an exciting legal battle.[35]

From the outset of the trial on May 25, 1896, it was clear that the case would drag on for months, if not years. Ryder's faltering mental and physical health (which county residents suspected was nothing more than a tactic to escape justice) and the absence of crucial defense witnesses repeatedly forced postponement. The delays led the *Atlanta Constitution* to warn that "the people feel outraged, and many of them have lost faith in the power of the courts to deal with criminals who are backed by money and influence."[36]

Finally, in September 1896, Ryder's health improved sufficiently to hold his trial. After seven days of testimony and argument, the jury retired for a short time and then found Ryder guilty of murder. The presiding judge sentenced him to be hanged in January of the following year. But two days after the trial concluded, defense lawyers announced that the sentence was illegal on the grounds of a technicality. After numerous conferences involving the court, the prosecution, and the defense, Ryder was resentenced and a new date of execution set.[37]

Before that date, however, the defense counsel appealed to the Georgia supreme court to overturn the sentence. In March 1897, the court finally ruled on the case and unanimously granted Ryder a new trial. When the trial began on July 19 in Talbotton, spectators filled the overflowing courtroom, and large crowds milled around outside the courthouse. But for the third time, the trial had to be postponed until the following September because crucial defense witnesses were not present. One of the prosecution lawyers announced with irritation that the defense was "monkeying with justice." [38]

That evening, two deputies took Ryder by carriage to a small town west of Talbotton, where they were to board a train to Columbus. A mob of fifteen men, who had organized as soon as it became evident that the continuance would be granted, met the deputies at the station and seized Ryder. Within a short distance of the station, the mob selected a suitable tree, tied a noose around Ryder's neck, and jerked him off the ground and watched him die. [39]

Contemporaries drew differing lessons from the lynching. The *Atlanta Constitution* argued that Ryder's murder was an outgrowth of Georgians' diminishing trust in their courts and that the community first had turned to the organized courts to seek justice. "But in this intense moment of public excitement they found 'technicality' taking the place of justice" and were angered by the "devious" methods used to defend him. The *Constitution* could draw only one lesson from the lynching. The people felt that they were being trifled with, and they demanded that the technicalities that bound the hands of justice be removed. "Until there is offered in the laws of the state a safe guarantee of speedy—not hasty—verdicts," the newspaper added, "the law will continue to find itself outraged." [40]

Newspaper editors also directed attention to the insanity plea. The *Brunswick Times* explained, "the insanity dodge doesn't fool Judge Lynch. . . , it is the biggest trump card being played by lawyers of the defense. . . . Away with such subterfuges." And even if some criminals were lunatics, the *Lumpkin Independent* argued, they were an expense and menace to society: "let their necks be broken to stop their further evil doings and the breed." [41] The *Constitution* questioned the very concept of the insanity plea. The newspaper worried that new theories of medicine were leading the public and justice "away from the stronghold of common sense." [42]

Many lawyers agreed that lynchings were in part the result of failings in the judicial system. In perhaps the most learned discussion of the Ryder lynching, Salem Dutcher, an Augusta attorney, offered detailed suggestions in several long letters to the *Constitution*. He contended that there had been few substantial changes in the Georgia penal code since 1833. Subsequent codes, including the most recent fifth edition, were merely "superimposed" on a code more than sixty years old. In many instances, penalties for crimes were so lax as to be farcical. Furthermore, many court procedures worked in favor of the defendant. Dutcher offered a number of specific reforms, such as compelling the accused to testify in court and limiting the defense's ability to challenge potential jurors, that would contribute to a cheaper and swifter penal system.[43]

The newspaper editors, ministers, and lawyers who complained of the "law's delay" tapped a deep reservoir of disenchantment with the legal system during the late nineteenth and early twentieth centuries. Many of the complaints about the criminal justice system reached a crescendo during the 1890s and struck a responsive chord throughout the nation. Beset by a host of serious problems during the late nineteenth century, the southern legal profession faced attacks from both within and without the legal community. At the same time that state law associations began the difficult processes of setting professional standards and weeding out "pre-professional" old-time lawyers, the profession was the target of harsh criticism from the Populist party and popular cynicism from the general citizenry.[44]

The surge in both crime and in mob violence in the 1890s added urgency to calls for reforms in the system of justice. Southern observers concluded that lynching was a response to problems that the courts were not meeting effectively. Leading southern legal scholars argued that mobs resorted to summary justice because of a profound and legitimate fear that due process of law actually hampered the suppression of crime and the punishment of criminals. Discontent focused on the complexities of the law of evidence and of trial procedure, both of which led to a staggering number of technical errors in criminal cases. State supreme courts had little choice but to reverse large numbers of decisions of lower courts routinely because of errors.[45] In addition to "shyster lawyers" who took advantage of every legal loophole and incompetent judges who failed to run their courts with a firm hand, many observers traced the law's delay to the simple fact that "men of education and good standing" often were exempted from jury duty in southern states.[46]

Governors' pardoning powers were no less suspect than the fairness of the courts.[47] A governor's respite or pardon of a condemned criminal frequently stirred communities to substitute their punishment for the less certain punishment of the state. On March 18, 1892, the governor of Virginia granted a reprieve to Lee Heflin and Joseph Dye, two white men who had been tried for and convicted of the murder of a white widow and her three children. The reprieve, made only a week before the scheduled execution, infuriated residents of Warenton, where the crime had occurred. When county authorities attempted to protect the prisoners by moving them to another jail, a mob overtook them, seized the prisoners, and hanged them. Newspapers all agreed that the mob had been motivated by the fear that "the course of the law might in some way be turned aside."[48]

The lynching of Leo Frank, a young Jewish industrialist, in Georgia on August 16, 1915, was an even more dramatic expression of the deeply rooted popular concerns about the courts and governors' pardoning powers. In 1913, Frank was accused of murdering thirteen-year-old Mary Phagan, a worker in his pencil factory. The lengthy legal battle of the Frank case attracted the attention of Tom Watson, the embittered former Populist leader, who stirred up xenophobic prejudices against Jews and fears that money and influence would prevent Mary Phagan's murderer from receiving his just deserts. In a trial marred by irregularities, Frank was found guilty of murder and sentenced to death. Subsequent appeals to the Georgia supreme court and the U.S. Supreme Court failed to overturn the sentence.

Two years later, in an act of great personal courage that destroyed his political career, Governor John Slaton enraged many Georgians by commuting Frank's sentence to life imprisonment. The nationwide campaign to defend Frank had offended many Georgians, and the commutation seemed to confirm Watson's warnings that chicanery would shelter Frank from justice while the honor of a common southern mill woman—or in Watson's endearing phrase, "a daughter of the people"—went undefended. On August 16, 1915, twenty-five masked men took Frank from his prison cell and lynched him near the home of Mary Phagan in Marietta. The controversy over Frank's commutation and his subsequent lynching confirmed many southerners' beliefs that mob violence protected society from both lawbreakers and a criminal justice system that failed to carry out its mandate.[49]

Some lawyers and judges lashed out against the notion that lynching was the result of slow and irregular justice. In response to the Ryder lynching, N. J. Hammond, a lawyer, stated succinctly, "the trouble is not in the law, but in the people." Another Georgia lawyer, Clyde Shropshire, argued that "the trouble [mob violence] exists in the. . . very innate being of our people."[50] If anything, the courts operated more swiftly than in previous times. There was one crime, however, for which the law's delay was frequent and lamentable—lynching. The only way to stop lynchings was to change the public sentiment that justified and excused them. The press had to stop apologizing for mob violence, and the pulpit had to "break its culpable silence."[51] Most important, members of lynch mobs had to be treated as the common murderers that they were. Until lynchers were confronted with prosecution and a hostile public, Georgia would be disgraced by "anarchy."[52]

The *Macon Telegraph* was one of the few newspapers in Georgia to reach similar conclusions. The newspaper asked, "are we not having altogether too much of mob law?" The legal system might not work as well as the public liked, but it was up to them to reform the laws through the legislature. "The people must have patience until they themselves correct the evils of which they complain." Lynchings offered no solution to any of the ills of the system of justice: "The way of reform is not through lynching bees."[53]

The significance of the lynchings of whites lies not in their tiny number, but rather in the way in which they both exposed and molded whites' attitudes toward mob violence. The occasional lynching of a white enabled defenders of mob violence to deny the obvious fact that race was central to most lynchings. By ignoring the significant differences that existed between the lynchings of whites and of blacks, many southern observers shifted the debate over the causes of mob violence from southern race relations to sweeping generalizations about the courts and the law.

The rationales for the lynchings of whites contributed in a large measure to the respectability of mob violence and spurred on demands for "a straight and narrow" system of criminal justice. Although exceptional in most regards, the crimes and lynchings of such whites as Dr. Ryder, W. W. Watts, and Abe Redmond were discussed as though these cases were typical of all lynchings. The "law's delay," shyster lawyers, and legal dodges all became stock defenses of mob violence. Between the advocates of legal reform and lynch mobs, a complex, symbiotic relationship existed. Concerned members of the legal profession and lynchers shared many of the same attitudes toward crime and punishment. They also were united by their broad general agreement on the principle that swift punishment was of paramount importance. Without the violence of lynch mobs, calls for legal reform would have lacked urgency. Without the learned justifications for summary "justice" provided by the legal profession and concerned observers, lynchers would have lacked an important justification for their violence. Moreover, this de facto collaboration of the southern legal profession and lynch mobs insured that "improvements" in the courts produced a system of criminal justice marked by the simplicity and severity of the mob. None of the conceivable reforms that the critics of the criminal justice system offered would have done anything to protect most of the white victims or virtually any of the black victims of mob violence. In fact, while the lynchings of whites played a crucial role in the justifications for the campaign for swift and rigorous justice, it was chiefly blacks who were victimized by a legal system that displayed a blatant disregard for even minor procedural safeguards. Thus, in both subtle and obvious ways, the rare lynching of a white contributed to an atmosphere in which blacks often faced the prospect of "legal lynchings" in the courtroom and mob murder in the streets.

Once unleashed, the attacks on the courts endured long after many of the original proselytizers for legal reform had moved on to other concerns. By roughly 1910, the southern legal profession had undergone more than a decade of professional purification, and the reputation of the legal profession had been largely restored. Law journals and newspaper editorial pages no longer harped on the theme of the law's delay and corrupt lawyers. Even so, many southerners remained acutely skeptical of the effectiveness of the criminal justice system and continued to exonerate and justify mob violence as the only remedy available to a provoked populace. As late as the 1920s and 1930s, opponents of mob violence still had to contend with charges that lynching was caused by "the chicanery of boot leg lawyers in corrupt courts" and warnings that mob violence would end only when elected officials saw to it that "the law does not dilly and dally." [54]

4

The Geography
of Lynching in Georgia

Many, if not most, white southerners either acquiesced to or openly celebrated mob violence, and yet white residents of different regions did not share the same proclivity to take the law into their hands. Virtually all observers and scholars of lynching suggest that whites resorted to mob violence to shore up caste lines in the face of some perceived threat, or, more simply, to "keep blacks in their place." If, as the Tuskegee Institute claimed, the frequency of mob violence is a barometer of race relations, then white fears about maintaining racial hierarchy varied considerably from region to region within the South.

Contemporaries and latter-day observers have offered a variety of explanations for regional variations in the levels of mob violence. Some students of lynching have traced its incidence to the most simple of demographic facts, the racial distribution of the population in a given area. Arthur Raper, the southern sociologist who headed the Southern Commission on the Study of Lynching in 1930, argued in his classic study *The Tragedy of Lynching* that blacks were most vulnerable to mob violence in areas where they comprised a small minority within the total population. As the proportion of the black population rose, the threat of lynching declined. He concluded that "statistically, per ten thousand population Negroes are safer from mob deaths in the old Black Belt, where more than half of the population is Negro, than anywhere else in the South."[1] More recently, Herbert Blalock, a sociologist, predicted that the occurrence of "symbolic or ritualistic forms of violence, such as lynching" were directly related to the proportion of the population comprised of blacks. As the proportion of blacks increased, he argued, the threat of lynchings did also. Thus, contrary to Raper, Blalock speculated that lynchings would be most common in precisely those areas where blacks made up the majority of the population, Raper's "old black belt counties."[2]

The incidence of lynching also has been traced to rural folkways that bred and, in turn, glorified mob violence. In the crude communities of the rural South, where poverty, ignorance, and isolation prevailed, frontier ethics combined with deep reservations about settling disputes through untrustworthy legal means to create an atmosphere in which vigilante justice thrived.[3] Frail social, educational, and religious institutions in these same mob-prone regions failed to promote responsible behavior. Rather than expressing a virile community spirit, mob violence exposed its conspicuous absence.[4] Moreover, lynchings were most likely to occur in sparsely settled rural counties where police protection was inadequate, if present at all, and local officials had neither the means nor the ambition to stop mob violence.[5]

Each of these interpretations holds much truth, and each offers clues toward the solution of the obviously complex problem of southern mob violence. But none of these explanations is adequate; each is beset with shortcomings. All seem to make the mistake of attempting to isolate specific demographic characteristics or rural conditions to explain a multifarious phenomenon. Attempts to explain lynchings as a measure of the racial profile of a community have either been marred by serious methodological failings or have failed to recognize that the symbolic significance of lynchings cannot be measured in proportion to population. Raper's conclusions, for example, fly in the face of the time-honored wisdom of whites and blacks alike that racial prejudice and oppression were most pronounced in those regions with the largest black populations.[6] And although Blalock correctly predicted that lynchings were most common in regions where blacks made up a majority of the population, there are significant exceptions that demand explanation. For example, blacks outnumbered whites in most counties in both coastal Georgia and the Cotton Belt of central Georgia, but the tone of race relations and the incidence of mob violence differed markedly in the two regions. Finally, the absolute number of lynchings in each area and the fear they generated, rather than the per capita rate, were the index of local race relations. There also are important flaws in the arguments that trace mob violence to specific rural conditions. Rural poverty, isolation, and weak government were manifestations of the economic and social foundations of the rural South rather than independent variables themselves. To emphasize these traits in explaining lynching is to mistake the symptom for the disease. Finally, there in the simple truth that lynching was rare in some portions of the rural South where poverty and isolation prevailed.

In reconstructing the forces that generated mob violence, it is crucial to recognize that the boundaries defining black behavior and keeping blacks "in their places" were products of historical developments that varied from region to region. To be sure, virulent racism and white economic and political dominance shaped race relations throughout the South, but significant variations existed in the tone of race relations and the status of blacks from region to region. The inherent ambiguities in racial lines allowed whites ample opportunities to define and redefine the code of racial etiquette to suit local circumstances. Thus, forms of black behavior that might spark white retribution in one region went unnoticed in another. In some areas of Georgia, for example, whites perceived black land-holding and economic autonomy, however modest, to be serious challenges to the racial hierarchy. But in other parts of Georgia and in Virginia, whites readily sold land to blacks, and neither black landownership nor economic independence merited undue concern.

The jurisdiction of the lynch mob typically extended from the back roads and open country to the small towns of the rural South. However, almost every city in Georgia and Virginia hosted at least one lynching, and even those exceptional cities that did not, such as Savannah and Richmond, still had to contend with numerous threatened lynchings. Clearly, southern city dwellers did not renounce the ethic of mob violence entirely. Lynchings or near lynchings occurred in such Virginia cities as Alexandria, Charlottesville, Danville, Fredericksburg, Newport News, Norfolk, Petersburg, Roanoke, and Wytheville, and in such Georgia urban centers as Americus, Athens, Atlanta, Augusta, Columbus, Macon, Milledge-ville, Rome, and Valdosta.

Urban racial conflict differed in degree and kind from the more persistent thread of violence in rural life, however. As contemporaries well understood, the character of race relations in southern cities differed markedly from that of the rural hinterland. The more elaborate and pervasive nature of urban segregation separated blacks and whites to a degree that was impossible in rural settings. Urban segregation demanded a different form of white vigilance than did rural racial boundaries, and although violence buttressed urban segregation, it usually was carried out by the police or rock-throwing youths rather than lynch mobs. These recurrent racial skirmishes, which reminded people of both races of the precise boundaries of their communities and proper conduct, only rarely erupted into full-blown race riots. Finally, the menace of lynchings degenerating into uncontrollable violence and disorder spurred urban officials and elites to discourage mob violence actively and to take preventative steps when confronted with the threat.[7]

Although mob violence in Georgia left no region of the state untouched, it occurred at different rates in the state's different regions. In the six counties that comprise coastal Georgia, thirteen lynchings occurred between 1880 and 1930. In neighboring southern Georgia, mobs executed 182 victims. In the Cotton Belt, which stretched across roughly the middle of the state, mobs claimed 202 lives. In the Upper Piedmont region, along the northern border of the Cotton Belt, forty-two people died at the hands of mobs, while in northern Georgia, nineteen victims were lynched. By 1930, mobs had claimed lives in 119 of the 159 counties in Georgia (Figure 6).

The pattern of mob violence can be explained by both subtle and conspicuous variations in the place of blacks in various local economies. At the heart of race relations throughout much of the rural South was agriculture and the role that blacks played in it. "Southern agriculture and southern race relations have been parts of one system," explains the sociologist Edgar T. Thompson, "the nature of one, in large degree, has determined the nature of the other." [8] The prevailing form of agriculture in each region, whether cotton cultivation or truck farming, set the tone of race relations, shaped the economic possibilities of blacks, and augmented or diminished the strength and cohesion of black communities. In turn, the social relations that were sustained and grew out of the different forms of southern agriculture produced varying degrees of racial conflict and violence.

The chronic, systematic mob violence that plagued much of central and southern Georgia was rooted in the day-to-day fabric of race relations. The hardcore of southern counties where lynch mobs carried on their bloody work year after year was comprised of large black populations and had economies dependent upon cotton cultivation. Periodic crises, whether local or national in origin, whether economic or social in character, heightened tensions and exacerbated violence but never were the primary causes of mob violence. Rather, lynchings in these areas testified to the dedication of whites to maintain and reinforce the sharply drawn racial boundaries fundamental to plantation society. Lynchings represented the continuing conflict between whites in the plantation districts of the South, who sought to consign blacks to a sharply circumscribed status, and blacks, who struggled to redraw those boundaries.

Elsewhere in the South, the catalysts for incessant mob violence were absent. By no means were blacks in those regions outside of the Black Belt free from the threat of lynch mobs, but mob activity occurred sporadically rather than continuously. The underlying causes of much of the intermittent violence in these regions can be traced to repercussions of the dramatic social and economic changes of the postbellum era. Various scholars have suggested that rapid change, whether from swift settlement, feverish industrial development, or painful economic depression, stimulated lynching, and ample evidence exists that change did generate racial tensions and violence in some regions of Georgia and Virginia.[9] But these

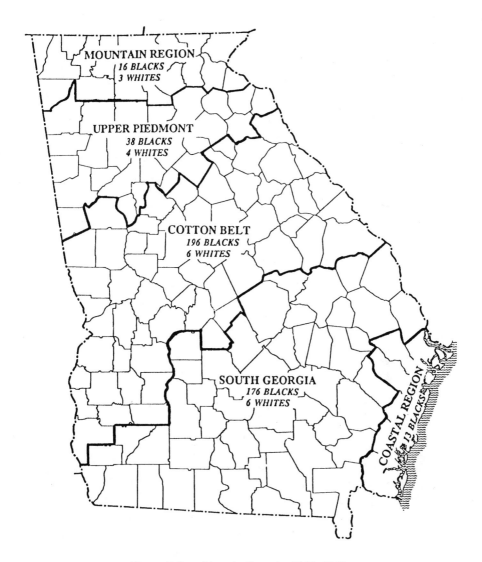

Figure 6. Lynchings in Georgia, 1880–1930

tensions were never adequate to sustain anything more than brief spasms of mob violence.

The connection between the socioeconomic status of blacks and mob violence is both complex and indirect. When Walter White, the courageous investigator of lynchings for the National Association for the Advancement of Colored People, proclaimed in 1929 that "lynching has always been the means for protection. . . of profits," he exaggerated the connection between economic forces and mob violence.[10] Specific alleged transgressions or crimes—rather than inchoate white fears about the economic status of local blacks—produced lynchings. But White recognized that regional variations in race relations and the status of blacks provided the context in which racial violence occurred and was understood.

Nowhere was racial violence more systematic than in the Cotton Belt and southern Georgia. Although the antebellum histories of the two regions differed greatly, profound social and economic changes in southern Georgia during the late nineteenth century recast the region in the mold of the Cotton Belt. Staple-crop agriculture, sharp caste lines separating white planters and black farm laborers, and a white population vigilant to suppress any threats to their rule created an atmosphere charged with latent conflict. Consequently, violence became integral to the ongoing struggle between whites intent on preserving their control and blacks desperately trying to escape white exploitation.

The Cotton Belt underwent little noticeable change during the late nineteenth and early twentieth centuries and became a byword for economic stagnation and social stasis. Bordered to the north by the rolling, red-clay hills of the Upper Piedmont and to the south by the vast plains of wire grass and stands of long-leaf pine of southern Georgia, the Cotton Belt was the heart of cotton cultivation in the state, both before and after the Civil War. Abolition initially unsettled plantation agriculture, but by the 1880s whites had established virtually unchallenged control over the resources of the region. Through a combination of subtle intimidation and outright violence, whites seized political power in spite of the very large black majorities in most counties. Extremely limited access to landownership consigned most blacks to tenantry. Rural laborers with aspirations beyond plowing, hoeing, and picking could find little satisfaction in a region largely bereft of either industrial or urban growth. Beyond the corporate limits of Augusta, Columbus, and Macon, which have been described aptly as "oversized towns," only small towns and hamlets interrupted the rural landscape.[11] Finally, whites, suspicious of any innovation that might threaten their dominance, created a system of public schools that challenged blacks to derive any benefit from education.[12]

The pressing issue white landlords faced following the Civil War was what system of labor would replace slavery. After experimenting with a variety of forms of labor, planters found that sharecropping and tenancy provided a compromise that satisfied the desire of freedmen to escape gang labor and to cultivate a tract of land apart from other tenants and, at the same time, allowed planters to control the planting, cultivating, and marketing of the crop. But as the rural labor system evolved during the late nineteenth century, the landlords' controls over agricultural laborers expanded, and rural workers' options diminished. A battery of prescriptive laws, which approached involuntary servitude in their intent if not in their effect, tightened the grip of landlords over sharecroppers. In addition, as staple-crop values plummeted, sharecroppers were rewarded with poverty and unrequited hopes of upward mobility on the agricultural ladder. In the wake of the new system of labor came stagnation, poverty, frustration, and an atmosphere saturated with suspicion on both sides of the racial line.[13]

Even in the best of times, the relationship between landlords and tenants was charged with tensions. Tenants and sharecroppers chafed under the close scrutiny of landlords. Although the degree of supervision varied with the size of the farm—supervision usually was less onerous on large plantations than on the smaller farms operated by resident landlords—planter authority everywhere was extensive. Moreover, even tenants left to their own devices might have to contend with a planter's exercise of previously latent powers at almost any time. Bitterness and conflict were the predictable products of the system of credit that planters advanced. Although most tenants managed to repay their advances each year, a small number found themselves mired in a cycle of debt peonage.[14]

Planters' prerogatives for dealing with laborers were vast, extending well beyond cultivation practices. The hierarchy of plantation agriculture, with the white owner at the top and sharecroppers at the bottom, sanctioned the discipline of black farmhands not only for economic reasons, but also for perceived transgressions only remotely connected to the economic functioning of the plantation. A planter kept close scrutiny over the conduct of a laborer because "when he steals, fights, assembles 'unlawfully,' plots, marries secretly, indulges in fornication, has illegitimate children, spends his time in gambling, cockfighting, or courting, the planter suffers some loss or threat of loss."[15] Planters assumed the right to regulate, prohibit, or punish these practices as they saw fit.

For all of the extraordinary authority planters claimed, they never achieved the degree of subordination and discipline of their laborers that they sought. They never managed to prevent sharecroppers and tenants from registering protests against real or fancied grievances by moving from one plantation to another. Nor were planters able to overcome the efforts of blacks to protect some aspects of daily life from white interference. Rural blacks established churches, social clubs, and fraternal organizations that partially shielded their social lives from white scrutiny. White uneasiness grew in proportion to the degree to which blacks were successful in carving out an independent social life. It is no coincidence that when racial violence erupted in plantation regions, white arsonists and mobs targeted such symbols of black strivings as black schools, churches, and club buildings.

Despite the changes that the abolition of slavery brought to the Cotton Belt, a thread of violence endured in the region's labor relations. Landlords, like their slavemaster predecessors, vouched for the healthy effects of intimidation and an occasional flogging of dilatory laborers. So rooted in the time-honored privileges of planters was violence that neither the courts nor public opinion impeded its routine application. Whipping and other forms of violent intimidation attracted the attention of local authorities only when they reached epidemic proportions and threatened to lead to an exodus of black laborers. The behavior of county officials reflected the widely shared belief that "any crime which occurs among the propertyless Negroes is considered a labor matter to be handled by the white landlord or his overseer." [16] A white planter might determine that a whipping was sufficient punishment for an offense, only to be confronted by black defiance. Deprived of the protection of local authorities and of any legal recourse, blacks turned to individual acts of self-defense to curb white violence. In such cases, the level of violence quickly escalated. Whippings and beatings were just increments on a continuum of violence that concluded with lynchings.

For the small white population in the Black Belt that was dependent on black labor, mob violence, as the sociologist Oliver C. Cox observed, was "the culminating act of continuing white aggression against the Negro." [17] Despite a secure grip on the Cotton Belt, whites felt the need to reassert dominance repeatedly with whipping sprees and lynchings. Violence was as central to the maintenance of white domination in the region as disfranchisement and black poverty. Not only were there more lynchings in the Cotton Belt than anywhere else in the state, but mob violence also became more frequent over time, increasing from an average of fewer than two incidents a year during the decade from 1880 to 1889, to four a year during the subsequent two decades, and seven a year between 1910 and 1919. [18]

Virtually every county in the Cotton Belt experienced at least one lynching, many more in most counties. Oglethorpe County, with three lynchings scattered over four decades, represented the average. In other, more mob-prone counties, lynchers claimed upwards of ten lives, and in the case of Early County, eighteen lives, between 1880 and 1930. The pervasiveness of lynching ensured that most people in the region had some personal exposure to mob violence, if only through the stories of bystanders or participants. That generation after generation of whites and blacks witnessed lynchings is borne out by the fact that 44 percent of the Cotton Belt counties had at least one lynching in each of three or more decades. What these statistics cannot convey adequately is the cumulative psychological toll that such commonplace extralegal violence took on the entire community.

The atmosphere of violence, so pronounced in Cotton Belt race relations, also was evident in the alleged crimes that provoked lynchings. Murder or violent assault, not rape, was the allegation most often leveled against mob victims in the region. Before 1900, alleged sexual offenses prompted the largest number of lynchings, but in the subsequent three decades murder topped the list of causes of mob violence. Between 1910 and 1919, for example, lynchers executed fifty-five victims for violent attacks and murders, nine for a variety of lesser affronts, and eight for sexual transgressions. Although it is impossible to know how common intraracial homicide was (given current knowledge of regional levels of crime in the period), it is clear that whites in the Cotton Belt chose to make the punishment of blacks charged with offenses against whites an object lesson for the entire black community.[19]

The seriousness with which Cotton Belt whites viewed black transgressions often found expression in the communal quality of lynchings. Actions by mass mobs comprised a greater percentage of lynchings in the region than anywhere else in the state.[20] With the exception of the first decade of the twentieth century, mass mobs committed the largest number of lynchings in each decade between 1880 and 1930. Given the small white populations in many Cotton Belt counties, the size of some of the mass mobs in the region is remarkable. If the mob of more than a hundred that stormed the Lee County jail on February 11, 1899 and lynched three blacks accused of rape in Leesburg, Georgia, was comprised of county residents, nearly one-tenth of the county's white population was present to witness and cheer on the extralegal execution. And if, as was likely, most of the mob was male, a substantial proportion of the 657 white men in the county was included. In May 1911, an even larger mob, estimated at more than four hundred, lynched Joe Moore in Taliaferro County, where the total white population numbered only slightly more than 2,300.[21]

Talbot County experienced a lynching which, as much as any single lynching could, revealed most of the characteristics of lynchings in the Cotton Belt. Located just to the east of the city of Columbus, Talbot County was a typical Cotton Belt county. The production of cotton dictated the rhythms of life for the county's roughly three thousand whites and eight thousand blacks. During the spring of 1909, many of the white planters in the northeast portion of Talbot County sensed dissatisfaction among their tenants. The planters concluded that the recent arrival of an elderly, blind, and apparently affluent black man who was living with William Carreker, one of the few black landowners in the area, was the cause for this new insolence. The old man, who was branded a "disorganizer," allegedly had been preaching to the neighborhood blacks that they still lived in slavery and that they could be free only if they were to break away from the white man. Convinced that the new undercurrent of impudence was much more than a temporary inconvenience, a group of whites, led by William Marshall Leonard, a prominent planter who boasted of his Virginia ancestry, met after church services and decided that steps had to be taken to prevent an "insurrection" among the blacks.

On the night of June 19, 1909, Leonard and a small group of whites surrounded Carreker's house. Leonard approached the house and demanded that the elderly man be turned over so that he could be whipped and forced to leave the county. News accounts later jovially explained that "it is not supposed that any unnecessarily harsh measures were contemplated—just a line of argument that would impress the negro with the necessity of ceasing such harmful and foolish tactics." Carreker pleaded with the whites not to hurt the old man, who, he explained, "didn't mean no harm. He jest' ain't got all his wits about him." Refusing to be put off, Leonard replied, "we have come after that voodoo preacher and we don't want no trouble." Then, as Leonard and the other whites advanced, someone in the house fired a shotgun blast, killing Leonard instantly and sending the rest of the whites into retreat.

By the following day, news of the killing had spread, and large numbers of white men from neighboring counties had gathered near Carreker's farm with the hopes of capturing and lynching Carreker and the old black man. Initially, Sheriff H. P. McDaniel deputized only fifty men to search for the men, but soon the posse had grown to include hundreds in small groups who fanned out through the county. One of the posses discovered the old black man hiding in a barn near the Carreker home. Ignoring his pleas for mercy, the men smashed his head with rifle butts, carried him a short distance to a bridge, shot him several times, and threw his weighted body from the bridge into the creek below. His death, the *Atlanta Constitution* recorded, was "accidental due to his falling from the bridge." In commemoration of the deed, the bridge thereafter was known as "Blind Man's Bridge."

Two days later, Carreker surrendered to a local white man he trusted and asked to be turned over to the sheriff. The sheriff took charge of Carreker and placed him in the tiny jail in Talbotton, the county seat. Sometime after midnight, the jailer was wakened by one of the men previously deputized by the sheriff, who claimed that he had captured a black witness to the Leonard slaying and requested the jail keys so that the prisoner could be jailed. The jailer "reluctantly" turned over the keys. A mob of approximately a hundred men proceeded to the jail, opened Carreker's cell, marched him to the courthouse square in Talbotton, and hanged him from the cross arm of a telephone pole. "When the [cell] doors were opened it was the work of but a few minutes to get the negro," the *Columbus Enquirer-Sun* reported. "It was all done quietly and in perfect order." [22]

The immediate cause of the lynching was the killing of the white planter. But the deeper cause of the lynching lay in the planters' reliance upon the threat of violence to silence black protests and secure a hold over subdued and inarticulate black laborers. When blacks refused to be cowed by the threat and either remained defiant or defended themselves, as William Carreker did, whites responded with swift and brutal retribution. The lynching of Carreker also exposed the undercurrent of hostility toward black landowners in the Cotton Belt. Moreover, the blatantly public character of the extralegal violence against him and the old black man, and the open complicity of local officials, typified mob violence in the region. Admittedly, none of these traits were unique to lynchings in the Cotton Belt, but nowhere else in Georgia were they so pronounced or routinely evident.

The racial violence of the Cotton Belt was nearly duplicated in southern Georgia, a region that was incorporated rapidly into the cotton kingdom following the Civil War. Southern Georgia, which includes the comparatively fertile lands of the southwestern corner of the state, the unrelieved expanse of the pine barrens, and the irreclaimable Okefenokee Swamp, escaped the antebellum era with only scattered incursions of the plantation agriculture that flourished along the tidal inlets and plains of the coastal region to the east and the Cotton Belt to the north. During the late nineteenth century, however, southern Georgia underwent a succession of rapid settlement and rural industrialization before taking on the familiar character of the Cotton Belt. The fluid, frontierlike conditions in the region attracted large numbers of upcountry whites, who envisioned better prospects in the wire-grass frontier, and blacks, who hoped to secure a foothold in the region's economy. Predictably, many whites viewed the ambitions of blacks as a direct threat to their own aspirations and to the fragile racial hierarchy. This tension between blacks' aspirations and whites' determination to replicate the social relations of the Cotton Belt fostered brittle race relations and fueled a half-century of violence. [23]

The catalyst for the economic development of southern Georgia was the expansion of railroads into the region during Reconstruction. The railroads, "those autocrats of civilization" as one pine barrens resident called them, facilitated the exploitation of rich natural resources, especially the great stands of pines that covered much of the region.[24] The forests also attracted the attention of lowland turpentiners, who furiously expanded the naval stores industry in the region. The lumber and naval stores boom lasted until 1910, when the wanton destruction of the forests was complete, and the industry moved on to the forests of Florida.[25]

Industrialization created a demand for unskilled black labor throughout the South, and the industries of southern Georgia were no exception. One observer explained, "The lumber mills. . . and turpentine farms have greater attraction to the average negro than the cotton field." Employment in lumber yards, turpentine orchards, and railroad crews required few skills and generally paid higher wages than agricultural labor. Moreover, many black laborers, especially turpentine hands, enjoyed the companionship of a largely black community of other workers.[26]

Between 1870 and 1900, the stream of black laborers and farmers increased the region's black population from 63,421 to 208,513. Cheap land and an open range for livestock provided ample incentive for black farmers. More blacks owned land in southern Georgia than in any other region in the state, save the coastal counties. In 1900, for example, 21 percent of blacks in the region owned land, compared to only 6 percent in the Cotton Belt. Although the number declined over time, as late as 1919 more than 40 percent of black farmers owned land in some counties in southern Georgia. Even along the northern and western boundaries of the region, where tenantry increased markedly, the percentage of black landholders exceeded that of the Cotton Belt.[27]

The new towns of southern Georgia also lured many black settlers because of the opportunities each offered for black artisans, laborers, and domestics. Blacks had a better chance of owning land in the growing towns of southern Georgia than in the Cotton Belt. Despite restrictions on property holding within the corporate limits of some towns and the thinly veiled hostility of whites, settlements of petty black landholders hugged the borders of many towns in the region.[28]

The influx of black laborers and the economic transformations gave particular gravity to the question of the "black man's place." The development of southern Georgia posed serious challenges to virtually all inhabitants. Long-time residents, many of them subsistence farmers, resented the harsh touch of "the ruthless hand of civilization."[29] They complained that the lumbermen and turpentine hands destroyed vital foraging grounds and drove away the wildlife that was a substantial part of their diet, and that the new industrial laborers, with their raucous lifestyle, threatened property and life. More recent settlers accepted black laborers as the inevitable but unpleasant consequence of development. For white farmers dependent on black labor, the wage-labor alternatives for blacks were constant sources of irritation. And all whites viewed with trepidation the violence that they believed was chronic among blacks and worried that rural industrialization and rapid settlement had failed to impose traditional restraints. At an early stage of the development of the piney woods, the *Valdosta Times* spelled out the danger the region faced. "The county is filled with a roving, thriftless class of vagabonds" who were progressing in "easy steps and with startling rapidity. . . from idleness and gambling to theft, from theft and dissoluteness to highway robbery and murder. We cannot afford to dally with this." Many such fears were not unique to southern Georgia, but the perception that controls on blacks in the region were either ineffectual or entirely absent made whites' fears strident, even urgent.[30]

As so often was the case with agricultural frontiers, inevitable conflicts occurred over dubious land titles, vague property boundaries, disputed hunting privileges, ownership of stray livestock, and the myriad of other tribulations that afflict rural folk. The confluence of the fluid conditions in southern Georgia in the late nineteenth century and of whites' ambition to establish their domination on a firm footing contributed to volatile race relations. In many racial disputes, it was not easy for blacks to know how best to act when confronted with circumstances for which traditional racial etiquette suggested no appropriate course of action. In such situations, a peaceful resolution was never a sure thing. The near-lynching of Welcome Golden and Robert Knight is an instructive example of how confusion over routine matters in the pine barrens of southern Georgia could intensify into a cycle of violence.

Golden and Knight's tragic misfortune was that they were swept into the center of a tangled land dispute between two white men. In October 1890, the two men, along with three other blacks, were hired by L. B. Varn, a major turpentine still operator in southeastern Georgia, to build crude shanties to house turpentine hands on a plot of land, known simply as Lot 2, in Ware County. Controversy immediately erupted because numerous individuals and companies had competing claims to the timber and the lot itself. Although Varn and Frank Stokes claimed the timber, Tom J. Sears and the Waycross Lumber Company claimed title to the land. The crux of the matter was that Varn, who had leased the land from the lumber company, planned to begin exploiting the timber on the lot while Sears simultaneously planned to take possession of the land itself. Efforts at compromise failed, and legal suits were initiated. Neither Varn nor Sears intended to wait for the outcome of the suits, however. Varn's decision to begin "boxing" the pines and collecting resin for turpentine brought matters to a head. Sears bitterly resented Varn's attempts to erect shanties only a short distance from the house that he was building, and he also worried that, once completed, the turpentine shacks would strengthen Varn's claim to the land.[31]

On the day after Knight, Golden, and the other hands began work, Sears resorted to violence in an effort to drive them off. He waited in ambush beside the road leading to Lot 2, and when Campbell Baker, one of the workers, passed on his return to Varn's camp, Sears shot twice, grazing the back of the black man's head. Baker later speculated, "I hadn't done anything to him at all. . . I guess he knew who I was working for and where I had been working." When Knight and the other workers heard about the incident, they were torn between seeking vengeance and abandoning the lot. Golden was unyielding, announcing that "they were going . . . to build that house for Mr. Varn and were going to stay there and nobody was going to run them off." Varn's willingness to arm his hands and to sanction their self-defense undoubtedly emboldened Golden and the other hands. In conversation a few days before Sears attacked Baker, Varn had announced that he had "a whole lot of trouble over there [Lot 2]. . . and if there was any shooting to be done that I would get the first shot or had a man that would." With the hope of heading off a showdown, the five black men armed themselves and visited Sears, as Knight later recounted, "to see if he was going to bother them anymore about the work." Both surprised and terrified by the sight of the armed black men, Sears vaguely agreed that he would stop harassing them and that he would seek a settlement directly with Varn.

On the following day, however, Sears recruited his distant relative and neighbor Berrien McLendon, James Hendricks, and two other white men to help him discourage Knight and the other black men from working on Lot 2. As a justification for asking McLendon to accompany him, Sears later claimed that McLendon "was a friend of Knight's and could do more with him than anyone else."

In fact, neither Sears or McLendon's intentions was as benign. Before joining Sears's private army, McLendon insisted upon completing breakfast, commenting that he was ready to go "kill those Varn niggers and that if he died he would die with his belly full." The five heavily armed white men turned a deaf ear on the pleas of McLendon's wife to not make further trouble and set off for Lot 2. When they arrived at Rob Knight's home, located a short distance from the disputed land, they surprised Knight and the other black men while they were playing cards. Without a word of warning, the whites advanced on the house, firing round after round from their shotguns and rifles. The blacks scattered in various directions, and someone in the house, probably Golden, began to return the fire. In the

exchange, some forty or fifty shots ripped into Knight's home, and two of the attackers, McLendon and Hendricks, were killed. Having suffered heavy casualties
and no longer enjoying the element of surprise, the surviving white men fled.

Knight hurried to Varn's turpentine still to let his employer know about the
shooting. Recognizing the potential for far greater bloodshed, Varn telegraphed
both the mayor of the nearby town of Waycross and the governor to plead successfully for the militia to be called out to maintain order. In subsequent weeks, the
shooting aroused considerable indignation in the white community, and "the air
was thick with threats of lynching." Knight later remembered, "the report out was
that there was a crowd of men out to kill my family. . . I was terrible uneasy."
At the spring term of the court in April 1891, Knight and the four other black
hands were tried for the murders of McLendon and Hendricks. (No charges were
ever brought against Sears for leading the attackers.) Knight received a sentence
of life imprisonment, Golden a sentence of death, and the other black men were
cleared of all charges.

Rumors of lynchings again circulated in Waycross in August 1891 following the
grant of a new trial to Knight and Golden. In December, only weeks before the
new trial date, fifty men battered their way into the Waycross jail and attempted to
smash open the door to the cell that held Golden and Knight. The sturdy cell door
held, and the mob had to settle for firing hundreds of rounds into the cell. Amaz-
ingly, Knight and Golden, escaped unharmed but, as a precaution against another
lynching, were removed to Savannah until their retrial.[32] In February 1892, under
heavy militia guard, they were returned to Waycross. Under advice from their
counsel, Knight and Golden pleaded guilty "to avoid being murdered by a mob
if they were cleared." Knight received a sentence of twenty years, and Golden a
life sentence. A week later the men began serving their terms as leased convicts
at the Dade Coal Mines of north Georgia. Finding humor in their pathetic plight,
the *Atlanta Constitution* smugly observed that they "appear glad to have the protection of the Dade mines." [33] Eleven years passed before their hopes for executive
clemency were fulfilled. In 1903, Governor Allen Candler reduced their sentences
to sixteen years. Finally, in 1908, eighteen years after the "difficulty" at Lot 2,
Knight and Golden were freed.[34]

Although the "Varn Mill Riot," as the event became known in local lore, did
not end with a lynching, it illustrates many of the tensions that bred mob violence
in southern Georgia during the late nineteenth century. The frontierlike character
of the region made for daily uncertainties; the dispute between Tom Sears and
L. B. Varn might just as well have been about livestock. In some cases, as was true
in the controversy involving Knight and Golden, blacks became convenient tar-

gets in disputes between white men.[35] In other instances, by refusing to surrender hard-won gains, by demonstrating ambition beyond their station, or by displaying a resolve to not be bulldozed, blacks placed themselves at risk. That many who became embroiled in disputes were itinerant laborers, in particular turpentine hands, made them doubly vulnerable to white hostility. Finally, the frontier atmosphere in the region encouraged many piney woods residents to scorn the tedious court system and resolve difficulties in time-honored, face-to-face fashion.

The mob violence that claimed one hundred and eighty-two lives in southern Georgia, then, was in part an expression of the deeply rooted tensions produced by the rapid settlement and development of the region. The most rapidly developing counties were the most prone to mob violence. Those in southern Georgia, where lynchings occurred, were more densely populated and (excepting the decade from 1880 to 1889) grew faster than did the region as a whole.[36] The most mob-prone counties also had larger black populations than did the region as a whole.[37] Finally, mob violence occurred in virtually all of the major towns, the most striking symbols of "progress and prosperity" in the region, as well as in smaller crossroad hamlets and industrial villages.

It would be a mistake to assume that the social stress fostered by rapid settlement and development alone was adequate to generate persistent mob activity. Between 1880 and 1900, the years of the most tumultuous development, sixty-three lynchings occurred. But between 1900 and 1920, when the hold of cotton cultivation on the region tightened, mobs murdered ninety-three victims. Almost certainly, the various socioeconomic transformations provoked whites' uncertainties about the security of the racial order, uncertainties that could only be assuaged by violently reminding blacks of the limits of permissible behavior. But the bloody record of mob violence in the region continued long after the boom years had given way to agrarian inertia. The legacy of the earlier, albeit ephemeral, openings for blacks meant that whites could not take for granted that the racial order of the Cotton Belt—with subdued, intimidated, and landless blacks on one side of the color line and white landlords on the other—would be recreated spontaneously in the backwoods of southern Georgia. The persistence and escalation of mob violence in twentieth-century southern Georgia is a measure of the stern methods that whites believed had to be taken to put blacks on notice that, despite the earlier avenues of advancement in the region, they would be put in their place.[38]

With the decline of timbering and turpentining, southern Georgia became an agricultural frontier. Cotton production rose with each decade, tenantry became increasingly common, and by 1910 southern Georgia had assumed many of the traits of the Cotton Belt. Ironically, the increasingly agrarian character of the region contributed to the persistence of mob violence. Whipping and other familiar methods of coercion became commonplace, and disputes between planters and black tenants, frequently ending with violence, became pretexts for an increasing proportion of lynchings.

Virtually every county in the region hosted at least one lynching; the four in Toombs County represented the average. Brooks County, with twenty-two, earned the unenviable reputation of the most mob-prone county in both the region and the state—and possibly even in the South. Forty-three percent of the counties in the region experienced at least one lynching in each of three or more decades; in the case of Emanuel County, mobs claimed lives in each decade between 1880 and 1930.

The crimes that provoked mob violence in southern Georgia also mirrored those in the Cotton Belt. Murders and violent assaults accounted for the majority, a trait that became especially pronounced between 1900 and 1920. During these two decades mobs murdered forty victims for alleged murders and only twenty-nine for all other crimes combined.[39]

For all of the similarities between mob violence in southern Georgia and in the Cotton Belt, lynch mobs in southern Georgia did manifest a few regional peculiarities. Although mass mobs were responsible for a substantial proportion of southern Georgia lynchings in each decade after 1890, they did not comprise as large a share of lynchings in the region as in the Cotton Belt.[40] However, this comparative divergence can in part be explained by the prominence of posses. Posses, which shared with mass mobs broad communal participation and support, claimed more lives in southern Georgia than in any other region of the state. This is not surprising, given the landscape, with its countless swamps and woodlands offering protection to fleeing suspects and, conversely, only obstacles to law officers and the paltry law enforcement forces in the region. Moreover, the tradition of man-hunting became for white men a welcome opportunity to demonstrate their civic commitment in a region where independence and isolation otherwise were the rule. Whites had long boasted that southern Georgia was "white man's country," and the pervasiveness of racial violence by mass mobs and posses demonstrated that large numbers of whites were only too ready to resort to violence in order to maintain the boast.

Each new economic transformation in southern Georgia brought new sources of tension between white and blacks. During the boom years of the late nineteenth century, whites struggled to establish hard and fast racial boundaries, while black resourcefulness constantly seemed to erode those very same boundaries. As turpentining and lumbering declined and cotton cultivation took root, land prices rose, and the quicksand of tenancy expanded, black opportunities faded. But with each new acre of cotton, the troublesome problem of securing and controlling black labor mounted. Whites in southern Georgia felt that a firm hand was needed to coax labor from the region's "shiftless" blacks, who, the *Savannah Morning News* grumbled, "work awhile and idle awhile. The easier life is for them the better they like it, and the standard of ease to which most of them bow is idleness." [41] As whites wrenched cotton from the sandy soil of the wire grass and pine barrens, they wrenched back, with violence when necessary, many of the gains that blacks had achieved.

The *Savannah Tribune* perhaps best captured the black impression of southern Georgia when it branded the region "the last gate to hell" and "A Hell Hole on Earth." [42] The area's depressing evolution, with its harsh and violent race relations, paralleled events in the pine barrens and wire-grass regions of Florida, Mississippi, Louisiana, and eastern Texas. [43] In each of these regions, the succession of expanding railroads, frantic timbering and turpentining, and burgeoning cotton cultivation went hand in hand with rampant mob violence. For generations of blacks, whether they lived in coastal Georgia or the Mississippi Delta, the "piney woods" became synonymous with frustrated hopes for independence and upward mobility, "piney wood peckerwood demons," and virulent and vicious white racism. [44]

It would be a grave error to assume that persistent racial strife and mob violence were inherent to staple-crop agriculture. The postbellum history of the Upper Piedmont underscores that not all portions of the cotton kingdom were hotbeds. The comparatively low levels of mob violence in the region, at least when compared to those of the Cotton Belt and southern Georgia, also demonstrate that rapid change did not inherently generate chronic mob violence. Certainly, few regions of the South underwent more rapid change than did the Upper Piedmont of Georgia during the late nineteenth century. While farmers in the region were drawn into market-driven cotton cultivation a period of sustained urban and industrial growth occurred. The cumulative effects of these agricultural and industrial transformations had far-reaching and unforseen consequences. But while these jarring changes produced serious social strains, including violence, they failed to produce a bloody record of mob violence as in other parts of Georgia.

The key to explaining the different levels of lynching in the Upper Piedmont and other areas of plantation agriculture was the absence of a rigid racial line separating landlords from tenants. The entire tone of labor relations, indeed, even race relations, was set by the sharpness of the color line separating these two groups.

If southern legal codes did not draw significant distinctions between the rights of black and white tenants, everyday practices did. In the Cotton Belt, where the color line divided white capital from black labor, landlords incorporated intimidation and violence into their routine methods of regulating labor. Only rarely were whites likely to be victims of such methods. But in the Upper Piedmont, the presence of growing numbers of whites mired in tenantry and sharecropping dictated that white landlords adopt different, less violent methods to manage their laborers.

Before the Civil War, the area's rolling hills sustained small-scale, semisubsistence agriculture, modest slaveholding, and large white majorities.[45] After the war, railroads expanded into the region and, in a transformation that foreshadowed the metamorphosis of southern Georgia, cotton cultivation rose dramatically. The swelling white population combined with the tribulations of cotton cultivation to place increasing pressures on hard-pressed yeoman farmers. They watched with frustration as many farmers sank into debt, as their farms shrank with each division among their children, and as cotton prices fell. Tenancy and poverty advanced in lockstep throughout the late nineteenth century.[46]

The rapid transformation of the Upper Piedmont's economy, the expansion of cotton cultivation, and the crop-lien produced severe social tensions but, strikingly, only limited mob violence. Class struggles among whites were as much a root of social tensions as were difficulties between the races. Although blacks comprised a large proportion of tenants in many counties, large numbers of whites also were caught in the web of tenancy. In several of the Upper Piedmont counties such as Gwinnett and Hall, white tenants outnumbered black tenants four to one. With such widespread tenantry, landlords confronted white laborers who were unencumbered by the racial etiquette that so sharply limited any expression of protest by blacks. White tenants enjoyed considerably greater leeway in challenging employers than did their black counterparts. If for no other reason, violent intimidation of tenants by planters almost certainly played a less significant role in labor relations in the Upper Piedmont.[47]

Violent coercion of white tenants, although undoubtedly not unheard of, flew in the face of the principles of white supremacy. Ned Cobb, a black Alabama farmer, drew from personal experience when he observed that white planters treated white tenants differently than blacks: "He [the white planter] don't want no white man on his place. He gets a nigger, that's his glory. He can do that nigger just the way he wants to, and the nigger better not say nothin against his rulins. . . . Well, a white man won't take that in this country off another white man. They go right up there toe to toe, and if it's a cussin frolic and a fallin out, why let it come."[48]

Of course, although these attitudes may have protected white tenants, they did not extend across the racial divide. Blacks in the Upper Piedmont, like blacks in the Cotton Belt, could make only guarded protests against either perceived injustices or mob violence. But neither whippings nor violence by landlords against blacks were systematic or pervasive.[49]

Racial tensions did flare in the region but seldom in the context of white landlord-black tenant relations. Rather, some of the violence expressed the rage and frustration of white tenants and sharecroppers. Landless whites, who chafed when they found themselves caught in a system of labor they believed fit only for blacks, insisted that they be in loftier positions on the agricultural ladder. But the evolution of Upper Piedmont agriculture almost certainly stripped most embattled poor whites of any hopes of acquiring land. They were left with the token advantages they received from white landlords—modestly better land to till and a degree of latitude denied blacks. Their pent-up discontent periodically surfaced in terrorist racial violence.

Such violence was a frequent phenomenon in the region and represented a larger proportion of lynchings in the Upper Piedmont than in any other region in the state. Whitecappings were particularly prevalent during the economic and social turmoil of the 1890s, but persisted well into the twentieth century.[50] Throughout the Upper Piedmont, especially along the borders of the region where mountain whites pressed down into the Upper Piedmont and in turn Upper Piedmont whites pushed into the Cotton Belt, white tenant farmers sporadically organized campaigns to drive black families off their landlords' land and ostracize the white farmers who rented to them. In 1912, for example, white tenant farmers in Forsyth County, a county on the northern border of the region, determined to force all black landowners to sell their farms and to drive all black tenants out of the county. They whipped and murdered an undetermined number of individuals, burned their homes and barns, and warned them to leave. The white planters who depended upon black laborers tried to prevent the exodus by refusing to hire white tenants or to extend credit to the leaders of the terrorist campaign, but even so, almost all blacks were driven out of the county.[51]

To be sure, the bulk of lynchings in the Upper Piedmont were not carried out by terrorist mobs of whitecappers. Serious alleged crimes prompted most of the mob murders in the region. Attempted rape or rape was the allegation leveled against seventeen of the thirty-five black victims of mob violence between 1880 and 1919. Lesser infractions comprised the next most common cause for mob violence. Twelve blacks and one white were lynched for overstepping the boundaries of acceptable conduct by arguing with an employer, informing revenue agents, or committing sundry affronts so obscure that they were not recorded. The remaining nine lynchings of three whites and six blacks were prompted by alleged attempted murders and murders. What these statistics reveal is that the alleged crimes that prompted violence in the Upper Piedmont differed markedly from the crimes that produced mob violence in the Cotton Belt and southern Georgia. Although alleged murders provoked 49 percent of the lynchings in southern Georgia and 55 percent in the Cotton Belt, they accounted for only 27 percent of the mob murders in the Upper Piedmont. Conversely, 30 percent of mob victims in southern Georgia and 27 percent in the Cotton Belt were accused of rape, whereas more than 42 percent in the Upper Piedmont were accused of the same offense. Clearly, the punishment of "violations" by black "beast-rapists" assumed particular importance in the Upper Piedmont.[52]

Precisely why alleged rapes were such a conspicuous cause of lynchings in the Upper Piedmont is hard to learn. The location of many of the lynchings for sexual offenses, however, is suggestive. Nearly half occurred either along the fringes of or within the environs of Atlanta and Rome, a small city on the northwestern corner of the region. These lynchings may have expressed the fears and frustrations of whites who lived uncomfortably on the fringes of urban life where rural and urban patterns of race relations came into conflict. That such fears existed would seem to be borne out by the fact that these same communities were prone to mob violence for other transgressions as well. Mobs executed two victims in Fulton County (of which, at the time, Atlanta comprised a part), nineteen victims in counties bordering on Atlanta, and three victims on the outskirts of Rome. The fifteen other lynchings in the region were scattered throughout nine other counties.

The lynchings on the periphery of Atlanta and Rome probably were testimony to the fears of whites that the day-to-day controls on black life in the countryside were losing their effectiveness and the conviction that symbolic violence was needed to restore black deference and fear. Atlanta and, to a lesser extent, the handful of other sizable towns in the region, threw the races together in competition for jobs, housing, and—as long as blacks retained the vote—political power. Moreover, fast-paced urban life also brought the races together in all manner of public accommodations and in varied settings in which the dictates of proper racial etiquette were ambiguous. The apparent erosion of race lines in Atlanta and other major towns, and the comparative affluence and what whites perceived to be the profligate decadence of urban blacks, all sharpened tensions. The steady migration of rural blacks through the bordering counties into the city and the simple fact of the proximity of Atlanta gave these fears particular immediacy. These conditions, the historian Don Doyle observes, "produced friction of a type and a scale rarely known before in the South, and it produced more vicious white reactions as a consequence." [53]

Despite mob violence along its boundaries and the constant threat of racial friction in the city, only two lynchings occurred in the heart of Atlanta. By no means was the city free from the threat of lynching attempts, but the combination of practical impediments to mob violence and the efforts of local leaders frustrated most lynch mobs. Law officers in Atlanta could muster their forces swiftly, and the fortresslike Atlanta jail posed a formidable challenge to any mob intent on lynching a prisoner. Most important, the desire to preserve the social order motivated Atlanta's civic leaders to marshall the police and, in an emergency, the militia to nip racial violence in the bud. [54]

Throughout most of the late nineteenth and early twentieth centuries, the forces in Atlanta that were committed to order managed to ensure that periodic minor racial clashes did not get out of hand. In September 1906, however, mounting racial tensions erupted in one of the bloodiest riots in southern history. Ignited by newspaper sensationalism and political opportunism, the Atlanta riot left at least ten blacks dead, sixty more wounded, and smoldering ruins in the black neighborhoods. While the riot itself demonstrated the explosive potential for violence against blacks in the city, the response of the white elite to the riot reflected concern about the dangers of uncontrolled mob violence. A relief committee was organized to assist victims, efforts were made to improve communication between the black and white communities, and the Fulton County grand jury, which investigated the riot, placed the blame for the riot squarely upon Atlanta newspapers, in particular the *Atlanta News,* for stirring up racial antagonism by printing sensational accounts of rumored crimes by blacks. W. E. B. Du Bois, who participated in some of the early interracial meetings following the riot, may have been on target when he complained that the meetings had been "gotten up primarily for advertising purposes." [55] The remorse of leading whites over the riot had less to do with the suffering of the black community than with the severe blow to the city's carefully nurtured progressive reputation. Thus, if only for "advertising purposes," local officials and leaders committed themselves to ensuring that no future racial disturbance scarred the city. [56]

Whatever the precise reasons for the periodic mob violence in the outskirts of the urban centers of the Upper Piedmont, when it did occur it often took the form of mass lynchings, replete with elaborate ritualism. Between 1900 and 1930, mass mobs summarily executed fourteen of the twenty-one mob victims in the region. And because the region's newspapers reported these lynchings with great relish and nauseating detail, their audience extended well beyond the crowds of lynchers, spectators, and souvenir-hunters who participated in the butchery.

In March 1900, for instance, the telegraph wires reported that a mob in downtown Marrietta that numbered at least 150 lynchers had executed John Bailey, a young black, for rape.[57] Newspaper correspondents counted mobs of two hundred, four hundred, and five hundred participants at other lynchings in the region.[58] In April 1902, a crowd estimated at four thousand poured into downtown Rome after rumors spread that Walter Allen, a local hotel porter, allegedly had attempted to rape a member of a prominent local family. (If he committed any crime at all, it was robbery and not attempted rape.) The crowd, "composed of citizens of high and low degree, without regard to friendship, politics, or social standing," stormed the jail, seized Allen, and lynched him "under the glare of an electric light on the principal street of the city." The ceremony concluded when the swinging corpse was fired upon by "every available gun and pistol in Rome." [59]

A mass lynching that incorporated many of the traits characteristic of lynchings in the Upper Piedmont occurred in September 1889 in East Point, a rough-and-tumble town that had grown up around the railroad yards on the southern outskirts of Atlanta. Warren Powers (sometimes also referred to as Powell), a fourteen-year-old "worthless fellow" who spent most of his time "loafing about in town," allegedly grabbed Ada Brooks, who was white, as she returned home after school. Before he could accomplish "his designs," her screams attracted workers from a nearby wagon factory and scared him off. Within an hour, a hastily organized posse captured Powers and turned him over to the East Point bailiff, who immediately telegraphed to Atlanta for orders from the sheriff and assistance from the police department. The bailiff locked Powers in the town jail, which was a small two-roomed addition to the rear of the post office, secured by a simple padlock and "as little calculated to withstand an attack as a smoke house." While the bailiff waited for reinforcements from Atlanta, a boisterous crowd of several hundred people gathered in front of the makeshift jail. Several hours passed before they rushed the building, smashed the padlock off with a hatchet, and dragged Powers from his cell. Ignoring the hysterical pleas of Powers's mother and father to spare him, the mob hustled their victim a distance from the jail before hanging him.[60]

If the lynching of Powers punished the most serious black depredation, there were many residents of East Point who believed that the mob's work was not done. Whites detected "that the negroes were mad and that they were bent on mischief." Jake Conley, a local leader, allegedly denounced the lynching and roared, "we ought to kill the bailiff and the mayor, and burn the town." Rumors that blacks planned to launch a mass attack from a nearby church kept tensions high, leading whites to prepare for the worst by stockpiling rifles and ammunition and by creating an informal militia to patrol the streets. When police arrived from Atlanta, most whites concluded that there was no longer any imminent threat to East Point. "Them negroes is never coming here," one lamented, "and we won't have any fun." Intent on having "some fun," groups of men, including, according to some accounts, the mayor and several prominent residents, invaded the nearby black districts, whipping and intimidating blacks under the pretext of searching for Jake Conley. By the end of the night, two buggy whips had been "entirely used up" in the flogging of at least fourteen people.[61]

Although the whippings provoked considerable outrage in Atlanta—obnoxious blacks, not random, inoffensive, hard-working blacks were the proper targets of a mob's fury—they had the intended effect. Many blacks fled East Point and the surrounding countryside and found shelter in Atlanta. Predictably, those who remained were intimidated and vigorously professed obedience. On the same day that a white mass meeting condemned the whipping spree but endorsed the lynching of Powers, a black mass meeting adopted resolutions that announced that Powers had "met with the fate such crimes deserve and the protection of virtue demands." The meeting also condemned "irresponsible" and "disreputable" local blacks who had attempted to incite "our race to riot and violence" and proclaimed that "we will do all in our power to protect the peace and harmony of the town." [62]

The crisis in East Point, beginning with the attempted "outrage" by a black youth corrupted by urban ways, followed by the communal punishment of black lust and the wanton terrorizing of convenient blacks, and closing with the public display of black intimidation and deference to white rule, epitomized the nature of mob violence along the urban frontier of the Upper Piedmont. But if white notions of extralegal violence were flexible enough to excuse lynchings, they did not excuse general mayhem or random acts against blacks. The forces of law and order might not have been sufficient to defend the flimsy jails in the rural hamlets, but they were adequate to prevent extended campaigns of terror against blacks.

For all of whites' fears about the sanctity of the racial hierarchy and their loathing of arrogant and insolent urban blacks, it is important to remember that mob violence in the Upper Piedmont never approached the levels of extralegal violence of either the Cotton Belt or southern Georgia. In part, this was because of the character of rural labor relations and the comparative effectiveness of local authorities and law officers in preserving the peace. A further, but more elusive, reason was that in portions of the Upper Piedmont the values that sanctioned mob violence— feminine virtue, family honor, white supremacy, and defense of community—

took on the coloration of urban life. The exigencies of urban life, which placed a premium on public order, and the unceasing preaching of urban progress and values by the prophets of the New South were powerful countervailing forces to the culture of mob violence. From the churches, colleges, and business groups—the sinew of the New South—came the staunchest opposition to lynching and the loudest calls for an ordered solution to the "negro problem." Legal segregation, it was argued, not mob violence was the balm for racial tensions. These critics were never large in number and they never won the majority of whites in the Upper Piedmont over to their vision of the New South, but their influence was evident in the editorial pages of the region's newspapers and when local authorities took forceful steps to prevent lynchings. In the atmosphere created by the historical conjunction of the genesis of an urban ethos and the economic evolution of the Upper Piedmont, the lynch mob endured but could not thrive.[63]

The social tensions played out to their violent conclusions in the Upper Piedmont had their counterparts in northern Georgia. During the late nineteenth century, northern Georgians were drawn simultaneously into the market economy and subjected to a new and intrusive imposition of federal authority when federal revenue agents set out to suppress illegal alcohol distilling. Whites in the region, like so many southerners, reacted to unwelcome change with resentment and outbursts of violence. The violence in northern Georgia, like the bloodshed in the Upper Piedmont, flared only sporadically, however. The social crisis that these deeply divisive innovations sparked left as its imprint on generations of mountain folk festering tensions that bred feuds, murders, and personal violence of all kinds, but not mob violence.

Before the Civil War, the steep ridges, short planting season, and isolation of northern Georgia checked the expansion of slavery and plantation agriculture. The largely self-sufficient white farmers who peopled the fertile valleys and hollows of the region had little need for black laborers, and consequently blacks never constituted a crucial part of the work force. In the immediate aftermath of emancipation, the small black population dwindled.[64]

After the Civil War, rail lines penetrated northern Georgia and simultaneously drew the region into the nation's expanding agricultural and industrial market economy and disrupted the prevailing subsistence economy. Improved transportation transformed the western corner of the region, while cotton cultivation expanded, commercial activity increased, and a handful of mill towns arose. Much of the eastern portion of the region, however, remained isolated. Corn, rather than cotton, was the major crop, and the abundance of corn and the isolation of most farms provided two of the essential ingredients to the moonshining industry that thrived in the mountains.[65]

Seemingly, the preconditions for racial violence should have been absent. The large white majority faced little serious threat, economic or otherwise, from the small and vulnerable black population. Yet during the late 1880s and early 1890s, racial violence in northern Georgia reached levels that equalled those elsewhere in the state. The history and magnitude of the bloodshed can be explained by the unpleasant innovations and unwelcome immigrants that mountain folk confronted when the isolation of their region gave way. During the late 1880s, the coincidence of aggressive tactics by federal revenue agents and the social dislocations that were a result of the national economic recession sparked extensive violence, including lynchings and whitecappings.[66] Rising sharply in 1889, the wave of violence that swept the region remained high from 1890 to 1892, reached a dramatic peak in 1893 and 1894, and then dissipated quickly thereafter. Nearly two-thirds of all the lynchings that occurred in the region took place between 1888 and 1894.[67]

The roots of the violence lay as much in social tensions that divided whites as in racial fears. Whitecappers used violence to silence and punish people suspected of informing federal revenue agents about illegal stills and to discipline the immoral, whether they were white or black. The racial fears that engrossed whites elsewhere also were evident; whitecappers whipped and murdered many blacks charged with transgressions ranging from indolence to miscegenation.[68]

Whitecapping violence was most pronounced in the western corner of northern Georgia, which had experienced rapid and complete economic transformation since the Civil War. The region also hosted the largest number of lynchings in northern Georgia. Eleven occurred between 1880 and 1930, and of these, nine took place between 1880 and 1894. The spate of lynchings, not coincidentally, occurred at the same time that the changes in the region had given rise to mounting concerns over the passing of the old order. Newspaper editors worried that indolence and lasciviousness would invade the budding towns of the region, and many locals resented surrendering local autonomy to the whims of the market autonomy. Finally, some whites were troubled by the vexing problem of blacks who did not always abide by the tenets of white supremacy. Thus, the spasm of lynchings and whitecappings against prostitutes, wife-beaters, petty criminals, "uppity" blacks, and revenue informers was all part of a futile rear-guard action to restore much-valued traditions and mores.[69]

Because whites suffered as often as blacks at the hands of the whitecappers, mobs during the late 1880s and early 1890s did not enjoy the widespread support that many did elsewhere in Georgia. Terrorist or private mobs were responsible for most of the mob murders in the region during the peak years of the whitecapping epidemic. Between 1888 and 1894, nine of the twelve mobs that murdered northern Georgians were either small private or terrorist mobs.[70] As whitecapping violence increased during the early 1890s, community opposition grew. Outraged ministers repeatedly denounced it, and in 1892, after a lynching in Dalton, exasperated citizens called a mass meeting there to protest the mob's actions and raise $750 to combat the mob (precisely how the money was used remains a mystery). Spurred on by local opposition to the mobs' depredations, local authorities managed to harass the whitecappers, and federal authorities even managed to bring several to trial. By 1895, the combination of federal suppression, local opposition, and the trials contributed to the decline in violence.[71]

Six lynchings occurred in the region after the flurry of violence during the early 1890s. Even after the crisis of the 1890s eased, whites still harbored many of the same fears of black criminality that whites did elsewhere in the state. The diffuse racial fears surfaced in communal responses to heinous crimes allegedly committed by blacks. Whites reacted to alleged sexual assaults and murders by blacks according to the brutal etiquette of race relations that justified lynching black rapists and murderers. In 1913, a mob of hundreds in Stephens County lynched two tramps who had killed a popular town policeman who tried to arrest them for loitering. In 1915, another mass mob executed Sam Stephens, a convict serving time on the chain gang, who allegedly had raped a sixteen-year-old white girl. Finally in 1916, in the last lynching in the region, a mob of a hundred lynched Henry White, a floater accused of raping a young white woman (the black *Chicago Defender* claimed that White and the woman had actually been lovers).[72]

Personal violence continued to plague the region, but, with the exception of a terrorist campaign by white farmers against black tenants and landowners in a few counties on the southern border of the mountains, blacks were not the victims. Like whites elsewhere in the state, whites in northern Georgia undoubtedly were committed to white supremacy, but the shrinking black populations in the mountains posed few economic or social challenges. If there was a black threat, it came from the occasional floater who strayed into the region. Once deprived of the fuel of social crisis, mob violence in northern Georgia was virtually extinguished. Statistically, in proportion to the total black population, blacks in the region were more vulnerable than were blacks anywhere else in the state. But size of population notwithstanding, generations of blacks lived in northern Georgia without suffering the ignominy of witnessing mob murder. In the last analysis, Gordon County blacks almost certainly would not willingly have surrendered a lifetime in a county free from the stain of lynching for the statistical safety of a Cotton Belt or south Georgia county. Northern Georgia may not have been a favorable environment for blacks to secure economic and social independence, but, if nothing else, they were relatively free from the ever-present threat of the noose and torch.

If there was any region of Georgia where whites seemingly should have felt a constant need to keep blacks in their places, it should have been coastal Georgia. Before the Civil War, white planters, with armies of black slaves, had carved out vast, lucrative rice and cotton plantations. With the war and Reconstruction, however, came social and economic upheavals as wrenching as any endured elsewhere. Yet comparatively tranquil race relations prevailed in coastal Georgia during the late nineteenth and early twentieth centuries. Although conditions for blacks were something less than the "black paradise" that the British traveler Sir George Campbell thought he found in neighboring coastal South Carolina, blacks in coastal Georgia escaped the furious bloodletting that characterized neighboring southern Georgia and the Cotton Belt. With only thirteen lynchings between 1880 and 1930, the low country had fewer lynchings than any other portion of the state.

Underlying the relative peace was a historical conjunction of economic forces and received culture. The postwar economic order, in which plantation agriculture played a diminishing role, no longer demanded the steady coercive labor practices of old. A combination of market forces, stiff competition from efficient plantations elsewhere, and the jarring transition to free labor crippled the efforts of low-country merchants and planters to restore past prosperity. With the eclipse of low-country plantations, an economy based upon lumbering, naval stores, shipping, and mixed agriculture emerged. As a result of this economic transformation, the control of black labor, which was the pressing concern of whites in the Cotton Belt, provoked only occasional hand-wringing among coastal whites. The *Savannah Morning News* summarized prevailing wisdom when it observed that black laborers "are not wanted as badly as in the middle section [the Cotton Belt] . . . because of the nature of the work that is demanded of them. This can be done as quickly and much more better by white men." Of course, black laborers were not as dispensable as the *Morning News* suggested, and white laborers were never in adequate supply, but the newspaper's comments did reflect the half-conscious desire of many coastal whites to replace the older labor practices, rooted as they were in plantation slavery, with flexible labor relations more appropriate to an emerging economy.[73]

Coastal whites entertained few fears that the new regional order threatened white domination. "Neither white government nor white civilization has anything to fear from the negro," the *Savannah Morning News* announced in 1906.[74] In contrast to whites who advocated terror and violence, low-country whites stressed the need for racial accommodation and harmony. Championing a conservative, fundamentally elitist definition of white supremacy, coastal elites entertained the notion that some whites posed as serious a social threat as did blacks. At a time when many southern whites either despaired of or firmly rejected the "uplift" of blacks, many coastal whites continued to believe that blacks were making progress with the help and encouragement of whites. In practice, this paternalistic ethos only went so far. It often amounted to little more than the avowed commitment to do what was best for blacks. Trivial support for black education, monotonous calls for the moral improvement of blacks, and episodic concern for the public health of blacks were the extent of coastal paternalism. But for all its limitations, white benevolence did stress the dangers of mob violence.[75]

At the root of white paternalism was a belief that coastal blacks should recognize that their status was determined by innate inferiority rather than arbitrary discrimination. "It is important not only that they [blacks] should be dealt with justly, but that they should feel that they are so dealt with," the *Morning News* stressed.[76] The touchstones of white rule—"conservatism, fairness, justice, and patience"—demanded that whites give "the negro a fair chance."[77] As a practical matter, this meant that racial peace could not exist as long as blacks believed that they were unjustly discriminated against by employers, the courts, or whites in general. Full justice for blacks required judicial impartiality and an end to mob violence.[78] "Criminals, white and black, must be treated alike," the *Morning News* editorialized, because otherwise the effect of blatant discrimination "tends to strengthen the race feeling."[79] Even as militant white racists became the dominant voice in southern race relations at the turn of the century, prominent whites in coastal Georgia called for a moratorium on "agitation on the race question" and steadfastly maintained that violence could never solve the region's problems.[80]

Both the paternalist ethos of coastal whites and the direction of the coastal economy were compatible with—and even conducive to—a greater degree of black assertiveness than was typical elsewhere in the state. Indeed, conditions in the region encouraged the full expression of black strivings, the stubborn defense of a hard-earned measure of social autonomy, and the creation of rich community bonds, qualities favorable to opposition—including collective resistance—to white violence.[81]

Underlying black independence in coastal Georgia was the heritage of both the peculiar form of slavery that flourished there and its upheaval following emancipation. During the Civil War, thousands of acres of confiscated and abandoned plantations in the region, under the administration of the Freedman's Bureau, were cultivated by freedmen. Although the federal government failed to satisfy the freedmen's aspirations for landownership, which flourished in such maroon communities as Sapelo Island, a substantial proportion of blacks succeeded in acquiring land. Prospective black landowners along the coast benefited from the waning of plantation agriculture and the failure of planters to adapt sharecropping to rice cultivation. As the plantations became unprofitable, whites readily sold portions of their landholdings to blacks. Nowhere in the state was black landholding more extensive than in the coastal region.[82]

The ownership of small plots of land, in itself, did not translate into economic autonomy, but it did provide a much-valued measure of independence from the vicissitudes of staple-crop agriculture. Moreover, landownership allowed blacks to offer their labor to the market under circumstances of their choosing. By tapping the varied resources of the fertile coastal environment, coastal blacks who owned only a small plot of land could eke out an impoverished but independent life. "The Negroes there," a Georgia planter ruefully observed in 1899, "will not work for wages, as they can live without work on fish, crawfish and oysters; a little patch of cotton furnishing them the means for tobacco and clothing."[83]

For large numbers of coastal blacks, the region's cities and towns offered economic, educational, and social opportunities seldom available in the plantation regions. Building upon foundations laid by antebellum free blacks and slaves, coastal blacks, especially in Savannah, worked to create viable businesses and social and religious institutions. Savannah and, on a much smaller scale, Darien and Brunswick harbored a growing, if vulnerable, black middle class of professionals and businessmen whose influence outweighed their small numbers. Although financially precarious and susceptible to white interference, black institutions, particularly newspapers, clubs, and churches, helped bind divided black communities together and provided forums for self-expression and protest. Black newspapers were especially prominent in urban activism. In particular, the *Savannah Tribune,* among the most influential southern black newspapers of the late nineteenth and early twentieth centuries, publicized injustices and, through the insistent call for social justice, strove to dispel disillusionment.[84]

Just as the economic and social opportunities for blacks set the coastal region off from many other regions of the South, so, too, did the continued political influence of blacks. During Reconstruction, the political clout of the large black population in the region sustained the fortunes of the Republican party and secured office for a substantial number of black politicians. Even the retreat from Reconstruction in the 1870s and the subsequent quarter-century-long campaign by white Democrats against black political participation failed to crush black political activism. Throughout the region, especially in McIntosh County, blacks continued to elect local officials until the end of the first decade of the twentieth century, when white Democrats, through a mixture of thuggery and adroit constitutional manipulation, effectively deprived blacks of their political rights.[85]

Despite the abundant signs of black strivings for autonomy, racial violence never became the preferred weapon of whites intent upon bullying. Although coastal Georgia was not free from lynchings, mob violence occurred only sporadically. Of the thirteen lynchings in the region, nine took place between 1880 and 1902. Twenty years passed until a small private mob from southern Georgia waylaid the Dodge County sheriff in 1922, seized the two prisoners he was moving to Savannah for safekeeping, and lynched them in Liberty County. The final lynchings in the region occurred in 1930, when the murder of the sheriff of McIntosh County led to the lynching of two black men. Lynchings in the low country were scattered between five of the six coastal counties, and only in Camden County, which borders on Florida, did no lynchings occur. If there was a portion of the low country that was mob-prone, it was the western part of Bryan and Liberty counties, where the low country gave way to the piney woods and the predominantly white population cultivated a reputation for hostility to blacks. Between 1888 and 1902, mobs claimed the lives of five blacks in this area.

In most regards, little distinguished individual lynchings in coastal Georgia from lynchings elsewhere in the state. The alleged causes of lynchings in the low country were apportioned among alleged murders, sexual offenses, and various "other crimes." [86] Private mobs and mass mobs carried out the bulk of the lynchings, while posses and terrorist mobs practically never surfaced in the region.[87] Thus, what is distinctive about mob violence in coastal Georgia is not where it occurred or the form it took, but that it took place so infrequently.

The event that most dramatically demonstrated the combination of forces that limited mob violence in coastal Georgia during the late nineteenth and early twentieth centuries occurred in McIntosh County in 1899. On August 21, Henry Delegale, a locally prominent black man, turned himself over to the sheriff after he learned that he had been charged with the rape of a white woman. That evening, a crowd of blacks gathered around the jail, intending to protect Delegale from any possible mob violence. On several occasions during the following two days the sheriff attempted to move Delegale to Savannah, allegedly for safekeeping. The crowd, certain that the move was a subterfuge to turn Delegale over to a mob, adamantly refused to allow the sheriff to move his prisoner.

On the second day of the standoff, the sheriff made a final attempt to remove Delegale but was discovered while in the act by a sentry who had been posted to watch the jail. Someone rang the bell of the black Baptist church as a signal, and in a short time hundreds of blacks, many armed, surrounded the jail. Although the crowd explained that its sole intention was to protect Delegale, local authorities decided to request that the governor call out the militia.[88]

Within hours, two hundred soldiers arrived in Darien and began patrolling the streets. The crowd surrounding the jail made no effort to interfere with the troops and, in fact, cheered the militia when they placed Delegale on a train bound for Savannah. In the following days the situation threatened to become even more explosive after Delegale's two sons shot two white men who had attempted to arrest them on trumped-up charges.[89] Under any circumstances in the South, the shooting of whites by blacks would excite local whites; McIntosh County whites had additional incentive to demonstrate unequivocally that black defiance would not be tolerated. But no lynchings or further bloodshed followed. Instead, a biracial effort by locally prominent blacks and militia officers worked to ease the clearly volatile situation.

Colonel Alexander R. Lawton, the ranking commander of the militia, took the first step in restoring order. To prevent the sheriff's posse from degenerating into a lynch mob, he persuaded the sheriff to enlist the militia in the Delegales' capture. Both the posse and the militia raced to apprehend the black family, but before the posse reached the Delegale homestead, the matriarch of the family met the advancing militia and pleaded with them to protect her family from the posse. The militia officers persuaded the posse, which included the brothers of the two men who had been shot, to surrender their arms and promise to refrain from violence against the family. The Delegales then surrendered and were moved without incident to the jail in Darien.[90]

Colonel Lawton also met with ten of the county's most prominent blacks and asked them to use their influence to calm the black community. The group, comprised of E. M. Brawley, Paul R. Mifflin, and J. P. Davis, all ministers in local Baptist churches; J. D. Taylor of the Presbyterian church; G. W. Butler of the African Methodist Episcopal church; F. M. Mann of the St. Cyprian Episcopal Church; Charles R. Jackson, postmaster of Darien; John C. Lawton, federal collector of customs for Darien; S. W. McIver, chair of the local Republican party; and James L. Grant, editor of the *Darien Spectator,* enjoyed excellent reputations in the white community.[91] These leaders collaborated on a circular that was posted throughout the county and widely published. They insisted that the troops were not present solely to protect "white interests" and called upon all local residents to refrain from any acts that might incite white violence and to uphold the law so as "to bring back to our city and county that peace and harmony between the races with which in the past we have been so signally blessed."[92]

The combination of the circular and the apparent intention of Colonel Lawton to prevent any mob violence eased tensions, and law officers began to round up the alleged black rioters who had surrounded the jail. During the next two days, fifty-eight men and five women were put in jail. Two days after the circular was issued, a special term of the superior court convened in Darien and took up the cases of the various participants in the "Insurrection." Although the charges against the forty suspected rioters were dropped, twenty-three were convicted and received stiff fines that ranged from $250 to $1,000, along with prison terms of twelve months' hard labor.[93]

The presiding judge then took up the cases of Henry Delegale and his two sons, ruling in favor of their motion for a change of venue and thereby ensuring a fairer trial than would have been possible in McIntosh County. At the close of the trials in nearby Effingham County, John and Edward Delegale, charged with shooting the two white men who had attempted to arrest them, received life sentences, but their brother and sister, who also had been charged with the crime, were acquitted. The jury also concluded that Henry Delegale was innocent of the rape charge that had precipitated the turmoil of the past month.[94]

The conclusion of the Darien Insurrection left little doubt that whites could suppress organized black protest. While white lynchers before and after the Insurrection acted with little fear of prosecution, the stiff penalties meted out to the "rioters" in McIntosh County were cruel reminders of the transparent racial bias of Georgia's courts. And the presence of state militia to restore order underscored the overpowering arsenal that whites had at their disposal.

Yet, the Insurrection also exposes several distinctive characteristics of race relations in the region. The restrained response of the local whites and the Savannah militia commander to the black protesters and their willingness to work with local black leaders to quell tensions typified the meticulously maintained tone and conventions of race relations in the region. In addition, the organization and militancy of coastal blacks also warned whites that they would not let mob violence pass without protest.[95]

The events in McIntosh County cast light on the comparative infrequency of lynchings in coastal Georgia during the late nineteenth and early twentieth centuries. When whites concluded that black behavior had exceeded appropriate boundaries, they had to rely upon the outside aid of the state to restore order and caste boundaries. That whites in McIntosh County felt compelled to take such steps is indicative not of their strength, but rather of their comparative weakness and the strength of the black community. Moreover, the reliance on state intervention contrasts sharply with the haste with which whites elsewhere in Georgia punished infractions with extralegal violence. Had blacks in southern Georgia, for example, ever staged an "insurrection," a wholesale pogrom would have erupted.[96]

Whites in coastal Georgia were no less vigorous supporters of white supremacy than were whites elsewhere—in fact, they were often more so—but they recognized that violence against blacks could have unintended and, more important, troublesome consequences. The combination of effective black leadership that strove to prevent racial conflict and the threat of black protest in the event of white violence convinced many local white leaders that racial violence posed an unwelcome threat to social tranquility.[97] Furthermore, white leaders gained legitimacy by stifling lynchings. They could allude to the alternatives to their benign rule by drawing comparisons with the brittle race relations elsewhere in the South in order to win the allegiance, albeit grudging, of black leaders.

Prominent blacks, like their white counterparts, shared a commitment to maintaining tranquil race relations. They only had to look elsewhere in the South to see how bad things could be. While they argued that the status of blacks in the coastal region demanded improvement, they strove to prevent any further erosion of the position of blacks. When racial conflict erupted in Darien, they worked diligently to diffuse the tension. At times, as in the crisis of 1899, they even had to mediate between whites and the black rank and file who bitterly resented abuse at the hands of whites.[98]

Coastal whites struggled to explain the events at Darien, but the straitjacket of white racism imposed rigid constraints on their understanding of the Insurrection. In a climate of heightened racial tensions, whites were unable and unwilling to admit that the stand blacks made represented anything but lawlessness. White newspapers in Savannah attempted to string together anecdotal accounts of black misdeeds in recent years to portray the blacks of McIntosh as dangerous and reckless. "We have often praised them as law-abiding and good citizens," the *Darien Gazette* complained, "and it is now with a feeling of sorrow that we are compelled to publish their outrageous proceedings."[99] Whites repeated incantations of white supremacy, but with the veiled recognition that their power was limited. In a slogan that succinctly captured the sentiments of most whites in the coastal region, the *Darien Gazette* explained that "the whites are going to rule and rule *justly.*"[100]

In editorial columns, white newspaper editors seemed to ignore sensational news descriptions of the black rioters in McIntosh County and instead stressed the importance of interracial cooperation in ending the Insurrection without greater bloodshed.[101] As one Savannah newspaper noted, the efforts of prominent blacks in Darien helped "to cement the peace and harmony which in the past has so signally blessed the relationship between the races in McIntosh County." [102] The lesson that the *Savannah Morning News* drew from the episode was that the two races had to work together to insure that "misapprehensions" of either did not produce similar outbursts in the future.[103] The infrequency of lynchings and other forms of racial violence during the next three decades testifies to the shared commitment of low-country whites and blacks to prevent such "misapprehensions" and perpetuate the region's distinctive racial harmony.

In 1903, the editors of the *Savannah Morning News* were struck by the regional variations in the treatment of blacks in the South. "The negro question presents different aspects in different states and even in different sections of the same state." The newspaper pointed out that Georgia itself—from northern Georgia, where there was "no negro problem," to central Georgia, where "the labor issue" dictated the tone of relations between blacks and whites—provided compelling evidence of the range of race relations. However sketchy the interpretation was, it did recognize the fundamental point that race relations varied greatly over time and place.[104]

Only by recognizing these important regional variations can the myriad of forces that underlay mob violence be fully revealed. Attempts to trace its origins to the depression of the 1890s, to the racial makeup of the population, or to the failings of rural government have tended to smooth over the regional variations in mob violence, leaving only broad generalizations about the "typical, mob-prone community." Historians, for example, have long assumed that the economic crisis of the 1890s was a catalyst for the bloodiest decade in the region's history. There can be little doubt that the depression contributed to worsening race relations by eroding the confidence of whites in their ability to maintain superior economic status and by provoking the most divisive political battles of the post-Reconstruction era. It is critical, however, to remember that the effects of the depression were not uniform across the South. In Georgia, for example, the effects were particularly severe in the Upper Piedmont and comparatively mild in southern Georgia. It seems doubtful that, without the additional irritant of the war on moonshining, the depression by itself would have provoked the wave of violence that gripped northern Georgia during the 1890s. Although the depression looms large in the mob violence of northern Georgia, it almost certainly was only peripheral to the far more savage violence of the Cotton Belt.

The steady toll of mob violence in the Cotton Belt and southern Georgia is testimony to the central role of lynching in the social and racial orders of the two regions. The heated debates among historians over the degree to which violence and intimidation were inherent in southern agricultural labor relations might profit from a greater recognition of the pervasiveness of racial violence in precisely those regions where plantation agriculture and the racial line separating white landlords and black laborers were most pronounced.[105] Across the South, the presence of staple crops, white landlords, and black laborers may serve as an index of mob violence. Unfortunately for southern blacks, their future in the South, as whites reminded them incessantly, was intimately bound to the very regions where racial violence was most pervasive. Until the effects of World War I precipitated the Great Migration to northern cities, many ambitious blacks migrated to southern cities, while others followed the agricultural frontier into the Mississippi and Arkansas deltas, the wire grass of southern Georgia, and the woodlands of East Texas. Tragically, by seeking upward mobility and personal success in these regions, they exposed themselves to the recurring butchery of the mob.

Outside of the Cotton Belt and southern Georgia, there was only a shallow, if volatile, reservoir of fuel for mob violence. During times of stress, the culture of racism sanctioned and focused white rage on black transgressors. The racial friction generated by the "urban frontier" of the Upper Piedmont and the class and racial cleavages opened by the tug of the market economy in north Georgia triggered spasms of mob violence. Once these tensions eased, however, it dwindled as well. Elsewhere in the South, such as eastern Tennessee, the upcountry of Arkansas, and the Piedmont of North Carolina, similar patterns are also apparent. By no means were race relations in these regions benign; Piedmont cities were the breeding ground of segregation, and whites in the rural upcountry were notorious for their enmity toward blacks. Mob violence, however, was not an essential characteristic of the racial order of these regions.

Finally, coastal Georgia offers a glimpse of the conditions that enabled some regions of the South to remain relatively free of unrelenting mob violence. The combination of the mixed economy of the region, the paternalistic ethos of whites, and the strength of the African-American community was a powerful brake on lynch mobs. Few regions aside from the South Atlantic low country, with its troubled plantations and exceedingly strong black communal traditions, enjoyed such propitious conditions for placid race relations. However singular the race relations of coastal Georgia, they are a reminder that whites committed to the maintenance of their domination did not always embrace mob violence as an ultimate weapon.

However considerable the regional variations in mob violence, blacks recognized that its potential threatened every black in the South. Blacks in coastal

Georgia almost certainly felt safer than blacks living in the Cotton Belt of Georgia, but newspaper accounts and oral testimonies of persistent violence elsewhere were vivid reminders of their oppressed status. Lynching was a powerful tool of intimidation that gripped blacks' imaginations, whether the blacks lived in a mob-prone county or in the relative safety of coastal Georgia. Neither W. E. B. Du Bois, from the shelter of the campus of Atlanta University, nor the author Richard Wright in Mississippi could escape the fear, insecurity, and rage provoked by distant racial violence.[106] As Wright later observed about his youth in the Deep South during the 1920s, "The things that influenced my conduct as a Negro did not have to happen to me directly; I needed but to hear of them to feel their full effects in the deepest layers of my consciousness. Indeed, the white brutality that I had not seen was a more effective control of my behavior than that which I knew." [107]

5

The Geography
of Lynching in Virginia

Perhaps there is no more telling illustration of the difference between the magnitudes of mob violence in Virginia and in Georgia than the simple fact that the number of lynchings in Georgia during the single year of 1919 exceeded the number of lynchings in Virginia during the entire twentieth century. Whereas mobs left their scars in virtually every county in Georgia, they left untouched numerous counties scattered throughout Virginia. Indeed, one-half of the ninety-five counties in the state never experienced a lynching, and fewer than one-quarter were the sites of more than one between 1880 and 1930.

The explanation for the comparatively limited scale of mob violence in the Old Dominion is not some innate law-abiding tendency among Virginians, for the record of racial violence in the state is too extensive to support such a conclusion. Moreover, lynchings in Virginia shared too many characteristics with lynchings throughout the South to be explained by any unique cultural pathology. Nor, given that white Virginians championed white dominance no less than other southern- ers, can the level of lynchings in the state be explained by an attenuated ethos of white supremacy.

However great the divergence of racial violence in Virginia may have been from the pattern in other southern states, eighty-three lynchings still occurred. Superficially, the rise in the incidence of lynchings in Virginia mirrored that of the South as a whole; the number peaked during the last decade of the century. But a closer look reveals that the ebb and flow of mob violence in Virginia differed in important ways from that in the rest of the South. Like the South as a whole, the 1890s was the bloodiest period in Virginia's history. However, that peak in lynching largely reflected a spasm of racial violence in the southwestern corner of the state. The frequency of racial violence elsewhere actually declined during the decade. Once the crisis of the 1890s passed in southwestern Virginia, the incidence of mob violence declined, and by 1910, lynchings in the Old Dominion, for all practical purposes, had become as rare as in Illinois or Arizona. In Georgia and Mississippi, by contrast, lynchings routinely punctuated day-to-day life well into the 1920s (Figure 7).

The different trajectory of mob violence in Virginia raises the question of whether the pattern of racial violence in the state may best be explained by forces specific to Virginia, or by forces felt first in the Old Dominion but that eventually influenced the whole South. In other words, was Virginia unique, or simply subject to developments that would filter down to the Deep South decades later? The answer, I believe, is that Virginia differed markedly from most of the rest of the South and that the conditions that precluded persistent mob violence there were shared by only the other border states. One of the ironies of the New South is that white Virginians during the late nineteenth century enshrined the Lost Cause and all things southern but at the same time set their state on a course of development that diverged in important ways from much of the South. In these changes, which contributed to distinctive labor and race relations, can be found part of the explanation for the substantial differences in the patterns of mob violence in Virginia and in Georgia and other southern states.

As the era of the New South unfolded in the Old Dominion, both the rural and the urban economies of the state became more complex and diversified. If Virginia lagged behind most northern states in such statistics as the extent of agricultural mechanization and the scale of industrial employment, the direction of the state's development was clear. Its future increasingly was directed northward by railroads, trade, and outlook. To a limited extent, such modernization fostered attitudes antithetical to lynching while it increasingly separated the state's labor relations from the Deep South. At the same time, the evolution of the economy had contradictory effects; while it generated racial friction in some regions, it removed sources of racial violence in others. In this regard, as in many others, Virginia shared much in common with such border states as Missouri, Kentucky, and Maryland. It is precisely because Virginia differed so conspicuously from most Deep South states that it provides such a valuable comparison.

Lynchings were less likely to occur in Virginia than in Georgia for the simple reason that white Virginians believed that racial boundaries could be maintained without the need to resort to persistent violence. At the heart of the comparatively calm race relations were labor relations that diverged from those in much of the South where mob violence was endemic. Unquestionably, the blight of sharecropping, poverty, and racism left its mark on rural Virginia. Virginia land-

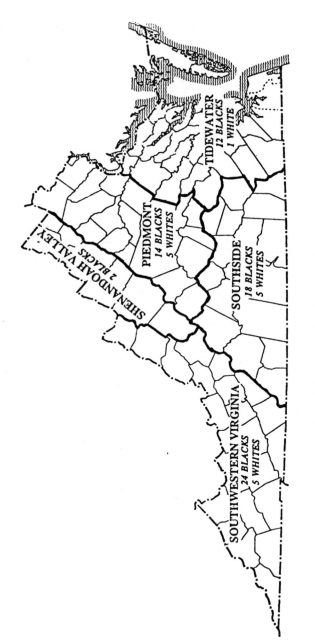

SHENANDOAH VALLEY
2 BLACKS

PIEDMONT
14 BLACKS
5 WHITES

TIDEWATER
12 BLACKS
1 WHITE

SOUTHSIDE
18 BLACKS
5 WHITES

SOUTHWESTERN VIRGINIA
24 BLACKS
5 WHITES

Figure 7. Lynchings in Virginia, 1880–1930

lords, like their counterparts elsewhere, devised a "web of restrictive legislation" to guarantee labor and limit its mobility.[1] But the diversified agriculture that prevailed shielded Virginians from the harshest poverty that bore down on staple-crop farmers elsewhere in the South. The evolution of agriculture in Virginia necessarily created a variant on the labor relations that prevailed in the plantation regions of the Deep South. As large numbers of planters shifted to diversified agriculture during the late nineteenth century, they increasingly turned away from long-term labor contracts and experimented with the use of casual day labor. The shift to ad-hoc day labor had far-reaching consequences, including a lessening of one of the chief sources of racial conflict—white landowners' intention to maintain, through extralegal means if necessary, the coercive labor practices that typified staple-crop agriculture throughout much of the South. In such a climate of race and labor relations, most whites could ignore the modest measure of autonomy blacks achieved because it posed no real threat.

Nowhere in Virginia was the incidence of mob violence more concentrated, both in place and time, than in the southwestern corner of the state. The twenty-eight lynchings that occurred there, more than in any other portion of the Old Dominion, reflected the desperation of whites to define the status of blacks in a region where blacks were still uncommon and furious social and economic change was taking place. The explicit racial inspiration for the violence was evident in who the mobs targeted as victims. In a region where whites outnumbered blacks by a margin of nine to one in 1900, the overwhelming majority of victims were black.

The arrival of railroads after the Civil War drew white residents in southwestern Virginia into the nation's expanding agricultural and industrial market economy. The previous patterns of economic life gave way, the isolation of the region broke down, and mountain folk confronted unpleasant changes and unwelcome immigrants. Before 1870, a single rail line ran down the valleys of southwestern Virginia. By 1900, railroads and mining companies, lured by vast lumber and mineral resources, had penetrated the entire region. In previously isolated mountain hollows, mining and lumber communities sprung up, often with astonishing speed. The Norfolk & Western Railroad, for example, created a celebrated boomtown by transforming Big Lick, a tiny village in 1880, into the city of Roanoke, with a population exceeding twenty-five thousand in 1890.[2]

Rural industrialization began to change the previously homogeneous population of southwestern Virginia. Company recruiters brought immigrants and blacks into the lumber camps and coal mines and created racially and ethnically mixed communities. Although the steady stream of black laborers did not represent a large-scale migration into the region, it still produced a significant increase in the black populations of some counties. Between 1880 and 1900, for example, the black population of Wise County grew from 101 to 1,965, and in Allegheny County, from 1,132 to 4,013. In counties not undergoing rapid economic development, however, black populations either remained small or declined. Thus, the 27 percent growth of the black population in the region between 1880 and 1900 actually represented a far more substantial increase within a few southwestern counties.[3]

That the influx of black laborers into predominantly white communities, together with the social and economic effects of rapid development, spawned deep social tensions is hardly surprising. Although some long-time mountain residents fought the advance of industrialization with tactics ranging from lawsuits to outright violence, others acceded to the transformations but retained grave concerns about the character of the immigrants. The editor of the *Abingdon Weekly Virginian,* after surveying the effects of the arrival of the railroad in his county, captured the uneasiness of many local residents with his observation that "along the tracks of the railroad there have congregated ex-convicts, robbers, cutthroats, and outlaws, the very scouring of the earth, until life and property are not safe." Elsewhere in the region, the fears of many whites were focused upon the influx of itinerant black lumber hands and miners.[4]

At first glance, the mob violence of the 1890s appears to have been the product of the collision of preindustrial values with the new industrial order and the shift of community life from stable self-sufficiency to dependency and exploitation. It has been argued that mountain residents, who watched as distant industrialists and their local political lackeys wrested control over the region from them, struck back violently against all manner of targets. Anger, frustration, social instability, and economic disruption ignited violence without bounds, ranging from feuds, killings, and labor violence to mob violence.[5]

There can be little doubt that more than coincidence explains the simultaneous phenomenas of rural industrialization and frequent lynchings in southwestern Virginia. But it is a mistake to assume that the mob violence expressed the dedication of deeply traditional mountaineers to defend their society against the unwelcome intrusion of the forces of modernity. The violence of the mountain lynchers was not an inarticulate, irrational reaction to inchoate fears, but rather a focused effort to control, not stop or reverse, change. Like their counterparts in southern Georgia, the whites who lived in the hollows and valleys of southwestern Virginia used violence as a tool to define boundaries in a region where traditional racial lines were either vague or nonexistent. There is ample evidence that the frustration and anger of the white residents of southwestern Virginia found its target with brutal precision.

The settings for many of the lynchings are suggestive of the tensions that helped fuel mob violence in the region. Had competition between white and black workers been at the root of the violence, lumber camps and coal towns should have been the sites of frequent lynchings. However, these communities, where the conflict was presumably most marked between the older, preindustrial values of mountain whites and the new order represented by imported black workers, were seldom the settings for mob violence. Until the history of all workers, black and white, in southwestern Virginia is written, it is difficult to know precisely why the economic competition and raw communal life in the mines and mills did not spark more racial violence. Nevertheless, growing evidence suggests that a surprising degree of racial harmony existed between the races in many industrial communities. The nature of the labor in the mines and mills and the considerable sense of community that developed in some industrial towns seems to have mitigated against the harshest forms of prejudice. Almost certainly, steady friction was present, but it seldom escalated into outright mob violence.[6]

Mob violence, rather than a form of backwoods or mining camp justice, typically occurred in the comparatively cosmopolitan towns of southwestern Virginia. Of the twenty-two counties in the region, only twelve had lynchings, and of these only six had more than one. The most mob-prone communities were the transportation, financial, and administrative centers for the surrounding countryside, typically much more than company towns dependent upon a single industry. Among the towns where lynchings occurred—in many cases, several extralegal executions—were Wytheville, Bluefield, Richlands, Clifton Forge, and Roanoke. The sites of the incidents tended to have a slightly higher percentage of black residents than was typical in the region and also a more rapid rate of population growth than was typical in counties that were free of mob murders. Lynchings in the region, then, occurred in precisely those communities that were the centers of change within the region.[7]

Just as most lynchings were not backwoods affairs, they also did not pit rustic mountaineers against townspeople who battled for law and order in the name of progress. Mobs enjoyed broad support in a majority of the lynchings, including those which occurred in towns. This communal nature of lynching is evident in the large proportion carried out by mass mobs, which executed 57 percent of all mob victims, a far larger percentage than in any other area of the state. Private mobs executed fewer than one-third of the victims, and on only one occasion did a terrorist mob claim a life.[8]

As was typical wherever mass mob violence was common, most lynchings were caused by murders and violent attacks. These two offenses provoked more than twice as many lynchings as did alleged sexual offenses, whereas minor offenses prompted only one.[9] The intentions of these mass mobs, of course, often went far beyond simply vengeance for the immediate crime and included blatantly prescriptive aims. The lynching of five black railroad hands in Richlands in Tazewell County in February 1893, for example, was intended to convey in unmistakable form the outright hostility of many whites in southwestern Virginia to the arrival of blacks. Four of the men had spent the evening before the lynching with two white store owners, carousing, drinking, and listening to "a disreputable white woman" play banjo. Later that night, as the white men stumbled home, the blacks allegedly robbed and beat them. On the following day, local law officers arrested and jailed one of the men. A mob quickly formed, easily overpowered the jailer, and captured the prisoner. Within hours the sheriff arrived with the other three alleged assailants. The sheriff, perhaps intimidated by the mob of eighty men or, more likely, sympathetic to their aims because one of the assaulted men was a cousin, readily turned over his prisoners.

The Tazewell County mob, which organized openly and made no effort to disguise its ranks, hardly represented a misdirected or veiled assault on the established order. At the front of the mob were James Hurt, a magistrate and a member of the Richlands town council, and James Crabtree, a prominent businessman in Richlands. The mob paused only long enough to allow a black minister to pray for the men before it hanged all four from the same tree. After the lynching, roaming whites claimed a fifth victim, an innocent black man, and posted signs throughout the county warning blacks to leave immediately or risk vigilante justice. In neighboring Buchanan County, whites also ordered blacks out, announcing "that Buchanan should be altogether a white county." [10]

Most often, lynchers intended to establish codes of acceptable black behavior rather than to purge the region entirely of blacks. The targets of the violence, as was so often the case, were young, itinerant workers whose raucous and sometimes violent life-styles provoked considerable concern. In the eyes of many whites, such behavior was doubly upsetting because it threatened life and property and was unpredictable.

The lynching of four black miners in Allegheny County in 1891 is but one instance of savage white retaliation provoked by nothing more than foolhardy black bravado in a region where the definition of acceptable conduct by blacks was very circumscribed. The incident began on the morning of October 17, 1891 in the boomtown of Clifton Forge. Six black mine workers from the nearby Big Hill

Mines came to town to enjoy their day off. Whites would later claim that the miners had a more sinister motive, "to take the town."[11] Like most black miners in the region, they had been lured from the fields of eastern Virginia by promises of good pay, new opportunities, and little racial discrimination. But as the men would discover, there were definite limits to the tolerance of whites for any conspicuous behavior.

The miners first relaxed at a bar and then, with considerable hoopla, had themselves photographed. A surviving photograph records Charles Miller, the leader of the group, with a pistol in each hand, his arms crossed on his chest, and three additional pistols stuffed in his belt. Beneath a broad-brimmed cowboy hat, he stares from the photograph as if self-consciously adopting the appearance of a wild west outlaw. One by one, the rest of the group seems to have followed Miller and adopted equally fierce poses for their photographs. After their visit to the photo studio, the men divided their time between shopping for flashy clothing and carrying out various pranks against convenient passersby on the street.[12]

Although Miller and his friends seem to have committed no specific crime beyond harassing a black boy who was selling chestnuts on a street corner, their boisterous, intimidating behavior did not pass unnoticed. A town police officer attempted to arrest the men, but was forced to retreat when they announced that "they would die before they were taken." Actually, the men seem to have had no interest in trouble. Sensing the danger they faced, they made their way out of town and quickly headed back to the mines. The officer, stung by his humiliation at their hands, gathered a posse and set out after them. A short distance from the Iron Gate mines, the posse overtook the blacks and ordered them to surrender. The details of the subsequent events remain vague, but there is no question that a lengthy gun battle took place and left two members of the posse wounded, one of them mortally. When news of the gunfight reached Clifton Forge, heavily armed white men poured from the town and began scouring the mountains for the miners. Throughout the afternoon the mountain sides rang with shouts and gunfire, and by late afternoon four of the "gang" had been captured and lodged in jail in Clifton Forge.[13]

It was obvious by early evening that an attempt would be made to lynch the men. At ten o'clock, a mob of perhaps three hundred surrounded the mayor's office and the jail that held the "desperadoes." Ignoring the mayor's meek protests, the mob systematically broke down the door of the jail and took command of three of the prisoners. After placing ropes around the necks of Miller, John Scott, and William Scott, the mob dragged them through the streets to a neighborhood known variously as Slaughter House Hollow or Butcher's Hollow. The lynchers allowed each man to pray and to confess before they yanked their victims up and fired hundreds of rounds into the swaying bodies. Despite three executions to its credit, the mob still was not appeased. The mob returned to the jail for Bob Burton, whose leg had been shattered by a bullet during the afternoon's gun battle, loaded him into a cart, and transported him to the tree where the mangled bodies of his three friends remained suspended. Despite his youth—he was only a teenager—and Miller's earlier confession that Burton had been forced to participate in the day's events against his will, the mob showed no pity. They hoisted him aloft beside the three corpses and riddled his body with shot.[14]

For several days following the lynchings, fear gripped Clifton Forge. Rumors that armies of black miners planned to march on the town led whites to station guards around the town and even to request the governor to order out the state militia. Gradually, the excitement waned, but the lynching was an indelible lesson for blacks. Both the mayor of the town and the local white newspaper editor agreed that the event had affected the black community, but they reached strikingly different conclusions about the precise nature of those effects. The mayor pointedly denied that the lynchings were evidence of "race prejudice." "If a party of white men had come here and acted as did the negroes. . . they would have shared the same fate."[15] But he hardly spoke for the blacks of Clifton Forge, who concluded that the lynchings were blatant expressions of "race prejudice." The fact that the mob had selected the site of the lynching because it was a black neighborhood and had dared blacks "to poke their heads out of doors" contradicted the mayor's claim.[16] The fury of the extralegal executions left local blacks intimidated; the local white newspaper editor noted that "not only were the negroes of the city quiet and orderly, . . . [but also they] have been seen less frequently on the streets." Moreover, following the lynching, "several quiet negroes have expressed a wish to leave the place as they do not feel secure."[17]

There was little ambiguity in the intended meaning of the Tazewell and Clifton Forge lynchings. Both mobs used the lynching as an opportunity to ensure that blacks were well aware that they remained in the region only with the sufferance of whites. The small pockets of black populations in the area were vulnerable both because their economic and social status appeared unstable and poorly defined and because by definition most blacks were "outsiders." In seeking to explain the lynching of the four men at Clifton Forge, the local newspaper noted that "a factor which helped to augment the desire for swift vengeance was the fact that all of the negroes were non-residents and had no friends here."[18]

As profound as the shock of rapid change was for many residents of southwestern Virginia, it produced only a temporary spasm of mob violence. As was the case in other areas undergoing rapid economic change, violence in southwestern

Virginia coincided with the period when industrialization was relatively new.[19] Of the twenty-eight lynchings that occurred in the region, twenty-two took place between 1880 and 1894, nine during 1893 alone. In the subsequent thirty years, only six lynchings occurred.

No precise explanation for the decline in mob violence is apparent. It seems probable, however, that the violent hostility of white residents toward blacks waned when blacks failed to secure a significant role in the region's changing economy. After the initial dramatic influx of blacks into the region, most preferred the coal fields of West Virginia, where they suffered less oppressive treatment at the hands of whites, to the industries of southwestern Virginia.[20] Whites in the region, unchallenged by black laborers, retained the dubious privilege of eking out a living in the mines and mills.

Thus, the mob violence in southwestern Virginia was no more a unique phenomenon rooted in a peculiar mountain culture than was the mob violence in the mountains of northern Georgia. Both regions were beset by sharp social tensions produced by rapid and profound change. But if the patterns of change in southwestern Virginia were similar to those found in other places, there were significant differences as well. Unlike Georgia, where the vast southern interior of the state and, to a lesser degree, the Upper Piedmont, underwent rapid transformation, the only portion of Virginia to experience a comparable impact from accelerated and dramatic change was the southwestern region. And unlike the transformations in the pine barrens of southern Georgia, the industrialization of southwestern Virginia did not initiate a sequence of changes in which blacks played a conspicuous and vital role. Lynchings only indirectly represented the responses of mountaineers to the advent of industrial capitalism.

The flurry of mob violence during the early years of industrialization was an attempt by whites to define the status of blacks, an effort that took on significance only because of the transformations within the region. The much larger issues of the social and economic injustice created by industrialization would have to wait for the gradual emergence of a powerful strain of labor activism. Once the effects of development became clear, residents of southwestern Virginia allied themselves either in support of or against the changes. The sporadic labor unrest and violence of the twentieth century signaled the advent of increasingly politicized protest directed against the people who spearheaded the change in the region and the inequities of industrialization itself.

The tensions that gave rise to mob violence in southwestern Virginia had no counterpart in eastern Virginia. Although eastern Virginia underwent considerable change during the late nineteenth century, most of that change represented the acceleration of developments already in progress rather than dramatic innovations in society. Even before the Civil War, the rural hinterland of eastern Virginia moved to the rhythms of commercial agriculture. The abolition of slavery, of course, set in motion substantial changes in the system of labor and agriculture. But for all of the similarities between labor relations in postbellum eastern Virginia and elsewhere in the South, there were important, if subtle, differences. The labor relations of eastern Virginia became at once flexible yet stable, firmly hierarchical yet seemingly looser than in many other regions of the South. These changes actually contributed to an amelioration rather than escalation of racial violence.

Drained by the many rivers, creeks, and streams that flow into the Chesapeake, and set off from the western hinterlands by the steep slopes of the Blue Ridge Mountains, eastern Virginia is the heartland of the state. From the sandy ridges along the brackish waters of the James River to the rolling meadows and woodlands of the Piedmont, from the manicured gentlemen farms of northern Virginia to the eroded sharecropping plots of the Southside, from the conspicuously traditional county seat of Culpepper to the burgeoning city of Newport News, from the overwhelmingly white Greene County, nestled against the Blue Ridge, to the overwhelmingly black Charles City County on the James, eastern Virginia is a region of great diversity.

Like other areas in the South, eastern Virginia participated in the headlong rush to create the New South. The forces of development were especially evident in the Tidewater. Comprised of roughly thirty coastal counties settled during the earliest years of the colonial era, the Tidewater had developed into perhaps the most diverse and complex region in the state by the late nineteenth and early twentieth centuries. Growing cities, particularly Richmond and Norfolk, became magnets for all Virginians and helped to make the region the most densely populated area of the state. With secure foundations as both rail centers and ports, Tidewater cities also became regional industrial centers. In the rural districts, agriculture ranged from truck farming to tobacco cultivation and subsistence farming. About half of the region's population was black, the highest percentage in the state, and they figured prominently in virtually all aspects of the economy.[21]

The counties situated to the west of the Tidewater and east of the Blue Ridge Mountains make up the middle section of the state. The James River divides the region into two distinctive areas. The twenty-odd counties north of the river, the Piedmont counties, were centers of diversified agriculture. Even before the Civil War, Piedmont farmers had begun to turn away from traditional plantation agriculture and toward raising grains, dairy products, fruits, and vegetables for urban markets. By the early twentieth century, they had achieved what one historian has described as "a happy balance of land, people, horses and mules, and a few tractors."[22] Land values and crop yields were high, at least in comparison to other regions in the South. Although the blacks in the region, fewer than a third of the Piedmont's total population, endured poverty and often were entangled in tenancy and sharecropping, most escaped the harshest throes of exploitation.[23]

Finally, below the James was the Southside, a distinctive rural land of corn, tobacco, and sharecropping. In many regards, the social effects of the cultivation of tobacco in the region were quite similar to those of cotton in Georgia. After the Civil War, white planters in Southside Virginia confronted the same labor difficulties that their counterparts in the Black Belt faced. By the late 1860s, they, too, had turned to a system of tenancy, sharecropping, and the crop lien to organize land and labor. The large black population of the Southside suffered the same hardships—crippling poverty, poor or nonexistent schools, and few occupational alternatives to agriculture—as blacks endured elsewhere in the plantation South.[24]

Given these notable differences within eastern Virginia, the region's race relations might be expected to have varied substantially. But differences were less important than similarities in the tone and character of race relations throughout eastern Virginia. Even the Southside, which was set off by its apparent similarities to the Deep South, had much more in common with the rest of Virginia than with the Deep South. Nowhere in eastern Virginia, not in the Tidewater, not in the Southside, and not in the Piedmont, was extralegal racial violence either prevalent or enduring. Although specific reasons explain the comparative absence of mob violence in each subregion of eastern Virginia, even more important common explanations exist for the pattern of mob violence in the entire region.

Throughout much of rural eastern Virginia, especially the Piedmont and the Southside, the adjustments to the effects of the Civil War had produced a rural economy rooted in what one historian has called "patronage capitalism." The void left by slavery was quickly replaced by a system that divided the population into patrons, who controlled virtually all of the ingredients short of labor needed to make a livelihood, and clients, who bargained for access to the jobs and resources controlled by the patrons. With such a tight grip on most sources of income, landlords could ensure that no truly free market in labor developed and that a fixed hierarchy of labor relations took root instead. Tenancy ensnared black and white alike wherever it occurred. Nowhere in eastern Virginia did the racial line and the line between landlord and tenant overlap precisely. Although blacks comprised the largest number of tenants in many counties, large numbers of whites also were caught. Even in the Southside, there were some counties where white tenants comprised more than 40 percent of all white farmers.[25] To this extent, there was little in the relationship between landlords and their clients that differed from sharecropping and tenancy in the upcountry of the Deep South.[26]

Although cut from the same fabric as the traditional system of agriculture associated with the Deep South, patronage capitalism in rural Virginia did have unique consequences. The complaints of eastern Virginia landlords about farm laborers may have echoed those of their counterparts in the Deep South, but many devised ways to overcome the obstacle of labor.[27] As planters shifted from tobacco to truck and livestock farming, their labor needs changed as well. Whereas tobacco was an exceedingly labor-intensive crop, the new crops required either less or only intensive bursts of labor. Rather than rely upon sharecroppers and tenants, landlords increasingly assumed direct management of their farms. Moreover, planters discovered that with greater reliance on day or seasonal labor they could diminish their obligations to the laborers as well.

This system of labor relations offered openings for laborers that were absent in many other areas of the South. Over the course of the late nineteenth century, substantial numbers of blacks succeeded in buying land. The ownership of small plots of land, by itself, did not translate into economic autonomy, but it did provide much-valued independence. At the same time, landlords learned that their interests were not threatened if they sold land to blacks. If anything, doing so helped bind black landowners even more closely to their white patrons. Landlords were quite willing to sell off portions of land to raise capital because they recognized that black land holdings, typically too small to sustain entire black families, did not jeopardize the pool of convenient and accessible black laborers. They could draw upon the black landowners when the need for laborers arose. Moreover, planters shrewdly recognized that when men on the lowest rung of the agricultural ladder bought land, they usually exhausted all of their wealth and were left, observed the historian Crandall Shifflett, land-poor.[28]

Nowhere in the South was black landholding more extensive than in the Tidewater, where the practice extended back to the antebellum period, when a rapidly growing number of free Negroes gained title to their farms. Although the federal government failed to meet the freedmen's aspirations for land after the war, a substantial proportion of blacks succeeded in acquiring land as a result of the postwar transformation of Tidewater agriculture. Black landownership in the Piedmont and the Southside, both in the antebellum and postbellum periods, did not match the levels in the Tidewater, but it still greatly exceeded that in most other areas of the South. Even in the Southside, where the grip of tenantry and tobacco cultivation was strongest, in all but three of the counties at least a third of the black farmers owned property, and more than 37 percent in the region owned land.[29]

To argue that many agricultural laborers enjoyed privileges denied their southern counterparts is not to say that the evolution of agriculture in eastern Virginia eliminated exploitation or poverty. But their characteristic forms were different in kind from those under which tenants and sharecroppers labored in the Deep South. Farm laborers in the Piedmont and Tidewater faced seasonal unemployment, poverty, and ever-present economic insecurity. Ironically, by allowing a degree of economic independence not available in the Deep South, landlords in eastern Virginia succeeded in gaining the grudging allegiance of their "clients," who so desperately needed patronage to enjoy the fruits of token independence. However much white landlords parroted the complaints of Deep South landlords about the quality of their farm hands, they managed to extract the labor they needed without resorting to the crudest forms of violent coercion. Moreover, the wide range of non-work-related activities, including schooling, religion, and fraternal gatherings, which provoked the irritation and suspicion of white planters elsewhere, attracted much less scrutiny in eastern Virginia. Quite simply, whites' definitions of acceptable black behavior were less narrowly drawn in eastern Virginia and hence less conducive to potentially violent interference. Although subject to poverty, ill-education, and crippling discrimination, blacks in the region were largely free from intrusive regulation, especially in its ugliest form, violence.

The system of rural labor relations that prevailed in eastern Virginia did produce tensions and periodic outbursts of raw class conflict, but it is striking how muted they were, at least in comparison to the rest of the South. Dissatisfaction occasionally found release in protest through anonymous barn-burnings, or more often in the steady stream of migrants leaving the countryside for the city. Otherwise, eastern Virginia escaped the late nineteenth and early twentieth centuries virtually untouched by the political convulsion of Populism, the agony of white-capping, and the turmoil that gripped the tobacco regions of Kentucky. Until the social and economic history of postbellum rural Virginia is fully charted, the precise reasons for the comparative tranquility will remain vague. Even so, it is clear that the complex legal and social relationships that kept laborers, tenants, and sharecroppers firmly in their places managed to dissipate incipient challenges with striking effectiveness.[30]

By no means was eastern Virginia free of the stain of mob violence. Mobs in the region claimed the lives of fifty-five of the eighty-five men lynched in the state. In the Tidewater, where mobs claimed thirteen lives, only ten of the thirty counties experienced lynchings, and only three had as many as two. In the Piedmont, where nineteen victims were lynched, mobs made their presence felt more widely than in the Tidewater; they murdered victims in eleven of the twenty-one counties. But in the Piedmont, multiple lynchings in just four counties (Alexandria, Albemarle, Loudoun, and Nelson) accounted for more than half of the lynchings. Finally, in the Southside, twenty-three individuals were lynched. Few counties there escaped without at least one incident; thirteen of the seventeen were sites of mob violence, and seven of those had more than one lynching.

Although the pattern of mob violence in eastern Virginia varied from the restricted bloodshed of the Tidewater to the much more widespread mob violence of the Southside, its frequency throughout the region followed similar patterns. Unlike southwestern Virginia, where the peak in racial violence in the 1890s coincided with that of the South as a whole, eastern Virginia became increasingly free of mob violence with each decade after peaking in 1880, when mobs claimed the lives of eighteen blacks and four whites. During the subsequent decade, eleven blacks and five whites were lynched, and in the first decade of the twentieth century nine blacks and two whites were murdered. Finally, three blacks were lynched in each of the following two decades. Clearly, the mobs of eastern Virginia were moving to a different rhythm than southwestern Virginia or most of the rest of the South.[31]

Whites in eastern Virginia were gripped by many of the same fears of black criminality that saturated the white South. Even so, the alleged offenses that inspired lynchings in the region differed from those in both southwestern Virginia and the South as a whole. In the Piedmont and the Tidewater, alleged sexual offenses precipitated well over half of all lynchings. Only in the Southside did murders lead to as many lynchings as did alleged sexual crimes.[32] Outside of the Southside, virtually no mob murders were prompted by the myriad of trivial offenses that incited lynchings in some areas of the South. And even in the Southside, the four victims lynched for nonviolent crimes—arson, burglary, and horse stealing—were perceived to have committed serious transgressions. Thus, nowhere in eastern Virginia did mob violence expand far beyond the narrow boundaries of punishment for alleged sexual offenses or murder.

Although often prompted by alleged rapes, fewer than a third of the lynchings in eastern Virginia were the acts of mass mobs. If anything characterized mob violence in eastern Virginia, it was private vengeance rather than communal execution. Small private mobs murdered more than half of all lynching victims in the region, while mass mobs executed fewer than a third of the total.[33] Even when the race of victims is taken into account (given that whites were only rarely lynched by mass mobs), private mob violence predominated. In keeping with the private—indeed, secretive—character of most lynchings in the region, public rituals of sadism were uncommon. News accounts of the fifty-five lynchings in eastern Virginia make no mention of torture, and in only four instances did a mob mutilate the corpse of its victim.[34]

The extralegal executions that typified rural eastern Virginia, then, were those in which the lynchers were few in number and meted out punishment with tight discipline. A typical lynching took place in July 1901, when a mob imposed "speedy justice" upon Joe Walton, a young black accused of attempting to rape his employer's daughter. Walton was placed in the Brunswick County jail in Lawrenceville, but before he could be tried a "band" of fifty masked men took him from jail and hanged him. The lynching, the news accounts reported, was so "orderly, well conducted and carefully planned" that "not a half dozen citizens [were] aware that it had occurred." According to rumor, the lynchers had stationed sentries around the town before they woke the jailer and took his keys. "In a quiet manner, no noise being made whatever," the mob removed Walton from his cell, marched him four miles from town to a bridge, tied a noose around his neck, and "swung him off." "The crowd then dispersed as quietly as they had come into town."[35] Because lynchings in eastern Virginia were infrequent occurrences and, like the Walton lynching, seldom public or conspicuously savage spectacles (at least by the standards of the day), they did not burn themselves into the collective memories of people as they did in Georgia.

Of course, a significant proportion of lynchings were not such tidy and orderly affairs as the lynching of Joe Walton. Many of the largest and most anarchic lynchings or threatened lynchings took place in cities. For example, in April 1897 a huge mob of enraged whites in Alexandria fought for several hours with policemen and, despite gunfire from the police, succeeded in battering down the jail doors and capturing Joseph McCoy, a black man who allegedly had raped his employer's daughters. McCoy was dragged from his cell and lynched from a lamppost at the intersection of two major downtown streets. Similarly, a series of alleged rapes in Portsmouth in August 1908 inspired a mob of sailors, dock workers, and other local whites to storm the jail in an attempt to lynch William King and Henry Smith, the two black men charged with the crimes. Although local law officers were completely overwhelmed by the mob, they did manage to spirit the men out of the city to safety. The outcome of these two mob attacks differed, however the potential for explosive mob violence in Virginia's urban settings is clear.[36]

The system of social and economic relations in rural areas, which seems to have defused tensions even if it failed to address them, did not extend to the urban centers. The lynchings and threatened lynchings in the towns and cities were testimony to the fears of whites that the day-to-day controls on black life in the countryside were losing their effectiveness and the conviction that symbolic violence was needed to restore black deference and fear. The tensions that accompanied industrialization and urbanization elsewhere in the South were also evident in the urban centers of eastern Virginia. The steady migration of rural blacks through the bordering counties into the city, and the perceived degeneracy of urban blacks all heightened racial animosities. Latent racial tensions, borne of competition for jobs, housing, and all manner of status, erupted periodically in racial violence, including lynchings and riots. In fact, mob violence or threatened mob actions occurred in virtually every major city in the region, including Richmond, Norfolk, Petersburg, and Lynchburg.[37]

But just as in the Upper Piedmont of Georgia, where devotees of the New South fretted about the threat mob violence posed to the smooth functioning of the regional economy, eastern Virginia city and state officials took steps to prevent serious social disorder. The exigencies of urban life and the commitment of the urban champions of the New South to progress and values were powerful countervailing forces to the culture of mob violence in eastern Virginia. As in the Upper Piedmont, ministers, educators, and businessmen voiced their opposition to lynching and called for a permanent solution to the "negro problem." Segregation, they promised, and not mob violence, would ease racial tensions. In eastern Virginia, the critics of mob violence exerted more influence than was typical elsewhere, which helped rouse local authorities to take forceful steps to prevent lynchings. Consequently, most of the lynching attempts in Lynchburg, Richmond, Norfolk, Fredericksburg, Petersburg, and other major towns were frustrated either by careful planning or outright brute force by local authorities.[38]

If any region in the South lacked the prerequisites for pervasive mob violence, it was the Shenandoah Valley. A valley of bountiful fertility, bordered by the jagged slopes of the Appalachians to the west and the Blue Ridge to the east, it was the richest region in the state. Settlers during the eighteenth and early nineteenth centuries never developed extensive plantations and consequently had made little use of slave labor. The affluent white farmers in the region tended to own their own land, which produced the largest crop yields in the state. Although blacks were scattered throughout the valley, their total numbers amounted to only slightly more than a tenth of the region's population. No where in Virginia were they less conspicuous than in the Shenandoah Valley.[39]

Their modest numbers in no way ensured that blacks in the region would be free from the threat of white violence, as blacks in northern Georgia well knew. But because few blacks in the Shenandoah Valley were tenant farmers or sharecroppers and most had carved out a largely independent social and economic world for themselves, there were few of the routine frictions that sparked mob violence in other areas of the South. Whites in the region still harbored many of the same fears of black criminality that whites did elsewhere, but only in exceptional circumstances did racial prejudice erupt in violent and unprovoked attacks on vulnerable blacks. On the two occasions when lynchings did occur in the Shenandoah Valley, mobs showed no more solicitude for their victims than did mobs elsewhere. In Page County in 1905, for example, a small group of whites accosted Henry Henderson, a tramp, for failing to abide by a tradition that forbade blacks to enter the community. The rock-throwing mob chased Henderson into a river, where they watched him drown without making any effort to rescue him.[40] The incident is a forceful reminder that even the Shenandoah Valley, where the most savage expressions of white racism were rare, was not free of the cancer of mob violence.

When Virginians during the late nineteenth century surveyed race relations in their state and looked for explanations for its comparatively limited racial violence, they typically emphasized both the good character of blacks and the efforts of public officials to maintain law and order. Few observers understood that the restraint of mobs in Virginia had at least as much to do with the absence of important catalysts of lynchings as to human intervention. With only a small portion of the state devoted to monoculture agriculture with all of its attendant evils, Virginia landlords were able to experiment with both new crops and new methods of securing labor. Neither the pursuit of economic justice nor the rejection of violence lay behind the apparent tranquility of agricultural labor relations in the Old Dominion. Rather, Virginia planters simply devised a system of labor that was exploitative, stable, and lucrative and yet did not rest upon the steady application of coercive methods. They discovered that the lash of wages was at least as effective as time-honored methods of coercive labor.

The evolving system of labor relations also promised a measure of independence to laborers even as it posed no challenge to planters' continued grip on the sources of wealth. Virginia landlords showed little interest in mimicking their Georgia counterparts, who assumed the prerogative to regulate violently virtually any area of black life. Thus, the enduring stimuli for lynching, so abundant in the Plantation Belt and southern Georgia, were largely absent from rural Virginia.

An additional explanation for the limited carnage of mob violence in Virginia is that the transformations of the late nineteenth century were far less disruptive there than in Georgia. Even in southwestern Virginia, where the aftershocks of industrialization generated a wave of mob violence, racial tensions were subsumed quickly by greater and more enduring tensions within the white community.

Similarly, there was no counterpart to the mounting land pressures in the Upper Piedmont of Georgia that pitted aspiring white farmers against black tenants. As a result, terrorist violence—especially whitecapping—was virtually unknown in Virginia. Although the color line was etched into the day-to-day reality of race relations, few whites believed that the upheavals of the late nineteenth century required violent, habitual defense of their property, livelihood, rights, or status from a black threat.

The differing levels of mob violence in Virginia and Georgia suggest patterns that may hold across the South. It would be a mistake to explain the geographical distribution of lynching by exaggerating the role of such social strains as economic depression, industrialization, or urbanization. Unquestionably, each of these processes generated serious racial friction, but they can explain, at most, only brief eruptions of mob violence and not the more than five decades of mob carnage. Rural industrialization, in particular, seems to have been a catalyst for racial antagonisms. The combination of the footloose workers in such rural industries as lumbering and turpentining and the challenge that the industrial labor practices posed to prevailing rural labor traditions predictably fostered ambivalence and hostility among many white residents in communities undergoing rural industrialization. And because rural industrialization did not require or encourage the expansion of local government or the development of anything that might be labelled as civic culture, neither institutions nor individuals were firmly committed to discouraging racial violence categorically. Because most rural industries had to move continuously in search of new resources, however, the social and racial traumas they generated also were transient. Thus, the repercussions of rural industrialization certainly may explain the brief explosions of mob violence in southern Georgia during the 1890s, and in parts of Florida and Mississippi after the turn of the century, but, almost certainly, they were not a principal cause of the phenomenon of lynching.

The effects of urban industrialization were even more contradictory than those of rural industrialization. Without doubt, black participation in industrialization in urban settings did engender job and housing competition between the races as well as a heightened concern over white status, all of which could, and did, explode in antiblack violence.[41] But those urban whites who were most committed to industrial and urban growth recognized the dangers of uncontrolled racial violence. They often may have condoned the practice of mob violence in theory and may even have believed that the occasional lynching in their city had a salutary effect upon blacks. But civic leaders recognized that unchecked urban mob violence could degenerate into a pogrom or a clear challenge to their authority and interests. The trauma of "mob anarchy" that business and civic leaders of Griffin, Georgia, confronted in 1899 is but one example of the potential for urban mob actions to escalate quickly beyond acceptable boundaries. When the management of a local cotton mill began to employ blacks in the mill, white workers organized a "Labor Regulatory Society" to overturn the new policy. The operatives whipped the new black employees, threatened the life of the mill superintendent, and issued a proclamation demanding that local white businesses fire black employees and replace them with whites. The violence escalated until local officials arrested several of the alleged ringleaders of the operatives and called out the state militia.[42] Southern urban elites, always suspicious of pluralism, labor activism, or any form of lower-class activism, were, predictably, apprehensive about events like those in Griffin. With the exception of the elites in a few southern cities, who skillfully turned mob violence to their own ends, the conservative social order that southern urban leaders favored was incompatible with chronic mob violence.[43]

As scholars have long recognized, the roots of lynching are to be found in the rural South. More precisely, lynch mobs seem to have flourished within the boundaries of the plantation South, where sharecropping, monoculture agriculture, and a stark line separating white landowners and black tenants existed. In such areas, mob violence became part of the very rhythm of life: deeply rooted traditions of violent labor control, unhindered by any meaningful resistance from either institutions or individuals opposed unconditionally to racial violence, sustained a tradition of mob violence that persisted for decades. In rough proportion to the degree that a particular region diverged from the plantation South, the likelihood of habitual mob violence in that region shrank. Thus, in large portions of Virginia, as well as parts of North Carolina, Tennessee, and Arkansas, where the evolution of agriculture and of labor and race relations diverged from the plantation South, the devastation wrought by lynch mobs pales in comparison to that of mobs in the Plantation Belt.

In Virginia, the fact that racial violence did not become a deeply rooted systematic feature of race relations had several important consequences. Confronted by a less pervasive practice than in other southern states, Virginians who were opposed to mob violence faced a much less daunting task when they campaigned for its suppression. For black Virginians, the terror of mob violence receded from personal experience much sooner than for blacks in the Deep South. Although they continued to view lynchings as a hideous reminder of their oppression in the United States, mob violence was not the ever-present threat that it was elsewhere.

Paradoxically, as the next chapter will explain, this comparative freedom provided an opening for vigorous opposition to mob violence even while it inspired a certain degree of cautiousness among many black leaders in Virginia, who had only to look southward to Georgia or Mississippi to be reminded of just how much better off their lives were.

6

"We Live in an Age of Lawlessness": The Response to Lynching in Virginia

Opposition to lynching in Virginia mounted slowly. Even at its strongest, it faced daunting obstacles. Opposition to mob violence was controversial everywhere in the South because virtually any discussion of the legitimacy of lynching touched upon white attitudes about race, crime, sexuality, and the very foundations of ordered society. Southern critics of lynching were always vulnerable to the charge that they were guilty of sectional treason, of pandering to the North, and of advocating "negrophilism." Meanwhile, the crippling dogma of white supremacy, the autonomy of county governments, and the weakness of state institutions all worked to frustrate opponents of mob violence.

The federal government, constrained by the prevailing constitutional doctrines and the absence of explicit antilynching statutes, was reluctant to play any role in suppressing lynching. Thus, any action had to be taken by state and local authorities. But both tradition and the intransigence of state legislators, who were jealous of any expansion of executive authority, held in check the powers of southern governors. With law-enforcement agencies limited to municipal police forces in the cities and county sheriffs in the rural areas, no statewide police forces could be relied upon either to prevent lynchings or prosecute mob members.

Yet, opponents of lynching in Virginia managed to overcome the obstacles of weak executive authority, entrenched localism, and hypersensitivity to criticism of southern institutions. Of critical importance was the limited role that mob violence and extralegal coercion played in the maintenance of the racial hierarchy. Neither violence nor intimidation were at the heart of the state's labor or rural race relations, as was the case in the plantation regions and the expanding agricultural frontiers of the South. In addition, whites in Virginia were more tolerant of black property-holding, mobility, and independence than was typical elsewhere.

Because most whites believed that traditional labor and race relations could be maintained without routine recourse to extralegal violence, opponents of mob violence faced less vociferous opposition than they did in Georgia and other southern states.

Of course, however comparatively favorable conditions for agitation against lynching were in Virginia, opponents still had to take advantage of opportunities to campaign against mob violence. They did so to a degree matched in only a few other southern states, exerting meaningful influence and contributing to the decline of mob violence decades before their counterparts in the Deep South even were able to organize. The earliest opposition came from black leaders, who battled the constraints imposed by virulent white racism and political impotence in protests against the brutality of white oppression. Their opposition reflected an urgent quest for freedom from white racism and for meaningful participation in the region's economic and political affairs. Initially, black agitation against mob violence was either assailed or, more often, simply ignored. But during the 1890s a growing number of conservative whites, concerned that lynching threatened the social tranquility and economic future of the state, decided that "the age of lawlessness" must end.[1]

Unlike the southern white opponents of mob violence during the 1920s and 1930s, conservative white critics of lynching in Virginia drew little inspiration from either religiously inspired social humanitarianism or any profound opposition to the southern racial hierarchy. Lacking in any formal organization, they were united by only their commitment to law and order. The theme of law and order provided an opening, although admittedly only a small opening, for a seemingly improbable common front of conservative white state and local officials and some black agitators in Virginia. The combined influence of governors who took steps against mob violence and local authorities who showed greater urgency in efforts to prevent lynchings helped speed the rapid decline of extralegal violence. Although similar tactics were attempted to varying degrees in most southern states, nowhere were they as successful as in Virginia.

During most of the late nineteenth and early twentieth centuries, black opposition to mob violence was uncoordinated and lacked any concrete program. The intertwined burdens of white racism and declining political influence posed formidable obstacles to any effective strategy opposing lynching. Not until the second decade of the twentieth century, when chapters of the National Association for the Advancement of Colored People (NAACP) were established in the state, did blacks create a permanent organization that pressed for improvements in their status and an end to mob violence. Despite these impediments, however, blacks in Virginia during the late nineteenth century did not respond to white violence with either resignation or submissiveness. Instead, they displayed great ingenuity in seizing the opportunities that did exist to challenge extralegal violence.

As long as Virginia's blacks retained any political leverage, they looked to the Republican party and the nation's conscience for remedies to the problem of white violence. During the 1860s and 1870s, the political clout of the large black population in eastern Virginia had sustained Republican fortunes and secured political office for a substantial number of black politicians. Despite the "redemption" of the state by white conservatives in 1873, the national retreat from Reconstruction in the 1870s, and the subsequent quarter-century-long campaign by white Democrats against black political rights, blacks continued to participate actively and in large numbers until the mid-1890s. Not until the turn of the century did white Democrats, through constitutional manipulation, effectively deprive them of their political rights. Until then, Virginia's blacks continued to exercise more local political authority than most southern blacks, even as they lost meaningful power over state and national affairs.[2]

Until the collapse of biracial Republicanism after the turn of the century, black Republicans attempted to goad state and local governments to suppress extralegal violence. For example, when they met in convention in Richmond in 1879 "for the purpose of considering matters connected with the welfare, rights and improvement of the colored race," they warned of an epidemic of black migration "provided our condition is not bettered." More to the heart of the matter, in 1880, Republican delegate Richard G. L. Paige of Norfolk County, frustrated by the failure of state and local authorities to prevent and investigate lynchings, tried unsuccessfully to prod the legislature to pass antilynching legislation.[3] These failed legislative efforts were important less because they impeded white violence against blacks—they did not—than because they reflected the continued belief and hope of many blacks that redress and protection could be gained through political activism and government intervention.

Deteriorating political fortunes and mounting frustration with the Republican party's failure to take meaningful action gradually eroded the institutional focus of black opposition to mob violence. Rising mob violence during the late nineteenth century exposed the limits of previous strategies against lynching. The surge of racial violence in southwestern Virginia and throughout the South as a whole during the early 1890s stimulated growing debate within the African-American community over appropriate tactics of protest and added urgency to their search for protection against violence.

Black leaders and local institutions attempted to fill some of the void left by the absence of any organized antilynching campaign. In sermons, public addresses, and convention reports, ministers and church members hammered away at the blatant hypocrisy of whites who claimed to be Christians while at the same time torturing and illegally executing blacks.[4] Black institutions in Virginian cities, with deeper pockets to dig into and more pressing needs to meet than organizations in rural areas, played a prominent role in sustaining activism during an era of worsening race relations. Although financially precarious and susceptible to white interference, such institutions, particularly newspapers, clubs, and churches, helped to bind together divided black communities and provide forums for self-expression sheltered from the hostile eyes of whites.[5]

Beginning in the 1880s, black newspapers assumed particular prominence in the campaign against mob violence. John L. Mitchell, Jr., the editor of the *Richmond Planet,* was particularly outspoken.[6] He used the *Planet* to publicize injustices and, through an insistent call for social justice, strove to dispel disillusionment. As black editors so often did, Mitchell turned his paper into a "safety-valve for the boiling black protest."[7] Even the masthead of the *Planet,* a drawing of a muscular black arm with a clenched fist, symbolized the newspaper's defiance. Mitchell published letters of protest from readers, accounts of sermons against lynching, and news of national organizations devoted to fighting black oppression. By publishing black eyewitness accounts of lynchings, the newspaper became the conduit for the rage of readers who could not remain silent in the wake of local mob violence. The newspaper's exposés of lynchings ensured that white news accounts, which routinely suffocated the truth of savagery with racist platitudes, did not become the sole historical record. In a real sense, Mitchell helped blacks to compile their own history of white repression.[8]

In editorials distinguished by both their passion and sardonic humor, Mitchell took it upon himself "to howl, yes, howl loudly, until the American people hear our cries."[9] His editorials offered blacks a crucial alternative to the often laudatory depictions of lynchings published in white newspapers. He lashed out at whites who failed to recognize the barbarism of lynch mobs. "Southern white folks have gone to roasting Negroes," he noted with disgust, "we presume the next step will be to eat them." And he offered nothing but reproach for elected officials who failed to take every possible step to prevent lynchings and prosecute lynchers.[10]

Mitchell's frustration led him to urge blacks to arm themselves in self-defense against mob violence. Although always careful to advocate only self-defense, his editorials, given the tenor of racial debate at the time, were incendiary: "You may say what you will, but a Winchester rifle is a mighty convenient thing when two-legged animals are prowling around your house in the dead of night." Every mob, he implored, should suffer the loss of "one or more of its members as a silent testimonial to the unerring aim of some Negro." [11]

Mitchell's sensational editorials were more than hollow rhetoric, for he was willing to back up his prose with action. In 1886, he received a threatening letter from a white who promised that he would be lynched if he were ever to set foot in Prince Edward County. In an act of bravado that gained wide attention, Mitchell armed himself and boldly traveled about the county. Although his visit to Prince Edward County was in keeping with nineteenth-century traditions of grandstanding newspapermen, it also conveyed to whites and blacks alike that Mitchell was, in his own words, a man "who would walk into the jaws of death to serve his race." [12] In addition, the flamboyant gesture was intended to demonstrate that fear should and could not intimidate blacks into surrendering either their rights or their dignity.

Mitchell also demonstrated his flair for activism in deeds of more enduring significance. In 1893, Isaac Jenkins, a black man accused of arson in Nansemond County, survived a lynching only to face trial as an arsonist. Mitchell seized upon the case as a blatant example of the injustices blacks suffered. With shocked disbelief, he complained that local authorities were more intent on persecuting Jenkins than on prosecuting the lynchers. He raised money for the black man's defense and published weekly accounts of his plight. When a jury finally acquitted Jenkins, Mitchell brought him to Richmond and organized speaking engagements so that Richmonders could hear a firsthand account of the horrors of mob violence.[13]

Mitchell recognized the serious limitations of the black press as a vehicle for protest. Beyond appealing to blacks to defend themselves against white attacks, few editors could offer practical methods to combat mob violence. Mitchell understood that white behavior, and not black conduct, needed to be altered, and consequently he attempted to prick the consciences of whites. But during the 1880s and early 1890s, his protests and those of other blacks fell upon deaf ears.

During the 1880s, the response of Virginia's governors to lynching in no way presaged the future opposition of their successors. Rather, the governors steadfastly ignored the rising tide of mob violence. Although mobs claimed an average of two victims a year during the decade, governors William E. Cameron (1882–86) and Fitzhugh Lee (1886–90) remained silent. Cameron was a member of the Readjuster party, a fragile biracial coalition of Republicans as well as whites outraged by the Democrats' solution to the state's debt problem. He failed to take any action against lynching almost certainly because he did not want to squander his limited political influence at a time when the Democratic party was ascendant. Moreover, Cameron could not count on support for any controversial steps against mob violence from within the Democratic-controlled House of Delegates. The silence of Lee, a Democrat, was in keeping with his unobtrusive style and firm commitment to avoid the exercise of authority whenever possible. As one historian has noted laconically, "Governor Lee seldom provided dynamic leadership." [14] Lee and the Democratic party were interested in consolidating power and had neither the inclination nor incentive to defend the rights of blacks. After all, the Democrats had regained political power in part through a strident white supremacist campaign that included healthy doses of intimidation and thinly veiled threats of violence. [15]

Governor Philip W. McKinney (1890–94) showed no greater proclivity for innovative or aggressive leadership than had Governor Lee. McKinney's administration coincided with the peak of lynching in the state, when nearly a third of all lynchings in the state's history occurred. Foremost of McKinney's aims was to ensure that the Democratic party gained complete hegemony in the Old Dominion. In a climate of sharpening racial tensions brought on by fears of increased federal intervention in southern affairs, worsening economic conditions, and the rise of a new generation of shrill white supremacists, McKinney possessed a peculiar ability to whip up racial tensions. [16]

McKinney's failure to speak out against mob violence provoked outrage among blacks. When he showed uncharacteristic energy in threatening to prosecute the organizers and participants in a Norfolk prizefight in 1892, the *Richmond Planet* bitterly contrasted his zeal in suppressing boxing bouts with his inaction on lynching. After a mob lynched five blacks in Tazewell County in February 1893, Mitchell again complained, "Governor McKinney is as silent as though he had suddenly turned to Venetian marble." [17]

Before 1893 there was little to suggest that either the effectiveness of black protests against lynching or white attitudes about mob violence differed in any meaningful way from the patterns elsewhere in the South. Like their southern counterparts, Virginia blacks initially had been committed to seeking redress through the political process. But as they met increasing frustration in the political arena during the late 1880s, efforts to capture the attention of white officials seemed to produce little more than white apathy. As long as no prominent whites, in particular governors, spoke out against lynching, local authorities had few incentives to risk social ostracism or violent retaliation by taking forceful steps to suppress mob violence.

Governor McKinney maintained his silence on mob violence until the close of his administration, when the Roanoke lynching riot in September 1893—"the greatest tragedy that ever darkened the city's chronicles"—virtually compelled him to address the issue.[18] On September 23, while the governor was out of state admiring the neoclassical wonderland of the Columbian Exposition in Chicago, a young black laborer named Thomas Smith allegedly choked, beat, and robbed Mrs. Henry Bishop, a "respectable" white woman, in the downtown of the industrial boom city of Roanoke. Within a short time, Smith was arrested and jailed. Throughout that afternoon, a surly crowd milled in front of the jail and demanded the prisoner. The pleas from the commonwealth attorney, the mayor, and the chief of police for the crowd to disperse were met with shouts and threatened violence. Realizing that open violence might break out at any moment, the mayor summoned his senior police officers for consultation. The chief of police suggested that Smith be transferred to another locale, but a city judge was quick to point out that a city of twenty-five thousand ought to guarantee the protection of its prisoners.

Mayor Trout, who had been critical of a lynching that had occurred in the previous administration and had been embarrassed by an attempted lynching during his own, was determined to maintain order. He ordered the entire city police force of fifteen to protect the prisoner and to resist, with firearms if necessary, any mob assault. In addition, he alerted the local militia. The first detachment of the Roanoke Light Infantry, some twenty men in all, arrived at five o'clock that afternoon. The presence of the soldiers, who advanced with fixed bayonets, temporarily reduced the size of the mob and partially cleared the congested streets in front of the jail.

Events, however, conspired to ensure that the mob's passions were kept at a fever pitch. Some of the demonstrators who refused to disperse were arrested, and then Mrs. Bishop's son whipped up the crowd by "shouting and hollering, 'Come on boys. . . they won't shoot." Finally, the enormous crowd, variously estimated at between 1,500 and 5,000 participants, advanced on the jail. They made a wild rush at the front and side doors while simultaneously hurling a barrage of rocks and missiles at a small group of militiamen upstairs. Shooting broke out, and in the chaos that followed, seven mob members were killed and at least twenty-five members of the mob and the jail's defenders were wounded, including the mayor, who had caught a pistol ball in his foot.[19]

Once the wounded and dead were cleared from the streets, the mob's fury was directed against two targets: the mayor, whom they believed had given the order to shoot, and the militia, which they believed had fired without provocation. With the danger of renewed violence an immediate threat, the commander of the militia dismissed his men with the instructions to change out of their military uniforms immediately and to go home quietly. The mob began a furious search for the mayor and ransacked both his home and the hotel to which he had been moved for medical care. Meanwhile, worried friends had convinced the mayor to escape by taking a special train to Lynchburg. Having failed to punish either the militia or the mayor, the mob set about locating Thomas Smith, who had been quietly removed from the jail during the chaos. Early the next morning, his hiding place was finally discovered, and he was captured and lynched. Only the timely intercession of a local minister prevented the mob from burying Smith's body—which bore the sign "Mayor Trout's friend"—in the front yard of the mayor's home. In the end, the mob satisfied itself by burning the body.

Smith's murder did nothing to eliminate the mob's grievances stemming from the previous night's clash. For three days, they remained encamped in front of the jail, demanding the removal of the mayor, the chief of police, and several police officers. During protracted negotiations between a committee of prominent city businessmen and leaders of the mob it was agreed that all officials but the mayor would be suspended pending the completion of a full-scale inquiry. Despite much grumbling, the mob accepted the terms and allowed the mayor to return from exile and resume authority.[20]

The mob's destructiveness and violent challenge to legal authority shocked the state.[21] The tension created by the riot only subsided with time; threats on the mayor's life continued to circulate, and members of the militia received letters that warned, "We want your blood. You shot our friends." Graphic reminders of the tragedy remained visible in downtown Roanoke: "the station house, the jail, and the courthouse have the appearance of being struck by a cyclone. . . the windows of the Mayor's office are filled with bullet holes and some of the glasses are broken out."[22]

During the turmoil in Roanoke, Governor McKinney was reluctant to comment on the lynching, and even after his return to Virginia he skirted the issue.[23] Finally, he addressed the problem in his final message to the general assembly. He admitted that lawlessness had prevailed during his administration and especially condemned the violence in Roanoke. He sternly cautioned that the law must be enforced through whatever means necessary and concluded, "let us profit from this terrible lesson, and learn in all cases to respect the authorities and obey the law."[24] McKinney's denunciation, the *Richmond Planet* lamented, was too little and too late to compensate for his years of silence.[25] That the governor felt compelled to issue any statement at all, however, bespoke the growing concerns of many whites that mob violence posed a serious challenge to social order in the state. The eleven other lynchings that occurred in 1893 provoked only modest comment or concern, but the attack on authority and the resulting anarchy in Roanoke simply could not be ignored. The *Richmond State* captured the urgent concern of many Virginians in an editorial shortly after the September lynching: "It seems that the time has come when every good citizen must enter his protest against such exhibitions of lawlessness. The situation is truly alarming and unless law-abiding citizens all assert themselves and exert the dignity and the majesty of the law, the time will come when the mob will rule and no man's life will be secure." [26]

When Governor McKinney's successor Charles T. O'Ferrall assumed office in January 1894, he quickly provided the leadership that had been absent during his predecessor's term. His administration proved to be the decisive turning point in the chief executive's stance on mob violence. Ironically, O'Ferrall shared many traits with McKinney. He was an old-fashioned Virginia gentleman and a Confederate war veteran. In political philosophy, he was a staunchly conservative Democrat who denounced with equal vigor free silver, Populism, and labor unions. Confronted, he believed, with a hydra-headed monster of social anarchy, he was quick to use the militia to chase Coxey's army, a protest organization of unemployed workers, from the state in 1894 and to suppress labor unrest in the southwestern coal fields in 1895. And like his predecessor, he was firmly devoted to white supremacy.[27]

But neither O'Ferrall's conservatism nor his devotion to white supremacy allowed for toleration of mob violence. He set the tone of his administration by announcing in his inaugural address that he would enforce the laws of the state, "let it cost what it will in blood or money." In each of his succeeding annual messages to the general assembly, he condemned lynching and called upon Virginians to stamp it out, as he explained in 1894, because "Christianity demands it; public morality requires it; popular sentiments exact it." [28]

For O'Ferrall and many other conservative whites, the upheaval in Roanoke was a clarion call for strong action against the excesses of mob violence. Simultaneously, elsewhere in the South, other white critics also struggled to be heard, but their pleas were drowned out by the violent rhetoric of the defenders of mob violence. In Virginia, however, the theme of law and order had a resonance that it lacked in most other southern states, and consequently conservative white opponents of lynching were able to exert decisive influence.

To a great extent, conservative opponents of lynching like O'Ferrall benefited from the peculiar tenor of Virginia politics, which throughout the late nineteenth and early twentieth centuries remained distinctly elitist. The state's ruling oligarchy demonstrated remarkable tenacity, even during the turmoil of Reconstruction. Virginia passed from military rule into the arms of the Conservative party (the pseudonym for the Democratic party until 1882) without ever experiencing Republican civilian rule. While the old, formerly established elites in other states had resorted to extensive and organized violence to regain power, conservatives in Virginia secured their rule largely through astute political maneuvers. Not only did they restore "home rule" without resorting to wholesale violence, but they also condemned the violence in other states.[29]

During the late 1870s and early 1880s, the oligarchy suffered defeat at the hands of the Readjuster party. The Conservative party, after renaming itself the Democratic party, responded vigorously and smashed its challengers in 1883. The bitter defeat taught the party to bend with prevailing political winds to head off political insurgency, all the while retaining its underlying commitments to elitist government, white supremacy, and economic orthodoxy. After the collapse of the Readjuster and Republican parties in the late 1880s and the stillbirth of the Populist party in the early 1890s, moderate and conservative Democrats enjoyed virtual hegemony. What political divisions there were existed along factional lines within the Democratic party.[30]

Unlike politics in many other southern states, leadership and political values were not transient in Virginia. The recruitment, development, and advancement of political leaders was orderly and predictable. Party leaders either committed themselves to the prevailing political orthodoxy or faced a rocky political future. The political scientist V. O. Key, writing in 1949, offered a description of Virginia politics that applied to the early 1900s no less than the 1940s. "The little oligarchy that rules Virginia demonstrates a sense of honor, an aversion to venality, a degree of sensitivity to public opinion, a concern for efficiency in administration, and so long as it does not cost much, a feeling of social responsibility." By means of an exceedingly effective machine organization that ran from the Virginia statehouse to the courthouse "cliques" and "rings," the homogeneous social values of the oligarchic leadership of the party dominated the legislature, the party machinery, and even city and county offices.[31]

Strident white supremacists, or to borrow the historian Joel Williamson's phrase "radical racists," never exerted the powerful influence, political or otherwise, in Virginia that they did elsewhere in the South. Among the Democratic leadership in Virginia, there were few racial extremists who strenuously proclaimed that blacks were retrogressing toward a state of bestiality and threatening the very foundations of white society. In states where racial extremists were ascendant, their attacks on opponents of mob violence hindered concerted efforts to suppress lynching. For such extremists, anything that whites might do to defend their supremacy was both justifiable and laudable. In Virginia, by contrast, opponents of mob violence were free to condemn lynching without fearing a backlash from strident racists.[32]

The oligarchic structure of government in Virginia was instinctively conservative and resistant to profound change. Regardless of faction, leaders within the party were drawn from the same patrician stock. By the early 1890s, the marriage of the Democratic party and the business interests of the state was nearly complete. Some party members remained suspicious of innovation, but most ardently embraced the industrial gospel of the age.[33] In keeping with their commitment to the doctrines of the New South, they believed that good race relations depended upon the state being left alone to solve the problem at its own pace and in its own way. In an age of violent, even hysterical, racism, the racial views of the Virginia Democratic leadership were moderate. Firm racial and class boundaries ensured social harmony, and in this fixed universe blacks were inherently inferior and naturally subordinate. Few seriously doubted that whites retained ample means to prevent blacks from threatening white dominance. Occasional slackness and lapses in the maintenance of racial lines, although not welcomed, could at least be tolerated because the party's leadership saw nothing too alarming in them as long as the established social order went unchallenged. In an editorial in February 1890, the *Petersburg Index-Appeal* vented its frustration with the fears of "negro domination" in the Old Dominion. The paper warned that "If all our interests, all our convictions are to be sacrificed to an African fetich [fetish] manufactured and erected by a set of political charlatans who still harbor or feign a foolish horror of the impossible," white Virginians would "cast aside the most beneficent measures and policies. . . because of a baseless *fear of the negro.*" The *Index-Appeal* stressed that the cry of "negro domination. . . is a great danger, and the democratic party will perish of it if it do[es] not shake off its childish 'make-believe' and attend to our real necessities." With power securely in Democratic hands, rabble-rousing and Negro-baiting were tolerated only so long as they did not imperil the tone of civility that constituted the heart of the state's political culture.[34]

Social unrest, whether the product of lynch mobs or labor unions, Virginia's elite concluded, retarded economic progress. In 1891, when the editors of the *Richmond Times* addressed the issue of "Mob Law," they saw a direct connection between labor unrest and lynching. The action of a crowd of striking Tennessee miners who liberated convict miners prompted the *Times* to label the action as "simply anarchism, pure and simple, and but the natural outcome of the contempt into which the courts have been thrown by various lynching cases." The wave of labor violence that swept the nation in 1894 stirred similar fears, arousing the *Times* to warn that "no one who has the least property or wishes to exercise with impunity his individual abilities to earn a living can hope to enjoy the property or work for his living as a free man unless that lawless and violent spirit is absolutely suppressed." It was not coincidental that in 1895 the leading Democratic newspaper in the state lumped labor unions, Coxey's army, illegal oyster fishing in the Chesapeake Bay, and lynching under the heading of anarchy and mob rule.[35]

This concern for social order also sustained the loud applause for Governor O'Ferrall's decision in 1894 to order the militia to drive encamped Coxeyites from Virginia at bayonet point. The Coxeyites, the *Richmond Dispatch* explained, demanded "a show of force" because "their way was to beg, bulldoze and steal, and thus. . . become terrors in the community afflicted by their presence." A year later, when O'Ferrall sent troops to preserve the order in the strike-torn town of Pocahontas near the West Virginia border, the *Dispatch* again warned of the persisting dangers of mob rule. "Cost what it may," the newspaper noted gravely, "the question to be decided at Pocahontas is whether our Virginia authorities shall enforce our laws and give protection to men who want to work, or shall surrender to a West Virginia mob." For these conservative white newspapers and much of the leadership of the Democratic party, mob lawlessness, in all of its many guises, threatened to overwhelm the entire social and economic order upon which the New South and Virginia rested. The choice before the South, the *Richmond Times* concluded in 1897, was quite stark: "We cannot serve two masters. Either the law or the mob must rule, and if we are to have mob rule, then let us abolish the law altogether." [36]

In light of the profoundly conservative inclinations of Virginia's elite, the absence of shrill advocates of racial extremism, and the clear threat to constituted authority that the mobs posed, it is hardly surprising that the Roanoke riot served as a catalyst for widespread demands for the suppression of social disorder. The major tenets of the conservative argument for law and order, of course, were not new. At least as early as 1871 the editors of the *Richmond Enquirer* had sketched with great clarity the threat that mob violence posed to the social order. Few subsequent calls by white conservatives seeking the suppression of mob violence would move far beyond the position taken by the *Enquirer*. When the lynching of a white horse thief in the Shenandoah Valley in 1871 provoked a debate over summary justice, a prominent lawyer had staunchly defended the mob's action in a letter to the newspaper: "It is simply an illegal performance of a deed, which, if legally done, could have met the approbation of all right-thinking men. No one was hurt who should not have been." The editors of the *Enquirer* dismissed such justifications as "sophistical." The crucial virtue of law, the newspaper observed, was to establish secure rules and standards of conduct that bound society together. "The dangers of this mob law is, that if you unchain the tiger, there is no telling whom it will tear." Social chaos was the inevitable consequence of a cavalier acceptance of the legitimacy of mob violence. "What human society wants is order and stability. The great point of the Law is, not that it is the best law, but that it affords a standard and fixes the tribunal of appeal between man and man." [37] Two decades later, the tragedy at Roanoke graphically drove home the precise dangers that unimpeded mob violence could pose to social stability and property alike in Virginia.

But even if some prominent Virginians believed that lynching could not be tolerated, these sentiments had to be turned into meaningful and direct action. Whites who opposed lynching never created an enduring organization to combat mob violence like those established elsewhere in the South during the 1920s. Instead, the burden of suppressing lynchings was placed on the governor and local authorities, who faced daunting obstacles when they attempted to act. The conspicuous limitations of executive powers placed considerable restraints on governors. Yet in the aftermath of the Roanoke lynching, Governor O'Ferrall demonstrated that even limited powers could be used to make important contributions to the suppression of mob violence. Spurred on by concerns for law and order, he placed the power of the state, however limited it may have been, firmly behind the suppression of lynching.

Each time a lynching occurred during his term, O'Ferrall undertook a careful investigation to determine if it could have been prevented. After a lynching in Alexandria in 1897, for example, he sent his personal aide to the city to inquire into the conduct of local authorities during the incident. The subsequent report exposed the incompetence and cowardice of the local police and the mayor.[38] Although the governor had no legal authority to punish the officials, he sharply criticized them in newspaper interviews and in his annual address to the general assembly.[39]

On several occasions, O'Ferrall's determination to crush mob violence led him to overstep the traditional powers of his office. In 1897, he sent troops to protect a black prisoner during a trial in Fairfax County, even though local authorities had not called for the militia. Once the troops had arrived, O'Ferrall convinced local authorities to make a formal request for their presence during the trial.[40]

In 1895, he went to even greater lengths to protect three black women in Lunenberg County charged with the murder of an elderly white woman. The "Lunenberg affair" reveals both the strengths and limitations of O'Ferrall's conservative opposition to mob violence. One noteworthy aspect of the episode was that it enabled a conservative white Democrat such as O'Ferrall to find common ground with the black firebrand John Mitchell. Certainly, the men were unlikely partners in a campaign against mob violence. But both shared concerns for the social order and the preservation of the sanctity of legal institutions, anxieties common among conservative whites and black opponents of lynching alike. For O'Ferrall, the protection of the three women became a symbolic defense of Virginia's legal institutions. For Mitchell, their defense was significant not only because mob violence threatened the integrity of Virginia's courts, but also because the women's plight exposed graphically the blatant injustices that blacks endured at the hands of white justice. Thus, O'Ferrall's concerns for suppressing social unrest provided an opening for John Mitchell, who skillfully took advantage of the real, if fragile, spirit of cooperation to nudge the governor to intervene on behalf of the women.

From the very beginning of the Lunenberg affair, it was clear that the plight of the three black women, Mary Abernathy, Porkey Barnes, and Mary Barnes, would be resolved either through lengthy court battles or through extralegal violence. Although the women all bore good reputations, they were arrested for the murder of Lucy Pollard after a fourth suspect, William Henry Marable, implicated them. In the first of the trials of the four murder suspects, Marable claimed that he had been with the three women when they committed the murder, but he denied any participation in the crime. The jury of ten whites and two blacks needed only nine minutes to find a verdict of murder in the first degree. During the subsequent trials, Marable was the principal witness for the prosecution and testified against each woman. Despite glaring discrepancies and erratic changes in his testimony, Mary Abernathy and Pokey Barnes were convicted and sentenced to hang, and Mary Barnes received a prison term.[41]

While covering the trials for the *Planet,* Mitchell determined that the women were innocent, the charges against them spurious, and the trials tainted by the threat of mob violence. His perceptions were shared by the commander of the militia troops that had stood guard throughout the trials to prevent lynching. The commander later reported that "threats were openly made that in the event of the acquittal of any of them. . . they would certainly have been lynched had they been without the protection of the troops."[42]

After starting a fundraising effort for money to hire attorneys to appeal the women's convictions, Mitchell appealed to George D. Wise, Henry W. Flournoy, and A. B. Guigon, three of Richmond's leading white attorneys, to take up their cases. By agreeing to do so, Wise, a former U.S. congressman and commonwealth attorney for Richmond, Flournoy, a former secretary of the commonwealth and judge in Danville, and Guigon, a member of the Richmond city council and school board, immediately drew local and statewide attention to the women's predicament. Various newspapers, most prominently the white *Richmond Times,* joined with the *Planet* and began to question the fairness of the trials.[43]

While the lawyers began the lengthy process of appeal, Mitchell methodically exposed the flimsy evidence that had convicted the women, the flagrant failures of the trial judge to follow established legal procedures, the dubious fairness of allowing some of the jurors to serve in more than one of the trials, and the extent to which threatened mob violence had intimidated the jurors. As one admitted in the *Planet,* he had voted for the guilty verdict because of "the excitement of the occasion" and in order "to go with the majority." [44]

Mitchell also alerted Governor O'Ferrall to the grave threat of mob violence that the women faced. Mitchell worked to convince the governor to delay the execution of Marable so that the condemned man could testify at the women's retrial. Despite strong misgivings about delaying the execution of a man he judged to be guilty, O'Ferrall acquiesced and delayed the execution. Throughout the ensuing months, while the legal battle wore on, Mitchell met with the governor and other prominent whites to discuss the case. In September 1895, when events took a surprising turn and the women again seemed threatened with mob violence, the governor decided to overstep the traditional powers of his office and take unorthodox steps to protect them. [45]

Drastic steps had become necessary because the commonwealth attorney of Lunenburg County, concerned that his prosecution during the women's trial might not survive a challenge in the Virginia supreme court, called for the return of the prisoners to Lunenburg so deficiencies in the trial record could be corrected. The warnings of defense lawyers that their clients probably would be lynched if returned to the county spurred O'Ferrall to declare that he would not allow their return without military escort. Sheriff M. C. Cardoza of Lunenburg County, however, refused to request troops and announced that he would transport the prisoners himself. [46]

When Sheriff Cardoza arrived in Richmond to retrieve the prisoners, the governor refused to allow them to be removed, explaining that "my sense of personal responsibility and public duty, and my obligation to protect the lives of these convicts. . . compel me to retain them in the city jail." After yet more complex legal wrangling, the Virginia supreme court ruled that the governor did not have the authority to prevent the prisoners from being returned to Lunenburg and ordered a retrial. [47]

O'Ferrall, who still harbored grave doubts about the safety of the women should they return to Lunenburg, sent a special message to the general assembly, defending his handling of the case and asking for the authority to take further steps to protect the women. Aware that his position might offend residents of the county, the governor forthrightly explained that "I would be unworthy indeed to hold the high and honorable position to which I have been called, if I stifle my sense of duty to avoid the censure of the thoughtless or to save the feelings of a community." He complained that he lacked authority to send militia without a formal request by the sheriff, and in this instance, the sheriff refused to make such a request. He entreated the legislature to amend the law immediately so he could order out troops at his own discretion. The legislators, by a large margin, refused his request.[48]

Without any further recourse, O'Ferrall could not prevent the women's return. Their trials, despite rumors of mob violence, were marked only by legal pyrotechnics. The team of defense lawyers succeeded in forcing the prosecution to drop the charges against two of the women. The third, Mary Barnes, who had chosen not to appeal her case because she refused to expose herself to possible mob violence at the retrial, remained in the state penitentiary. O'Ferrall, who felt compelled by "every mandate of justice and dictate of conscience," pardoned her shortly after the conclusion of the retrial in Lunenburg. When Mary Barnes finally was released from jail in 1896, Mitchell escorted her to the capitol, where they personally thanked the governor.[49]

The complexities of the Lunenburg case and its large number of participants should not obscure the governor's prominent role. On behalf of three blacks convicted of the murder of a white woman, and on tenuous legal grounds, he ordered state officials to defy county authorities. Moreover, he urged the legislature to expand the powers of his office so that he could take more forceful steps to prevent lynchings. John Mitchell of the *Planet* heaped unrestrained praise on the governor for his efforts. "The final release of Porkey Barnes and Mary Abernathy," he wrote, "is. . . an everlasting tribute to that spirit of justice and fair play which. . . is ever present and vigorously manifest in the actions of Governor O'Ferrall."[50]

The Lunenburg case, although a dramatic example of O'Ferrall's dogged determination to stop mob violence, also demonstrated the obstacles he faced. It alerted him to the modest powers of his office when local authorities appeared to be unwilling to take necessary steps to prevent mob violence. He concluded that "the spirit of lynching will never be eradicated in any state until there are stringent laws against it, so enacted as to be enforceable."[51] In 1895 and again in 1897, he proposed several laws to force local officials to suppress mobs. Local jurisdictions, he argued, should be subject to fines for lynchings that occurred within their borders and also be liable for costs incurred in calling out the militia. He also urged that law officers who gave up prisoners be subject to summary suspension and jury investigations. Furthermore, a prisoner who was mobbed— or the prisoner's heirs—should have the right to sue the officer for damages, and the burden of proof in any trial should be on the officer. O'Ferrall's reforms found little support in the general assembly, where legislators, who steadfastly championed limited executive powers and the autonomy of county governments worried that his proposals would unduly centralize power.[52]

Although many conservative whites in Virginia recognized the seriousness of the problem of mob violence, their anxiety over the issue was never sufficient to inspire them to support far-reaching reforms in state power. The only significant measure that the legislature passed to address the issue of mob violence during the 1890s was a law that raised the penalty for attempted rape from imprisonment to death. The justification for the law, the *Richmond Dispatch* explained, was that the "severe and expeditious" law would prevent both attacks on women and, in turn, lynchings.[53] But state legislators would not go beyond this measure. By their very nature, most conservative white opponents of mob violence shied away from any dramatic innovations in meeting its threat. Even O'Ferrall's advocacy of the modest expansion of state authority offered no suggestions beyond the timid antilynching laws enacted in some other southern states, laws that almost certainly would have accomplished no more in Virginia than they did elsewhere. Moreover, because O'Ferrall and other conservative whites believed that the campaign against mob violence amounted to little more than a struggle between lawlessness and order, they saw a victory for law and order whenever punishment was meted out by the courts rather than mobs. Thus, the mantra of law and order served as an inspiration to suppress mob violence while simultaneously as a damper on any reform that would have addressed the root causes of mob violence. Their intentions, then, were a far cry from what either John Mitchell and other black agitators sought or from the aspirations of the antilynching movement in the Deep South two decades later.

With pardonable vanity, O'Ferrall boasted in his autobiography that he "had broken down almost entirely the spirit of lynching that had prevailed to an alarming extent in the state so long."[54] Certainly, a partial explanation for the sharp decline in the number of lynchings during his administration must be traced to his campaign against mob violence. Whereas twenty-seven men had died at the hands of mobs during his predecessor's four-year term, mobs executed only three black men and one white man during O'Ferrall's term.[55] Moreover, his outspoken opposition and aggressive efforts to squelch lynching set the standard against which the actions of all later governors were judged. His frequent denunciations of lynch mobs, his appeal to local authorities to make use of the state militia, and his unorthodox actions during the Lunenburg case showed that the governor, despite limited powers, could find ways to take effective steps to curtail mob violence.

Governor O'Ferrall's hope that the "mob spirit" had been crushed proved to be overly optimistic. During the term of his successor J. Hoge Tyler, mobs executed seven blacks and three whites. Tyler privately lamented, in May 1898, that "the lynch spirit is so strong again." [56] The resurgence coincided with racial tensions over the role of blacks in the military during the Spanish-American War and agitation over segregation and disfranchisement.[57] Mob violence also plagued Tyler's successor, Andrew J. Montague (1902–6), who deeply regretted that the lynchings of seven blacks marred his administration. Mob violence finally declined sharply during the administration of Claude A. Swanson (1906–10), and no more than three lynchings took place during any subsequent governor's term.

The governors who succeeded O'Ferrall showed more scrupulous concern for the limits on their powers than he had, but they were equally vigorous in pressing local authorities to prevent lynchings and punish lynchers. When local authorities requested troops, governors sometimes responded with dramatic displays of force. In 1904, when the rape of a white woman in Roanoke, allegedly by a black man, threatened to lead to mob violence, Governor Montague ordered nearly eight hundred troops to protect the man during his trial.[58] In 1907, when a threatened lynching and race riot in Accomack County induced local authorities to request the militia, Governor Swanson responded not only by sending troops but also by traveling overnight on a police boat to reach the scene of the disturbance on the Eastern Shore peninsula. Swanson addressed a crowd in the town, warning that he would "stay a week, a month, or even spend the summer. . . to keep the peace." [59] More often, governors chose to work closely with local authorities by carefully arranging adequate militia protection for the transportation and trial of alleged criminals.[60]

O'Ferrall's legacy was most apparent in the widespread conviction among all Virginians that governors had a personal responsibility to prevent lynchings. Any that could have been prevented by state intervention were viewed as blots on the governor's record. Governor Tyler, for example, suffered sharp criticism for his indecisiveness during a lynching in Greenville County in 1900. In March 1900, Walter Cotton, a black murderer, escaped from jail in Portsmouth and, while a fugitive, killed two more people. On March 22, local authorities in Greenville County arrested both Cotton and Brandt O'Grady, a white tramp from Boston who was Cotton's suspected accomplish. Threats of mob violence soon compelled the sheriff and judge of the county to request troops. A militia company from Richmond quickly responded and reached Emporia, the county seat of Greenville County, within hours. After witnessing the emotion-charged atmosphere in the town, the militia commander suggested that the prisoners be moved to Richmond, but local authorities refused, claiming that any such attempts would enflame the mob.[61]

Conditions worsened the following morning. After the militia commander wired for reinforcements on his own initiative, county officials ordered him to withdraw the troops. He immediately sent Governor Tyler a telegram describing the crisis and expressing his firm conviction that the withdrawal of the troops would result in the lynching of the prisoners. The governor ignored his warnings and ordered the troops to comply with the wishes of county officials. The militia commander, after a last-ditch effort to convince county officials that the troops should remain, assembled his men and marched away. Within minutes of their departure, a mob made up of both blacks and whites stormed the jail and hanged Cotton and O'Grady.[62]

The tragedy at Emporia immediately provoked a bitter and lengthy dispute over the governor's handling of the crisis. The *Richmond Times* lamented that "the state of Virginia has been disgraced and Governor Tyler is responsible for it." The *Portsmouth Star* charged that Tyler had permitted, even invited, the lynching by withdrawing the troops. His subsequent attempts to defend his actions led the paper to conclude "his foot has the proverbial proclivity for filling his mouth." Perhaps the sharpest criticisms came from Samuel C. Mitchell, a history professor at Richmond College (now the University of Richmond). In a sermon delivered at the Second Baptist Church in Richmond, Mitchell assailed Tyler, complaining that he lacked both courage and vision and that his handling of the Emporia affair was "the most criminal instance of official incapacity to be found in the annals of Virginia." Mitchell concluded that Governor O'Ferrall would have easily prevented the lynching at Emporia.[63]

Governor Tyler was not without defenders. The *Richmond Dispatch* and the *Norfolk Virginian-Pilot* consistently defended him while roundly condemning the local authorities in Greenville County. Prominent citizens from throughout the state also wrote to the governor to express support and sympathy. But even some supporters admitted that the governor had made a mistake in judgment by withdrawing the troops.[64] Tyler's defenders repeated traditional refrains about the supremacy of local authorities and the dangers of executive tyranny, but they, too, were critical of the county officials and condemned the lynching as "an element of barbarism which causes a shudder in the heart of every good man and woman." [65]

Although Virginians entertained different opinions about how far governors should go to suppress lynching, the controversy over events in Emporia demonstrated that by 1900 widespread sentiment held that mob violence posed a serious threat to social order and that governors had to assume a large responsibility for the prevention of lynching. Whereas in many southern states governors passed off the prevention of lynchings as the responsibility of local authorities, governors in Virginia did so at the risk of public censure.

Of course, if mob violence were to be suppressed, local authorities, as well as state officials, had to respond swiftly and decisively to prevent lynchings and punish lynch mobs. As long as sheriffs and public authorities displayed indifference or actively participated in lynchings, mob violence would continue unchecked. Local authorities in Virginia, like their counterparts throughout the South, felt the pull of powerful forces that militated against vigorous opposition to mob violence, yet many struggled to uphold the law with a determination that too often was absent elsewhere.

Local officials were spurred on by pressure from state officials and fear of state-wide censure by governors and newspapers for any dereliction of duty. Almost certainly, many believed that the preservation of social order and the maintenance of respect for legal authority demanded the suppression of lynching. They were also loath to admit that they could not control their community during a lynching. Even if lynchers committed no serious damage or destruction of property, local officials knew that mobs challenged their role as guardians of the community and the dignity of the law. Many suffered from divided allegiances when they faced lynch mobs. Community ties often led them to sympathize with the mob's objectives; even if they did not, any vigorous steps to prevent a lynching or punish lynchers could provoke social ostracism or even violent retaliation. They also might face political retaliation if they angered local residents by their handling of a lynching. Finally, many local officials held a conception of law and order that neither stressed the abstract principles of justice nor drew precise distinctions between legal and extralegal justice. Instead, many saw mob violence as a means of carrying out the spirit of formal law, if not the letter.[66] Thus, local authorities often felt the tug of competing forces both to stifle mob violence and to ignore, or even aid, lynch mobs.

Virtually all of the lynchings in Virginia were the result of the failure of local officials to protect their prisoners adequately. Sometimes, law officers made little pretense of preventing mob violence, whereas in other instances, they and county officials displayed glaring incompetence. Many incidents resulted from open complicity between local law officers and the mob. Occasionally, however, conscientious sheriffs and jailers were simply caught off guard and overpowered by well-organized and heavily armed mobs.

If some local authorities withered in the face of lynch mobs, many managed to thwart them. By far the most effective immediate action local authorities could take, particularly in rural areas, was to remove a threatened prisoner to a distant and secure jail. For example, in 1895 local authorities in Bristol protected a black man accused of assaulting a white girl by rushing him out of town before he fell into the hands of a mob. Similarly, by quickly moving two suspected arsonists to nearby Rockingham County, Augusta County officials managed to forestall a lynching in 1897. On countless other occasions, prudent law officers protected their prisoners either by hiding them or by simply outrunning the mob.[67]

When flight became impossible, authorities faced a potentially explosive situation if they insisted on protecting a prisoner. Officials often bargained with mobs to let the law take its course, promising that, if tried, the alleged criminal would receive the death penalty.[68] For most local authorities there was nothing unseemly about essentially agreeing to "legal lynchings" at the hand of the state. After all, they were more concerned about preserving the sanctity of the courts and legal authority than the rights of threatened prisoners. During a threatened lynching in Glen Wilton in 1909, for example, a local official and prominent businessman addressed the mob. "I wouldn't lift my little finger to save this nigger," he announced, "but it will be the greatest shame on the county and the greatest setback to law and order. . . if we let this fellow be lynched. . . . I'll give you my word of honor. . . that if a shyster lawyer gets him off, . . . I'll lead the lynching party, and we'll hang the negro and the shyster to the same branch of one tree." With shocking regularity, local authorities resorted to similar pledges to persuade mobs that lynching was unnecessary.[69]

Resolute law officers sometimes refused to offer any concessions to the mob and resorted to force to thwart a lynching. In 1895, the deputies protecting a prisoner in Clarke County had to fire warning shots before a mob threatening the jail dispersed. Five years later a Mecklenburg County constable showed perhaps more courage than prudence when he stood off a mob by drawing his pistol and warning that he intended to defend his prisoner "to the last extremity." And in 1920, in Wise County, a mob ignored the machine gun mounted atop the jail and opened fire on the sheriff and his deputies, who were protecting the building. They returned the fire, killing one mob member and wounding another.[70]

With growing frequency, local authorities turned to the state militia to quell mob violence during the 1890s. Although a mere show of force usually quieted threatening mobs, troops had to demonstrate readiness to use their weapons on several occasions. Militia called out in Norfolk in 1888 succeeded in clearing the streets around the jail only after they marched in ranks with fixed bayonets.[71] And the Roanoke militia had fired on a mob in September 1893, killing seven and wounding at least twenty-five. Between 1880 and 1908, sheriffs, superior court judges, and mayors requested militia from the governor to protect prisoners and disperse mobs on forty-three occasions, a total that far exceeded the totals for every other southern state, with the exception of Texas.[72]

Virginia's urban authorities, undoubtedly concerned about the potential damage and bloodshed if mob violence went unchecked, were particularly conscientious opponents of lynching. When mobs appeared in the streets and threatened jails, mayors usually were quick to request troops from the governor. City authorities also adopted various tactics of crowd control, such as ordering fire companies to turn their hoses on a mob or ordering police to arrest its members. In 1904, police in Fredericksburg arrested two members of a mob that had attempted to break into the town jail and murder a black prisoner. Also in 1904, a well-organized mob in Danville tried to take advantage of the absence of the local militia, but the mayor had eighteen of the mob members arrested. Several received sentences ranging from thirty days in jail to a $50 fine and sixty days in jail. Similarly, in 1908, the mayor of Portsmouth had several members of a mob arrested when they tried to lynch two blacks charged with assault. Although several belonged to prominent local families, the mayor insisted on prosecuting them. To his great irritation, however, a jury refused to convict any of them.[73]

After lynchings, local authorities typically showed little inclination to prosecute mob members. County officials recognized the potential political costs and social ostracism they might be subjected to if they did so. Nevertheless, commonwealth attorneys or city officials ignored local sentiment on several occasions and attempted to prosecute lynchers. Following the Roanoke lynching riot of 1893, for example, local authorities brought charges against sixteen members of the mob, but only three were convicted. Even the stiffest sentences only amounted to thirty days' imprisonment and a $100 fine. In 1902, the commonwealth attorney of Loudoun County endured harsh criticism when he prosecuted fifteen men accused of participating in the lynching of a black. After a long and often bitter trial, the jury acquitted them all. Yet in a few exceptional instances, prosecution of mob members resulted in convictions. In 1898, the commonwealth attorney of Patrick County successfully prosecuted six men who had participated in the lynching of a white man charged with rape, and in 1920, the commonwealth attorney of Wise County secured the conviction of the leader of a mob that had murdered a black.[74]

That commonwealth attorneys often failed to convince juries to convict mob members underscores the frustrations that conscientious authorities confronted when local sentiment supported mob violence. Yet, their efforts indicate the deliberate if lonely struggle that many local officials waged to harass and punish lynchers. Moreover, such attempts at prosecution are in marked contrast to the inaction of local officials in Georgia and other southern states.[75]

The motives that drove local authorities to prevent lynchings or prosecute mob members remain obscure in most instances. Concern for the preservation of social order and the maintenance of respect for legal authority almost certainly were paramount. Humanitarian concern for victims either was absent or never admitted publicly. Whatever the particular motivations, by moving prisoners, calling out the militia to protect alleged criminals during trials, or promising mobs that prisoners would receive a speedy trial, local authorities did help to curb lynching.

The commitment to law and order that played such a prominent part of any white opposition to mob violence also provided an opening for blacks to combat lynching. Just as a shared devotion to institutional justice enabled Governor O'Ferrall and John Mitchell to work together, so, too, it sometimes roused blacks and whites alike to diffuse racial tensions and prevent lynchings in communities gripped by hysteria in the aftermath of a crime. For example, in 1909, in the town of Glen Wilton in western Virginia, a murder allegedly committed by a black miner threatened to provoke a wholesale pogrom against all blacks in the community. Local blacks, including several ministers, met with concerned local whites, in particular a prominent woman. By posting signs warning that "all bad negroes must quit town," the black community hoped to mollify white concerns about black lawlessness. Local officials moved the alleged murderer to a safe jail, and tensions subsided. As one white later observed, "what's the use of having race trouble when the good negroes want to be good?"[76]

There were clear limits, however, beyond which whites would not accept black tactics against mob violence. For rural blacks, the only available recourse often was spontaneous and unorganized protests. As long as indirect forms of protest were adopted, white anger usually was not aroused. For example, in late August 1917, after a mob lynched a black in Northumberland County, blacks refused to work for the leader of the mob even though he offered them double wages.

When blacks employed more militant methods, however, they risked the severest sanctions. Individuals sometimes fended off mobs fiercely and, in other cases, organized into unofficial militia to protect jailed blacks.[77] In 1904, for example, following the murder of a local black man at the hands of a small mob of whites, aroused blacks in a suburb of Norfolk took to the streets to protest both the lynching and the police's apparent complicity in the murder. Local authorities, who failed to intimidate the crowd, requested state militia "to restore order." Only after several tense days and numerous melées did a semblance of tranquility return.[78]

The black press proudly reported these incidents and urged readers to emulate such defiant stands. But the hazards of armed self-defense were obvious; it usually provoked local authorities to act swiftly to suppress any organized black opposition and, in addition, only rarely was countenanced by even conservative white critics of mob violence, who saw it as nothing more than another expression of lawlessness.

Not until the outbreak of World War I, when urban African-American activists in the state founded chapters of the NAACP, did permanent institutional opposition replace the spontaneous protest of the past. As early as 1914, students and faculty at Virginia Union University in Richmond had organized the first branch of the NAACP in the state, but interest in starting branches elsewhere was sporadic. The turning point for the organization in Virginia came in 1917, when the NAACP launched a drive to expand membership in the South. James Weldon Johnson, who was appointed field secretary and organizer for the NAACP in December 1916, set out on a strenuous speaking and organizing tour that included mass meetings in Richmond and Norfolk. He later recalled that his tour had not been "overwhelmingly successful," but that, at the very least, it had demonstrated that "everywhere there was a rise in the level of the Negro's morale." [79]

In the aftermath of Johnson's trip, blacks in Norfolk and Richmond established NAACP branches in 1917. The "quickening effect" that Johnson perceived among the southern black population increased during the war years, organization grew rapidly, and branches were organized in many of Virginia's most important cities and towns. By the end of 1918, branches had been chartered in the smaller cities of Charlottesville, Danville, Lynchburg, Portsmouth, Roanoke, and Salem, and in the following year branches opened in Alexandria, Graham, Louisa County, Martinsville, and Petersburg. Although enthusiasm seemed to wane during the immediate postwar years, blacks in Arlington, City Point, Leesburg, Newport News, and Staunton stirred up enough local interest to establish branches in their communities by 1921. [80]

The initial enthusiasm for the NAACP in Virginia eroded during the 1920s, and many branches succumbed to apathy, ineffective leadership, and white hostility. In Norfolk, for instance, after the initial fervor evoked by its founding faded, the local branch became moribund. After several failed attempts, it finally was revived in 1926. [81] In nearby Portsmouth, branch president David Harrell bitterly complained of the hurdles that he had to overcome in his decade-long struggle to sustain the organization. After its founding in 1918, the Portsmouth branch had to be revived and reorganized in 1927 and 1933. [82] The same pattern of early enthusiasm and slow disintegration held in Leesburg, Martinsville, Salem, and Staunton.

The Lynchburg, Roanoke, Richmond, and Norfolk (after 1926) branches, however, survived lapses in membership enthusiasm and, along with the national headquarters in New York, played important roles in voicing black anger over racial violence and organizing against discrimination in the courts.

In most regards, the arrival of the NAACP in the region did not mark a dramatic departure from earlier methods of agitating against mob violence. As a staunch defender of law and order, the organization typically was circumspect rather than confrontational. It attempted to reform racial inequities by pressuring white officials to prevent or punish mob violence, by providing legal representation for alleged black criminals, and by publicizing racial outrages. The infrequency of mob violence in Virginia by the early twentieth century led local branches to devote their resources to pressing urban problems, and only rarely did the organization extend its reach into the countryside.

Residential segregation, rather than lynching, was the preeminent concern of most branches of the NAACP in Virginia.[83] In 1917 the Virginia Union University branch gave an early indication of the priorities of many Virginia branches when it appealed to national headquarters to return a recent contribution to the national antilynching fund. "Now that the segregation fight is on," the vice president of the branch asked, "we would like to know if it would not be better for us to use that money in this present fight."[84] With attention understandably focused on urban problems, rural blacks, for all practical purposes, had to continue to rely upon their own strategies of defense against white attacks. Especially egregious attacks did stir urban NAACP branches to assist rural black communities, however, and the organization worked diligently to support efforts to investigate and prosecute participants in seven lynchings that occurred between 1918 and 1927.[85]

The mixture of caution and activism that typified the activities of the NAACP in Virginia was also evident in the antilynching activities of P. B. Young, the editor of the *Norfolk Journal and Guide* and one of the most influential blacks in the state during the 1920s and 1930s. After assuming the editorship of the newspaper in 1909, Young gradually turned the *Journal and Guide* into the most widely read black newspaper in Virginia, while at the same time gaining the attention and respect of prominent whites in Norfolk. Young's influence grew in direct proportion to his attempts to discourage the Great Migration northward during World War I and dismiss expressions of black militancy. In numerous editorials, he assured southern blacks that their brightest political and economic future lay in the South. At the same time, he openly appealed to Louis Jaffé, editor of the *Norfolk Virginian-Pilot,* and other prominent Norfolk whites—the "best white citizens"—to accept their obligations to blacks and, in particular, "to forestall bloodshed and riot."[86] Although a member of the Norfolk branch of the NAACP, Young disavowed the "agitation and protest" he associated with the national leaders of the organization and instead preferred to work for black advancement by building ties to the white establishment locally. He discovered common ground with Jaffé on the race relations issue in general and on lynching in particular. Jaffé almost certainly was in complete agreement with Young's belief that "able and safe" black leaders should join with "good white people" and "the best blood of the Old South" to preserve Virginia's "happy race relations." United both by their contempt for mob violence and its effects on blacks and whites alike, as well as by their opposition to any federal antilynching statute, the two men joined forces in their editorial columns to denounce lynching tirelessly.[87]

The immediate effectiveness of Young's editorials and the NACCP's actions against mob violence was modest. In an era when few whites welcomed outspoken attacks by blacks on the racial hierarchy and when the civil rights of blacks were repeatedly abridged, blacks in Virginia and elsewhere in the South lacked sufficient leverage to halt mob violence. But black agitators in Virginia, unlike those in many other states in the South, were not systematically intimidated or silenced, and some whites were attentive to at least some of their concerns. Some, especially John Mitchell, warned whites that lynching would not be endured silently and implied that black discontent could not be ignored. Others, including P. B. Young, urged that the races collaborate to crush extralegal violence. Some whites found the tone of these protests, especially Mitchell's, shrill, but others were sympathetic to an appeal to the best class of whites to blunt vicious racist attacks.

Blacks in Virginia in the early twentieth century, like their counterparts in other border states, confronted a dilemma when they campaigned for improvement in the comparatively peaceful race relations in the Old Dominion. They needed only look to the Deep South to see how dire conditions could be, including levels of persistent mob violence that were unheard of in Virginia, even at the end of the nineteenth century. Their challenge was to call for the advancement of blacks and yet not alienate white Virginians by appearing to be ungrateful troublemakers. However suffocating the paternalistic character of white concern, many black leaders adopted a strategy of defending the status quo which, for all of its shortcomings, remained preferable to the worst that the South had to offer.

The evolution of opposition to lynching in Virginia is but another reminder of the complexities of southern mob violence. Just as there is no one explanation for a phenomenon with as many insidious permutations as mob violence, so, too, no single explanation can explain either the opposition to or demise of lynching. For the practice of lynching to cease in Virginia or, for that matter, in the South as a whole, strong steps were needed either to suppress mob violence or to address the underlying socioeconomic tensions that were its catalysts. Mob violence would persist until legal authorities imposed social order or until whites repudiated the bloody practice.

The forces that mobilized against mob violence in Virginia during the 1890s were by no means without counterparts in other southern states. But, with the possible exception of Kentucky, circumstances in few other southern states were as favorable to opponents of mob violence as in Virginia. The demise of lynching in the state cannot be separated easily from the conditions that gave rise to lynching in the first place. Of crucial importance was the simple fact that mob violence was not nearly as integral to the logic of socioeconomic and race relations in Virginia as it was in many other southern states. It was because lynching was never as deeply rooted in Virginia as in Georgia, for example, that the unorganized opposition to mob lawlessness in the Old Dominion, with its theme of law and order, was ever effective at all. Throughout the South during the 1890s and early 1900s, various governors, including Andrew H. Longino of Mississippi, Emmett O'Neal of Alabama, and Duncan C. Heyward of South Carolina, championed law and order. Unlike Virginia's governors, however, they met with frustration and failure. While they pleaded endlessly for defense of the sanctity of the courts, their pleas alone could not supplant mob justice with court-imposed justice. Lynching in Mississippi and South Carolina was too deeply embedded in the fabric of social and economic relations to be disposed of by rhetoric alone. Moreover, Longino, Heyward, O'Neal, and other "law and order" governors faced severe—even withering—criticism for their stands against mob violence.

In Virginia, by contrast, ardent critics of mob violence faced only isolated criticism. The elitist, temperamentally conservative character of Virginia politics created precisely the sort of environment in which opposition rooted in fears about social order could take root and flourish. Moreover, the theme of law and order, at the heart of conservative white opposition to mob violence, allowed whites to ignore troubling questions about the sources of mob mentality. The issue for them quite simply was anarchy, not racism. Whereas later antilynching organizations in the Deep South took tentative steps toward revealing the complex causes of lynching by applying the methods and insights of the social sciences to the problem of mob violence, most white opponents in Virginia saw lynching as little more than glaring evidence of the absence of adequate popular devotion to legal authority.

Unlike later white opponents of lynching, only a few prominent Virginians recognized that mob violence raised the most profound questions about the values and traditions of southern whites. A small group of Baptist academics and ministers in Richmond did voice strong opposition to lynching on humanitarian grounds and worked to nudge the Baptist churches of the state to condemn mob violence publicly. In 1904, the group, led by Samuel C. Mitchell, who four years earlier had criticized Governor Tyler so sharply for his mishandling of the Emporia lynching, composed a "Protest Against Lynching" that was later adopted by the Virginia Baptist General Association. However, they were unable to move the association to do anything further, and it issued no subsequent declarations until the 1920s.[88] Although individual white ministers sometimes spoke out against mob violence in the aftermath of lynchings in their communities, none of the white churches in Virginia made any organized or sustained efforts to convince its members of the incompatibility of Christian values and mob violence. Thus, white opposition was largely bereft of compassion for either the black victims of mob violence or the black community that endured the wrenching pain of vigilante violence.

Because of the simple solution they proposed—justice at the hands of the courts rather than the mob—conservative white opponents of lynching in Virginia had no need to create enduring organizations. Instead, all that was needed was effective law enforcement and the temporary mobilization of all right-thinking citizens in mob-threatened communities. Whites even were willing to work with members of the black community as long as the intended goal was to defend the courts and legal authority from mob violence. Few believed that anything more than modest reforms in state laws aimed at strengthening the hand of state authorities was needed. These attitudes were hardly conducive to the creation of any progressively inclined white organizations committed to opposing mob violence. Consequently, in the 1920s when the Commission on Interracial Cooperation (CIC), with its program of interracial harmony and antilynching activism, spread across the South, Virginia whites responded tepidly at best. One of the organizers of the CIC in the state explained at a regional convention that Virginia was one of the most difficult states to organize because it was "one of the most conservative." The comparative infrequency of many of the most extreme forms of racial oppression—in particular, lynching—by the 1920s convinced many whites that race relations in Virginia hardly merited attention. As a CIC supporter noted with regret, white Virginians typically doubted that there was "any need of an inter-racial committee." The sheer lack of interest led CIC organizers "to pursue a course of safety rather than speed," and as a result the CIC was virtually stillborn in Virginia.[89] It should come as no surprise, then, that white Virginians, residents of the southern state in which mob violence had met with early opposition and had hosted the fewest lynchings, would play only the most inconspicuous role in any of the major antilynching organizations of the twentieth century.

Nothing more fully reveals the character of white opposition to mob violence in Virginia than the circumstances surrounding the passage of the first antilynching law in the state's history in 1928. The force behind the passage of the statute was not an antilynching organization, but rather was Louis I. Jaffé of the *Norfolk Virginian-Pilot*. A spate of lynchings during the mid-1920s troubled Jaffé, prompting him to launch a relentless editorial campaign denouncing extralegal violence. Although his editorials touched upon the barbarity of lynch mobs, he dwelled upon the theme that lynching was "a crime which is plainly destructive of guarantees which have been regarded as inviolate in Anglo-Saxon thinking and jurisprudence since Runnymede."[90]

Following the lynching of Leonard Woods in southwestern Virginia in November 1927, he implored Governor Harry F. Byrd to "find a means to force a showdown on this outrage." Jaffé's advocacy prompted the governor to request from the editor a draft proposal of antilynching legislation. The governor adopted the outline of Jaffé's legislation and, after modest changes, pushed the bill through the Virginia General Assembly. The new antilynching law, signed on March 14, 1928, gave the governor the authority to use state officers to investigate lynchings and try mob members. Furthermore, the legislation declared participation in a violent mob equivalent to committing a comparable crime as an individual. Jaffé took great pride in the passage of the antilynching law, which he viewed as the culmination of his advocacy for legislation making "the punishment of lynchers . . . a primary obligation of the State." In 1929 he was rewarded with the Pulitzer Prize for his editorials "on the lynching evil and [his] successful advocacy of legislation to prevent it." He had no doubt that the law was "an epochal measure" and was proud of the fact that no lynchings took place in Virginia after the law was adopted.[91]

The passage of the antilynching law was in equal measures the product of Jaffé's single-minded persistence and of new attitudes toward executive authority. The expansion of the governor's powers during the Byrd administration, of which the antilynching statue was part, reflected new notions of executive power that moved considerably beyond the narrow conceptions of the past.[92] Moreover, the Virginia law was a calculated effort to help stave off federal antilynching legislation, which Congress was threatening to pass, by demonstrating that the southern states had the means and the will to suppress mob lawlessness. The Virginia antilynching law is the culmination of a nearly forty-year campaign for social order rather than any victory for racial enlightenment.

On balance, then, the virtual demise of lynching in the state by 1904 did not mark a new era of racial harmony and tolerance. After all, the criminal justice system continued to punish blacks harshly, executing them with frightful regularity. Blacks, moreover, continued to bear the burdens of disfranchisement, segregation, poverty, and pervasive racism. Yet, the demise of lynching in Virginia lifted one of the most onerous badges of black oppression.

7

The Struggle against Lynching in Georgia, 1880–1910

It is ironic that although opposition to lynching in Georgia developed later than it did in Virginia, the challenge it posed to the state's traditions and institutions was far more profound. The sheer scale of lynching in Georgia, where mobs continued to claim large numbers of victims well into the twentieth century, demanded broader antilynching strategies and a more sustained effort than in Virginia. With each passing decade, the unremitting pervasiveness of lynching compelled critics to challenge conventional justifications for lynching and conceive of increasingly elaborate tactics to suppress mob violence. Neither repeated incantations of the slogan "law and order" nor simple solutions could end this complex and deeply embedded form of brutality.

The evolution of attitudes toward mob violence among Georgians suggests those elsewhere in the South. Throughout the 1880s, the course of debate and opposition to lynching followed similar lines. But during the 1890s, the response to lynching in Georgia and other states in the Deep South diverged sharply from that in Virginia. While opposition to mob violence mounted in Virginia during the 1890s, the ascendance of strident racists in Georgia intimidated persons opposed to lynching and greatly hampered efforts to turn public opinion against extralegal violence. The rise of extremist racism was not the single, sufficient reason for the astonishing levels of mob violence in Georgia between 1895 and 1910. But the intellectually sanctioned racial hysteria of the late 1890s and first decade of the new century legitimized the practice to a degree that was without parallel in Virginia. Opponents of lynching in Georgia faced the enormous task of finding an effective strategy to combat mob violence, while at the same time waging a continuous skirmish with ardent defenders of lynching.

Between 1880 and 1894, mobs in Georgia claimed the lives of one hundred and eleven people. The annual toll of mob violence rose from two lynchings in 1882 to fifteen at the end of the period, leaving virtually no region of the state unscarred. It was during the early 1890s that mob lawlessness peaked outside of the heartland of lynching in southern Georgia and the Cotton Belt and claimed victims from the mountain hollows of northwestern Georgia to the suburbs of Atlanta and the black hamlets along the coast.

The rise in the frequency of lynching did not go unnoticed. The worsening economic conditions and bitter political struggles that fanned class and racial tensions during the early 1890s provoked heated debates over the region's ills, including lynching. Despite the increasingly shrill tenor of the exchanges, publicly expressed attitudes toward lynching varied considerably. Outspoken advocates were few; instead, most Georgians who aired their views in public evidenced uneasiness about the prevalence of mob violence in their state.

The tone of race relations during the 1880s and early 1890s reflected the conservatism of the ruling Bourbon Democrats, in power since the close of Reconstruction. During the 1880s, their rule seemed to pacify the state and provide economic leadership and a solution to the "Negro problem" that dovetailed with the national mood. Henry W. Grady, the editor of the *Atlanta Constitution,* perhaps expressed most articulately the Bourbons' attitude toward race relations. He championed the supremacy of the white race but pledged that it would dominate "not through violence, not through party alliance, but through the integrity of its vote and the largeness of its sympathy and justice through which it shall compel the support of the better classes of the colored race." Similarly, in 1888, Governor Alfred H. Colquitt explained: "The people of the southern states are not so foolish as to believe that their peace, prosperity, or even their safety can be assured if a moiety [half] of the population is treated with injustice and denied its rights in the state." The Bourbons, who found hope for improved race relations in the progress that blacks had made since slavery, prophesied that, given time and freedom from meddling by northerners, they would oversee an era of harmonious race relations in the South.[1]

Many white newspaper editors embraced the Bourbon philosophy and urged whites to refrain from the flagrant violations of the legal rights of blacks. Lynching, they warned, bred disrespect for the law, disrupted social stability, and provoked blacks to seek revenge. In December 1889, after an unusually violent Christmas holiday, the *Savannah Morning News* pleaded with whites to "cultivate the best of feeling between the races, and the best way to do that is for the stronger race to treat the weaker one with absolute fairness and justice." Similarly, the *Atlanta*

Constitution cautioned that "just so long as a few reckless citizens are allowed to charge around assuming the functions of the courts, the South will be a veritable Poverty Flat, and capital and enterprise will refuse to cross our borders."[2]

However sincere the commitment of the Bourbons to tranquil race relations, their limited vision of the role of the state impeded any truly effective steps to protect blacks from white violence. The Bourbons in Georgia inherited an exceedingly weak state government and only marginally strengthened it before passing it along to their successors.[3] Because they possessed an inveterate fear of executive authority and centralized power, they displayed little capacity for effective leadership. Certainly none of the Bourbon governors demonstrated any resolve in the face of mounting mob violence.

Perhaps the best illustration of the limitations of the Bourbons' conception of the measures needed to suppress white violence is Governor Hugh D. McDaniel's handling of a lynching in Troup County in July 1884. On July 11, 1884, near the town of LaGrange, Willis Harden, a black farmhand, was arrested on the charge of raping a white woman. After a citizens' meeting to determine Harden's fate degenerated into a bloodthirsty mob, a friend of Harden's sent the governor a desperate telegram requesting protection. The governor responded by wiring the county sheriff that it was his sworn duty to protect the life of his prisoner. On the following day, the governor was again beseeched to use his authority to protect Harden, but this time the plea came from sheriff and mayor of LaGrange. Rather than sending the militia to LaGrange, the governor answered, with what to many must have been embarrassing naiveté, that "a proper use of municipal authority, aided by the sheriff and supported by law-abiding citizens" would preserve order. With no state aid forthcoming, the mayor ordered the sheriff to remove Harden from the town limits, whereupon a mob captured and hanged him. McDaniel's listless response typified the inaction of Bourbon leaders throughout the 1880s. None did more than offer rewards for information leading to the arrest of lynchers, perfunctory steps that produced neither evidence against nor convictions of mob members.[4]

The growing incidence of mob violence and the failure of state authorities to suppress mobs incensed blacks. Black leaders in Georgia loudly denounced lynching, but, like their counterparts elsewhere in the South, had great difficulty devising an effective strategy to combat mob violence. The Republican party in Georgia was degenerating into a "quarrelsome lot of office-seekers and contentious factionalists," and blacks could not count on it to protect their civil rights.[5] During the late 1880s, many black Republicans, often at loggerheads with white party members, increasingly resented the party's neglect. As the editor of a black newspaper in Valdosta fumed, "The Negro's vote keeps the Republican party in power yet the party does not protect him. He's lynched every day in the South. It should not surprise anybody if to save his life and property he goes over to the third party [the Populists] or the Democrats." [6]

Blacks continually entreated white leaders to live up to their paternalistic rhetoric by suppressing lynching. They struggled to build protest organizations that could pressure whites while simultaneously appealing to the "best class" of whites to uphold the law and protect them from mob violence. In public meetings, editorials, sermons, and even in an occasional demonstration, they condemned increasing white violence. And in exceptional instances blacks armed themselves to protect alleged criminals threatened with violence. In 1882, for example, a group in Athens led by William A. Pledger, a prominent black politician and editor, rescued from the clutches of an angry mob two black men who had shot and killed a white university student. Similarly, in 1892, armed blacks congregated around the Macon city jail to protect a black man charged with the murder of a white. For whatever reasons, in both instances no lynching occurred. [7]

More often, blacks voiced their protests at local and state conventions. On at least three occasions, blacks in Atlanta organized meetings to protest white attacks and call upon state authorities to guarantee that the perpetrators would be prosecuted. [8] In January 1888, upon the call of the Reverend William J. White, editor of the *Augusta Georgia Baptist,* 350 black Georgians met in Macon to address the pressing problems their race faced. The convention strongly denounced lynchings, as well as inadequate schools and the racism of the criminal justice system. It also urged the state's blacks to support only those candidates who would endorse reform of the criminal justice system, full civil and political rights for blacks, and legislation to suppress lynching. [9] Evidently nothing came of either the Macon convention of 1888 or the various Atlanta meetings. Yet, indirectly, these and other smaller protests glaringly demonstrated that mob violence was of paramount concern to blacks.

Whether it was because of political expediency, a dilatory sense of justice, or the tug of paternalism, some white politicians responded to black concerns about mob violence. At a time when black Georgians still retained the vote, the hotly contested political battles between the Populists and Democrats during the early 1890s encouraged politicians to compete vigorously for their favor. By promising to take strong action against lynchings, both the Populist and Democratic parties hoped to sway black voters. In 1892, and again in 1894, the two parties took similar stands on lynching. In 1894 the Populist party passed a resolution denouncing the "evil practice of lawless persons taking the law into their own hands," while the Democratic platform condemned "every form and species of mob violence and lynch law." [10]

More important, political expediency and contempt for the lawlessness of mobs prompted the Democratic governor, William J. Northen, to campaign for reelection in 1892, stressing opposition to mob violence and, following his election victory, to use his annual address to the legislature to call for laws against lynching. Although Governor Northen had been elected as part of an agrarian backlash against the Bourbon leadership in power, neither his beliefs nor his actions marked a dramatic break with his predecessors. In many regards he represented the most humane face of Bourbon democracy. Descended from wealthy planter stock in the Cotton Belt, Northen first achieved distinction as a champion of agricultural reform and as a religious leader. From the time of his conversion in 1853, he served the Baptist church throughout his life, rising to hold the offices of president of the Georgia Baptist Convention, the Southern Baptist Convention, and vice president of the American Bible Society.

Although his political and economic beliefs were thoroughly conventional, Northen displayed a vague understanding of the changes underway in Georgia and a commitment to modest measures to ameliorate the dislocations they caused. His instinctive conservatism, as evidenced by his unshakable faith in the Democratic party, was complimented by his instinctive devotion to the paternalistic stewardship of hard-pressed rural Georgians. Like Governor O'Ferrall of Virginia, with whom he shared many traits, Northen found no justification for lynching in the shrill cry for white supremacy. That Northern was troubled by the mounting carnage in Georgia was but another expression of his conservative sensibilities and paternalistic Christian impulses. [11]

Governor Northen was far more active than previous governors in trying to find a way to suppress mob violence. In 1893 the legislature answered his request for antilynching legislation by passing a law requiring law officers to summon a posse to prevent mob violence. Sheriffs who failed to follow the law could be charged with a misdemeanor; participants in the mob could be charged with committing a felony, or, if death resulted from their actions, murder. After the passage of the antilynching statute, Northen sent a letter to all Georgia sheriffs, informing them of the new law. On one occasion, at his own expense, he had a black man who was threatened by a mob rushed to Atlanta for safekeeping. He repeatedly denounced lynchings and warned that he would call out the militia to disperse mobs if necessary. The governor's prodding seems to have had some effect; for the first time, local authorities began to request troops to prevent lynchings. [12]

Neither Northen's public stand nor the antilynching law halted mobs from taking the law into their own hands, however. The antilynching law was too broad and left the prosecution of lynchers and derelict sheriffs to local authorities, who were unlikely to prosecute. Some legislators recognized these shortcomings and later in the decade offered various amendments to strengthen the law, but their attempts failed, and even if the revisions had passed they would have accomplished little. As Sol C. Johnson, editor of the black weekly the *Savannah Tribune* bitterly observed, "negroes in Georgia were lynched before the proclamation, after the proclamation, and will continue to be lynched so long as the State winks at the lawlessness of her citizens." [13]

By nature cautious and suspicious of innovation, the Bourbon leaders of Georgia were not well suited to handle the problem of swelling mob violence. As much as possible they preferred to overlook racial violence and other signs of racial tensions, electing instead to emphasize their paternalistic guardianship of blacks. Even Governor Northen, who refused to disregard lynching, could not envision the broad measures needed to suppress mob violence. Unable to comprehend fully the society they sought to lead, both the Bourbons and Northen assumed that once law-abiding communities were armed with the appropriate sanctions, they would stamp out lynching. Their antilynching remedies, including the 1893 antilynching statute, rested upon the untested assumption that most Georgians could be relied upon to oppose extralegal violence. But, of course, in much of Georgia, where violence and intimidation were woven into labor and race relations, it was patently absurd to assume that some vague commitment to law and order would prevail over the far stronger conventions of localism and routine extralegal violence. Moreover, the Bourbon ethos failed to win the allegiance of the mass of white Georgians and, when challenged by popular attitudes that were increasingly hostile to blacks, it quickly collapsed.

At first glance, responses to lynching in Georgia and Virginia between 1880 and 1894 are similar. During the 1880s, while frustrated blacks railed against the savagery of white mobs and the inaction of state authorities, conservative white Democrats ignored the worsening violence in their states. When the level of mob violence could no longer be ignored, whites in power finally took steps to confront the problem. In their respective states at nearly the same moment, Governors Northen and O'Ferrall pleaded for respect for law and order and proposed measures to suppress mob violence. But beyond this, the similarities break down. The myriad conditions that contributed to the success of state and local authorities in Virginia were largely absent in Georgia. No counterpart to the Roanoke lynching stirred deep fears of anarchy, and there was neither the unity within the Democratic party nor the broad commitment to the New South's creed to ease the work of conservative whites opposed to lynching. Just how formidable the obstacles to any antilynching efforts in Georgia were would become evident during the next two decades.

Between 1895 and 1910 a decisive shift occurred in the tone and substance of discussions of race relations in Georgia and throughout much of the South. A wave of harsh racism swept away the Bourbon notion of race relations and revolutionized popular attitudes toward blacks. Racial violence swelled to record levels. One hundred and fifty four blacks and six whites were lynched in Georgia in the fifteen years under discussion. On average, mobs executed ten victims a year, and in 1899, the bloodiest year of mob violence in the state's history, mobs claimed the lives of twenty-six victims. Serious race riots also broke out in several Georgia cities, including the particularly violent Atlanta race riot of 1906.[14]

That racial violence persisted, and even worsened after the depression of the 1890s had eased and a degree of prosperity had returned to the state, is testimony to the depth of the social tensions. The continued violence of mobs also confirms John W. Cell's observation that historians should be wary of relying on the agricultural distress of the 1890s to explain such complex phenomena as disfranchisement, segregation, and racial violence. The specific forces that poisoned race relations in Georgia included the rise of a new generation of racial extremists, the bitterness borne of the collapse of Populism, the uneasiness of whites prompted by the training and stationing of black troops in the state during the Spanish-American War, and the anger of southern whites aroused by the racial policies of the Republican administrations of William McKinley and Theodore Roosevelt.[15]

To a great extent, the taproot of the inflamed debate over race relations was the bitter legacy of the political struggles of the 1890s. Both Populists and Democrats had stooped to blatant racial demagoguery during their political clashes. In one example of Democratic fulminations, Senator John B. Gordon, a Confederate war hero and the embodiment of the Bourbon Democrats, charged Tom Watson, the state's most prominent Populist, with weakening white supremacy and thereby threatening "our spotless, pure and peerless southern womanhood." [16] Even the Populists, who initially shied away from openly racist appeals, lashed out with racist invective at their opponents. In the most extreme instance, during the gubernatorial campaign of 1896 they charged Democratic Governor William Y. Atkinson with encouraging blacks to rape white women. They offered the governor's pardoning of a black man convicted of rape as evidence for their remarkable claim.[17]

The escalating racist rhetoric was legitimized and elaborated by a group of racial extremists, including intellectuals, politicians, and rabble-rousers. In Georgia, the most prominent radicals were journalists and politicians, whose large audience extended well beyond the boundaries of the state. Among the journalists were Charles E. Smith, better known by his pseudonym Bill Arp, of the *Atlanta Constitution;* Rebecca Lattimer Felton of the *Atlanta Journal;* and John Temple Graves of the *Atlanta News.* The loudest political expressions of the racist dogma came from Governor Hoke Smith, also editor of the *Atlanta Journal,* and the increasingly embittered Tom Watson.[18]

In an era of rising violence, these strident racists offered both an explanation and a justification for the barbaric acts of whites against blacks. They replaced the assumptions of Bourbon race relations with a portrait of the black as "beast-rapist who needed to be held down by force as he degenerated toward extinction."[19] Convinced that there was a natural antipathy between the races and that an alleged epidemic of black crime exposed the enmity that the new generation of blacks harbored against whites, the racial extremists exhorted whites to use all tools at their disposal to meet the black "threat." The menace that provoked the greatest concern was the black rapist, who, the radicals argued, was the product of black participation in politics, of vagrancy, and of "free schools with the Boston social equality attachment."[20] In an exercise in rhetoric that could have served as the creed of the extremists, Rebecca Lattimer Felton linked the black rapist to pandering white politicians, who purchased black votes with liquor. Black men, whose passions were inflamed by the ill-gotten whiskey, attacked white women in a vain attempt to satisfy their lust for social equality.[21] Thus the radicals warned that the black threat was an outgrowth of the host of social ills that afflicted the South and must not be viewed merely as isolated crimes by aberrant blacks.

In light of the magnitude of the alleged threat to whites, the strident racists loudly defended lynchings as the justifiable response of a desperate people. In 1897, Rebecca Lattimer Felton attracted national attention by announcing during an address to the State Agricultural Society of Georgia that "if it takes lynching to protect women's dearest possession from drunken, ravening human beasts, then I say lynch a thousand a week if it becomes necessary."[22] Bill Arp echoed Mrs. Felton: "As for lynching, I repeat what I have said before, let the good work go on. Lynch em! Hang em! Shoot em! Burn em!"[23] In these and other emotional pleas, the radicals shifted the defense of lynching from a necessary evil to a positive good.

The hysterical ranting of the racial extremists almost suffocated dissenting opinions regarding mob violence. The journalist Wilbur Cash went so far as to suggest that during the late nineteenth century the South succumbed to a "savage ideal" of racial orthodoxy, "whereunder dissent and variety are completely suppressed and men become, in all their attitudes, professions, and actions, virtual replicas of one another." [24] Ready with acerbic pens and race-baiting oratory, the radicals savaged any southerners who dared to criticize mob violence. In 1898, when Dr. J. B. Hawthorne, a prominent Methodist minister in Nashville, discounted the views of Rebecca Lattimer Felton and others as unrepresentative of popular opinion, Mrs. Felton responded furiously by labeling him a "slick-haired, slick-tongued Pecksniffian blatherskite." Henceforth, she carried on a protracted feud with Hawthorne and never missed an opportunity to malign him in her weekly newspaper column and her correspondence. In the most notorious radical assault on the free discussion of race relations, Andrew Sledd, a young professor at Emory University, endured a hail of public scorn for writing an article in the *Atlantic Monthly* in 1902 that called for an end to lynching and a calm, reasoned discussion of race relations. The ever-vigilant Mrs. Felton, infuriated by Sledd's willingness to criticize the South in a northern journal, led the campaign that finally forced him to resign his position and move North.[25]

Racial extremists found ready allies within the ranks of rural newspaper editors. They sensed the growing divisions between rural and urban Georgians and spoke in terms that resonated across the rural hinterland. By giving mob violence the loftiest of justifications for lynching, at least in the eyes of contemporary whites, the radicals provided rural editors with illusionary explanations that ignored the role that lynching played in the exploitation of black labor. Moreover, by parroting the radical defense of lynching, most rural editors rebutted even the slightest hint of condemnation of their communities after a lynching. They scoffed at urban critics who, they claimed, lived in policed cities safely removed from the daily dangers that blacks posed to rural whites. As the editor of the *Crawfordville Advocate-Democrat* asked of Georgians who publicly lamented lynchings in 1903, "What's the use of forever apologizing for doing something that is necessary and proper." The *Statesboro News* observed that although the many urban editors in Savannah and Atlanta were opposed to the rhetoric and philosophy of the extreme racists, "the people are not." [26]

The radicals' charge that critics of mob violence were prissy urbanites carried more than a germ of truth. Prominent among the opponents of lynching were urban newspaper editors, ministers, and influential jurists and lawyers. Opponents of lynching included conservatives who remained committed to a nostalgic paternalism and moderates who advocated a more humanitarian direction in race relations. Even as they remained devoted to the ethos of white supremacy, some urban whites watched with mounting anxiety the persistent barbarity of lynching in the state. Although urban leaders shared much in common with elites throughout the state, they placed different meaning and emphasis on social stability. Increasingly, they worried that extralegal violence was an expression of a crude, irrational, and dangerous rural culture. Moreover, as urban elites in Georgia began to confront such problems as high crime rates and social unrest, problems created by urban growth, their toleration for lawlessness began to evaporate.[27]

Most white Georgians who opposed lynching agreed with the radicals that the origins of mob violence in the postwar South could be traced to the predictable, even laudable, response of whites to attacks by black men on white women. But, the opponents argued, whites showed a worrisome tendency to expand upon the crimes they defined as punishable by rope and torch. If left unchecked, the critics warned, uncontrolled mob violence would lead to anarchy. Thus, many whites who protested against lynching emphasized their concern about the scale of mob violence but did not denounce lynching categorically.[28]

Opponents of lynching also cautioned that continued racial violence would prompt northern interference in southern race relations. They were especially troubled by federal prosecution of the participants in lynchings in Huntsville and Chattanooga and of southern planters charged with violating federal peonage laws. Although federal prosecution was forthcoming only in very rare instances in which mobs trampled federal authority, critics hoped that the fear of northern intervention would provoke local authorities to act against lynching and persuade public opinion to shift away from an open embrace of mob violence.[29]

Despite the best intentions, the white opponents of lynching during this period stumbled because of their lack of understanding of the underlying roots of mob violence. Instead of addressing the pervasive racism of both the criminal justice system and labor relations, most critics of lynching viewed segregation, prohibition, and disfranchisement as the best solutions to the problem of racial violence. In an era of vituperative, fanatical racism, segregation and disfranchisement seemed to offer an alternative to continuous racial strife. By separating the races as much as possible and by depriving blacks of liquor—the alleged inspiration for black crime—it was believed that the dangerous friction that produced racial violence would be removed. The connection between mob violence and segregation as a solution to the problem of racial violence was made explicit in Augusta in May 1900 after the murder of a prominent young white man by a black man. The murder, which followed an altercation over seats on a streetcar, prompted editors of the city's white dailies to denounce the absence of streetcar segregation in the city. In short order, the murder roused the Augusta city council to pass a Jim Crow law segregating the street cars and a mob to lynch the alleged killer.[30]

Aside from Jim Crow reforms, white critics of lynching offered few solutions or strategies to combat the problem of mob violence. A few Georgians, including Governor William Y. Atkinson (1894–98), argued that, in light of the almost universal failure of local authorities to prevent lynchings, state authority must be expanded to meet the challenge of mob lawlessness. In his five annual and special messages to the state legislature, Atkinson called for laws providing for removing from office any official who surrendered a prisoner to a mob, stiffening the punishment for men who failed to respond to summons to form a posse to protect a prisoner, and giving a mob victim's family the right to sue to recover damages. In his last address he scolded lawmakers for failing to fulfill campaign promises to enact laws against lynching, but Atkinson's tongue-lashing failed to move the legislators to act on his proposals.[31]

Opponents of lynching made frequent appeals for the creation of a statewide rural police force to prevent crime, preserve order, and assuage the fears of rural whites who felt threatened by roving black criminals. But such proposals flew in the face of the state's traditions of entrenched localism, dispersed authority, and parsimonious government. However reasonable the idea of state police may have been, it was too innovative for contemporary notions of the state.[32]

Finally, critics routinely called for the establishment of an organization devoted to suppressing lawlessness. The only attempt to create law-and-order committees, however, was a conspicuous failure. After the Atlanta race riot of 1906, former governor William J. Northen led a short-lived campaign to combat lawlessness and improve race relations. Drawing upon the example of the Christian League, an interdenominational organization in Atlanta with both white and black members, Northen proposed that local leagues be created throughout the state as forums in which whites and blacks could voice their grievances and nurture sentiment against mob violence.[33] He traveled to more than eighty counties in the state, delivering speeches that denounced lynching and outlining his proposal for local committees. His visits were so well received that he concluded that "public opinion on law & order is rapidly changing for the better."[34]

Northen's campaign did lead to the creation of committees in many towns and counties, but they disappeared after initial interest waned. More important, Northen's personal campaign lacked both an enduring organization and any tangible goal beyond drumming up support for the suppression of crime. Characteristically, Northen and other white critics of mob violence failed to organize carefully as they and their contemporaries had done to combat such other troublesome social problems as public health and child labor.[35]

Underlying the failure to devise a strategy was the general agreement with some of the basic tenets of the racial extremists. Governor Allen D. Candler, whose term in office coincided with the bloodiest years of mob violence in the state's history, exemplified the contradictory character of the moderate's views on lynching when he denounced the epidemic of mob violence that broke out in 1899, while at the same time blaming blacks for provoking whites by rampant criminality and persistent striving for social equality. Even a dedicated opponent of lynching like Governor Northen was so deeply disturbed by the rampant violence he saw in black communities and the threat that it posed to whites that his speeches against lynching left many of his contemporaries believing that he condoned mob violence.[36]

A prickly defensiveness toward northern criticism contributed to the confused arguments of white opponents of lynching. Moderates bitterly resented the apparent moral hypocrisy of northerners who turned a blind eye on the widespread lawlessness in the North while censuring all southerners for lynching. At their worst, the harangues of moderates against northern critics lapsed into the same vitriolic defense of white supremacy and regional chauvinism that characterized the fulminations of the racial extremists.[37]

Such confused and timid white opposition to lynching provided little incentive for Georgia's state officials to take forceful steps against mob violence. Although most governors spoke out against lawlessness, they had little effect. With few exceptions, chief executives during the period were men of modest distinction, little achievement, and no great prestige or influence in the state. Consequently their public denunciations of lynching appear to have exerted little influence. They also were shackled by the weak powers of their office and the absence of virtually any administrative apparatus. Moreover, whenever a governor publicly condemned mob violence or boldly dared exercise his limited powers to suppress lynching, he faced the stinging criticism of the racial extremists.[38]

The impotence of state officials was clearly illustrated in 1904, when Governor James M. Terrell (1903–7) punished several state militia officers who had failed to prevent the lynching of two black men in the south Georgia town of Statesboro. At the request of local authorities the governor had sent militia companies from Savannah to protect Paul Reed and Will Cato, turpentine hands charged with the murder of a white family. The militia prevented any lawlessness during the trial of the men, but at its conclusion a mob stormed the courthouse, overpowered the troops, and seized the prisoners. The mob then took the men out of town, chained them to a stump, and burned them alive.[39]

The mob's blatant contempt for state authority, and the shocking incompetence of Captain Robert M. Hitch, the militia commander, provoked disbelief and outrage in the ranks of the militia and among those Georgians already troubled by the persistent lawlessness in the state. Governor Terrell quickly appointed a commission to investigate the lynching and determine if Hitch and his subordinate officers should be court-martialed. When the governor accepted the commission's recommendation for a court-martial, defenders of mob violence immediately rallied in support of Captain Hitch. Mob members, who openly boasted of their participation in the lynching, dared the state to attempt to prosecute them and even raised money to buy Hitch an engraved sword as an expression of their esteem. (Whether the sword was ever delivered to Hitch remains a mystery.) John Temple Graves and the editors of country weeklies throughout the state leaped to the defense of Statesboro's reputation and excoriated the governor for wasting state funds to punish honorable white soldiers rather than black rapists. Editorials went so far as to urge Hitch to campaign for the governorship that fall. Indeed, some voters did scratch out Terrell's name on the ballot and wrote in his name. Support for Hitch and his officers remained high even after the governor dismissed them from the militia, and they pilloried Terrell in a widely printed public letter.[40]

Unlike the Roanoke lynching of 1893, which raised concern about mob rule and led many Virginians to call for stronger action to suppress mob violence, the Statesboro lynching only fueled the continuing debate between critics of lynching and its defenders. In contrast to the response to the Emporia lynching in Virginia in 1900, when Governor Tyler was rebuked for failing to do enough, Governor Terrell was criticized for taking eminently justified—if modest—steps to punish state officials for obvious incompetence.

Local authorities who bucked tradition and attempted to prevent lynchings were just as likely to face condemnation. Sheriffs who transferred prisoners to distant jails for safekeeping could expect to endure considerable local criticism. Similarly, courageous sheriffs who faced down angry mobs in turn faced the prospect of defeat when they ran for reelection. And local authorities who requested local militia to disperse a mob met with criticism for wasting county and state funds to protect the lives of black criminals.[41]

The failure of state and local authorities to protect blacks from mounting white attacks predictably bred resentment, frustration, and anger in the black community. Whereas political expediency and a commitment to the Bourbon code of race relations had led some white politicians during the 1880s and early 1890s to accept the legitimacy of black demands for the suppression of lynching and the punishment of lynchers, most state or local politicians during the late 1890s and the first decade of the twentieth century displayed little if any sympathy for any expressions of black protest. For example, in April 1899, following the gruesome lynchings of Sam Holt and several other blacks in the state, a group of prominent blacks in Atlanta, including W. E. B. Du Bois, then a professor at Atlanta University, entreated Governor Candler to use his influence and authority to protect blacks. His response is revealing only because it was so regrettably conventional. Despite the deferential tone of the plea and the stress it placed upon the seemingly noncontroversial issue of the preservation of law and order, Candler responded with a statement that parroted the prosaic wisdom of the most strident racists. With all seriousness, the governor announced that "the whole trouble of these disorders is traceable to politics." "The prime cause of all friction" between whites and blacks, he explained, was the "scalawags and carpet-baggers, who came here and took charge of him [the negro], filled his head full of false ideas, characterized him the ward of the nation, and for partisan purposes, induced him to believe that he would be protected by the general government." As far as Candler was concerned, the legislature could do little more than had already been done with regard to mob violence. The only solution was for "good negroes" to build up "a sentiment in their race against the diabolical crimes which are always at the back of these lynchings."[42] Thus, the only possibility for common cause by state authorities and blacks that Candler offered was a campaign against black moral degeneracy, a campaign that even the most conservatively inclined blacks could not easily join without condoning the most debilitating racist stereotypes.

The boundaries, then, which circumscribed black protest were drawn much more tightly in Georgia than in Virginia. Moreover, the limited extent of black landownership, the pervasiveness of poverty, and the precariousness of black institutions in the regions where lynching was most deeply rooted all impeded vigorous black activism. This is not to suggest that blacks did not find opportunities to denounce mob violence; they were hardly complacent in its face. However, the strategies they adopted in much of Georgia were necessarily different than those blacks followed in Virginia or even in Atlanta. It is a mistake to look to the Cotton Belt or to southern Georgia for sustained campaigns against mob violence by such reformers as John Mitchell, or even spontaneous demonstrations of the magnitude of the 1899 "Insurrection" in the coastal town of Darien. Given the pervasiveness of white violence and white scrutiny of black conduct, blacks necessarily adopted furtive means to condemn attacks. At best, protest in most of rural Georgia released some repressed anger and preserved blacks' sense of dignity. For all of their creativity and courageousness, however, they could not halt or even seriously impede whites intent on violence.

Blacks in rural Georgia, like their counterparts throughout the South, sought protection through a variety of strategies, ranging from flight to self-defense, but the specific social environment of each region made each response unique. An appeal for protection against extralegal violence on grounds of need to maintain the sanctity of the courts made no sense in the Cotton Belt and southern Georgia, where legal rights for blacks were little more than abstractions. Merely criticizing mob violence openly could incite white retaliation.[43]

The consequences of violent resistance for the black community extended beyond just those individuals who brazenly defied whites. Black communities and institutions frequently became the targets of destruction by marauding whites in the aftermath of acts of self-defense. Even black fraternal organizations were threatened.[44] Although whites had laid waste to black institutions throughout the late nineteenth century, the magnitude of attacks during the early twentieth century reached levels comparable only to those of Reconstruction. The cumulative effect of the pogromlike attacks on black communities, the dynamiting of black churches and lodges, and the razing of black schools was profound and far-reaching. The violence committed against individual insubordinate blacks, in conjunction with the havoc inflicted upon black institutions, became an object lesson for entire black communities and drove home the repercussions of rebelliousness.

Fully aware of the costs of overt resistance, rural blacks had few alternatives but to seek the protection of whites from lynch mobs. Because few planters were willing to renounce extralegal violence categorically, there was little chance to create a coalition to suppress lynching. Appeals for protection necessarily entailed a sacrifice of black independence because they could not be separated from a planter's prerogatives or paternalism. For rural blacks who lacked—or refused to depend upon—white protectors, flight was one of the few responses to white violence that was independent of whites and yet typically did not inspire retaliation. In countless instances, news of impending mob actions prompted blacks to flee their homes and hide in isolated forests or swamps.[45]

In many instances, whites ignored black protests, but on occasion they violently suppressed them. The repressive atmosphere bore down on virtually all blacks who questioned the practices that relegated them second-class citizens. Black editors, among the most persistent crusaders for black rights, were occasional targets of white hostility. In 1900, a mob threatened the life of William J. White, editor of the *Augusta Georgia Baptist,* after he denounced a local lynching. In 1906, a white mob, inspired by news of the Atlanta race riot, again threatened White and forced him to flee the city. Similarly, J. Max Barber, editor of the periodical *Voice of the Negro,* was compelled to abandon his magazine and leave the city after he aroused the anger of whites in Atlanta in 1906 by blaming the city's race riot on several local newspapers.[46]

In light of the immense obstacles to black activism against lynching during the era of ascendant racial extremism, it is difficult to know how to measure the short-comings and achievements of black antilynching efforts. Through both design and habit, whites thwarted such efforts at every turn. Black activists were ignored or ridiculed, whites were unable or unwilling to create their own organizations to carry on the struggle against mob violence, and white authorities all too often were blind or even sympathetic to the violent intimidation by white mobs.

Perhaps the best measure of the achievements of black antilynching efforts between 1880 and 1910 is that blacks unequivocally refused to accept the legitimacy of white justifications for mob violence. While the attitudes of Georgia blacks toward the tightening noose of segregation, disfranchisement, and strident racism ranged from pragmatic acceptance to black nationalism, none made any conces-sions to white justifications. The survival of a vision of dignity and freedom from violence and coercion in the midst of a hostile, racist environment must stand as the signal accomplishment and enduring legacy of black antilynching efforts between 1880 and 1910.

From the vantage point of Georgians who opposed mob violence, there was little reason for optimism at the end of the first decade of the twentieth century. The tally of mob executions remained at virtually the same level as the previous de-cade's: mobs murdered one hundred and one Georgians between 1900 and 1909, compared with one hundred and thirteen during the 1890s. Moreover, there was little visible evidence that popular sentiment against mob violence had shifted. What "progress" had been made in public attitudes toward lynching was riddled with compromises with the very values that gave legitimacy to mob violence. Contemporaries would have needed the skills of a trained logician to distinguish most public criticisms of mob violence from justifications. The tortured arguments of whites who did not unequivocally champion mob violence reflected the tug of competing values. Torn between a commitment to law and order and sympathy for the traditional justifications for mob violence, concerned whites were immobi-lized by indecision and confusion. When a mob executed a black man accused of rape in the nearby town of Cordele in February 1912, the editor of the *Americus Times-Recorder* felt called upon to assess the future of mob violence in the state. Lynching, he soberly explained, "is unlawful, it is, in a sense, a black spot on the state, it has its injurious effect on the public mind in more ways than one. . . .

We may deprecate them as much as we will, pulpit, press and bench may unite in urging their cessation, appeals may be made day after day that the law be allowed to run its course—but when such assaults occur. . . the rapist will meet his death at the hands of a mob representing the outraged sense of the community. After all it is but natural that this should be the case." [47]

In his catalog of conventional wisdom about lynching, the *Times-Recorder* editor exposed the continuing grip of traditional explanations. By 1910, white Georgians might periodically wring their hands over the excesses of mobs, but they retained faith that mob violence was essentially beyond control and that, when all was said and done, lynching was in the natural order of things.

8

Turning the Tide: Opposition to Lynching in Georgia, 1910–30

After months of travel through Georgia and the South to investigate race relations during the first decade of the twentieth century, the northern journalist Ray Stannard Baker wrote optimistically that "the Negro problem is not unsolvable; it is being solved, here and now, as fast as any human problem can be solved."[1] The glacial speed of improvements in race relations before World War I, however, would seem to have flown in the face of Baker's sanguine conclusions. And yet, he correctly discerned that the broad social transformations in the South during the late nineteenth century were inspiring a new generation of social activists. In a drawn-out and halting process, these new activists began to challenge the orthodox wisdom of the strident racists. The most profound changes in attitudes about race relations, and lynching in particular, would take place after the war, but the tentative initiatives taken by activists in the previous decade were of seminal importance.

The new activists envisioned social and cultural rehabilitation on a scale far beyond the modest vision of conservative whites committed to the slogan of law and order. Conservative whites' understanding of racial violence, like that of their Virginia counterparts, was woefully shallow, and their strategies hopelessly narrow. In contrast, the antilynching reformers of the early twentieth century drew upon a diverse body of ideas, only one of which was a narrow dedication to law and order. Inspired by greater faith in the power of government, convinced of the virtues of something vaguely defined as "progress," and armed with the methods drawn from both the social sciences and religious reform, these activists condemned lynching as a primitive, barbaric holdover that had no place in the New South.

Despite contradictory aims, white businessmen dedicated to economic progress, white reformers animated by a vision of Christian social justice, and black activists committed to color-blind justice all agreed that public action to elevate community morals was needed if any campaign against lynching were to succeed. In keeping with their sweeping conception of their mission, these activists set about creating networks of institutions which, for the first time, could awaken opposition to lynching, even in the hinterlands of Georgia. Thus, in striking contrast to Virginia, where much of the drive behind the antilynching campaign came from state officials, the antilynching campaign in Georgia was first and foremost waged by social reformers.

The decline of lynchings during the 1920s and 1930s reflects the effectiveness of antilynching activists. Of course, social and economic exigencies contributed to the success of agitation against lynching. The decline of mob violence was precipitated by the aftershocks of the Great Migration of rural blacks to the North, the expansion and maturation of business and middle-class values of all kinds, and far-reaching economic changes in the region during the 1930s.

Even without the activities of antilynching activists, mob violence almost certainly would have diminished across the twentieth century. But the most satisfying explanation for its decline in twentieth-century Georgia emphasizes the dialectical relationship between the broad social transformations and the cumulative effects of decades of antilynching agitation by blacks and whites alike. It is important to keep in mind that these broad social forces in themselves might have diminished the sources of racial violence without calling into question any of the values that previously had condoned and justified racial violence. The signal contribution of opponents of lynching was that they accelerated its demise while they exposed the grisly reality behind the facade of white violence, thereby challenging some of the South's most ingrained cultural conventions.

The emerging campaign against mob violence in Georgia drew upon the values of social harmony, efficiency, and orderly progress that were the order of the day following the turn of the century. Many white southerners, as participants in the southern variant of the Progressive reform movement, developed greater confidence in the ability of government and established institutions to address the social and economic ills of the region. With blacks confined to a lower and separate status by Jim Crow laws and disfranchisement, white southerners congratulated themselves for solving the "Negro problem." The persistence of lynching and other forms of mob violence despite the "reforms" of segregation and disfranchisement, however, called into question many of the traditional rationales for mob violence. Moreover, there was the troubling evidence that the number of lynchings provoked by alleged sexual crimes was declining sharply even while mobs continued their barbarism.[2]

The reform spirit of the Progressive Era in Georgia did not intrinsically challenge most racial attitudes. Indeed, the reforms that captivated progressives both expanded and codified segregation, especially in towns. For instance, the city planning and "city beautiful" movement in Atlanta, which did spruce up the city's drab and congested landscape, went hand and hand with an elaborate system of residential segregation. Moreover, most of the implemented progressive reforms did not so much increase the influence of the politically powerless as reinforce the power of already dominant elites. But the thrust of progressivism, in particular the emphasis placed upon the link between economic development and social harmony, also reduced the tolerance of some southerners for the most strident forms of racial extremism, including extralegal behavior.[3]

The appearance of the first regionwide organized opposition to mob violence reflected the Progressive Era's enthusiasm for specialized organizations of like-minded individuals. Earlier opposition was limited by its lack of stable organizations and committed grass-roots organizers. Although there had been periodic calls for the creation of organizations committed to battling lynching for more than a decade before 1910, the groups that were established floundered for lack of both membership and effective strategies. After roughly 1910, however, conditions were far more favorable for the creation of a network of institutions that would both directly and indirectly challenge mob violence and the values that sustained it. In time, a fragile web of institutions carried the fight against mob violence into even the most benighted corners of the South.

The founding of the various business, civic, and reform organizations, groups that represented "the characteristic social unit of the modern city," can best be seen as a part of the modernization of the South during the twentieth century.[4] Urbanization and industrialization exerted contradictory influences on southern life, and, to a greater extent than elsewhere, modernization in the American South was uneven, incomplete, and impeded by tenacious traditions. The tensions between progress and tradition were especially evident in the cities and county seats of Georgia. The growing economic importance of the state's urban centers coincided with the emergence of what one historian has called "the commercial-civic elite."[5] Members of this group would play an important role in the gradual shift in attitudes toward lynching. By no means did this burgeoning middle class, small and unrefined as it was, harbor sentiments of racial liberalism that were far in advance of the existing racial order. Rather, as cultural and economic intermediaries between the major urban centers and the rural hinterland, its members were self-conscious promoters of the values and behavior that would, they believed, ensure growth and prosperity in their communities. By participating in Rotary, Kiwanis, and Civitan clubs, and similar groups that mushroomed across the state, Georgians took part in a process that replaced the older localistic and informal definition of community with a newer, institutional-based sense of community. These organizations, despite their often provincial outlook and primitive structure, were the opening wedge for values that compromised traditional individualism, independence, and localism.[6]

The expansion of various reform, religious, or business associations across the South—a process that gathered strength after 1910—contributed to a growing divide between urban and rural dwellers. Although the perception of worsening rural distress was not unique to the South, it was particularly significant there because of the inescapably rural character of the society. For many whites sympathetic to reform, much more was at stake than just the problem of race relations. As a North Carolina professor explained, "The problem is not so much what to do to elevate the inferior race as it is to save the whites from the blighting influences of narrow-mindedness, intolerance, and injustice."[7] For the small, self-conscious middle class in the region's towns and cities, rural traits and habits only recently perceived as marks of traditional values became instead the stigma of degeneracy. As the cultural gulf between the middle-class townspeople and rural dwellers widened, mob violence increasingly became a sign of backwardness, not civilization; of rural decadence, not virtue.

The impetus behind the reevaluation of rural life and race relations came from disparate sources, including "uptown" business groups, religious reformers, activist academics, and liberal journalists. The social values that propelled reform in early twentieth-century Georgia, which ranged from orderliness, economic expansion, and middle-class moralism to humanitarianism, were at once diverse and contradictory. As a result, although the various reform groups hardly moved in lockstep—the deeply etched race line remained, fundamentally dividing the efforts of black and white opponents of lynching—the cumulative effect of their attacks on mob violence was to strip away much of the legitimacy of lynching. Moreover, by bringing new and innovative methods to bear on the problems of the rural South and race relations, the various antilynching activists, black and white alike, finally overcame many of the daunting obstacles that had for so long hindered opposition to mob violence.

The response of white Atlantans to the Atlanta race riot of 1906 offers an early and telling illustration of the interrelationship of the "commercial-civic" ethos and the commitment to reform in race relations. Reeling from the national and international attention the riot had received, members of Atlanta's white elite set about restoring the city's reputation and promoting their own version of interracial harmony. Within three days of the end of the riot, Samuel P. Jones, president of the Atlanta Chamber of Commerce, organized a meeting of hundreds of the city's "leading citizens." Meeting at the Fulton County Courthouse, the all-white group condemned the rioters as murderers and promised aid for the victims of the riot. Another committee, led by W. G. Cooper, secretary of the Chamber of Commerce, and George Muse, a prominent merchant, carried out an investigation and issued a report that tallied the devastation wrought by the rioters and recommended that strong measures, ranging from the continued stationing of militia in the city to the closing of all barrooms, be taken to preserve order.[8]

In the weeks following the riot, white civic leaders concerned themselves with restoring public order and business activity. Roused by the committee's report, city officials set out to purge many bars and restaurants. They targeted in particular barrooms that catered to blacks, under the assumption that liquor had been the catalyst for the alleged assaults by blacks, which, in turn, had provoked the rioters. More than a hundred black bars and restaurants were shut down, and within two weeks of the riot fewer than twenty black saloons and no integrated bars remained in the city. At the same time, authorities successfully prosecuted a handful of the white rioters, although no meaningful action was taken against most of the hundreds of whites who had participated in the event. For all practical purposes, the riot initially served as a pretext for concerned whites and local authorities to reexert authority in the black neighborhoods and initiate a civic reform movement. In this regard, events in Atlanta differed little from the previous responses of whites elsewhere in the South to other serious outbreaks of racial violence.[9]

In the months that followed the riot, however, a few prominent whites began to place some blame on their own failure to develop a program for race relations. John E. White, a Baptist minister, warned that occasional informal discussions between the races could no longer take the place of a coordinated effort for interracial communication. As long as the "best white people" of the South were idle, lawless whites would be emboldened by the "inaction they see in the ranks above them." Invoking "the standards of the Christian Gospel," White appealed for the white "conscience to support a program of basic righteousness."[10]

The first steps toward turning White's plea into a practical program were taken by the "Committee of Ten," which included such prominent businessmen as Sam D. Jones; J. W. English, president of the Fourth National Bank; Forrest Addair, a real estate developer; H. Y. McCord, a wholesale grocer; Charles T. Hopkins, a prominent lawyer; and A. B. Steele, a lumber merchant. In what Ray

Stannard Baker described as "the first important occasion in the South upon which an attempt was made to get the two races together for any serious consideration of their differences," the committee met at the Colored Young Men's Christian Association with twenty leading blacks, including the prominent ministers H. H. Proctor, E. P. Johnson, E. R. Carter, J. A. Rush, and Bishop Lucius Henry Holsey; B. J. Davis, the editor of the black weekly, the *Atlanta Independent;* and Booker T. Washington, who had traveled to the city in hopes of using his influence to foster interracial cooperation.[11]

The principal concern of the white committee members was to ensure that Atlanta, and its reputation as the symbolic capitol of the New South, was not scarred by another race riot in the future. The black spokesmen, who had broader aims in mind, made it clear that quick and token measures were unlikely to produce harmonious race relations, and that immediate steps should be taken to end such routine practices as police brutality and violence against blacks who rode streetcars. Washington privately reported that "the colored people did not mince their words; they told the whites in no uncertain terms the way the colored people had been grievously injured. The whites were equally frank; they acknowledged their sins of omission and commission and promised in most sincere terms to make amends for the future."[12] In short order, city authorities reorganized the police force and discharged nearly a fourth for participating in the riot. At the same time, the streetcar companies promised that their employees would treat blacks better and claimed to have devised methods to segregate the races with less discomfort for black passengers.[13]

Charles T. Hopkins, a white lawyer for Atlanta University and one of the participants in the impromptu meeting between the white committee and the black leaders, concluded that the city needed an organization that would encourage an enduring dialogue between "the better white elements" and "the best Negroes of the city." On Thanksgiving Day 1906, Hopkins founded the Atlanta Civic League and enlisted more than a thousand white Atlantans in the new organization. The preservation of law and order was a driving motivation behind the league, as became clear when members oversaw severe measures—bars were ordered closed and blacks were "encouraged" to stay off the streets at night—to prevent racial incidents during the Christmas holidays of 1906. The league also committed itself to providing lawyers to defend poor blacks in the courts and pointed to its success in winning the acquittal of a black man wrongly accused of the rape of a white woman in December 1906. In addition, the organization initiated a monthly meeting of twenty of its members and twenty members of the Colored Co-operative Civic League. Established by H. H. Proctor, pastor of the upper-class First Congregational Church, the Colored League quickly attained a membership nearly as large as its white counterpart. In monthly meetings, members of the two organizations discussed municipal problems, including the black community's continuing grievances concerning police, streetcars, and public accommodations in general.[14]

Prominent white religious leaders also threw their support behind efforts to rehabilitate Atlanta. After organizing a prayer meeting of prominent white and black clergymen, William J. Northen, former governor and president of the Atlanta Business Men's Gospel Union, established the biracial Christian League. In addition to holding weekly interracial prayer meetings at the Colored YMCA, the Christian League also set aside the second Sunday in December as a day when every minister in the city should preach a sermon in favor of civic duty, good will, and law and order. On December 6, the appointed Law and Order Sunday, Booker T. Washington returned to Atlanta and joined Northen in calling for the interracial audience at Friendship Baptist Church to continue to support the campaigns for racial conciliation of the Civic and Christian leagues.[15]

From Washington's perspective, the response of white and black leaders in Atlanta to the riot represented "the most radical, far-reaching, and hopeful solution of the race problem that has ever been undertaken by Southern white people." [16] In fact, a northern reporter came closer to the truth when he observed that "a few men have dreamed a dream, that's all." [17] White participants attempted to achieve racial harmony on the basis of voluntarism without addressing the underlying conditions of social and economic inequity and racial injustice. Within two years of the riot, interracial meetings between the various civic organizations became infrequent, and dialogue among leaders became largely symbolic. For W. E. B. Du Bois, John Hope, and several other Atlanta blacks, the riot itself was glaring evidence of the failure of precisely the rhetoric and methods of the interracial movement. Moreover, none of the cosmetic reforms that the movement accomplished could offset the subsequent effects of the disfranchisement of blacks, the codification of residential segregation, and the continued discrimination in public services. Perhaps the movement's signal accomplishment was to restore, in the eyes of the city's elite, the progressive image of Atlanta.[18]

It would be a mistake, however, to overlook the significant innovation that the Atlanta interracial movement represented in Georgia. By calling for an organized campaign to improve race relations, White and Hopkins dismissed the notion that occasional gestures of paternalism would ensure social peace. They recognized that as the chasm between the races widened, only the most attenuated sense of community united blacks and whites. As they and other white leaders of the movement probably only vaguely understood, the exigencies of southern urban life demanded more formal methods of communication between the races. Hopkins implied as much when he admitted his ignorance of black opinion after the first interracial meeting following the riot: "I believe those Negroes understood the situation better than we did. I was astonished at their intelligence and diplomacy . . . I didn't know there were such Negroes in Atlanta." [19] (And this from the lawyer for one of Atlanta's major black colleges!)

Although the effort to mobilize the business and religious elite of Atlanta soon sputtered and lost momentum, it subtly but permanently shifted the attitudes of the city's white upper class toward racial violence. As they justified the increasing segregation of southern society, they also advanced the provocative notion that practical steps could be taken to improve the status of blacks. These modest steps, which rested upon the implicit assumption that blacks should become self-reliant citizens, distinguished the white reformers from earlier paternalists by opening the door for more meaningful dialogue. Finally, the enduring resonance of the values of the interracial movement among some circles in Atlanta helps to explain the prominence of Atlantans in subsequent antilynching efforts.

No campaign against mob violence was likely to succeed until white southerners reevaluated the region's race relations in general and the function of lynching in particular. Beginning around the turn of the century, southern academics from various disciplines joined together to turn the cold light of modern science on the region's social ills. Although few in number and subject to periodic attacks from conservative critics, these intellectual pioneers were participants in the larger intellectual transformation from the Victorian values that had dominated southern discourse during the late nineteenth century to a set of cautiously modern values far less encumbered by the regional chauvinism and prejudices of the past. In their quest to overcome the ignorance of the masses and enlighten public opinion, they pioneered many arguments and techniques that became staples in the campaign against lynching.[20]

The intellectual awakening in the South penetrated deepest on campuses in North Carolina, Virginia, and Tennessee, but it also touched institutions in Georgia. What innovations there were in the state took place at the University of Georgia, where Chancellor Walter B. Hill and then David C. Barrow replaced the traditional classical curriculum with a more practical and flexible curriculum and oversaw the rapid expansion of the school's professional and graduate facilities. With the encouragement of the chancellors, faculty members set out to apply their scholarship to the pressing issues of the day, including the contentious issue of race relations. During the Barrow administration in particular, several faculty members, including R. J. H. DeLoach, Robert Preston Brooks, C. J. Heatwole, and Barrow himself actively participated in various groups committed to racial reform.

In addition, in 1912 the recently founded, northern philanthropic Phelps-Stokes Fund picked the University of Georgia to receive one of the two Phelps-Stokes Fellowships, to be granted to white students who would spend a year researching some aspect of race relations. In subsequent years, the Phelps-Stokes research papers were published as pamphlets and became an important part of the emerging social science literature on the race problem. Beyond the campus of the University of Georgia, however, there were few signs of any broad movement of new racial awareness among the faculty at the state's other colleges. Emory College (after 1915, Emory University), for example, remained a liberal but conventional Methodist institution and, under the careful watch of Dr. James E. Dickey and Bishop Warren A. Candler, escaped contagion from the more disruptive progressive currents felt at other Methodist institutions such as Vanderbilt and Trinity (now Duke).[21]

Even otherwise deeply traditional campuses in Georgia were exposed, however, if only at a distance, to the new currents of thought on the region's race problems. To a great degree, the catalysts for campus concern were regional organizations like the Southern Sociological Congress (SSC) and the University Commission on Southern Race Questions, both of which combined a broad concern for social welfare with a commitment to race reform. Established in Tennessee in 1912, the two organizations attracted great attention in southern reform circles and newspapers and inspired some observers, including Ray Stannard Baker, to announce a "new departure in southern attitudes toward the Negro."[22] The founding of the organizations reflected conditions in Tennessee that were especially propitious for the development of more sophisticated approaches to social problems, including the election of the avowed reformer Benjamin W. Hooper as governor, the maturation of Vanderbilt as an increasingly independent-minded, secular university, and the emergence of a cluster of urban reformers in Nashville. Moreover, these Tennessee reformers were committed to fostering social reform beyond the boundaries of their state, and in 1912 invited hundreds of academics, ministers, and reformers to Nashville for the first meeting of the Southern Sociological Congress.[23]

Committed to practical solutions rather than theoretical questions, members of the SSC pledged their loyalty "to study and improve social, civic, and economic conditions in the South." The organization pioneered interracial meetings and published hundreds of thousands of pamphlets and folders on various issues of race relations, including lynching. At the second annual congress in Atlanta in

1913, for example, nearly a thousand people, including more than four hundred blacks, attended four days of meetings. The central theme of the gathering was race relations, and a "Statement on Race Relationships" was issued denouncing lynching, lamenting the treatment blacks received from southern courts, and calling for improvements in black education. Six years later in Knoxville, at the eighth meeting of the congress, the organization produced a resolution on lynching and the outlines of "a Program for the Improvement of Race Relations." The program represented the summation of the ideas and proposals raised at previous congresses but added a new call for the establishment of biracial committees to address local problems.[24]

A spinoff of the SSC, the University Commission attempted to extend the influence of the congress and its program onto college campuses. The membership of the commission included one member from a state university in each southern state. Initially, R. J. H. DeLoach, professor of agriculture at the University of Georgia, represented the state, but in subsequent years Robert Preston Brooks and C. J. Heatwole, also professors at the University of Georgia, filled DeLoach's place. Meanwhile, David C. Barrow, the chancellor of the university, served with two other southern university presidents on the commission's advisory committee. Although strapped for funds and hampered by a lack of staff, the commission met annually and issued letters that addressed lynching and other social problems. It also developed innovative college courses treating the problems of race relations.[25]

By rejecting the traditional rationales and excuses for lynching, the SSC and University Commission worked to dispel the notion that black crimes prompted lynchings. In 1916, the University Commission issued a widely published letter that drew upon information supplied by the Tuskegee Institute to reveal the trivial offenses that served as pretexts for extralegal violence. Calling upon college students to lead the crusade against mob rule, the letter stressed that civilization rested upon obedience to law and the substitution of reason and deliberation for impulse and passion. Both the SSC and the University Commission maintained that social forces, such as illiteracy, poverty, and hidebound rural traditionalism, were to blame for mob violence. Only economic development and expanded public education could produce a revitalized South, and in turn lead to the decline of mob violence. Both organizations recognized that such broad social transformations would take years, and that mob violence would persist during that time. In the meantime, they urged whites to break their silence and openly denounce racial injustices.[26]

After 1920 the SSC and the University Commission lost much of their earlier focus and for all practical purposes became moribund. For as long as they existed, neither managed to overcome members' chronic paternalism, genteel racism, and instinctive moderation. Despite these evident shortcomings, the sociologist Howard W. Odum found cause to label the SSC as one of the most important southern organizations of the period. The two organizations played a modest but noteworthy role in the campaign to end lynching by creating a forum for the exchange of ideas. The organizations also provided for the apprenticeship for many whites who would become members of the antilynching movement in Georgia, including Thomas J. Woofter, who participated in the University Commission while a student at the University of Georgia; Lily H. Hammond, a leading Methodist activist in the state; and Will W. Alexander, a Methodist reformer who would later head the Commission on Interracial Cooperation in Atlanta. Moreover, the fruition of the methods of the SSC became evident in the late 1920s and 1930s when a generation of southern academics, in particular sociologists, began to unmask the deepest roots of the region's social and racial distress. The far-reaching regional analysis that would later be evident in the sociological studies of Woofter, Rupert Vance, and Arthur Raper, including Raper's masterpiece *The Tragedy of Lynching,* would have been inconceivable without the precedent established by the SSC and University Commission. Perhaps Josiah Morse, a professor at the University of South Carolina and one of its members, offered the most perceptive assessment of the commission—and, by extension, the SSC—when he wrote that it was "not so much what the commission has actually done, as what it hoped to do, and the spirit in which it has gone about its work." [27]

The growing commitment to reform within the academic community cannot easily be separated from the social gospel movement within southern Protestantism. Throughout the period from 1910 to 1930 a symbiotic relationship existed between religious reformers and virtually all secular groups committed to social "uplift." Religious reformers provided much of the inspiration for reform and, equally important, the means by which the message of reform could reach far beyond the confines of academic or reform circles. Given the sheer pervasiveness of religious institutions in southern life, no reform movement could ignore the potential power of churches to mobilize popular sentiment.

However much southern religious institutions supported and reinforced the region's "cultural unity," they nonetheless were the seedbed for a more socially active Christianity during the twentieth century. Not even the fundamentalist churches could escape the social implications of even the most narrowly based moral reforms. As the historian Timothy Smith explains, "the quest for personal holiness became in some ways a kind of plain man's transcendentalism, which geared ancient creeds to the drive shaft of social reform." [28] Within some Protestant denominations—the Methodist church in particular and even the Baptist church—liberal factions took tentative steps to reconcile the claims of modern science and philosophy with classical theology.

One consequence of the incipient social gospel movement within the South was that, beginning around 1900, a growing number of Methodists and Baptists adopted a broader interpretation of the Christian mission toward blacks. Frustrated by most southern religious leaders who cloaked their sense of social responsibility in a commitment to the preservation of the status quo, the reformers urged southern churches to organize and agitate for moral reforms. They cautiously attempted to bridge the gulf separating the races and move their churches beyond "their nineteenth-century attitude of ignoring the Negro's very existence." [29]

Lily Hardy Hammond, a member of the South Carolina aristocracy and the wife of the president of Paine College, a black Methodist college in Augusta, and a prominent Methodist reformer in her own right, personified the peripatetic course of most religiously inspired reformers who moved beyond Christian piety. Like many Methodist women, she discovered a powerful social message in John Wesley's teachings but, because of her gender, was denied any formal exercise of power. She and many women like her—often to the consternation of church elders—seized upon the new opportunities that Methodism's social work provided and grasped a measure of autonomy from male oversight while pressing for social activism. Lily Hammond was first active in women's prayer groups and aid societies before she became the first superintendent of the Methodist Bureau of Social Service in 1899. In part because of her experiences at Paine College, while serving as superintendent she increasingly directed her attention to the problems of southern race relations. [30]

In 1914 Hammond outlined her unconventional attitudes toward race relations in a book entitled *In Black and White*. In tone and substance, her book gave voice to the growing conviction in some religious circles that improved race relations were the greatest test of the social gospel. She attacked race prejudice, catalogued the injustices suffered by blacks, and, by drawing upon her experiences as a social worker, explained the role that economic discrimination played in perpetuating black poverty and mistreatment by whites. Lynching aroused Hammond's deepest concern about the social conscience of the South. Although she believed that many southerners opposed lynching, she castigated them for not making concerted efforts to suppress the crime. If she failed to offer viable solutions to the problems of the black community, she recognized that expressions of right-thinking attitudes alone were inadequate to suppress the culture of mob violence. Hammond steadfastly participated in virtually all of the major race reform organizations founded by whites after 1910, including both the SSC and the University Commission, and was the guiding spirit of the Southern Publicity Committee, an organization that served as a news service to publicize black achievements and the accomplishments of race reform organizations.[31]

Lily Hammond's growing social concerns were shared by other white religious activists, including John E. White and M. Ashby Jones, prominent Baptist ministers in Atlanta who advocated taking tentative steps toward ameliorating the harshness of southern race relations. Although White, the pastor of the Second Baptist Church in Atlanta, lacked Hammond's empathy or vision and retained what one scholar has referred to as "the more grating aspects of the older, paternalistic approach to race problems," his strongly voiced moderate attitudes toward matters of race exerted a powerful influence. White's early reform interests did not include the "Negro problem," but after the Atlanta race riot of 1906, he came to realize that social reform could not easily be separated from the South's race problem. Between 1906 and 1920, he lectured widely and published numerous articles that sketched out his program for improved race relations. He tirelessly called for better education for blacks and, as he had since the Atlanta race riot, pleaded for the white elites to use their prestige to foster biracial communication.[32]

Although far less prolific than White, M. Ashby Jones, the pastor of the Ponce De Leon Baptist Church, was even more ardently committed to denouncing mob violence. Before moving to Atlanta, Jones had served as a minister in Richmond, where, in 1900, he publicly opposed new segregation laws for public accommodations. In 1904, he joined with Samuel C. Mitchell in pushing the Virginia Baptist General Association to campaign against lynching. In 1906, Jones moved to Columbus, where he ministered to the First Baptist Church until 1908. He then moved to the First Baptist Church of Augusta, where he served until moving to Atlanta in 1917. Between 1917 and 1926, when he moved yet again to a church in St. Louis, Jones "made interracial understanding one of the basic thrusts of his ministry."[33] For most of his career, Jones left little public record of his ideas about race, but instead directed his views to his congregation and church councils. Only after World War I, when he became an active organizer of the interracial reform movement, did Jones begin to publicize his views. By the end of the 1920s, he had rejected the prevailing pseudo-scientific notions of white racial superiority and come out in favor of extending all the benefits of citizenship to blacks, including the right to vote.[34]

Neither White nor Jones were able to shed their powerful sense of paternalism and firm belief in racial "integrity" (i. e., segregation), but they voiced sentiments which, in light of the earlier tenor of debate, were moderate and even enlightened. By throwing their considerable prestige behind efforts to create an interracial reform movement, White, Jones, and Hammond hoped to inspire leadership in the campaign from an element of southern society—religiously inspired white elites—which, although qualified to provide it, had long failed to do so.

For some young white Georgians, particularly a small but active group of women college students, contact with religiously inspired social activism and racial reform stimulated new lines of thinking on race relations that ran far in advance of the paternalism of White and Jones. While the Young Men's Christian Association (YMCA) demonstrated a "slow but quickening" concern for racial issues, the Young Women's Christian Association (YWCA) went much further and awakened—at least in a few Georgia women—the courage to "shake off [the] dominion [of] sacred racial mores." For Katherine Lumpkin, a student at Brenau College in Gainesville, and Augusta Roberts, a student at Agnes Scott College in Atlanta, membership in the YWCA before World War I set in motion a profound reappraisal of southern race relations and in time led them to dismiss the "separate but truly equal" doctrine espoused by most southern liberals of the day.

In national and regional conferences, Lumpkin, Roberts, and other Georgia YWCA members came into contact with the national currents of thought on social and racial reform alike. In part because the YWCA lacked a formal program of interracial work until the 1920s and, more important, remained segregated until the late 1940s, Lumpkin and Roberts were struck by the incongruity between the Social Gospel foundation of the organization and the social practices, including racial discrimination, that it tacitly condoned. Increasingly conscious of the desperate need for social reform in the South, a small cadre of women in the YWCA began to view themselves as something more than dilettante reformers. Years later, Augusta Roberts recalled, "We . . . followed the pattern of building a small but committed network" who went "into society with a very different approach to issues." Certainly, before the 1920s the YWCA's social activism had little immediate impact on the pressing racial problems of the day, but the YWCA, like the SSC and the University Commission, contributed significantly to the emergence of an expanding network of southern activists.[35]

The message of racial activism and humanitarianism hardly reached beyond the members of a few urban congregations, the readers of a few journals of reform, and the participants in a few exceptional campus programs in Georgia before World War I. Not until the 1920s did opposition to mob violence rooted in the churches emerge in a full-blown regional movement. Even so, the writings and activities of Hammond, White, Jones, and other religiously inspired critics countervailed what Lily Hammond complained was the failure of "the pulpits of the South. . .[to]

speak of those [racial] problems which press upon us all, and for which there is no solution outside the teachings of Christ." [36]

If the spiritually inspired church reformers provided the most humane face of the emerging antilynching movement, white businessmen represented the conservative impulse behind opposition to lynching. The urban and small-town businessmen who populated the Chambers of Commerce, the Kiwanis, the Rotary Clubs, and various other voluntary business groups were the core of what might be called the uptown opposition to mob violence. Enthusiasm for law and order and orderly progress had always been present among business circles in Atlanta and Savannah, but during the first decades of the twentieth century, when Georgia was suffering its first extensive labor unrest, the problem of mob rule took on new urgency. [37] At the forefront of the businessmen's concern was the fear that mob law threatened both social and economic stability. Although Governor Joseph M. Brown (1909–11, 1912–13) did not draw his political support from the urban business community, his hostility toward mob law, whether lynching or labor militancy, meshed seamlessly with uptown attitudes about the need for social order. During his two terms as governor Brown demonstrated an "almost unseemly eagerness" to call out the militia to squash labor strikes. [38] A timid man who had previously avoided any public speaking, Brown found in the issue of mob law a cause that appealed to his deeply conservative values. While he was governor and after he left office he delivered countless speeches and wrote several articles denouncing labor unrest and lynch mobs as "training school[s] of anarchy." As a solution, Brown proposed a variety of state laws unfavorable to labor unions, swift use of law officers and militia to preserve law and order, and a campaign to convince Georgians of the urgent need for respect for the rule of law. [39]

The suppression of mob violence, of course, was never a principal, or even major, concern of Georgia's business community. For Atlanta businessmen, who set the pace for their counterparts elsewhere in the state, the pressing task was to foster a gung-ho boosterism widely known as the "Atlanta spirit." In March 1916, the president of the Atlanta Chamber of Commerce provided a definition of the Atlanta Spirit, explaining that the business community must commit the city "to a policy of city building, both material and ideal—materialistic in those things that merely show the visual growth of Atlanta, and idealistic in the development of a city striving for the intellectual, artistic, industrial, and moral development of our people." [40]

In language drenched with moral fervor and materialistic zeal, Atlanta business elites set out to whip up a powerful civic spirit that would bind together city residents, regardless of race. By the 1920s, the Chamber of Commerce in Atlanta had begun to turn vague rhetoric on interracial harmony and respect into reality. Paul Norcross, the group's president in 1924, explained that the business community was obliged to participate in interracial cooperation because it was "a matter of equity, a matter of right, a matter of justice." By fulfilling their civic duty, he predicted, white businessmen in turn would reap benefits for themselves and Atlanta: "we must recognize that it is our obligation and privilege to instruct and train his race in the needs of community requirements, thereby reaping a mutually beneficial civic reward." [41] In practical terms, the uptown commitment to interracialism amounted to modest contributions to a few social agencies that worked in black neighborhoods and elaborately polite meetings between white and black chambers of commerce. [42]

Despite repeating mantralike the continuous achievements that accompanied civic solidarity and racial harmony, business organizations could not ignore the simple fact that racial violence, especially mob violence, persisted. Even clubs noted for chronic boosterism managed to denounce specific lynchings or even condemn mob violence in general. After a terrorist mob went on a rampage and destroyed black churches and property in Laurens and Dodge counties in 1919, for example, the Laurens Chamber of Commerce called for county officials to punish the mob members and promised that the organization would contribute funds to rebuild destroyed churches and lodges. Members of the chamber also publicly requested that the county commissioners appropriate county funds to contribute to the rebuilding. Following a lynching in 1922, the Civitan Club of Macon, roused by appeals of various speakers for citizens to uphold the law, passed resolutions attacking mob violence and offering its services to local authorities to assist in law enforcement. In the same year, the Athens Kiwanis Club threw its support behind efforts to secure the passage of a new antilynching law. Local businessmen also assumed the lead in organizing mass meetings held to condemn mob murders. In 1915, the businessmen of Montecello, for example, called a mass meeting that "greatly deplored" the recent lynching of an entire black family in the town. In the next year, businessmen in Clarksville chaired a mass meeting that declared that "the true citizenry of our state does not countenance or condone such wanton and uncivilized methods [as lynching]." [43]

A prevailing sense of both optimism and conservatism ensured that such denunciations were timid and seldom went beyond advocating a stern dose of law and order. Even so, they called into question the prevailing assumption that lynch mobs acted on behalf of entire outraged communities. By adopting resolutions condemning mob violence, local business elites attempted to distance themselves from mob violence and the values that fueled it. They denied approval of or responsibility for the mob's actions. In distinguishing between the law-abiding and the lawless, between behavior that advanced the South and that which set it back, the opponents of lynching within the business community in Georgia contributed in a small but nonetheless meaningful way to diminishing the legitimacy of mob violence.[44]

Without the constant promotion of journalists and newspaper editors, the various expressions of opposition to mob violence, whether token gestures like those of business groups or the more substantial actions of the SSC, would have had little impact. Although the editors of several urban papers in Georgia had long pleaded with their readers to refrain from taking the law into their own hands, they had also argued that segregation and disfranchisement would produce calmer, less violent relations between blacks and whites. But the persistence of lynching long after the passage of Jim Crow laws and the elimination of black voting exposed the fallacy of such arguments, and the editors recognized the need for a sustained crusade to end mob violence.

The urban dailies, such as the *Atlanta Constitution* and *Macon Telegraph,* took it upon themselves to propagate a version of the era's urban boosterism, complete with appeals for civic spirit and law and order. In 1916, for example, the *Telegraph* agreed with the secretary-manager of the Georgia Chamber of Commerce when he speculated that if newspapers devoted enthusiastic attention to "civic development . . . Georgia would take on a civic impetus that would take it further than man could measure during the next ten years." [45] As self-conscious defenders of the reputations of their communities, urban editors were all too aware of the national scorn that lynching brought upon the region. Concern for Georgia's reputation and the desire to mollify regional and national critics stirred urban editors to proselytize for organized efforts to suppress lawlessness.

Impetus for the mounting newspaper opposition to lynching came from the unwelcome national and international attention during the trial and lynching of Leo Frank in 1915. Frank, a Jewish industrialist in Atlanta, was wrongly charged with the murder of a young white girl. His trial and conviction appalled citizens throughout the country and directed withering criticism at the state, criticism that was further exacerbated when a small mob, angered by Governor John M. Slaton's commutation of Frank's sentence, removed Frank from prison and lynched him.[46] Stung by editorials in prominent national journals that suggested that "a state that has bowed to the will of the mob. . . is no longer worthy to be called a state" and that the only hope for Georgia "was a heavy inoculation of civilization," the *Atlanta Constitution* dejectedly observed that "not only are the people of Georgia being branded as barbarians at the North, but the attacks and criticisms of our own neighbors and friends here at home are little milder than those that come from a distance." In an era of boundless optimism about future prosperity the lynching of Leo Frank was an unwelcome reminder to newspaper editors that the outmoded traditional values that sustained lynching threatened the smooth, orderly progress of Georgia.[47]

Urban newspaper editors attempted to turn lynching into a political issue but met with little success. In 1916, the *Atlanta Constitution* sent letters to all gubernatorial candidates, requesting their opinions about lynching and the steps they would take as governor to combat mob violence. In 1918, urban dailies also strongly supported a new antilynching law that would allow the governor to remove any sheriff who failed to prevent a lynching through incompetence or connivance with the mob. In August, the antilynching bill, after running aground on the constitutional fundamentalism of the legislators, was tabled by a vote of 122 to 39 in the legislature. Yet editors continued to call for state action and supported each of the many antilynching bills that failed to pass in succeeding years. Their greatest hope, however, was placed in campaigns of public education against mob violence.[48] For these journalists the elimination of lynching promised to improve race relations, build better cooperation between black and white leaders, and reduce the possibility of federal intervention. Most important, by marshalling a host of practical reasons why Georgians should halt lynchings, the editors created an atmosphere in which antilynching organizations could work without facing crippling white hostility or provoking charges of pandering to the North.

The emergence of a network of activists was by no means restricted to the white side of the color line. Despite tremendous obstacles, African-American activists in Georgia created a fragile network of self-help, religious, and civic institutions during the first two decades of the twentieth century. The longstanding barriers to black protest groups remained: opposition from local whites, the absence of experienced organizers, and, finally, what W. E. B. Du Bois referred to as the "narrow repression" and "provincialism" of the region itself.[49]

All the myriad impediments to reform were apparent in the failure of the Equal Rights Convention of 1906 and the troubled early years of the National Association for the Advancement of Colored People (NAACP) in Georgia. In February 1906, William J. White, the editor of the black denominational weekly the *Georgia Baptist,* organized a meeting of some four hundred black participants at the first Equal Rights Convention in Macon. The meeting marked the emergence of a more militant spirit among many of Georgia's black leaders and was a sign of their growing frustration with Booker T. Washington's philosophy of accommodation. With White, a staunch critic of Washington, providing direction to the convention, the collected ministers, teachers, professionals, and farmers endorsed a program of action that owed much to the ideas and presence of W. E. B. Du Bois, John Hope, J. Max Barber, Bishop Henry McNeal Turner, and other black militants. The delegates approved an "Address to the American People" that urged blacks to "agitate, complain, protest and keep protesting against the invasion of our manhood rights" and to organize into "one great fist which shall never cease to pound at the gates of opportunity until they fly open." A second convention met the following year to make plans for creating organizations in every county in the state. But the stirring rhetoric of the convention failed to reach beyond the small number of blacks who subscribed to black newspapers, and the few local branches that were established quickly collapsed. By 1908 the organizers of the 1906 convention recognized the futility of any further statewide meetings.[50]

The failure of the fledgling NAACP to take hold in Georgia before World War I also bespoke the difficulties that all-black protest organizations had to overcome. After decades of unsuccessful attempts to create a national organization committed to promoting black rights through political pressure, agitation, and legal action, a group of intellectuals and reformers, both black and white, formally organized the NAACP in 1909. In 1913, W. R. Scott, founder and owner of the Atlanta *Daily World,* had contacted NAACP headquarters about organizing a branch in Atlanta, but as late as 1916 no action had been taken. Efforts were apparently hindered by the divisions between supporters and opponents of Booker T. Washington's accommodationist program. Washington's prestige and considerable influence gave his opposition to the NAACP and its aims, which he angrily dismissed as "nonsense," great weight among black leaders in the city. Not until after his death and World War I did the divisions between the pro- and anti-Washington camps narrow sufficiently to enable the NAACP to take root and expand throughout the state.[51]

The difficulties that beset the Equal Rights Convention and the NAACP, however, did not preclude the organization of a variety of civic, religious, and social organizations before the war. Although none of these groups was principally concerned with mob violence, they could not remain silent about lynching and racial violence. The black civic organizations in Atlanta, Savannah, and Macon periodically condemned racial violence and lynching as they devoted attention to sanitation, health, and educational conditions.[52]

In Atlanta, Lugenia Burns Hope, the wife of the president of Atlanta Baptist (now Morehouse) College, founded the Neighborhood Union, perhaps the most notable black reform organization in the state. The union was simultaneously a center of educational, social, and political activities and the training ground for a generation of activist black women. With an agenda that extended from improving sanitation to lobbying for recreational facilities for black children, the union focused most of its energy on the many problems of Atlanta's black community. But concern for the evils of mob violence, particularly in light of the deep scars left by the Atlanta race riot of 1906, surfaced in many union meetings and activities. It was not coincidence that Lugenia Hope and other women active in the organization would play important roles in the interracial opposition to lynching following World War I. Many of the women were also members of the National Association of Colored Women's Clubs, an organization incorporated in 1904. The NACWC gave impetus to black women's clubs and reform groups throughout the country, and its meetings and publications provided forums where deplorable conditions, including mob violence, could be discussed.[53]

The hard-won achievements of these various black organizations produced no immediate decline in the incidence of mob violence in the South. Before World War I, activists in Georgia continually confronted their inability to gain the attention of whites. Years later, W. E. B. Du Bois recalled, "Well, it was difficult to do anything as a Negro organization. What influence could we have on white public opinion?"[54] And yet, as understandable as Du Bois's frustration was, the years of institution-building, especially between 1900 and 1920, were not without their lasting accomplishments. The organizations, although few in number and unable to reach out to the bulk of Georgia's black population, enabled a small number of activists to develop grass-roots organizational skills that would undergird protest during the 1920s and 1930s. Without the important precedent established by these various organizations, black antilynching efforts following World War I almost certainly would have remained tragically handicapped by inexperienced leadership and a fragile institutional foundation.

World War I marked a turning point in the history of racial violence in much of the South, especially in Georgia. The war initiated broad social changes that cut deeply into the fabric of race relations in the state. The historian George Tindall has observed that the "immediate effect of the war on the South was to create situations of dynamic change in an essentially static society."[55] At the onset of the war, few contemporary observers would have claimed that opposition to lynching had achieved any tangible reduction in its incidence. Between 1910 and 1917, mobs claimed the lives of ninety-seven blacks and three whites; in other words, lynchers executed an average of fourteen people a year during the period. Not only had opponents of mob violence failed to move Georgia from the head of the list of mob-prone states, but they also had failed to pressure local and state authorities to take any meaningful steps to prosecute lynchers.

Black participation in the war effort and the higher wages that blacks were able to command in the tight wartime labor market revived concerns among whites about the extent of their domination. In a climate poisoned by the national government's efforts to manufacture war frenzy, white southerners all too often took rumors and reports of blacks circulating German propaganda seriously. Lynchings and racial violence erupted with a ferocity unmatched since the racial hysteria that accompanied the Spanish-American War twenty years earlier. Thirty-nine blacks died at the hands of mobs between 1918 and 1919, and race riots broke out in cities and towns throughout Georgia.[56]

As the war ignited racial violence it also set in motion an exodus of southern blacks, a momentous event that posed an implicit challenge to the prevailing racial order in the South. When the war halted European immigration, northern businessmen turned to southern blacks to ease the shortage of unskilled labor. The new economic opportunities in the North, which continued even after the war ended, lured thousands in the vast population shift known as the Great Migration. While the scale of migration from Georgia is difficult to determine accurately, as many as 250,000 blacks may have left the state between 1917 and 1924. In the first four months of 1923 alone, according to the State College of Agriculture, more than sixty-eight thousand set off.[57]

The precise motivations that led Georgia's blacks to uproot themselves and migrate to northern cities were as varied as the migrants themselves. How racial violence stimulated the exodus remains a matter of debate. Writing at the time of the Great Migration, the black sociologist Charles S. Johnson concluded that the migration's "basic impetus has remained economic." There can be little doubt that Johnson was correct to stress that the migration was the "symptom of [the] wholesome and substantial life purpose" of southern blacks intent to "improve their states." But there is also considerable evidence, both anecdotal and scholarly, that Johnson underestimated the role of racial violence.[58]

Blacks themselves routinely observed, in the words of a church elder from Macon, that the "unjust treatments enacted daily" were "driving the Negro from the South." R. J. Bennett, a migrant from the Upper Piedmont town of Austell, spoke for many when he explained that he was "truly tired of Living in a country where the Poor negro has no Privalige." [59] Such testimony that racial violence contributed to the exodus is borne out by recent quantitative evidence. A careful survey of Georgia and South Carolina concludes that black migration was not uniform across the two states. In fact, it was heaviest from precisely those counties where mob violence was most lethal. Racial violence did not trigger the migration, but the exodus of blacks, once precipitated by the new economic opportunities in the North, represented a variation on a traditional form of silent protest and self-defense. For generations, blacks had resorted to short-term flight to escape white violence. What was unprecedented about the Great Migration was its scale and permanence.[60]

The exodus surprised many white Georgians, but they easily understood its implications for the region's labor relations. As train load after train load of blacks made the trip north, white Georgians became deeply concerned about the prospect of an acute labor shortage. During the war years, they resorted to legal harassment, intimidation, and outright violence to stem the exodus. But when these traditional methods of intimidation failed to impede the movement in any meaningful way, whites concluded that the war and migration had altered life permanently.[61]

In fact, many fears were exaggerated and unfounded. The migration produced a decline in the overabundance of cheap, unskilled labor in Georgia rather than any drastic shortage of labor. Despite appearances, it is not at all clear that the war and migration produced fundamental changes in the labor practices of the South.[62] But in this instance, the appearance of change was every bit as important as the far less revolutionary reality. James Goodman, a historian, has observed that planters, who relied upon "a very amiable peasantry," were understandably concerned about the flight of laborers from the state. "Migration simultaneously threatened the ready availability of that peasantry and planted doubts about its continued amiability."[63] Expediency alone prompted Georgia's whites to attempt to appease restive black laborers. A contemporary government report observed that many "see in the growing need for Negro labor so powerful an appeal to the self-interest of the white employer and the white planter as to make it possible to get an influential white group to exert itself actively to provide better schools; to insure full settlements between landlord and tenant. . .; to bring about abolition of the abuses in the courts."[64] "Landlords," Jack Temple Kirby suggests, "were forced more each year of the exodus to compete with northern employers, and to treat black croppers and laborers as valued employees and laborers rather than as a child race."[65]

The intertwined effects of the war, the Great Migration, and the anticipated labor shortage all lent gravity to the public discussion of race relations in Georgia and created the opening for the small fraction of the population that sought to combat racial violence and increase racial understanding. Although the war did not generate profound or even enduring changes in the fundamental underpinnings of the economy, the opening for race reform that the conflict created, short-lived as it was, was of seminal importance to the campaign against lynching.

At the forefront of the quickening crusade against lynching in Georgia was the newly invigorated NAACP. During the war years, a consensus of purpose emerged in the black community, and new branches were organized in all of Georgia's most important cities and towns. By 1920 the state boasted the second largest number of branches in the nation. Much of the inspiration for organizing new branches may be traced to James Weldon Johnson's tour of the South in January 1917. When Johnson reached Atlanta, he met with a group of blacks, led by Walter White, a recent graduate of Atlanta University and the cashier of the Standard Life Insurance Company, a leading black insurance firm; Harry Pace, an executive of Standard Life; and Herman Perry, the founder of the firm, who had launched a successful drive to form an Atlanta branch of the NAACP in December 1916. The "quickening effect" that Johnson had perceived was "especially noticeable" in Atlanta. At the time of his visit, the Atlanta branch already had initiated a highly visible and ultimately successful campaign to improve public education facilities for blacks. Elsewhere in Georgia, Johnson's visit was the catalyst for the organization of local branches. Blacks in Savannah, Augusta, Athens, and Macon warmly welcomed him and responded by forming branches in their cities. By the end of 1918, the organization had spread even to the smaller cities of Brunswick, Columbus, Hawkinsville, Rome, Thomasville, and Waycross. The expansion continued in the following year, and branches opened in Albany, Americus, Cordele, Dublin, Milledgeville, and Valdosta.[66]

With local enthusiasm for the NAACP at a fever pitch in the immediate postwar years, branches initially grew rapidly. Within two years of its founding, for example, the Atlanta branch listed more than a thousand members. But after only a few years of activity, many branches, like their counterparts in Virginia, succumbed to indifference, weak leadership, and white hostility. In Augusta, for example, initial fervor gave way to virtual chaos. By 1919 the branch was moribund, and repeated efforts in 1926, 1927, and 1930 failed to revive it.[67] Similarly, the Macon branch collapsed in 1919 and was not restored permanently until 1926. The same pattern of early fervor and gradual dissolution held with the Albany, Americus, Brunswick, Hawkinsville, Valdosta, and Waycross branches.[68] The Atlanta, Savannah, and Rome branches, however, survived lulls in membership enthusiasm, and—along with the national headquarters in New York—played a crucial role in undermining, bit by bit, the legitimacy of extralegal violence.[69]

The NAACP's principal motive for investigating and publicizing lynchings was to win public support for federal antilynching legislation. The organization also prodded efforts to prosecute lynchers and made sure that reports of racial violence were not suppressed by increasingly publicity conscious local authorities.[70] With the expansion of the NAACP around the periphery of the Cotton Belt and southern Georgia, the struggle against lynching in the region was transformed. As long as rural blacks had to rely upon their own limited resources they could make little headway in securing protection from white mobs. By waging a campaign for the passage of a federal antilynching law, the NAACP performed the vital task of whittling away at white justifications for extralegal violence. More immediately important to blacks in the most mob-prone regions, however, was the existence of an organization that investigated and exposed otherwise slighted or ignored instances of mob violence.

By drawing upon the tiny number of black professionals and the much larger number of black ministers scattered throughout rural Georgia, the NAACP was able to reach deep into the plantation hinterland. For the first time, indignant blacks did not have to remain silent in the aftermath of local incidents of lynching. For example, following the mass lynching of eleven blacks in Brooks County in May 1918, S. E. McGowan, a black undertaker; Dr. Athens N. Grant; the Reverend Samuel S. Broadnax; Dr. Maurice H. Cobb; and a Reverend Wilson, all of Quitman, worked with the national office of the NAACP to gather evidence about the lynchers, protect important witnesses, and shield the black community against any further reprisals.[71] In this case and in others, the organization became a conduit for the rage of rural blacks and, through the organization's exposés, enabled them to insure that white newspapers did not become the sole historical record of lynchings. Whereas in the past disgusted blacks had written to their state governor, or even the president of the United States, to plead that rural lynchings be investigated, they now could write to a responsive and trustworthy organization and, in a real sense, begin to compile their own history of white repression.[72]

The NAACP exposé of the lynching of Berry Washington in 1919 illustrates the effects that the organization could have in providing a full accounting of an event. Washington, a seventy-two-year-old black in the town of Milan, Telfair County, aroused the fury of a white mob when he shot the mayor's drunken son, who was attempting to rape a young black woman. After Washington surrendered himself to the police, a mob seized and hanged him.[73] County officials and the mayor convinced local editors to suppress the story, but the Reverend Judson Dinkins in the nearby town of Cordele contacted both the NAACP and the Tuskegee Institute in Alabama (the institute was known widely for gathering statistics on mob violence) about the affair.

After securing an affidavit from Dinkins, the NAACP released a full account of the lynching to newspapers throughout the nation. The editorial protests of the *Atlanta Constitution* and the *Macon Telegraph,* which severely criticized the way that local authorities handled the incident, provoked the superior court judge of Telfair County to issue a strong charge to the county's grand jury to investigate the lynching. The grand jury promptly indicted the county's sheriff for negligence and his deputy for being a ringleader of the mob. The deputy sheriff, however, could not be prosecuted—he had been killed while attempting to arrest a criminal—and the sheriff, whose negligence could not easily be proven without the testimony of his dead deputy, was acquitted.[74]

The legal protection that NAACP branches attempted to provide for black criminals also posed a direct challenge to mob violence. By exposing the trumped-up charges that blacks routinely faced, the NAACP called into question the justifications of lynching that stressed the pervasiveness of serious black crime. As the NAACP revealed in case after case, all too often the courts punished infractions that could only be construed as crimes in an atmosphere where fundamental civil rights for blacks went unrecognized. The lengthy efforts of the Savannah branch of the NAACP to secure legal aid and protection for two black youths, Joe Jordan and James Harvey, revealed with tragic clarity the interconnectedness of southern legal traditions and mob violence.

During the summer of 1921, Harvey and Jordan had hiked throughout the Deep South before stopping to work for a few months in Wayne County in south Georgia. The young men, one of whom was a war veteran, quickly became ensnared by the worst forms of the coercive practices of southern agriculture and were unable to compel their white employer to pay them. In September, apparently after the men had demanded their wages, their employer's wife brought charges against them for attacking and raping her. Three days after the alleged crime, the suspects having been removed to Savannah, a special term of the court was held. The case was argued before the court by an appointed counsel who made no attempt to gather evidence or secure testimony for the defense of his "clients." Not surprisingly, when Harvey and Jordan were tried even while they remained incarcerated in the Savannah jail, the jury found them guilty, and they were sentenced to death.[75]

The uncle of James Harvey contacted the NAACP, pleading for aid in overturning this miscarriage of justice. Dr. Alexander, president of the Savannah branch, and L. E. Williams, president of the Wage Earners Savings Bank, with the aid of Harry H. Pace, the president of the Atlanta branch, hired James A. Harolds, a white lawyer in Jessup, to represent the two men and launched a campaign to win a retrial. Harolds succeeded in bringing the case before the supreme court of Georgia on appeal, but the court affirmed the judgment of the lower court. By May of 1922, the continuing efforts to defend Jordan and Harvey had awakened the concern of several prominent white women in Wayne County who, disturbed by the injustice of the convictions, petitioned for a new trial on the grounds that new evidence had been discovered. When the Wayne County judge turned down the petition, the men's lawyer and the NAACP had no recourse but to petition Governor Thomas W. Hardwick for executive clemency. On the day of their scheduled execution, the governor granted the men a reprieve and sentenced them to life imprisonment.[76]

Even this victory proved short-lived. On July 1, while the Wayne County deputy sheriff transported the two men to Savannah for safe-keeping, a mob of fewer than fifty men seized them and hanged them beside the roadside. Unwilling to let the case drop, members of the Savannah branch of the NAACP traveled to the site of the lynching, saw to it that Jordan and Harvey were properly buried, and began gathering evidence against the lynchers. The investigations left little doubt that the deputy sheriff and policemen who had been transporting the prisoners were complicitous in the event. Numerous local witnesses claimed that the two officers had waited for hours at the site of the lynching until the mob arrived and "seized" Harvey and Jordan. Although the names of several of the lynchers were revealed, attempts by the NAACP to win the conviction of the officers and the lynchers produced few results. At the very least, the details of the case became grist for the NAACP's campaign to convince the nation of the need for a federal antilynching law.[77]

Given the impediments to protest in rural Georgia, the impact of the NAACP was greater than most historians have recognized. Of course, without profound changes in southern agriculture, mounting concern over the migration of blacks out of the region, or broader conceptions of state and local political authority, the NAACP's efforts to create an atmosphere hostile to previously accepted forms of white violence would have come to naught. The achievements of the NAACP in rural Georgia must be measured according to a different standard than that used for black reform organizations in Atlanta, for example. The organization's tactics, which in the context of Atlanta were riddled with limitations and contradictions, assumed a radical character in the context of the Cotton Belt. It therefore comes as no surprise that whites in the Cotton Belt and southern Georgia lashed out at the organization and its informers.[78] Even though the NAACP failed to secure either the convictions of lynchers or the punishment of law officers guilty of complicity, it helped direct the spotlight of national scorn on rural communities where lynching persisted. In a myriad of ways the NAACP worked to remove what a later civil rights activist in the region would call "the mental block in the minds of those who wanted to move but were unable for fear." [79]

Like the NAACP, the Commission on Interracial Cooperation (CIC), founded in 1919 under the auspices of a group of prominent white ministers, educators, and social workers in Atlanta, attempted to take advantage of the opening for reform provided by the adjustment to the war and its consequences. Unlike the NAACP, the CIC was an entirely southern and largely white organization. It grew to include local and state interracial committees throughout Georgia and the South as a whole by carefully steering clear of any appearance of challenging white supremacy. The commission announced that it was "absolutely loyal . . . to the principle of racial integrity." Even so, it created an enduring and effective organization devoted to campaigning against mob violence.[80]

The organization of the CIC represented the culmination of a revival of the interracial movement in Atlanta at the time of World War I. Beginning in 1916, white ministers in Atlanta, organized as the Committee on Church Cooperation, had met with black ministers to discuss and find solutions for the range of urban ills that bore down on blacks. Within two years the informal meetings gave way to more formal meetings of the Christian Councils, comprised of representatives from both races and officials of the YMCA, YWCA, and the Salvation Army, which endeavored to stimulate communication between white and black congregations.[81]

In January 1919, the concern that readjustment to peace after the war might be impeded by racial friction led several members of the Committee on Church Cooperation to initiate the Atlanta Commission of Interracial Cooperation, the immediate forerunner of the CIC. Under the leadership of John J. Eagan, a prominent Atlanta manufacturer, and Plato Durham, former dean of the Candler School of Theology at Emory University, the commission brought together a number of Atlantans who had long demonstrated an interest in "developing better conditions in the South." [82] Among the founders were M. Ashby Jones; Cary B. Wilmer, rector of St. Luke's Episcopal Church; Richard O. Flynn, a Presbyterian minister; Will A. Alexander, a member of the War Work Council of the YMCA and a former Methodist minister in Tennessee; and Richard H. King, executive director of the Southeastern Department of the YMCA War Work Council. During the remainder of 1919, Jones, Eagan, and especially Alexander, for whom the interracial campaign became a crusade, worked to accumulate enough financial backing to expand the Atlanta program across the South. Finally, in January 1920, adequate funding was secured from the Laura Spelman Rockefeller Memorial and the Commission on Interracial Cooperation was formally organized, with Alexander its executive secretary.[83]

Like the NAACP, the local committees of the CIC began in a frenzy of activity that subsided after a few years. Although the CIC typically failed to take root outside of the main cities of the South, local committees in Georgia endured, and indeed even flourished. In large part, the easy access to and constant attention from the headquarters' staff in Atlanta explain the development of effective local committees. Furthermore, the state committee benefited from the skilled leadership of Thomas J. Woofter, Jr., a recent doctoral graduate in sociology from Columbia University; Clark H. Foreman, the grandson of the founder of the *Atlanta Constitution;* and Arthur F. Raper, a product of Howard Odum's sociology program at Chapel Hill. In few other southern states were the combination of talent and resources more favorable for the work of the CIC.[84]

The commission set out to tackle a broad host of "negro problems," of which lynching was but one. The aims of the CIC including pledging financial aid to blacks who had been victimized by the courts, campaigning for better public facilities such as sewers and playgrounds, drawing attention to police brutality against blacks, improving social services for blacks, and crusading against mob violence. With such diverse aims, the organization necessarily adopted a variety of tactics, ranging from carefully orchestrated publicity campaigns that emphasized black "progress" to drawn-out legal battles to defend blacks accused of crimes.

Local branches of the CIC relied upon an equally wide variety of tactics in the fight to end mob violence. Whatever method adopted, however, commission members intended to demonstrate that an influential constituency in Georgia was dedicated to suppressing lawlessness. Branches of the organization periodically led public panels with local law officers to inform concerned citizens "How to cooperate with sheriffs and other peace officers to prevent mob violence." [85] CIC members routinely urged prominent whites in communities where lynchings might occur to exert influence to preserve law and order and pointedly remind sheriffs and other local law enforcement officers of the necessity to protect prisoners. When commission members were unable to prevent mob violence, they investigated lynchings and, when possible, secured indictments against mob leaders.[86] The state headquarters also assumed a prominent role and achieved notable victories. In 1922, for example, the legal assistance it provided led to the indictment of twenty-two white men and the conviction of four of them for participating in a lynching in Liberty County. The following year the state committee again provided legal assistance to secure indictments against whites who had participated in lynchings, although none of the men were convicted.[87]

Central to the CIC's campaign against mob violence was a program of public education to turn sentiment against lynching. The organization became a clearinghouse of information on the subject. In 1921, at the urging of Will Alexander, Governor Hugh M. Dorsey (1917–21) used CIC records to provide the basis for a speech and a pamphlet that described 135 instances of the mistreatment of blacks in Georgia, including lynchings and violent intimidation. Although typically not a bold critic of Georgia's race relations, Dorsey was at once encouraged by the work of the CIC and deeply discouraged by the upheavals of the Great Migration and the heightened racial violence after World War I. Conditions had reached a point, he concluded, where "to me it seems that we stand indicted as a people before the world."[88] The pamphlet, which attracted national attention, called for a comprehensive state antilynching law, including the creation of a state police force under the governor's control. The Georgia CIC drew up an antilynching statute, which was introduced into the 1926 legislature by Alexander R. Lawton, a member of the Savannah branch of the organization, but the bill, like previous attempts, failed to pass.[89]

A notable feature of the antilynching campaign of the CIC was that it supplemented the efforts of the NAACP. However much the NAACP and the CIC took issue with each other's aims, the diversity of membership that the two groups could mobilize was salutary, indeed essential, to the progress of the antilynching effort.[90] The CIC's refusal to challenge segregation and the NAACP's militant support for a federal antilynching law reflected deep-seated differences between the two organizations. The differences were no less evident in the membership of the two groups. Attempts to make the CIC interracial in fact as well as in name often failed. Lugenia Burns Hope found that blacks outside Atlanta were very wary of participating on local committees. Even so, the leadership of the CIC periodically communicated and worked with the NAACP. Sometimes the cooperation across the race line was the product of advance planning or formal organization; at other times, cooperation occurred because circumstances demanded it. Without question, leaders of both organizations deliberately took advantage of different tactics to apply the fullest possible pressure on whites who otherwise would have been opposed to or uninterested in the antilynching campaign. The more moderate methods of the CIC complimented the provocative tactics of the NAACP, virtually compelling whites caught in the glare of publicity to respond.[91]

An apt illustration of the ongoing communication between the organizations is the behind-the-scene maneuvers following an attack on Asbury McClusky, a black farmer, near the town of Statham in the spring of 1922. The trouble began after McClusky became involved in a legal dispute with the county bailiff over the ownership of an organ. Soon thereafter, the bailiff and several other white men whipped and shot McClusky and fired as many as thirty-five shots into his home. Although he survived the attack, McClusky was forced to flee. When Thomas J. Woofter learned of McClusky's plight, he decided to attempt a new tactic to combat white violence. On behalf of McClusky, the CIC filed a $50,000 damage suit and a petition for a restraining order against the men who had perpetrated the attack.[92]

As the case made its way through the courts, Woofter concluded that it would be a mistake for the CIC to arouse local sentiment by issuing provocative statements. Moreover, Woofter was worried about angering Governor Hardwick with critical publicity about race relations in Georgia at a time when "we need him particularly. . . because of the possibility of the introduction of a bill giving him the power to remove negligent sheriffs." Yet at the same time Woofter also believed that the McClusky suit represented "a test case" that deserved wide publicity. With this in mind, he wrote to Walter White, assistant secretary of the NAACP, in a thinly veiled attempt to encourage him to draw national attention to the new tactic to fight mob violence. He collected newspaper clippings about the case and sent along a detailed account from the CIC's files. Although he did not spell out precisely what he had in mind, Woofter's intent was clear. After stressing that the governor "is especially sensitive on the subject of outside publicity," he coyly advised White that he could use the information on the McClusky case "in any way you see fit."[93]

As the case bogged down in the courts, it became obvious that restraining orders were costly, time-consuming, and, of course, could not prevent determined mobs from acting. The outcome of the trial was a bitter disappointment: "The jury refused to find their neighbors guilty. They [the Klansmen] went scot free."[94] The case, however, reveals that at least as early as 1922 the two principal national antilynching organizations had begun a productive exchange of information and tactics. It was no small matter that, despite significant differences in aims and membership, the CIC and NAACP enjoyed a working relationship marked by shared respect and even a degree of healthy competition. Certainly, had the two organizations been pitted against one another and had the CIC become a voice of southern chauvinism, the campaign against lynching would have been debilitated by rivalry and jousting that might well have become a regular distraction and wasteful diversion.

Just what effect the campaigns of the NAACP and the CIC had on public attitudes is difficult to determine, but two organizations almost certainly contributed significantly to the growing intolerance of Georgians toward lynching. When appraising the significance of the CIC in 1936, the sociologist Howard Odum stressed that "the value of the C. on I. C. has come from. . . [its] continuous, uninterrupted major effort constantly under the same management and motivation. . . . It has modified that culture in vigorous and constructive ways." [95]

Odum might just as well have extended his conclusions to include the NAACP. By keeping the issue of racial violence under public scrutiny, the two organizations ensured that concern over lynching did not evaporate. Moreover, the massive lobbying effort of the NAACP for the passage of a federal antilynching statute was deeply troubling to many white Georgians. Fearing federal interference in southern affairs if an antilynching bill passed Congress, prominent white journalists desperately pointed to southern antilynching efforts as proof of the South's ability and desire to halt the evil practice without a federal antilynching law. [96]

In a variety of both subtle and conspicuous ways, the changing public sentiment toward lynching became evident during the 1920s. In rituals that became increasingly common during the decade, residents of communities scarred by lynching held public meetings to denounce the mobs. That the meetings were often organized by local Rotary Clubs, Chambers of Commerce, or newspapers is hardly surprising. These self-appointed guardians of civic reputation took it upon themselves to assure the rest of the state that their communities, with the exception of a lawless minority, were committed to the rule of law. On occasion, the public meetings called for steps to be taken against parties involved in a lynching. In one instance, citizens in Colquitt County in 1922 filed a petition with the board of the county commissioners urging the removal of a county policeman who had participated in a lynching. Although cynics dismissed these protestations as little more than public relations ruses, they actually were evidence of the growing sentiment that extralegal violence was no longer acceptable. [97]

The legitimacy of mob justice also came under attack from church congregations and ministers in communities that had witnessed lynchings. Such willingness to go on record protesting against mob violence marked a significant departure from the past. Although a small number of social reformers in the upper ranks of southern Protestantism had condemned lynching and called for the just treatment of blacks, most southern congregations had remained untouched by any comparable social awakening. [98] Walter White, who served briefly as the NAACP branch secretary in Atlanta and then for years as the administrative officer of the national organization, was guilty only of slight exaggeration when he lamented the "depressing picture of an ignorant, prejudiced, intolerant ministry. . . stirring up racial and religious antagonisms to the point of frenzy." [99]

Against such a background, the first gestures of opposition to mob violence from within local congregations during the 1920s predictably were often tentative and restrained. Although no congregations appear to have disciplined or expelled mob members, many did go on record to condemn local lynchings and the individuals responsible for them. In 1920, the executive committee of the Council of Churches in Atlanta denounced the lynching of George King, a black, by a small white mob and demanded that city authorities and Governor Dorsey take steps to uncover and punish the murderers. The committee concluded that "neither aristocratic nor bolshevistic Russia has ever presented a more flagrant violation of the fundamental right of citizenship than the execution of this negro." After a mob in Athens in 1921 burned at the stake John Eberhardt, a black accused of murder, the Athens Ministerial Association met and labeled the lynching as "barbarism" that was "subversive of every interest we hold precious." A year later, following a lynching in Macon, numerous ministers in the city delivered sermons condemning the event, and Sunday school classes in at least seven churches passed resolutions denouncing the lynching and pledging support for legal authorities. For T. B. Stanford, pastor of the First Street Methodist Church in Macon, the explanation for the lynching was simple: "These upheavals of passion that make men lose their heads are calculated to destroy the very basis of our civilization. They are born of the devil." [100]

In at least a few instances, outraged ministers went so far as to denounce local authorities who failed to prevent mob violence. Following the lynching of James Harvey and Joe Jordan in Liberty County in 1922, P. T. Holloway, pastor of the Midway Methodist Church, blasted officials in neighboring Wayne County who had been transporting the prisoners through Liberty County when they were seized. In his sermon and then in a widely published letter, the minister excoriated the incompetence and disingenuousness of the law officers. Almost certainly, Holloway's public criticism contributed to the impetus behind the prosecution of several of the alleged lynchers and those authorities suspected of complicity. [101]

The accumulated weight of denunciations of mob violence by ministers, newspaper editors, business groups, and antilynching organizations pushed local law officers and authorities to take meaningful steps to prevent lynchings. Before the 1920s few law officers in Georgia showed any inclination to jeopardize their local standing by protecting black prisoners at all costs. To do so would have been both potentially dangerous and without reward because there was seldom any significant constituency that prized the defense of the legal process. But during the 1920s conscientious law officers increasingly could count on a modicum of local support if they stood up to mobs. As a result, they were emboldened and surrendered their prisoners significantly less often than had been the case in the past. Between 1900 and 1914, for example, 63 percent of all lynching victims were seized by mobs while in the custody of law officers. Moreover, 38 percent of all mob victims had been removed from jails. But between 1915 and 1930, the percentage of mob victims taken from law officers fell to 42 percent, and fewer than 25 percent were taken from jails.[102] In short, the likelihood that black prisoners in the custody of law officers would fall into the hands of lynchers declined markedly during the 1920s.

The increased effectiveness of law officers reflected both new tactics for dealing with mobs and greater devotion to preserving law and order. Law officers continued to move prisoners to distant jails for safekeeping, but instead of relying upon railroads as they had previously, conscientious officers now used fast automobiles and followed circuitous, unpredictable paths to the jails. Because the routes and schedules of railroads were common knowledge, it was therefore virtually impossible to move prisoners secretly on trains. The advent of the automobile age did not mark the end of the practice of mobs relieving officers of their prisoners on Georgia's back roads, but it did significantly improve the odds that black prisoners would survive the trip to a safer jail.[103]

Local authorities, fearful of disorder, also demonstrated a new willingness to request militia troops to disperse mobs. The militia on occasion even resorted to force. In 1923, for example, a mob of several hundred gathered around the city jail in Savannah, intent on lynching a black man charged with the rape of a white woman. Authorities requested the militia to be called out, and when it arrived at the jail, city policemen began arresting members of the mob in front of the jail. The mob, however, was not quelled until one of its members was shot and forty-eight others were arrested. That authorities felt no need to justify the stern measures they took, including bloodshed, and that newspapers throughout the state applauded their actions is strong testimony to the increasing willingness of legal authorities to confront the issue of mob violence.[104]

Finally, local authorities showed a considerably greater interest in prosecuting mob members than had been the case previously. Throughout the decades between 1880 and 1920, there were occasional attempts to prosecute lynchers; a few exceptional cases were even successful. In virtually all of these instances, the lynchers that faced prosecution had participated in either terrorist or private mobs—mobs that typically lacked broad local legitimacy. Participants in posses or mass mobs responsible for lynchings remained virtually free of any threat of prosecution. Although the same pattern of prosecution generally held true after World War I, local authorities demonstrated far greater interest in trying mob members. After twenty of the sixty-nine lynchings between 1919 and 1930, authorities secured indictments against members of lynch mobs. In addition, members of foiled mobs were also indicted. Authorities even began to experiment with innovative tactics against mobs.[105] For example, in May 1922, Judge Blanton Fortson of Athens granted a temporary injunction restraining several men from further mob violence against a black man in neighboring Barrow County. In a few instances, mob members even were convicted. In April 1922, three members of a mob that had fatally wounded Will Jones, a black farmer in Schley County, were convicted of attempted murder and sentenced to one to four years in prison. Four men in Savannah received three-to-four-month sentences in 1924 for leading the mob that had attacked the jail the previous year.[106]

The first conviction of mob members for murder followed the lynching of Dave Wright in August 1926 in Coffee County. Wright, a white man with an unsavory reputation as a moonshiner, shot a white woman who had testified against him for violating prohibition statutes. A week after the crime a small mob seized Wright from the local jail and murdered him. State and local authorities used the opportunity to make examples of the lynchers. The superior court judge for the county immediately summoned a grand jury and exhorted them to indict the mob members. During the next three months, the state's attorney "built up such a case that the leader and eight of his associates felt constrained to enter pleas of guilty." The leader of the mob and another of its members received life sentences, while the seven other men received sentences ranging from four to seven years.[107]

Newspapers across the state trumpeted the convictions and argued that a precedent had been set for the punishment of all lynchers, regardless of the race of their victims. The *Douglas Enterprise* warned that "lynching henceforth is murder in Georgia, and the same laws will cover both." The *Augusta Herald* declared that "since 1889, Georgia has had 433 lynchings; if there should be another, we trust that members of the mob will be given the extreme penalty of death." Newspaper editors also saw the convictions as vindication for their claims that Georgians "are as strongly in favor of law enforcement as the people in any other section of the country."[108] Much of the editorial response was marred by chronic exaggeration of the significance of the case. That the lynchers had been a motley collection of whites who had murdered a white man whose crime had created little sensation in the community goes far to explain the successful prosecution. Moreover, the editorial accolades for the Douglas County authorities were aimed at demonstrating that there was a new commitment to law and order in Georgia and that federal antilynching legislation was unneeded.

The significance of the trials of lynchers in Douglas County and elsewhere in the state during the 1920s must not be overestimated. If mob members were more likely to be indicted, they still were rarely convicted. Cases often floundered because of squabbles between county and state officials over legal jurisdiction, flimsy evidence, perjured alibis, and sympathetic juries who refused to convict. Even so, it is important to recognize the increasing efforts to prosecute lynchers measured the declining legitimacy of mob violence. At the very least, the trials of mob members marked an advance over the virtually complete legal silence that had previously surrounded lynchings and initiated the gradual process by which the punishment of lynchers, even if only private mob members, became the legitimate concern of local authorities. The attempted prosecutions and convictions of lynchers during the 1920s recall nothing so much as Samuel Johnson's reference to the dog walking on its hind legs: What matters is not that it is done well, but that it is done at all.

The cumulative effect of the various efforts to suppress lynchings is apparent in the declining frequency of lynchings in Georgia during the 1920s. Forty lynchings occurred in the state between 1920 and 1922, but during the succeeding four years, mobs murdered only ten victims. And beginning in 1927 and continuing through 1929, Georgia enjoyed the first lynching-free years in five decades. However difficult it is to determine the precise roles that the Great Migration, the NAACP, the CIC, and emerging local opposition to mob violence played, their effects were clear. The accelerating shift from outright glorification of mob violence to defensive embarrassment can be traced across the early twentieth century. During the 1920s, the legitimacy of the noose and torch as appropriate weapons for an indignant, civilized community came under attack from both within the South and from without. For all of the divergent, even contradictory, aims of black activists and white critics of mob violence, they and a growing number of southerners all agreed that lynching could no longer be ignored, justified, or condoned.

By no means were the traditions of mob violence entirely uprooted in Georgia during the 1920s. Defenders of the practice, often deeply suspicious of the changes that had brought lynching into question, continued to justify it with arguments that had changed little since the late nineteenth century. In 1916, the editor of the Cordele Dispatch foreshadowed the arguments of the defenders of mob violence in the following decades. "Commercialism seems to be the ruling spirit of the day," he observed, "we may, and doubtless will, suffer for our loyalty to our women, but we will suffer to the end, and will not CHANGE!" [109]

Traditionalists vehemently denounced the antilynching campaign; the sheer innovation of the organizations and the values they proselytized predictably bred uneasiness and hostility. In 1921, for example, when Governor Dorsey issued his exposé cataloging shocking instances of cruelty toward blacks, the Dixie Defense Committee leaped to the defense of the state, and Governor-elect Hardwick, a devoted member of the Ku Klux Klan, branded the pamphlet "infamous slander." [110] The lawlessness of the Klan during the 1920s also underscored the persistence of deeply rooted traditional values that had not been touched by the efforts of the antilynching reformers. [111] Georgia's brief respite from mob lawlessness ended in 1930, when mobs murdered seven blacks. In isolated, impoverished communities in the state, whites tenaciously clung to the ethos of mob violence and resorted to extralegal measures when sufficiently provoked by rumor or deed. Lynchings continued sporadically throughout the 1930s and 1940s, and not until 1946 did the last lynching occur in Georgia. But with each passing year, the defenders of mob violence moved toward the periphery of southern society, no longer able to claim the unquestioned allegiance of the white masses.

The history of opposition to lynching in Georgia contrasts markedly to opposition in Virginia. In Virginia, elected officials, motivated by fears about the unraveling of social order during the turbulent decade of the 1890s and with the warm support of the state's newspapers, assumed leadership of the opposition. In Georgia, conservative opposition to lynching also arose during the 1890s but failed to survive the cyclone of racial hysteria at the end of the decade. The powerful influence of the racist radicals in Georgia stifled effective opposition to lynching until the second decade of the twentieth century.

When a new campaign against mob violence did evolve, it was driven as much by humanitarian zeal as by a concern for social order. A small group of dedicated antilynching reformers worked to dissolve the attitudes that perpetuated lynching. By 1910, many Georgia editors had moved from grudgingly defending it as a natural response of an outraged citizenry to labeling it an affront on civilization. Antilynching reformers, with the eager support of journalists, hammered away at the backwardness of lynching and the threat that it posed to the advancement of whites, no less than blacks.

The lengthy campaign to persuade Georgians and other southerners to stop mob violence could not have succeeded without important political and economic developments. Across Georgia in communities untouched by the antilynching campaign, whites confronted the repercussions of the Great Migration. As blacks streamed northward, planters felt compelled to promise improvements in the treatment of those who remained behind. Economic exigencies seemed to demand that whites no longer acquiesce to mob violence against blacks.

The looming threat of an antilynching bill also strengthened the resolve of southerners to halt mob violence. A symbiotic relationship of sorts developed between the supporters of a federal antilynching bill and southern white opponents of lynching. The protracted struggle to secure a federal antilynching law gave antilynching advocates credibility. They could say, with sincerity and some justification, that if southerners did not stop lynchings, others would.

The crusade to make race relations in Georgia more equitable and humane by ending lynching was intended to pose no more of a challenge to white supremacy than had the efforts of opponents of lynching in Virginia. Yet, ironically, just when the antilynching campaign in Georgia and elsewhere in the Deep South was achieving its greatest successes during the 1930s, many of its leaders began to confront the stumbling block of segregation. Although most shied away from attacking segregation, they had challenged white complacency, urged forward racial reform, and pioneered many of the techniques that would contribute to the ultimate demise of segregation and white supremacy.

Epilogue:
The Passing of a Tradition

By the end of the 1930s, the demise of lynching was irreversible. During the decade, the combination of the continued efforts of antilynching activists and profound changes in the southern economy delivered the decisive blows to the tradition of mob violence. Contemporaries recognized that the practice of lynching was ending, but, understandably, few opponents were willing to wait idly for its disappearance. If anything, the diminishing incidence of lynching during the decade only spurred the efforts of antilynching activists.

The first lynching of 1930 in the south Georgia town of Ocilla gave no indication of any diminution of the ferocity of mobs. On February 1, the news wires carried graphic accounts of the lynching of James Irwin, a black charged with the rape and murder of a white woman. After seizing Irwin from the sheriff's custody, the mob had tortured him by cutting off his fingers and toes and by ramming a red-hot poker into his throat before finally burning him to death. From the standpoint of many concerned observers, the Irwin lynching, the six other lynchings in Georgia, and the fifteen lynchings elsewhere in the South during the next eight months threatened to erase the gains made in the struggle against mob violence during the preceding decade.[1]

The flurry of activity by antilynching activists during the 1930s represented the culmination of a decade of reform efforts. Activists did not adopt new tactics so much as apply familiar methods with a newfound urgency. For example, Will Alexander, the chair of the CIC, proposed that the organization carry out detailed investigations of each lynching in 1930 in order to determine the precise causes of mob violence. The CIC had already made it a practice to investigate lynchings, as had the NAACP. What distinguished the new campaign, which was labeled appropriately the Southern Commission on the Study of Lynching, was the prestige and influence of the participants. Among the members were the Pulitzer Prize-winning journalist Julian Harris of the *Atlanta Constitution;* John Hope, the president of Atlanta University; and B. F. Hubert, president of Georgia State College. In addition, research on each lynching was to be carried out by two trained social scientists, Arthur Raper, a young white sociologist educated at the University of North Carolina, the emerging center of southern liberalism, and Walter R. Chivers, a black professor at Morehouse College in Atlanta.[2]

The commission's findings appeared first in *Lynchings and What They Mean,* released in the fall of 1931, and then in fuller form in Raper's *The Tragedy of Lynching,* published in 1933. Both served to codify the conclusions of southern white liberals and antilynching activists about the causes of mob violence and the best way to suppress it. There was little that was strikingly new in Raper's interpretation of the phenomenon of lynching; in fact, Walter White and the NAACP had reached similar conclusions years before. But, by virtue of scholarly methodology and scientific tone, the commission's findings became the definitive contemporary analysis of lynching—at least in the eyes of concerned southern whites. What was most significant about Raper's conclusions was that they provided, in the words of the *Chattanooga News,* "all the necessary facts concerning the malady which has made the South a synonym for barbarity in other countries."[3] In Raper's hands, the evidence from the lynchings of 1930 was clear; illiteracy, poverty, and cultural stagnation were the root causes of mob violence. He disposed of the shibboleths of conventional white supremacy and hammered home the central point that lynchings could not be separated from the region's far-reaching social and economic difficulties. Presumably, only the modernization of the southern economy would eradicate many of the causes of mob violence. In the meantime, the commission's conclusion that "the primary responsibility for the lessening of crime and eradication of lynching rests upon that portion of the white population which controls political, social, and economic conditions" added legitimacy to the CIC's campaign to encourage influential whites to fight against mob violence.[4]

The founding of the Association of Southern Women for the Prevention of Lynching (ASWPL) in Atlanta in 1930 was an expression of the new vigor with which white antilynching activists set out to liberalize the attitudes of white southerners. The new organization also represented the logical evolution of the campaign by white women reformers to address the intertwined issues of racial and gender discrimination in the South, a reform tradition that extended at least as far back as the turn of the century and the efforts of Lily Hammond and others. Worried by the sharp rise in the number of lynchings during 1930, and convinced of the vital need for white women to repudiate forthrightly the "code of chivalry" that was "being used as shield behind which our own men committed cowardly acts of violence against a helpless people," several women members within the CIC formed the organization. Under the vigorous leadership of Jesse Daniel Ames, the ASWPL grew to have a membership of forty-three thousand women scattered throughout the South. When Ames assumed leadership in 1930, she had already established herself as one the South's leading social activists, first as a campaigner for suffrage and progressive reforms in Texas and then, following World War I, as a leader of the struggle for racial justice in the CIC throughout the 1920s. With her "aggressive" and "forthright" personality, Ames was perfectly suited to directing the day-to-day operations of the association and its skeleton staff.[5]

The ASWPL worked diligently to raise public consciousness about the evils of mob violence and pressure local authorities to prevent lynchings and prose-cute lynchers by expanding on the tactics for fighting mob violence developed by the CIC and mobilizing a network of concerned churchwomen throughout the South. With a membership that consisted of respectable women active in religious and civic organizations and who typically had ties of family and friendship with prominent local men, the organization skillfully recruited precisely those citizens most likely to be able to dissuade lynchers and prod law officers to uphold the law. In Georgia, prominent ASWPL members such as Dorothy Tilly of Atlanta, Julia Collier Harris of Atlanta, Ida-Beall Neel of Forsyth, as well as Ames herself used their personal influence in church and social organizations to cultivate support for the organization's aims. Elsewhere in the South, state chairwomen such as Bessie C. Alford and Ethel F. Stevens of Mississippi and Kate T. Davis of South Carolina effectively used the skills and influence they had gained from political and reform activism to carry the message of the ASWPL into their states.[6]

One illustration of the effectiveness of the ASWPL's program was the preven-tion of a lynching in central Georgia in December 1934. On Christmas Day, an Associated Press editor called Jessie Daniel Ames with a warning that a black man had killed a law officer in Schley County and that a lynch mob was forming to track down the suspect. Ames immediately contacted Mary Addie Mullino, a member of the ASWPL and a prominent member of the Methodist Woman's Missionary Society who lived in Macon County, which borders on Schley County. Rather than attempting to face down the mob in person, Mullino took advantage of her per-sonal contacts in Schley County and telephoned a number of ministers and other "public-spirited" county residents, urging them to do anything they could to pre-vent the lynching. She also contacted the sheriff and his deputies, reminding them of their oath to uphold the law and pointing out that lynching was never justified.

When law officers captured the man later in the day, the success of Mullino's tactics was clear. Her telephone calls and mobilization of local citizens had almost certainly convinced law officers that they would be subjected to a barrage of unfavorable publicity if they failed to uphold the law. The sheriff also understood that he might risk alienating influential local citizens if he failed to make a sincere effort to protect the man. Mullino's diligence was by no means uncommon among ASWPL members; in numerous other instances their timely intercession deterred possible lynchings. The combined tactics of publicity and mobilization of local women activists throughout Georgia and the South were decidedly effective in reducing the numbers of lynchings. In particular, the organization's efforts to prod law officers to uphold the law was notably successful in lessening the proportion of lynchings in which prisoners were taken from custody.[7]

The vision and methods of white antilynching activists during the 1930s reflected the maturation of the social critique of the South, which had its roots in the Progressive Era at the turn of the century. The vision combined a powerful yearning for order and control with a sincere desire to eliminate the social ills of mob violence and brutal racial discrimination. Raper's statistics and evidence demonstrated that lynching went hand in hand with a rural culture corrupted by drunkenness, irreligion, illiteracy, poverty, and excessive license. The object of the reformers was to inculcate values that were all too obviously absent in a region where mobs committed such inhuman acts of brutality as the lynching of James Irwin. The most earnest members of the CIC and ASWPL envisioned a South in which there would be no lynchings, no mob intimidation of the courts, no extralegal violence in labor relations, and far less racial discrimination overall. To achieve such a South, they believed that the virtues of sobriety, piety, education, industry, and restraint would have to be instilled in southerners. In many regards, the white antilynching activists, like earlier middle-class reformers elsewhere in the nation, had a conspicuously restrictive moral vision. Yet, simultaneously, the reformers also offered a liberating vision, nowhere more evident than in the ASWPL's head-on challenge to southern racial and sexual conventions. For all of the limitations of the antilynching campaigns of white southerners during the 1930s—and there were many—it must be remembered that they still came far closer to understanding racial violence and offering ways to stop it than had any previous generation of southerners.

Complementing the regional campaigns of the ASWPL and CIC was the national campaign for public mobilization waged by the NAACP. If anything, the NAACP's influence increased during the 1930s when its modest resources could be used more effectively as the level of mob violence decreased. Dormant branches of the organization throughout the South, including many in Georgia, were revived and began again to defend the legal rights of alleged black criminals both in and out of the courts.[8] More important, after the bitter failure to secure a federal antilynching statute during the previous decade, the organization launched another relentless campaign to win the passage of a federal statute. To garner support for the Wagner-Costigan antilynching bill, the NAACP intensified its campaign to publicize the horrors of mob violence. For the most part, efforts during the 1930s differed from the organization's earlier methods only in scale. For example, the extent of publicity that the NAACP generated following several notorious lynchings during the decade, including the exceptionally gruesome lynching of Claude Neal in Florida in 1934, was without precedent. No longer could southern communities rest assured of the security of relative anonymity or of only a brief and spasm of condemnation following a lynching; instead there was the certain prospect of a flood of hostile national publicity, much of it generated by the NAACP.[9]

However much the persistent efforts of the CIC, ASWPL, and NAACP succeeded in bringing lynching into increasing disfavor in the nation at large and in the South in particular, they could not address the underlying socioeconomic causes of mob violence. By the 1930s, virtually all antilynching activists recognized that impersonal economic and social forces lay behind lynching, but few antilynching activists were certain of how best to confront such a vast and seemingly intractable problem as the impoverished southern economy. Yet profound changes took place during the 1930s, even without the guiding hands of antilynching activists, changes that contributed in crucial—if virtually unrecognized—ways to the effectiveness of the campaign against lynching.

One of the jarring but unintended consequences of New Deal programs in the South was that the existing system of agriculture, especially the plantation system, was virtually revolutionized. It is hardly surprising that two distinctive features of the South, mob violence and an agricultural economy based on the tenant plantation, should pass away simultaneously. Planters had long resisted powerful forces at work on the archaic traditions of southern agriculture, but until the New Deal, few had either capital or compelling incentives to bring their farming and labor practices into line with those of the rest of the nation. As a result of New Deal agricultural programs, especially the cotton and tobacco crop-reduction and subsidy programs administered by the Agricultural Adjustment Administration (AAA), the southern economy lost many of its most exaggerated characteristics. For the first time, strong economic forces encouraged planters to adopt mechanical farming methods and wage labor and raise wage levels. Beginning in the fall of 1933, a protracted process of tenant evictions, increasing reliance on hired labor, and gradual adoption of mechanization led inexorably to capital-intensive agriculture throughout the South.[10]

This process of "adjustment" came at great human cost. Although landlords were supposedly committed to dividing government crop-reduction payments with their tenants, the wave of tenant evictions was stark evidence of failure to do so. In the short term, the modernization of southern agriculture intensified the smoldering tensions in relations between landlords and tenants. Displaced sharecroppers and tenants had few opportunities to protest the effects of the economic changes. They did not sit on any of the boards that oversaw the government programs, and when they attempted bold measures of protest, as in the Southern Tenant Farmers' Union, they were systematically and ruthlessly silenced. For black farmers who could not find a place as hired laborers or who refused to become part of the large pool of surplus labor in the countryside, there were few alternatives aside from moving to the city or going North.[11]

The cumulative effect of these broad changes was to reshape rural labor and race relations. Planters in the old plantation areas of the South learned what their counterparts in Virginia had known for decades; the appearance of the cash nexus in the countryside by no means signaled the end of their control. Traditional methods of marshaling labor, including the healthy applications of violence, gave way to less personal and paternalistic techniques of what now became known as "farm management." Indeed, an army of federal agricultural agents educated planters in how best to use farm labor and modern farming techniques. Coercion and violence were hardly excised from rural labor traditions, but much of the labor violence that flared in the rural South during the 1930s was no longer unique to the region. Jack Temple Kirby, a historian, has pointed out that when southern planters and local authorities stamped out the protest organizations of the rural downtrodden, they were mimicking the actions of large farmers and local authorities in the Southwest.[12] Thus, planters did not so much renounce violence as they increasingly relied upon the support of local and state law enforcement and judicial institutions to crush most challenges to their power.

Conversely, despite the ingrained conservatism of planters and other rural whites, the unsettling effects of the modernization of southern agriculture during the 1930s failed to breed widespread concerns about the preservation of white authority. The contrast with the 1890s is striking. Although the changes in rural society during the 1930s were at least as profound as those during the 1890s, there were no counterparts to either the Populist movement or the radical racists during the 1930s. The demise of older forms of plantation agriculture, and with it the acceleration of the depopulation of the same regions, reduced many of the persistent causes of mob violence without at the same time generating new sources of extralegal violence. The implication of these broad changes was momentous. The economist Gavin Wright has noted, "The economic underpinnings and social glue that had kept the [southern] regional economy isolated were no longer present in 1940." [13] As the modernization of the rural economy of Georgia and the Deep South gained speed, one of the most significant obstacles to the campaign against lynching was removed. As long as traditional methods of organizing rural labor had persisted, the efforts of antilynching activists had been challenged by deeply ingrained traditions of coercive labor practices. Thus, although antilynching activists were unable to address the economic causes of lynching effectively, the painful process of rural modernization had the salutary effect of sharply diminishing the socioeconomic roots of mob violence.

In addition to bringing about fundamental changes in the rural South, the New Deal also set a precedent for greater federal intervention to punish lynchers. Although no federal antilynching law passed during the 1930s (in part because of President Roosevelt's refusal to alienate southern congressmen by supporting the legislation), staff members of the Department of Justice began to explore ways to apply the equal protection clause of the Fourteenth Amendment to the crime of lynching. Partly to appease black voters in the North who were outraged by lynchings and partly as an expression of the emerging federal commitment to protect the rights of minorities, the Department of Justice took the unprecedented steps of investigating the lynchings and pressing charges against mob members. Beginning in the aftermath of the lynching of Cleo Wright, accused of an attack on a white woman in southwestern Missouri in 1942, the Federal Bureau of Investigation investigated the lynching and, even more extraordinary, the Civil Rights Section of the Department of Justice brought charges against members of the lynch mob.

The failure of the case against Wright's lynchers, and the fact that the Department of Justice had only a limited mandate from Roosevelt to investigate lynchings, demonstrate that the newfound federal concern about lynching had clear limits. But to countless southern racists unlearned in the law, the meaning of the Department of Justice's investigations into the Wright lynching seemed clear: the federal government had thrown its support behind outside agitators and against mob violence. The investigation of Cleo Wright's death, the historian Dominic Capeci has argued convincingly, "signified the transition of the Justice Department's role in civil rights: instead of sitting on their law books, Justice Department lawyers interpreted them." [14] Even without a federal antilynching statute, administrators found legal pretexts for the expansion of federal authority to include the investigation and prosecution of lynchers. As they reinterpreted the government's obligation to protect the civil rights of blacks, they took a crucial, although admittedly tentative, step in placing federal power in opposition to mob violence.[15]

Given the seemingly static quality of southern society, the disappearance of lynching by 1950 was momentous. It marked the passing of one of the most significant rituals of black degradation. The decline, of course, did not mean that white violence against blacks stopped. But as the number of lynchings declined sharply during the 1940s, the tradition of mob murders by mass mobs, with their attendant public rituals, virtually came to an end. Lynching became the particular province of small, secretive mobs that carried on the tradition of terrorist mob violence. There were no more assaults on jails, no more extended public rituals of torture and mutilation of mob victims, and no more carnivalike gatherings to witness the victim's corpse. Instead, when lynchings did occur, they were the actions either of law officers who exceeded even traditional standards of police violence against black suspects or of a small number of mob members who displayed conspicuous concern for the concealment of their identities. As the practice changed during the 1930s and 1940s, the line between lynching and murder became obscure, indeed almost arbitrary. Perhaps the most revealing illustrations of the changing character of mob violence were the slaughter of four blacks at the hands of a small mob near Monroe, Georgia, in 1946, and the mass execution of black convicts by law officers near Brunswick, Georgia, in 1947.

Much about the lynching near Monroe is tragically familiar; the immediate causes of the lynching and the complicity of the law officers with the mob followed convention. In July of 1947, Roger Malcolm, a black tenant farmer in Walton County, an Upper Piedmont county located between Athens and Atlanta, angrily confronted his wife with the charge that she was having an affair with Barney Hester, the son of Malcolm's white landlord. When Malcolm's wife fled to Hester's home for protection, Malcolm followed and in short order the two men began to fight. Precisely what happened next was never determined, but the outcome of the fight was clear: Malcolm had stabbed his landlord's son. He was arrested, but not before a small mob of Hester's neighbors had savagely beaten and nearly killed him. During the next ten days, several half-hearted attempts were made on the Walton County jail where he was held, but none amounted to much and they were easily foiled.[16]

If the days of sheriffs openly turning their prisoners over to mobs had passed, whites intent on lynching still could expect success by resorting to the traditional clandestine methods of private mobs. On July 25, J. Loy Harrison, the landlord of Malcolm's brother-in-law, presented himself at the county jail in Monroe and agreed to pay Malcolm's bail and to make him "work off" the debt on Harrison's farm. There was nothing unusual about Harrison's act (planters had long taken advantage of southern jails for cheap labor), and, after all, both Malcolm's wife and brother-in-law had pressed Harrison to take custody of Malcolm. Accompanied by Malcolm and his wife, sister, and brother-in-law, Harrison drove home to his farm by way of a maze of unpaved back roads.

Several miles from Monroe, a parked car blocked the road, forcing Harrison to stop his car. A small group of armed white men surrounded the car, dragged Malcolm and his brother-in-law aside, and bound them with ropes. When one of the black women recognized one of the gunmen and pleaded with him to spare the men's lives, the leader of the mob shouted, "get those damned women, too." The lynchers dragged the four blacks a short distance from Harrison's car (Harrison claimed that he was covered with a shotgun by one of the gunmen) and lined them up. Then, as Harrison later recalled, "I could see the Negroes four abreast. I could see the back of the men's hands. I heard the leader say 'one, two three' and then 'boom.' He did that three times." [17] When the firing ended, the riddled bodies of the two women and two men lay crumpled on the ground. Once the execution was completed, the lynchers politely ordered Harrison to turn his car around and drive away. When Harrison called the Walton County Sheriff a short time later, all he had to say was, "they just hijacked me and killed my niggers." [18]

The brutal slaughter provoked immediate and loud condemnation throughout Georgia and the nation. Governor Ellis Arnall ordered the Georgia Bureau of Investigation (GBI) to investigate and offered a reward of $10,000 for information leading to the conviction of the murderers. The reward fund soon totaled more than $30,000 after the NAACP, the Congress of Industrial Organizations, the American Civil Liberties Union, and the Mariners Union added to it. Even President Harry S. Truman denounced the lynching and ordered the FBI to try to secure sufficient evidence to prosecute the lynchers for violating the civil rights of the four victims. The FBI and GBI collected incriminating evidence against a deputy sheriff, who almost certainly was involved in the planning of the executions, and against Harrison, who almost certainly had not just happened to drive to the spot where the lynchers waited. There was good reason to believe that Harrison had deliberately brought along Malcolm's wife and sister with the intention that they could testify later that he had not participated in the murders. (But, of course, when one of the women recognized a mob member, they too had to be executed.) Months of collecting evidence, however, failed to produce any indictments, and even the attempt by U.S. Attorney John Cowert to secure indictments from a federal grand jury in Athens came to naught. In the end, no charges were ever bought against any of the twenty men rumored to have participated in the lynching.[19]

The Walton County lynchings of 1946 demonstrated both the continuities in mob violence as well as the important changes in the response to lynching. There was little about the cause of the lynching or the carefully planned subterfuge of the mob to distinguish it from the pattern of private mob violence that had persisted in Georgia for at least a half-century. But the volume of criticism and the resources brought to bear in the investigation of the lynching were unprecedented. The emergence of new southern law enforcement agencies such as the GBI, of the federal concern about mob violence as demonstrated by the FBI's investigations, and of the maturing coalition between national labor unions and civil rights organizations as evidenced by the contributions to the reward fund, ensured that the Walton County incident would not be just another lynching in the eyes of the nation. The cumulative impact of these various forces was to drive mob violence in Georgia as well as in the South virtually underground.[20]

Just slightly less than a year after the executions in Walton County, the emerging character of racial violence that defied easy characterization was revealed when guards at the Anguilla Prison Camp mowed down at least fifteen black convicts, killing eight and wounding the rest. The events were far removed from the violence of a frenzied mass of lynchers storming a jail, but, in many ways, the actions of the guards represented the evolution of the ruthless violence that southern posses and lawmen had inflicted upon black suspects for generations.

The slaughter at the camp followed the refusal of twenty-odd prisoners on a work detail to work in a snake-infested swamp without boots. When the protesting prisoners were returned to an enclosure at the camp, the prison warden, who apparently was "half-drunk," ordered the five "ring-leaders" of the protest to come forward so they could be punished. In light of the warden's threat to one of the prisoners—he taunted Willie "Pee Wee" Bell, "I want to kill you"—the men predictably refused to step forward. Enraged by the prisoners' defiance of authority, the warden and the guards armed themselves with pick handles, iron bars, an ice pick, and at least one submachine gun. The warden then shot down Bell, setting off a mad rush by the convicts to seek cover. As the prisoners scrambled, the warden ordered, "Let em have it," precipitating a barrage of gunfire, including several machine gun bursts. Eight men died almost immediately, while many more (the exact number remains unclear) collapsed with severe wounds.[21]

Had it not been for the NAACP, the bloodshed at the Anguilla Prison Camp probably would have attracted only passing attention. The local newspaper, the

Brunswick News, called for state and local officials to investigate the deaths and expressed some doubt about the "official" account of the incident. At least one local politician stated publicly that "This is murder" and indignantly complained that the warden and guards had not been arrested or relieved of their duty. But it was members of the Brunswick branch of the NAACP who carefully gathered evidence, including a letter smuggled from the camp describing the horrifying conditions there. The NAACP's findings left little doubt that the prison staff had slaughtered the prisoners without any justification whatsoever. But, as had happened so often in the past, evidence alone, no matter how compelling, did not ensure that charges could be brought against whites guilty of violence against blacks, especially black criminals. NAACP activists had difficulty even mobilizing support within the local black community because, as one NAACP investigator explained, "they felt we were defending habitual criminals." [22] Moreover, efforts to publicize the "massacre" provoked the increasingly familiar debate over whether such incidents of violence should be properly labeled lynchings, murders, or, in the Anguilla case, prison uprisings. Against this background, few were surprised when a coroner's jury, a superior court grand jury, and a special committee of the state legislature all separately concluded that the warden and his guards had taken steps "necessary to end a mutiny and prevent a mass escape." [23] At a time when lynching was rapidly losing the patina of legitimacy in the South, the Anguilla killings reaffirmed that law officers still could participate in lawless executions secure in the knowledge that they would escape harsh local condemnation or punishment.

It is tempting to see the Anguilla massacre as an obvious example of how the state began to assume the role previously held by mobs. Long before mob violence had begun to decline, whites frequently had substituted "legal lynchings" and violence by posses in its place. That the number of executions in many southern states rose sharply as the number of lynchings fell during the 1930s would seem to suggest a direct relationship between an increase in state-inflicted punishment and the decline of extralegal violence. [24] Certainly, the notorious Scottsboro case during the 1930s attracted national and international attention to the mockery of justice that blacks often received from the southern legal system. In time, the uproar caused by the blatant miscarriage of justice prevented the black men in the Scottsboro case from being executed, but in countless other instances that failed to attract attention, blacks charged with serious crimes faced perfunctory trials and likely execution. [25]

Even so, violence by state authorities, in the form of legal executions or legal lynchings, differed in fundamental ways from most earlier lynchings and should not be interpreted as the continuation of lynching under another guise. First, there is no evidence that any statistically important increase in state executions compensated for the decline in lynchings.[26] Admittedly, as long as public executions persisted in the South they were intended to convey lessons in civil and social order. But by the beginning of the twentieth century, authorities in most southern states, including Georgia and Virginia, had moved executions out of the public eye and behind prison doors. As in many other cultural transformations, the abolition of public executions in the South took place decades after the question had been settled in the rest of the nation. With the advent of private executions, which the historian Louis Masur has described as "private mechanisms of order and control," state-inflicted capital punishment could no longer serve as a surrogate ritual for lynching.[27] In fact, state authorities in the South specifically abolished public executions because they all too often were taken over by crowds and degenerated into macabre festivals of disorder. In condemning demands for the public execution of a black man convicted of murdering an Atlanta policeman in 1903, the *Atlanta News* summarized the justifications for abolishing public executions. "Public hanging would tend to martyrize the principal actor therein," the *News* warned, whereas "the mystery and silence of a private execution is more effective than the blare and blazon of a public gallows."[28] By adopting private executions, southern states sought to promote the values of restraint, discipline, control, and order, values that were undermined by public executions and conspicuously absent from most lynchings.

Moreover, the continuing practice by southern law officers of ruthlessly murdering black prisoners on the slightest pretext could never affirm in any communal way the traditions that many lynchings previously had. Such murders, like lynchings, were intended to intimidate and silence individual blacks and black communities alike. At least until the 1960s in many areas of the South, police brutality retained a degree of community sanction that mob violence had long lost. But police brutality was an instrument of terror, not a violent ritual that could give expression to or harness the deepest fears and convictions of the white community. The violence of law officers, as in the Anguilla massacre, often was as horrific as that of any lynch mob in Georgia's history, but, by virtue of its quasi-legal legitimacy and its isolation from public view, it could never fulfill the role lynching had played.

A ritual of a different kind was played out in southern courtrooms whenever blacks were punished in the trials that made a mockery of justice. Court proceedings and transcripts routinely displayed the manifest racism that prevented blacks from receiving anything that approached full justice at the hands of southern courts, but no legal lynching could convey the full, frightful symbolism of white supremacy that lynching by seething mobs had once conveyed. There can be no doubt that proper trial procedure, rules of evidence, and adequate legal representation for defendants were absent in most trials involving blacks. Yet, the ritual of the courthouse was far different from the ritual of mob violence.

The very existence of legal procedures imposed constraints, however limited, upon whites that neither tradition nor community sentiment imposed upon mobs. Throughout the late nineteenth and early twentieth centuries, the dockets of southern supreme courts included large numbers of appeals by blacks who had been victims of mock justice. Too few of these appeals were heard, but there were even fewer instances in which lynch mobs had second thoughts and released their victim unharmed. Moreover, once the fight for color-blind justice moved from the streets to the courtroom, civil rights activists could use the legal process itself to challenge racial discrimination in the courts.

Beginning in the 1930s, when black lawyers began to provide competent—indeed, superb—representation for black defendants, the courtroom became the setting for rituals that called into question in profound ways white notions of black inferiority. When Charles H. Houston, the brilliant Howard University law professor, skillfully defended a black man charged with the murder of two white women in Virginia in 1936, his legal and intellectual prowess could not be ignored. The *Richmond Times-Dispatch* had to admit that "there are negro lawyers in the country who can be courageous without being obsequious, lawyers who can make a fight without arousing racial antagonisms." The newspaper concluded, "that of itself gave the trial a certain educational value." [29] Throughout the 1930s and 1940s there were countless trials, most of them unheralded, in which other black lawyers began to reclaim the courtroom in the name of fair and full color-blind justice. However much the odds were stacked against black defendants, the gathering momentum of the campaign to secure equal justice ensured that the odds of the courtroom were considerably better than those of the mob.[30]

In 1953, after two successive years free from mob violence in the United States, the Tuskegee Institute announced that "lynching as traditionally defined and as a barometer for measuring the status of race relations in the United States, and particularly in the South, seems no longer to be a valid index of such relationships." [31] During the 1950s, lynchings became so extraordinary that each incident provoked national outrage. The lynchings of Emmett Till in 1955, of Mack Charles Parker in 1959, and the murder of three civil rights workers in 1964 became national causes célèbres.[32] Racial violence again flared across the South during the civil rights struggles of the 1950s and 1960s, but it typically was terrorist violence that drew upon but simultaneously differed from the tradition of mob violence. If anything, the violence of the period harkened back to the explicitly political character of violence during Reconstruction a century earlier.[33] Assassinations, church-burnings, bombings, acts of police brutality, and mob-inflicted beatings were the order of the day, the preferred victims were black activists and their white allies, and the preferred targets were churches and buildings used by civil rights workers. The carnage left by this terrorist violence was considerable, but it utterly failed to produce the submission and resignation among southern blacks that white terrorists intended. Moreover, the sordidness of the terrorist attacks, such as the bombing of Birmingham's Sixteenth Street Baptist Church and the resulting deaths of four black children, produced revulsion, even among many southern whites.[34]

In the end, terrorist violence, for all of its horrors, could not preserve or reestablish white racial hegemony, in large part because the southern political economy had undergone sweeping changes in the three decades following the depression. A tradition of violence that in the past had played an integral role in the South's peculiar regional economy became a liability at a time when southern political and economic leaders were intent upon attracting outside capital and labor. According to the historian Numan Bartley, "In 1940 the raison d'être of southern state governments was the protection of white supremacy and social stability; thirty years later their central purpose was the promotion of business and industrial development."[35]

In some locations, notably New Orleans, urban business leaders nearly abdicated leadership during the late 1950s and early 1960s and failed to exert their influence to secure smooth and peaceful desegregation. But in many other parts of the South, the reluctant commitment on the part of conservative white businessmen to peaceful change deprived white extremists and terrorists of any claim to speak for the white community.[36] Without any cloak of legitimacy, terrorist violence could not become the counterrevolutionary instrument that it had been a century earlier. There is every reason to believe that the failure of terrorist violence to halt the gains of the civil rights movement during the 1960s assures that there will be no renewal of mob violence in the South. But it is worth noting that the hanging of a black youth in Alabama by the Ku Klux Klan in 1981 suggests that deeply rooted traditions of mob violence, although languishing, have not been entirely uprooted.[37]

Perhaps nothing about the history of mob violence in the United States is more surprising than how quickly an understanding of the full horror of lynchings has receded from the nation's collective historical memory. As early as 1953—the first year on record in which the nation did not suffer a lynching—at least one American intellectual displayed evident fatigue with the whole topic in, of all places, a defense of the trial and execution of Julius and Ethel Rosenberg. Leslie Fielder fumed that the Rosenbergs were being elevated to the status of legendary victims of American injustice by those who needed "martyrs" to replace the exhausted symbols of lynched blacks.[38] At the moment when the actual practice of lynching virtually ceased, the trivialization of lynching gathered momentum. Few Hollywood westerns were complete without a scene depicting a mob of stern frontiersmen administering their ruthless but honest brand of backcountry justice upon desperadoes and other deserving criminals. As westerns lost popularity during the 1970s, Hollywood found a new setting for vigilante violence that could tap the deepest fears of audiences troubled by urban decay and crime. The conspicuous success of recent American movies that graphically glorify vigilante violence and urban vigilantes is a troubling warning that the process of revising the place of mob violence in American history has not ended.

During the twentieth century we have become accustomed to measuring the numbers of victims of inhumane violence in millions. The casualties of genocide during this century—Armenians, Jews, Cambodians—almost elude the grasp of the human mind. Lynching in the United States, which claimed somewhere between four and five thousand victims, may appear modest in scale by these modern standards. But the atrocity of lynching has left an indelible mark on American life. For blacks, lynching epitomized the hypocrisy of a nation that prided itself on respect for the natural rights of humanity. In song and literature such black artists as Billie Holiday and Richard Wright found in lynching a tragic symbol of the American capacity for savagery. For whites, lynching was either a relapse into barbarism that stood in contradiction of their faith in the continued ascent of the human race, or an expression of their determination to crush what they perceived as a threat to the advance of civilization. With the decline of lynching, many southern whites renounced the inhumanity of the mob, preferring instead to rely on the harsh justice of the state. The history of lynching inspires pessimism and skepticism about the values of a society that could unleash the dark forces of mob violence. Yet it also fosters a degree of hope that the demise of lynching has emancipated African Americans from a gnawing fear and demonstrates that lapses into barbarism are not irreversible.

Appendix A
Tables

1 *Mob Victims, 1880–1930*

Mob Type	Georgia		Virginia	
	Black	White	Black	White
Terrorist	56	3	3	—
Private	126	12	29	12
Posse	50	1	1	—
Mass	155	3	32	2
Unknown	54	—	5	2
Total	441	19	70	16

2 *Number of Lynching Victims, 1880–1930*

Number Lynched	Mob Type					
	Terrorist	Private	Posse	Mass	Unknown	Total
Georgia:						
1	42	103	36	102	48	331
2	10	6	4	22	6	48
3	3	12	—	18	—	33
4	4	4	—	4	—	12
5	—	5	—	5	—	10
7	—	—	—	7	—	7
8	—	8	—	—	—	8
11	—	—	11	—	—	11
Total	59	138	51	158	54	460
Virginia:						
1	3	39	1	25	5	73
2	—	2	—	—	2	4
4	—	—	—	4	—	4
5	—	—	—	5	—	5
Total	3	41	1	34	7	86

3   *Lynchings of Blacks, 1880–1930*

	Category of Alleged Offense		
Decade	Murder	Sexual	Minor
Georgia:			
1880–89	10	31	10
1890–99	45	40	21
1900–1909	44	27	28
1910–19	82	18	37
1920–29	21	7	13
1930	3	1	3
Total	205	124	112
Virginia:			
1880–89	8	11	3
1890–99	14	11	2
1900–1909	6	5	2
1910–19	1	2	—
1920–29	2	4	—
1930	—	—	—
Total	31	33	7

4   *Lynchings of Black Women in Georgia, 1880–1930*

Mob Type	Number
Terrorist	1
Private	2
Posse	2
Mass	4
Unknown	1
Total	10

5   *Lynchings of Whites by Region, 1880–1930*

Georgia		Virginia	
Mountain Counties	3	Tidewater	1
Piedmont	4	Piedmont	5
Plantation Belt	6	Southside	5
Southern Georgia	6	Shenandoah Valley	0
Coastal Georgia	0	Southwestern Virginia	4
Total	19	Total	15

6   *Alleged Crimes of White Mob Victims, 1880–1930*

Crime	Georgia	Virginia
Assault	1	2
Incest	2	0
Murder	8	6
Unknown crime	3	0
Rape/Attempted rape	3	2
Rape/Murder	1	3
Rape/Robbery	0	2
Wife Abuse	1	0
Total	19	15

7   *Lynchings of Whites, 1880–1930*

Mob Type	Georgia	Virginia
Terrorist	3	0
Private	12	11
Posse	1	0
Mass	3	2
Unknown	0	2
Total	19	15

8   *Lynchings in Cotton Belt Georgia, 1880–1930*

Decade	Mob Type					Total
	Posse	Private	Mass	Terrorist	Unknown	
1880–89	1	5	7	2	4	19
1890–99	3	7	25	5	4	44
1900–1909	3	17	9	9	7	45
1910–19	8	26	27	4	7	72
1920–29	5	3	8	4	2	22
Total	20	58	76	24	24	202

9   *Average Population Density in Southern Georgia, 1880–1930*

	All Counties (Percent)	Counties with Lynchings (Percent)
1880–84	7.8	15.8
1885–94	10.6	17.5
1895–1904	16.0	24.8
1905–14	28.4	37.5
1915–24	41.3	49.5
1925–30	44.6	39.6

Source: Federal Census

10   *Average Population Growth in Southern Georgia, 1880–1930*

	All Counties (Percent)	Counties with Lynchings (Percent)
1880–90	+34.6	+26.8
1890–1900	+3.0	+52.6
1900–1910	+12.7	+18.3
1910–20	+7.0	+11.3
1920–30	+5.2	+8.9

Source: Federal Census

11   *Percent Black Population in Southern Georgia, 1880–1930*

	All Counties	Counties with Lynchings
1880–84	23.6	39.2
1885–94	26.8	40.8
1895–1904	28.1	43.1
1905–14	35.3	44.4
1915–24	39.6	45.7
1925–30	41.3	46.2

Source: Federal Census

12   *Lynchings in Southern Georgia, 1880–1930*

Decade	Mob Type					Total
	Posse	Private	Mass	Terrorist	Unknown	
1880–89	2	17	1	—	5	25
1890–99	4	11	14	5	8	42
1900–1909	2	10	19	5	6	42
1910–19	18	10	13	8	4	53
1920–29	2	7	4	2	1	16
1930	—	2	2	—	—	4
Total	28	57	53	20	24	182

13   *Lynchings in Upper Piedmont Georgia, 1880–1930*

Decade	Mob Type					Total
	Posse	Private	Mass	Terrorist	Unknown	
1880–89	—	1	4	2	—	7
1890–99	1	6	—	6	1	14
1900–1909	—	—	8	1	—	9
1910–19	1	1	4	1	2	9
1920–29	—	1	1	—	—	2
1930	—	1	—	—	—	1
Total	2	10	17	10	3	42

14   *Lynchings in Northern Georgia, 1880–1930*

Decade	Mob Type				Total
	Private	Mass	Terrorist	Unknown	
1880–89	3	—	1	1	5
1890–99	3	3	3	—	9
1900–1909	1	—	—	—	1
1910–19	—	4	—	—	4
Total	7	7	4	1	19

15   *Lynchings in Coastal Georgia, 1880–1930*

| | Mob Type | | | | |
Decade	Private	Mass	Terrorist	Unknown	Total
1880–89	1	—	—	—	1
1890–99	—	3	—	1	4
1900–1909	1	1	1	1	4
1910–19	—	—	—	—	0
1920–29	2	—	—	—	2
1930	1	1	—	—	2
Total	5	5	1	2	13

16   *Average Population Growth in Southwestern Virginia, 1880–1930*

	All Counties (Percent)	Counties with Lynchings (Percent)
1880–90	15.3	21.2
1890–1900	26.3	33.8
1900–1910	13.9	33.6
1910–20	—	—
1920–30	13.0	15.0

Source: Federal Census

17   *Percent Black Population in Southwestern Virginia, 1880–1930*

	All Counties	Counties with Lynchings
1880–84	12.7	14.3
1885–94	11.0	16.7
1895–1904	10.9	11.8
1905–14	9.9	00.0
1915–24	7.9	8.2
1925–30	6.5	6.5

Source: Federal Census

18   *Lynchings in Southwestern Virginia, 1880–1930*

Decade	Mob Type				Total
	Mass	Private	Terrorist	Unknown	
1880–90	1	4	—	1	6
1890–99	12	2	1	2	16
1900–1909	2	1	—	—	3
1910–19	—	—	—	—	—
1920–29	2	1	—	—	3
Total	17	8	1	3	29

19   *Lynchings by Race in Eastern Virginia, 1880–1930*

Decade	Race of Victim		Total
	Black	White	
1880–89	18	4	22
1890–99	11	5	16
1900–1909	9	2	11
1910–19	3	—	3
1920–29	3	—	3
Total	44	11	55

20   *Lynchings by Mob Type and Decade in Eastern Virginia, 1880–1930*

Decade	Mob Type					Total
	Posse	Private	Mass	Terrorist	Unknown	
1880–89	—	13	5	—	4	22
1890–99	—	9	6	1	—	16
1900–1909	—	7	3	—	1	11
1910–19	1	1	1	—	—	3
1920–29	—	1	2	—	—	3
Total	1	31	17	1	5	55

21 Number of Times Militia Aid Given to Civil Authorities to Prevent Lynchings, 1886–1908

	Alabama	Arkansas	Florida	Georgia	Louisiana	Mississippi	North Carolina	South Carolina	Tennessee	Texas	Virginia
1886	—	—	—	—	—	—	—	—	—	—	—
1887	1	—	—	—	—	—	—	—	—	—	—
1888	3	—	—	—	—	—	—	—	—	2	1
1889	1	—	—	—	—	—	—	—	—	4	1
1890	—	—	1	—	—	—	—	—	1	1	4
1891	1	—	—	1	—	—	1	—	—	—	4
1892	—	—	1	1	—	—	—	—	—	—	2
1893	—	—	—	—	—	—	—	—	—	—	2
1894	—	—	1	4	—	—	4	4	—	—	3
1895	—	—	—	—	—	—	—	—	1	—	3
1896	*	—	1	1	—	—	—	—	—	1	—
1897	*	—	1	3	1	—	—	—	—	3	3
1898	*	—	—	—	—	—	—	—	—	2	—
1899	*	—	—	2	1	—	—	—	—	3	—
1900	*	—	—	2	—	1	—	2	—	3	4
1901	*	—	1	3	—	1	—	—	—	5	1
1902	*	—	2	2	1	3	—	2	—	4	2
1903	*	—	1	3	—	1	—	3	—	3	2
1904	*	—	1	7	1	4	—	—	—	2	1
1905	*	—	1	1	—	5	—	—	—	3	—
1906	*	—	—	—	1	1	—	1	1	2	5
1907	1	—	2	1	2	—	—	—	—	3	4
1908	*	—	—	3	—	1	—	3	—	3	1
Total	7	0	13	34	7	17	5	15	3	45	43

*Not reported

Sources: Winthrop Alexander, "Ten Years of Riot Duty," *Journal of the Military Service Institution* 19 (July 1896): 1–25; Report of the Army War College 9744-C, "Duty Performed by Organized Militia in Connection with Domestic Disturbances, 1894–1908," General Staff War College Division RG 165, Box 476, National Archives, General Catalog, Washington, D.C.; *Report of the Adjutant General of the Commonwealth of Virginia, 1880–1908*; *Report of the Adjutant General of the State of Georgia, 1880–1908*.

22   *Lynching Victims in Georgia, 1880–1930*

Region: Crime Category:
  NG   North Georgia   M   Alleged murders or assaults
  UP   Upper Piedmont   O   "Other" crimes and alleged
  CB   Cotton Belt   minor transgressions
  SG   South Georgia   S   Alleged sexual crimes
  C   Coastal Georgia   U   Unknown offenses

Date	Race	Name	County	Region	Crime and Category		Mob Type
07/29/1880	B	Milly Thompson	Clayton	UP	Unknown Offense	(U)	Terr.
09/20/1882	B	Gus Knight	Johnson	SG	Rape	(S)	Private
12/17/1882	B	Richmond Roberts	Burke	CB	Attempted Rape	(S)	Posse
08/10/1883	B/W	Harry Bradley, Rueben Robinson, Joe Fulford (W)	Miller	SG	Murder	(M)	Private
08/26/1883	B	Lewis Warren	Miller	SG	Attempted Rape	(S)	Unknown
09/04/1883	B	Frank Fountain	Miller	SG	Attempted Rape	(S)	Unknown
10/13/1883	B	Henry Kyle	Decatur	SG	Rape	(S)	Private
02/04/1884	B	Jeff Rogers	Walker	NG	Rape	(S)	Private
05/14/1884	B	Hardy Grady	Effingham	SG	Attempted Rape	(S)	Private
07/11/1884	B	Aaron Coachman	Early	CB	Attempted Rape	(S)	Mass
07/11/1884	B	Willis Harden	Troup	CB	Rape	(S)	Mass
07/18/1884	B	Samuel Gibson	Troup	CB	Incest	(S)	Private
08/06/1884	B	Richard Cuff	Calhoun	CB	Unknown Offense	(U)	Unknown
08/20/1884	B	Jack Johnson	Carroll	UP	Rape	(S)	Private
03/15/1885	B	George Rouse	Dooly	SG	Murder	(M)	Unknown
07/24/1885	B	Peter Stamps	Douglas	UP	Miscegenation	(S)	Mass
07/29/1885	W	Thomas Brantley	Decatur	SG	Wife Abuse	(O)	Private
07/31/1885	B	Jack Hopkins	Jasper	CB	Assault	(M)	Private
08/09/1885	B	Henry Davis	Randolph	CB	Rape	(S)	Mass
09/17/1885	W	Willis Dyar	Franklin	UP	Unknown Offense	(U)	Terr.
11/17/1885	B	Cap Hamilton	Johnson	SG	Arson	(O)	Private
11/26/1885	B	Alex Etheridge	Hancock	CB	Theft	(O)	Unknown
08/13/1886	B	Henry Smith	Effingham	SG	Rape	(S)	Posse
08/13/1886	W	James Moore	Bibb	CB	Rape	(S)	Mass
09/14/1886	B	Joe Jones	Pierce	SG	Attempted Rape	(S)	Unknown
09/14/1886	B	S. Wilkinson	Burke	CB	Attempted Rape	(S)	Private
10/05/1886	B	Thomas Israel	Screven	SG	Attempted Rape	(S)	Private
12/20/1886	W	Frank Sanders	Franklin	UP	Murder	(M)	Mass
01/16/1887	B	Tom Tench	Merriwether	CB	Rape	(S)	Private
03/12/1887	W	Peter Reynolds	Macon	CB	Murder	(M)	Mass
05/17/1887	B	Will Hood	Merriwether	CB	Attempted Rape	(S)	Unknown
07/09/1887	B	Ross Griffin	Oglethorpe	CB	Attempted Rape	(S)	Mass
07/27/1887	B	Reuben Hudson	Dekalb	UP	Rape	(S)	Mass
01/13/1888	B	Henry Burney	Laurens	SG	Theft	(O)	Private
02/08/1888	B	Unknown Man	Liberty	C	Arson	(O)	Private

Date	Race	Name	County	Region	Crime and Category		Mob Type
03/08/1888	B	Tom Ruffin	Dade	NG	Attempted Rape	(S)	Private
05/01/1888	B	Henry Pope	Chattooga	NG	Rape	(S)	Private
06/03/1888	B	Allen Sturgis	McDuffie	CB	Theft	(O)	Private
06/26/1888	B	Edward Clark	Worth	SG	Attempted Rape	(S)	Posse
09/05/1888	B	Sam Long	Colquitt	SG	Rape	(S)	Mass
10/13/1888	B	Bill Johnson	Pulaski	CB	Rape	(S)	Mass
10/14/1888	B	Lewis Edwards	Wayne	SG	Murder	(M)	Private
12/01/1888	B	Tom Smith, John Coleman	Wilkes	CB	Debt Dispute	(O)	Terr.
07/10/1889	B	Martin Love	Whitfield	NG	Attempted Rape	(S)	Unknown
08/31/1889	B	Robert Mitchell	Mitchell	SG	Unknown Offense	(U)	Unknown
09/04/1889	B	Warren Powers	Fulton	UP	Attempted Rape	(S)	Mass
09/30/1889	B	John Duncan	Murray	NG	Miscegenation	(S)	Terr.
10/10/1889	B	Bill Moore	Wayne	SG	Assault	(M)	Private
11/08/1889	B	James Thomas	Emanuel	SG	Attempted Rape	(S)	Private
11/16/1889	B	John Anthony	Lincoln	CB	Attempted Rape	(S)	Unknown
12/25/1889	B	William Fluid, Pete Jackson, William Hopps	Wayne	SG	Murder	(M)	Private
02/27/1890	B	Brown Washington	Morgan	CB	Murder	(M)	Mass
03/22/1890	B	Sim Bell	Johnson	SG	Murder	(M)	Private
06/05/1890	B	George Penn	Madison	UP	Rape	(S)	Private
06/27/1890	B	Andrew Robinson	Clinch	SG	Attempted Rape	(S)	Unknown
10/24/1890	B	General Williams	Burke	CB	Murder	(M)	Private
10/30/1890	B	Owen Jones	Pulaski	CB	Rape	(S)	Posse
10/30/1890	B	Will Lowe	Lowndes	SG	Attempted Rape	(S)	Mass
11/18/1890	B	Jim Simmons	Thomas	SG	Attempted Rape	(S)	Private
02/21/1891	B	Wesley Lewis, Henry Jackson	Glynn	C	Assault	(M)	Mass
02/25/1891	B	Allen West	Dodge	SG	Attempted Rape	(S)	Private
05/03/1891	B	Hosea Jones	Murray	NG	Unknown Offense	(U)	Terr.
06/30/1891	B	Dan Buck	Clay	CB	Attempted Rape	(S)	Mass
08/29/1891	B	Cato Simmons	Decatur	SG	Informing	(O)	Terr.
09/27/1891	B	Charlie Mack	Emanuel	SG	Rape	(S)	Mass
11/01/1891	W	Larkin Nix	Mitchell	SG	Murder	(M)	Private
12/14/1891	B	Henry Daniels	Cobb	UP	Murder	(M)	Unknown
02/26/1892	B	Jones	Echols	SG	Murder	(M)	Private
05/17/1892	B	Jim Redmond, Gus Roberson, Bob Addison	Habersham	NG	Murder	(M)	Mass
07/08/1892	B	Issac Flowers	Wayne	SG	Wild Talk	(O)	Terr.
08/22/1892	B	Benjamin Howard	Liberty	C	Attempted Murder	(M)	Unknown
09/06/1892	B	Jesse Williams	Dodge	SG	Attempted Rape	(S)	Mass
10/23/1892	B	Jack Wilson	Whitfield	NG	Unknown Offense	(U)	Terr.
04/13/1893	B	Unknown Man	Quitman	CB	Unknown Offense	(U)	Unknown
04/13/1893	B	Unknown Man	Quitman	CB	Murder	(M)	Mass

Date	Race	Name	County	Region	Crime and Category		Mob Type
05/18/1893	B	Bill Dennis	Coffee	SG	Unknown Offense	(U)	Unknown
05/22/1893	B	Ephraim Mitchell, Unknown Man	Coffee	SG	Murder	(M)	Unknown
05/22/1893	W	Junius Lawrence	Washington	CB	Unknown Offense	(U)	Terr.
06/14/1893	B	Warren Ross	Early	CB	Murder	(M)	Private
10/17/1893	B	Bill Richardson, Jim Dickson	Chattooga	NG	Murder	(M)	Private
10/22/1893	B	Arthur Bennett	Clayton	UP	Attempted Murder	(M)	Private
11/29/1893	B	Newt Jones	Appling	SG	Murder	(M)	Unknown
12/02/1893	B	Lucius Holt	Pike	CB	Murder	(M)	Mass
12/13/1893	B	Will Ferguson	Berrien	SG	Informing	(O)	Terr.
12/26/1893	B	Calvin Thomas	Decatur	SG	Rape	(S)	Private
02/10/1894	B	Bob Collins	Oglethorpe	CB	Enticing Servant	(O)	Terr.
03/05/1894	B	Sylvester Rhodes	Tattnall	SG	Murder	(M)	Mass
04/06/1894	B	Dan Ahren	Greene	CB	Rape	(S)	Mass
04/20/1894	W	Henry Wooley	Gilmer	NG	Informing	(O)	Terr.
04/22/1894	B	Robert Evarts	Glynn	C	Rape	(S)	Mass
05/21/1894	B	Unknown Man	Miller	SG	Attempted Rape	(S)	Private
06/17/1894	B	Owen Ogletree	Monroe	CB	Rape	(S)	Mass
06/24/1894	B	George Franklin	Mitchell	SG	Rape	(S)	Mass
09/19/1894	B	Dave Goosby	Lowndes	SG	Murder	(M)	Mass
11/08/1894	B	Lee Lawrence	Jasper	CB	Rape	(S)	Mass
12/23/1894	B	Sam Taylor, Eli Frazier, Harry Sherod, Sam Pike, George Fritz	Brooks	SG	Murder	(M)	Mass
01/09/1895	B	George Coldhand	Colquitt	SG	Murder	(M)	Posse
03/02/1895	B	Chas. Robertson	Wilkinson	CB	Murder	(M)	Unknown
03/13/1895	B	Amos Gibson	Monroe	CB	Attempted Rape	(S)	Private
05/22/1895	B	William Connell	Montgomery	SG	Murder	(M)	Posse
08/12/1895	B	John Harris	Mitchell	SG	Murder	(M)	Mass
11/09/1895	B	Lewis Jefferson	Clinch	SG	Attempted Rape	(S)	Private
11/22/1895	W	L. W. Perdue	Montgomery	SG	Rape	(S)	Private
05/10/1896	B	Bill Hardee	Ware	SG	Assault	(M)	Terr.
06/01/1896	B	Jesse Slayton, Will Miles	Muscogee	CB	Rape	(S)	Mass
10/07/1896	B	Charles Williams	Emanuel	SG	Murder	(M)	Mass
10/15/1896	B	Henry Milner	Spalding	CB	Attempted Rape	(S)	Mass
11/05/1896	B	Unknown Man	Colquitt	SG	Unknown Offense	(U)	Posse
01/07/1897	B	Anthony Henderson	Dooly	SG	Murder	(M)	Unknown
01/22/1897	B	Charles Forsyth, William White	Twiggs	CB	Murder	(M)	Mass
07/19/1897	W	Dr. W. L. Ryder	Talbot	CB	Murder	(M)	Private
07/22/1897	B	Oscar Williams	Spalding	CB	Rape	(S)	Mass
09/03/1897	B	Sam Teott	Echols	SG	Cattle stealing	(O)	Terr.

Date	Race	Name	County	Region	Crime and Category		Mob Type
09/12/1897	B	Charles Gibson	Bibb	CB	Rape	(S)	Mass
11/19/1897	B	Josh Ruff	Glascock	CB	Theft	(O)	Private
02/13/1898	W	Whit Dillard	Fannin	NG	Murder	(M)	Private
03/23/1898	B	James Allen	Colquitt	SG	Attempted Rape	(S)	Unknown
05/28/1898	B	Peter Shaw	Troup	CB	Rape	(S)	Private
08/08/1898	B	John Meadows	Spalding	CB	Rape	(S)	Mass
08/19/1898	B	Jim Neely	Henry	CB	Assault	(M)	Terr.
08/20/1898	B	Hamp Hollis	Sumter	CB	Murder	(M)	Mass
08/22/1898	B	Tom Miller	Brooks	SG	Attempted Rape	(S)	Posse
09/11/1898	B	George Burden	Spalding	CB	Attempted Rape	(S)	Posse
10/02/1898	B	Unknown Man	Madison	UP	Unknown Offense	(U)	Posse
11/22/1898	B	Ed Merriwether	Jasper	CB	Murder	(M)	Mass
12/07/1898	B	Jake Glover	Jasper	CB	Murder	(M)	Private
12/25/1898	B	Jeff Bolden	Jackson	UP	Attempted Murder	(M)	Private
01/29/1899	B	Charles Martin	Madison	UP	Unknown Offense	(U)	Terr.
02/11/1899	B	George Bivens, William Holt, George Foot	Lee	CB	Rape	(S)	Mass
03/16/1899	B	Bud Cotton, Tip Hudson, Henry Bingham, Edgar Brown	Campbell	UP	Arson	(O)	Terr.
04/23/1899	B	Sam Hose	Coweta	CB	Murder	(M)	Mass
04/24/1899	B	Lige Strickland	Campbell	UP	Murder Accomplice	(M)	Private
04/27/1899	B	Alf Thurman	Lee	CB	Informing	(O)	Terr.
04/27/1899	B	Enoch Daniel	Lee	CB	Wild Talk	(O)	Terr.
05/20/1899	B	Tom Linton	Fayette	UP	Unknown Offense	(U)	Terr.
06/14/1899	B	Dave Clark	Wayne	SG	Assault	(M)	Unknown
06/16/1899	B	Williams	Wayne	SG	Attempted Rape	(S)	Private
07/15/1899	W	Si Smith	Hall	UP	Murder	(M)	Private
07/23/1899	B	Lewis Sammin, and Two Men	Early	CB	Rape/Robbery	(S)	Mass
07/25/1899	B	Charles Mack	Early	CB	Rape/Robbery	(S)	Mass
08/03/1899	B	Lewis Henderson	Early	CB	Attempted Rape	(S)	Unknown
08/11/1899	B	Will McClure	Carroll	UP	Attempted Rape	(S)	Private
09/14/1899	B	Ed Henderson	Worth	SG	Attempted Rape	(S)	Mass
10/23/1899	B	Albert Harris	Monroe	CB	Unknown Offense	(U)	Unknown
10/26/1899	B	John Goolsby	Twiggs	CB	Assault	(M)	Private
11/20/1899	B	Unknown Man	Butts	CB	Attempted Rape	(S)	Posse
03/18/1900	B	John Bailey	Cobb	UP	Attempted Rape	(S)	Mass
04/03/1900	B	Allen Brooks	Chatham	C	Rape	(S)	Unknown
05/04/1900	B	Marshall Jones	Coffee	SG	Assault	(M)	Private
05/13/1900	B	William Wilson	Columbia	CB	Murder	(M)	Private
06/08/1900	B	Simon Adams	Muscogee	CB	Attempted Rape	(S)	Private
06/11/1900	B	Renny Jefferson	Thomas	SG	Attempted Rape	(S)	Private
06/26/1900	B	Jordan Hines	Pike	CB	Unknown Offense	(U)	Unknown

Date	Race	Name	County	Region	Crime and Category		Mob Type
07/02/1900	B	Abe Sebens	Pierce	SG	Unknown Offense	(U)	Unknown
07/24/1900	B	Jack Hillsman	Crawford	CB	Attempted Rape	(S)	Mass
08/19/1900	B	Bill Cato	Colquitt	SG	Attempted Rape	(S)	Mass
10/24/1900	B	James Greer, James Callaway	Pike	CB	Rioting	(O)	Terr.
12/08/1900	B	Bud Rufus	Floyd	UP	Rape	(S)	Mass
01/02/1901	B	Dobson	Brooks	SG	Rape	(S)	Mass
01/03/1901	B	George Reede	Floyd	UP	Attempted Rape	(S)	Mass
01/03/1901	B	Sterling Thompson	Campbell	UP	Informing	(O)	Terr.
02/28/1901	B	John Moody	Bryan	C	Leaving Employer	(O)	Terr.
03/13/1901	B	Sherman Harris	Randolph	CB	Murder	(M)	Private
04/15/1901	B	Kennedy Gordon	Bulloch	SG	Attempted Rape	(S)	Private
05/08/1901	B	Henry Johnson	Lowndes	SG	Assault	(M)	Private
06/28/1901	B	Unknown Man	Quitman	CB	Attempted Rape	(S)	Private
07/25/1901	B	Frank Earle	Montgomery	SG	Theft	(O)	Private
08/10/1901	B	Joe Washington	Bryan	C	Attempted Rape	(S)	Mass
11/01/1901	B	Theo Booth	Wilkinson	CB	Attempted Rape	(S)	Mass
04/01/1902	B	Walter Allen	Floyd	UP	Attempted Rape	(S)	Mass
06/10/1902	B	Frank Thomas	Coffee	SG	Unknown Offense	(U)	Private
07/25/1902	B	Arthur McCauly	Harris	CB	Unknown Offense	(U)	Unknown
07/28/1902	B	John Wise	Bryan	C	Rape	(S)	Private
08/31/1902	B	John Brown	Jasper	CB	Scared White Girl	(O)	Private
09/06/1902	B	Bill Mobley	Dooly	SG	Attempted Rape	(S)	Private
10/23/1902	B	Ben Brown	Haralson	UP	Attempted Rape	(S)	Mass
02/07/1903	B	Lee Hall	Johnson	SG	Attempted Murder	(M)	Unknown
02/23/1903	B	Will Frambo	Spalding	CB	Indecency	(S)	Terr.
04/21/1903	B	Andrew Rainey	Decatur	SG	Arson	(O)	Private
06/08/1903	B	Banjo Peavy	Houston	CB	Murder	(M)	Mass
06/26/1903	B	George McKinney, Garfield McCoy, Wiley Annett	Baker	SG	Murder	(M)	Mass
07/14/1903	B	Ed Claus	Dodge	SG	Rape	(S)	Posse
10/16/1903	B	Mitchell Gilbert	Dooly	SG	Unknown Offense	(U)	Unknown
05/15/1904	B	John Cumming	Columbia	CB	Rape	(S)	Mass
06/01/1904	B	Arthur Thompson	Calhoun	CB	Murder	(M)	Unknown
08/16/1904	B	Paul Reed, William Cato	Bulloch	SG	Murder	(M)	Mass
08/17/1904	B	Albert Rogers, Son of Rogers, Rufus Lesuere	Bulloch	SG	Unknown Offense	(U)	Terr.
08/22/1904	B	Jim Glover	Polk	UP	Rape	(S)	Mass
08/28/1904	B	A. L. Scott	Wilcox	SG	Murder	(M)	Mass
08/29/1904	B	Sebastin McBride	Bulloch	SG	Unknown Offense	(U)	Terr.
09/18/1904	B	John Ware	Franklin	UP	Attempted Murder	(M)	Mass
09/21/1904	B	Ed Martin, Jack Troy	Talbot	CB	Unknown Offense	(U)	Terr.

Date	Race	Name	County	Region	Crime and Category		Mob Type
06/29/1905	B/W	Rich Robinson, Lewis Robinson, Claude Elder, Sandy Price, Rich Allen, Gene Yerby, Robert Harris, Lon Aycock (W)	Oconee	CB	Murder/Theft	(M)	Private
10/08/1905	B	Tom Seabright	Decatur	SG	Rape	(S)	Mass
10/28/1905	B	Gus Goodman	Decatur	SG	Murder	(M)	Mass
05/13/1906	B	Will Morman	Dodge	SG	Rape	(S)	Mass
05/19/1906	B	Unknown Man	Berrien	SG	Murder	(M)	Posse
07/11/1906	B	Ed Pierson	Emanuel	SG	Attempted Rape	(S)	Mass
07/31/1906	B	Floyd Carmichael	Fulton	UP	Scared White Girl	(O)	Mass
09/07/1906	B	Charles Fuller	Monroe	CB	Attempted Rape	(S)	Unknown
05/07/1907	B	Charlie Harris	McDuffie	CB	Murder	(M)	Posse
05/21/1907	B	Sam Padgett's Wife and Son	Tattnall	SG	Murder	(M)	Mass
07/01/1907	W	Dock Posey	Whitfield	NG	Incest	(S)	Private
10/27/1907	B	John Walker	Houston	CB	Assault/Robbery	(M)	Unknown
01/09/1908	B	Issac Webb, Thomas Coley	Pulaski	CB	Attempted Murder	(M)	Posse
02/26/1908	B	Jim Harris	Echols	SG	Assault	(M)	Private
03/05/1908	B	Curry Roberson, John Henry Pinkney, Jerry Buchan	Pulaski	CB	Murder	(M)	Mass
06/27/1908	B	Albert Baker	Ware	SG	Rape	(S)	Mass
06/27/1908	B	Unknown Man	Ware	SG	Wild Talk	(O)	Mass
06/27/1908	B	Walter Wilkins	Ware	SG	Unknown Offense	(U)	Mass
07/29/1908	B	Alonzo Williams	Toombs	SG	Attempted Rape	(S)	Mass
08/09/1908	B	Charles Lokie	Tift	SG	Wild Talk	(O)	Terr.
08/25/1908	B	Vincent Williams	Jefferson	CB	Murder	(M)	Private
09/05/1908	B	John Towns	Early	CB	Attempted Theft	(O)	Terr.
09/21/1908	B	George Thomas	Clay	CB	Attempted Murder	(M)	Private
10/11/1908	B	Henry White	Dodge	SG	Assault	(M)	Unknown
03/03/1909	B	Joseph Fowler	Early	CB	Assault	(M)	Unknown
04/10/1909	B	Alfred Iverson	Randolph	CB	Leaving Employer	(O)	Terr.
05/24/1909	B	Albert Aiken	Lincoln	CB	Assault	(M)	Mass
06/19/1909	B	Joseph Hardy	Talbot	CB	Wild Talk	(O)	Terr.
06/22/1909	B	William Carreker	Talbot	CB	Murder	(M)	Mass
06/25/1909	B	Albert Reese	Randolph	CB	Assault	(M)	Private
07/02/1909	B	Henry Issac	Brooks	SG	Attempted Theft	(O)	Private
07/20/1909	B	John King	Dodge	SG	Attempted Rape	(S)	Mass
07/31/1909	B	Simon Anderson	Houston	CB	Vouyerism	(S)	Terr.
08/27/1909	B	Ben Clark, John Sweeney	Montgomery	SG	Murder	(M)	Unknown

Date	Race	Name	County	Region	Crime and Category		Mob Type
12/01/1909	B	John Harvard	Pulaski	CB	Murder	(M)	Unknown
03/01/1910	B	Will Williamson	Toombs	SG	Attempted Murder	(M)	Posse
04/14/1910	B	Albert Royal, Charlie Jackson	Turner	SG	Debt Dispute	(O)	Terr.
07/31/1910	B	Unknown Man	Grady	SG	Attempted Theft	(O)	Private
09/01/1910	B	Unknown Man	Madison	UP	Attempted Theft	(O)	Unknown
11/07/1910	B	William Barnes	Macon	CB	Murder	(M)	Mass
11/08/1910	B	Bob Bryant	Macon	CB	Murder Accomplice	(M)	Unknown
12/15/1910	B	Will Atwater	Pike	CB	Unknown Offense	(U)	Terr.
01/22/1911	B	William Johnson	Unknown	Unk.	Murder	(M)	Private
02/25/1911	B	Chas. Jones, John Veazey	Warren	CB	Murder	(M)	Mass
04/01/1911	B	Cheatham	Decatur	SG	Informing	(O)	Terr.
04/07/1911	B	Charlie Hale	Gwinnett	UP	Rape	(S)	Mass
04/08/1911	B	Dawson Jordan, Charlie Pickett, Murray Burton	Schley	CB	Murder	(M)	Private
05/13/1911	B	John McLeod	Emanuel	SG	Murder	(M)	Mass
05/21/1911	B	Ben Smith	Emanuel	SG	Assault	(M)	Posse
05/22/1911	B	Joe Moore	Taliaferro	CB	Murder	(M)	Mass
06/21/1911	W	Lawrence Crawford	Jasper	CB	Rape	(S)	Posse
06/27/1911	B	Joe Watts	Walton	UP	Attempted Rape	(S)	Mass
06/27/1911	B	Tom Allen	Walton	UP	Rape	(S)	Mass
06/30/1911	B	Unknown Man	Brooks	SG	Unknown Offense	(U)	Terr.
07/11/1911	B	William McGriff	Mitchell	SG	Murder	(M)	Mass
08/18/1911	B	Unknown Man	Early	CB	Aiding Criminal	(O)	Terr.
08/29/1911	B	Will Davis	Clay	CB	Murder	(M)	Posse
10/05/1911	B	Frank Mack	Dodge	SG	Attempted Rape	(S)	Posse
10/07/1911	B	Andrew Chapman	Wilkinson	CB	Attempted Rape	(S)	Private
10/07/1911	B	Unknown Man	Dooly	SG	Unknown Offense	(U)	Unknown
10/19/1911	B	Jerry Lovelace	Merriwether	CB	Assault	(M)	Private
12/23/1911	B	John Warren	Decatur	SG	Murder	(M)	Unknown
01/22/1912	B	Burrell Hardaway, John Moore, Gene Harrington, Dusty Crutchfield	Harris	CB	Murder	(M)	Private
01/30/1912	B	Albert Hamilton	Crisp	SG	Rape	(S)	Mass
02/04/1912	B	Charlie Powell	Bibb	CB	Attempted Rape	(S)	Mass
02/06/1912	B	Homer Stewart	Toombs	SG	Murder	(M)	Mass
03/21/1912	B	Homer Howell	Pulaski	CB	Murder	(M)	Private
04/17/1912	W	Lee Chitwood	Crisp	SG	Incest	(S)	Private
04/24/1912	B	Henry Etheridge	Monroe	CB	African Colonization	(O)	Terr.
06/24/1912	B	Ann Bostwick	Crisp	SG	Murder	(M)	Mass
08/13/1912	B	T. E. Cotton	Muscogee	CB	Murder	(M)	Private
09/10/1912	B	Robert Edwards	Forsyth	UP	Murder Accomplice	(M)	Mass

Date	Race	Name	County	Region	Crime and Category		Mob Type
10/05/1912	B	Babe Yarbrough	Sumter	CB	Attempted Rape	(S)	Private
11/30/1912	B	Sidney Williams	Telfair	SG	Attempted Murder	(M)	Private
02/28/1913	B	Unknown Man	Habersham	NG	Murder	(M)	Mass
03/04/1913	B	George McDonald	Brooks	SG	Assault	(M)	Private
05/06/1913	B	John Henry Moore	Columbia	CB	Assault	(M)	Private
05/13/1913	B	Sam Owensby	Troup	CB	Murder	(M)	Unknown
06/21/1913	B	William Redding	Sumter	CB	Murder	(M)	Mass
07/27/1913	B	John Shake	Houston	CB	Assault	(M)	Mass
08/15/1913	B	Robert Lovett	Calhoun	CB	Murder	(M)	Private
08/25/1913	B	Virgil Swanson	Merriwether	CB	Murder Accomplice	(M)	Private
11/24/1913	B	Unknown Man	Walton	UP	Attempted Rape	(S)	Unknown
05/07/1914	B	Charlie Jones	Columbia	CB	Theft	(O)	Private
09/26/1914	B	Nathan Brown	Wilcox	SG	Murder	(M)	Unknown
01/15/1915	B	Dan Barber, Jesse Barber, Eula Charles, Ella Charles	Jasper	CB	Resisting Arrest/ Assault	(M)	Mass
01/22/1915	B	Peter Morris	Early	CB	Murder	(M)	Posse
04/17/1915	B	Caesar Sheffield	Lowndes	SG	Theft	(O)	Private
06/14/1915	B	Sam Stephens	Stephens	NG	Rape	(S)	Mass
07/04/1915	B	Alonzo Green and Son	Jones	CB	Unknown Offense	(U)	Mass
07/15/1915	B	Peter Jambo, James Jackson	Bleckley	CB	Aiding Criminal	(O)	Unknown
08/17/1915	B	John Riggins	Decatur	SG	Rape	(S)	Posse
08/17/1915	W	Leo Frank	Cobb	UP	Murder	(M)	Private
12/20/1915	B	Sam Bland, Willie Stewart	Dodge	SG	Murder	(M)	Mass
12/30/1915	B	Grandison Goolsby, Mike Goolsby, Ulysses Goolsby, Hosh Jewell, Charles Holmes, James Burton, Early Hightower	Early	CB	Murder	(M)	Mass
01/20/1916	B	John Seymour, Felix Lake, Frank Lake, Dewey Lake, Major Lake	Lee	CB	Murder Accomplice	(M)	Private
02/12/1916	B	Marvin Harris	Twiggs	CB	Murder	(M)	Posse
02/25/1916	B	Jesse McCorker	Bartow	CB	Attempted Theft	(O)	Private
08/18/1916	B	Lewis	Lowndes	SG	Attempted Theft	(O)	Posse
09/20/1916	B	Elijah Sturgis	Randolph	CB	Unknown Offense	(U)	Posse
09/20/1916	B	Henry White	Walker	NG	Miscegenation	(S)	Mass
09/20/1916	B	Pete Hudson	Randolph	CB	Murder	(M)	Mass

Date	Race	Name	County	Region	Crime and Category		Mob Type
09/27/1916	B	Moxie Shuler	Decatur	SG	Attempted Rape	(S)	Private
10/04/1916	B	Mary Conley	Calhoun	CB	Murder Accomplice	(M)	Unknown
03/01/1917	B	Linton Clinton	Thomas	SG	Scared White Girl	(O)	Posse
03/28/1917	B	Joe Nowling	Mitchell	SG	Unknown Offense	(U)	Terr.
09/18/1917	B	Rufus Moncrief	Clarke	CB	Gambling Dispute	(O)	Private
11/09/1917	B	Jesse Stater	Brooks	SG	Writing Letters to White Girl		Terr.
11/17/1917	B	Mack Johnson, Collins Johnson	Mitchell	SG	Argument	(O)	Private
12/15/1917	B	Claxton Dekle	Candler	SG	Murder	(M)	Posse
02/17/1918	B	Bud Cosby	Fayette	UP	Kidnaping/Theft	(O)	Posse
05/17/1918	B	Will Head, Will Thompson, Hayes Turner, Chime Riley, Mary Turner, Eugene Rice, Simon Schuman, Sidney Johnson, Three Unidentified Men	Brooks	SG	Murder Accomplice	(M)	Posse
05/18/1918	B	Tom Devert	Unknown	Ukn.	Attempted Rape	(S)	Posse
05/22/1918	B	Jim Cobb	Crisp	SG	Murder	(M)	Mass
05/22/1918	B	Spencer Evans	Taliaferro	CB	Rape	(S)	Private
05/24/1918	B	John Calhoun	Pike	CB	Murder	(M)	Posse
08/12/1918	B	Ike Harden	Miller	SG	Attempted Rape	(S)	Private
09/03/1918	B	John Gilham	Bibb	CB	Attempted Rape	(S)	Private
09/24/1918	B	Sandy Reeves	Pierce	SG	Scared White Girl	(O)	Mass
04/13/1919	B	Willie Williams, Joe Ruffin, Andrew Ruffin	Jenkins	SG	Murder Accomplice	(M)	Mass
05/01/1919	B	Benny Richards	Warren	CB	Murder/Assault	(M)	Mass
05/15/1919	B	Jim Waters	Johnson	SG	Leaving Employer	(O)	Mass
05/25/1919	B	Berry Washington	Telfair	SG	Murder	(M)	Private
08/02/1919	B	Charles Kelly	Fayette	UP	Argument	(O)	Terr.
08/03/1919	B	Unknown Man	Bleckley	CB	Wild Talk	(O)	Terr.
08/14/1919	B	Jim Grant	Wilcox	SG	Assault	(M)	Unknown
08/27/1919	B	Eli Cooper	Laurens	SG	Organizing Black Farmers	(O)	Terr.
09/10/1919	B	Obe Cox	Oglethorpe	CB	Murder	(M)	Mass
09/22/1919	B	Ernest Glenwood	Dooly	SG	Wild Talk	(O)	Terr.
10/06/1919	B	Jack Gordon, Will Brown	Lincoln	CB	Murder Accomplice	(M)	Mass
10/06/1919	B	Mose Martin	Lincoln	CB	Murder	(M)	Posse
10/07/1919	B	Eugene Hamilton	Jasper	CB	Attempted Murder	(M)	Mass

Date	Race	Name	County	Region	Crime and Category		Mob Type
10/18/1919	B	Unknown Man	Marion	CB	Intimacy with White Woman	(O)	Unknown
11/02/1919	B	Paul Jones	Bibb	CB	Rape	(S)	Mass
11/20/1919	B	Wallace Baynes	Morgan	CB	Murder	(M)	Posse
12/01/1919	B	Jack Ridicer	Wilkinson	CB	Attempted Murder	(M)	Unknown
12/20/1919	B	Charles West	Sumter	CB	Murder	(M)	Private
06/21/1920	B	Phillip Gaithers	Effingham	SG	Murder	(M)	Mass
08/13/1920	B	John Grant	Emanuel	SG	Wage Dispute	(O)	Terr.
09/22/1920	B	George King	Fulton	UP	Unknown Offense	(U)	Private
09/24/1920	B	Felix Cremer	Greene	CB	Aiding Criminal	(O)	Mass
09/26/1920	B	Bob Whitehead	Sumter	CB	Attempted Murder	(M)	Posse
11/17/1920	B	Willie "Boney" Ivory, Minnie Ivory, Alex Byrd	Coffee	SG	Murder	(M)	Private
11/24/1920	B	Curly McKelvy	Mitchell	SG	Murder Accomplice	(M)	Private
01/02/1921	B	Jim Roland	Mitchell	SG	Attempted Murder	(M)	Posse
01/06/1921	B	Sam Williams	Talbot	CB	Unknown Offense	(U)	Unknown
02/16/1921	B	John Lee Eberhardt	Oconee	CB	Murder	(M)	Mass
05/14/1921	B	Rawls Ross	Coweta	CB	Murder	(M)	Mass
06/18/1921	B	John Henry Williams	Colquitt	SG	Murder	(M)	Mass
12/05/1921	B	Aaron Birdsong	Oconee	CB	Murder Accomplice	(M)	Posse
12/05/1921	B	Roy Grove, Wes Hale	Oconee	CB	Aiding Criminal	(O)	Mass
02/13/1922	B	Will Jones	Schley	CB	Wild Talk	(O)	Terr.
02/17/1922	B	John Glover	Lowndes	SG	Murder	(M)	Posse
03/12/1922	B	Alfred Williams	Columbia	CB	Attempted Murder	(M)	Posse
05/18/1922	B	Charlie Atkins	Washington	CB	Murder	(M)	Mass
05/29/1922	B	Will Bryd	Wayne	SG	Murder	(M)	Mass
06/30/1922	B	Joe Jordan, James Harvey	Liberty	C	Debt Dispute	(O)	Private
07/14/1922	B	Shake Davis	Colquitt	SG	Miscegenation	(S)	Private
07/24/1922	B	Will Anderson	Colquitt	SG	Attempted Rape	(S)	Private
08/02/1922	B	Cocky Glover	Monroe	CB	Murder	(M)	Mass
09/02/1922	B	Jim Reed Long	Barrow	UP	Attempted Murder	(M)	Mass
09/28/1922	B	Jim Johnson	Washington	CB	Rape	(S)	Private
12/30/1922	B	M. B. Burnett	Wilkes	CB	Wild Talk	(O)	Terr.
02/03/1923	B	George Butts, Clinton Chambers	Hancock	CB	Murder/Robbery	(M)	Posse
08/17/1923	B	Aaron Harris	Bleckley	CB	Attempted Rape	(S)	Private
08/17/1923	B	Lee Green	Houston	CB	Rape	(S)	Mass
03/19/1924	B	John Haynes	Crisp	SG	Attempted Rape	(S)	Unknown
04/03/1924	B	Beach Thrash	Merriwether	CB	Murder	(M)	Unknown
06/23/1924	B	Marcus Westmoreland, Penny Westmoreland	Spalding	CB	Argument	(O)	Terr.

Date	Race	Name	County	Region	Crime and Category		Mob Type
03/02/1925	B	Robert Smith	Screven	SG	Attempted Rape	(S)	Mass
09/21/1925	B	Willie Dixon	Baldwin	CB	Murder	(M)	Private
07/06/1926	B	Willie Wilson	Toombs	SG	Unknown Offense	(U)	Terr.
08/30/1926	W	Dave Wright	Coffee	SG	Murder	(M)	Private
02/01/1930	B	James Irwin	Irwin	SG	Murder	(M)	Mass
07/29/1930	B	S. S. Mincey	Montgomery	SG	Political Dispute	(O)	Private
09/08/1930	B	George Grant	McIntosh	C	Murder	(M)	Mass
09/09/1930	B	William Bryan	McIntosh	C	Unknown Offense	(U)	Private
09/24/1930	B	Willie Kirkland	Thomas	SG	Attempted Rape	(S)	Mass
09/28/1930	B	Lacy Mitchell	Thomas	SG	Testifying against Whites	(O)	Private
10/01/1930	B	Willie Clark	Bartow	UP	Murder	(M)	Private

23   *Lynching Victims in Virginia, 1880–1930*

Region: Crime Category:
P   Piedmont   M   Alleged murders or assaults
S   Southside   O   "Other" crimes and
SH   Shenandoah   alleged minor transgressions
SW   Southwestern   S   Alleged sexual crimes
T   Tidewater   U   Unknown offenses

Date	Race	Name	County	Region	Crime and Category		Mob Type
01/19/1880	B	Arthur Jordan	Fauquier	P	Miscegenation	(S)	Private
02/18/1880	B	Page Wallace	Loudoun	P	Rape	(S)	Mass
04/12/1880	B	James Black	Dinwiddie	S	Attempted Rape	(S)	Private
10/03/1880	W	George Lowry, David Thomas	Nelson	P	Rape & Robbery	(S)	Unknown
12/06/1881	B	William Allen	Warwick	T	Murder	(M)	Private
10/02/1882	W	Jim Rhodes	Albemarle	P	Murder	(M)	Private
04/12/1883	W	William M. Crockett	Wythe	SW	Murder	(M)	Private
01/04/1884	W	E. D. Atchison	Highland	SW	Assault	(M)	Private
02/05/1884	B	Peter Bland	King William	T	Assault	(M)	Private
08/02/1884	B	John Fitzhugh	Rappahannock	P	Assault	(M)	Unknown
02/05/1885	B	Ivy Jackson	Bland	SW	Murder	(M)	Private
05/18/1885	W	Hairston Terry	Bedford	S	Murder	(M)	Private
11/15/1885	B	Noah Cherry	Princess Anne	T	Murder	(M)	Mass
11/30/1885	B	Henry Mason	Campbell	S	Murder	(M)	Private
02/06/1886	B	John Wilson	Patrick	S	Horse Thief	(O)	Private
04/19/1886	B	Kellis Moorman	Henry	S	Assault	(M)	Private
07/27/1887	B	Reuben Coles	Surry	T	Rape	(S)	Mass
07/11/1888	B	William Henry Smith	Wythe	SW	Rape	(S)	Private
07/27/1888	B	Bruce Younger	Halifax	S	Attempted Rape	(S)	Mass
09/02/1888	B	Archie Cook	Prince Edward	S	Rape	(S)	Unknown
03/14/1889	B	Magruder Fletcher	Accomack	T	Rape	(S)	Private
04/02/1889	B	Martin Rollins	Russell	SW	Murder	(M)	Mass
04/23/1889	B	Scott Bailey	Halifax	S	Attempted Rape	(S)	Mass
06/08/1889	B	John Forbes	Nottoway	S	Burglary	(O)	Private
09/14/1889	B	Samuel Garner	Tazewell	SW	Attempted Rape	(S)	Unknown
11/08/1889	B	Orion Anderson	Loudoun	P	Frightened White Girl	(O)	Private
11/23/1889	B	Robert Bland	Prince George	T	Attempted Rape	(S)	Private
12/02/1890	B	Thaddeus Holmes	Charlotte	S	Murder	(M)	Mass
02/23/1891	B	Scott Bishop	Nottoway	S	Murder/ Robbery	(M)	Mass
04/06/1891	B	Tom Pannell	Pittsylvania	S	Unknown	(U)	Terr.
10/17/1891	B	Charles Miller, John Scott, Robert Burton, Unknown Black Man	Alleghany	SW	Assault & Riot	(M)	Mass

Date	Race	Name	County	Region	Crime and Category		Mob Type
01/11/1892	B	George Towler	Pittsylvania	S	Miscegenation	(S)	Private
02/12/1892	B	William Lavender	Roanoke	SW	Attempted Rape	(S)	Mass
03/18/1892	W	Lee Heflin, Joeseph Dye	Prince William	P	Murder	(M)	Private
04/06/1892	B	Issac Brandon	Charles City	T	Attempted Rape	(S)	Private
07/06/1892	B	Joe Williams Anderson	Louisa	P	Attempted Rape	(S)	Private
10/12/1892	B	Phillip Young	Fluvanna	P	Murder	(M)	Mass
11/29/1892	W	Burgess and Lucas	Russell	SW	Murder	(M)	Private
02/01/1893	B	Jerry Brown, Spencer Branch, John Johnson, Sam Ellerson, Sam Blow	Tazewell	SW	Assault	(M)	Mass
02/26/1893	B	Abner Anthony	Bath	SW	Attempted Rape	(S)	Private
04/16/1893	B	Arthur Morgan	Tazewell	SW	Murder	(M)	Unknown
05/11/1893	B	George Halsey	Smyth	SW	Rape	(S)	Mass
06/13/1893	B	William Shorter	Frederick	SH	Attempted Rape	(S)	Private
09/15/1893	B	Jesse Mitchell	Amelia	S	Rape	(S)	Private
09/20/1893	B	Thomas Smith	Roanoke	SW	Assault	(M)	Mass
11/01/1893	W	Abe Redmond	Charlotte	S	Assault	(M)	Private
05/17/1894	B	Samuel Wood	Scott	SW	Unknown	(U)	Terr.
04/23/1897	B	Joeseph McCoy	Alexandria	P	Rape	(S)	Mass
09/06/1897	W	Henry Walls	Patrick	S	Murder	(M)	Private
06/20/1898	W	[?]Howlet	Carroll	SW	Murder	(M)	Private
07/12/1898	B	John Henry James	Albemarle	P	Rape	(S)	Mass
09/12/1898	W	Lee Puckett	Patrick	S	Attempted Rape	(S)	Private
08/08/1899	B	Benjamin Thomas	Alexandria	P	Attempted Rape	(S)	Mass
01/05/1900	W	W. W. Watts	Warwick	T	Rape	(S)	Private
03/24/1900	B/W	Walter Cotton, Brandt O'Grady (W)	Greenville	S	Murder	(M)	Mass
09/14/1900	B	Pinkney Murphy	Nelson	P	Attempted Rape	(S)	Unknown
12/07/1900	B	Dan Long	Wythe	SW	Rape	(S)	Mass
03/19/1901	B	Hubert Wailer	Halifax	S	Arson	(O)	Private
07/01/1901	B	Joe Walton	Brunswick	S	Attempted Rape	(S)	Private
04/06/1902	B	James Carter	Amherst	P	Assault	(M)	Private
06/05/1902	B	Wiley Gwynn	Wise	SW	Attempted Rape	(S)	Private
07/31/1902	B	Charles Craven	Loudoun	P	Murder	(M)	Mass
01/13/1904	B	Elmore Moseley	Prince George	T	Murder	(M)	Private
08/04/1904	B	Andrew Dudley	Nelson	P	Attempted Rape	(S)	Private
10/24/1904	B	George F. Blount	Nanesemond	T	Assault	(M)	Private
02/27/1905	B	George Henderson	Page	SH	Unknown Cause	(U)	Terr.
12/26/1909	W	Henry Pennington	Buchanan	SW	Murder	(M)	Mass
08/16/1917	B	William Page	Northumberland	T	Attempted Rape	(S)	Mass
08/17/1917	B	Walter Clark	Pittsylvania	S	Murder	(M)	Posse
11/24/1918	B	Allie Thompson	Culpepper	P	Attempted Rape	(S)	Private

Date	Race	Name	County	Region	Crime and Category		Mob Type
11/14/1920	B	Dave Hunt	Wise	SW	Rape	(S)	Mass
08/03/1921	B	Lem Johnson	Brunswick	S	Murder	(M)	Mass
10/13/1923	B	Horace Carter	King William	T	Rape	(S)	Private
03/20/1925	B	James Jordan	Sussex	T	Rape	(S)	Mass
08/15/1926	B	Raymond Bird	Wythe	SW	Miscegenation	(S)	Private
11/30/1927	B	Leonard Woods	Wise	SW	Murder	(M)	Mass

Appendix B
Regions of Virginia and Georgia

Historians have long recognized the significance of the regional diversity of the South. Certainly, the regional variations in Georgia and Virginia and their effects upon the histories of the two states are as pronounced as in any southern states. Few would question that important regional differences were apparent in the expansion of slavery before the Civil War, in the depth of popular support for the Confederacy, or in the speed and scale of industrialization and urbanization in the postbellum period. Similarly, I have attempted to demonstrate that there were significant regional variations in the pattern of lynching. In light of the emphasis I have placed on these regional variations, a word on the criteria for defining the regions in Georgia and Virginia is in order.

The boundaries of the regions in Virginia may be drawn on the basis of easily recognizable natural features. The state may be divided into five geographical regions: the Tidewater, the Piedmont, the Southside, the Shenandoah Valley, and southwestern Virginia. The Tidewater consists of a coastal plain that extends westward to the fall line, which marks the limit of the tidal surge as well as the beginning of the Piedmont. In the Piedmont, the sandy, loamy plains of the Tidewater give way to rolling hills and soils that range from very rich to very poor. Although a region of considerable diversity, the Piedmont is clearly defined by the fall line to the east and the Blue Ridge mountains to the west.

Although Southside Virginia is the southern extension of the Piedmont south of the James River, its socioeconomic development is so distinct from most of the Piedmont to the north that I have treated it as a distinct subregion. Across the Blue Ridge Mountains lies the Shenandoah Valley, the broadest and most fertile portion of the Valley of Virginia. The distinctive geography, the north-south axis of trade, and the northern origins of many of the region's settlers sets the Shenandoah off from counties to its east. The valley extends ribbonlike to the southern border of the state, but below Rockbridge County (which technically is in the James River Valley and not the Shenandoah Valley), it is much narrower and socioeconomic development followed different lines than in the valley to the north. To the west and south of the valley are the Appalachian ridges of southwestern Virginia. In practical terms, the isolation of much of the region from eastern Virginia and the constraints upon agriculture imposed by the landscape separated the region from both the Shenandoah Valley and the Piedmont.

In addition to these important geographical features, the various regions in the state also are distinguished by differing population characteristics. In simple terms, the proportion of blacks to whites diminishes in Virginia from east to west, with the largest numbers of blacks living in the Tidewater and Southside and the fewest in the valley and southwestern region. The regional divisions used in this study are informed by the detailed survey of Virginia's historical geography in Jean Gottmann, *Virginia in Our Century* (Charlottesville: University Press of Virginia, 1969), especially part 1.

Although the regional variation in Georgia is at least as marked as in Virginia, few conspicuous boundaries separate the regions. Historians typically have relied upon the 1880 United States census report on cotton production, which divides the state into seven regions on the basis of soil types and climactic patterns. The seven regions, from north to south, are Northwest Georgia, the Blue Ridge, Middle Georgia, the Central Cotton Belt, Lime-sink Uplands, Pine Barrens, and the Coastal Counties. More recently, agricultural historians have refined these regional categories by adding four more regions: the Cumberland Plateau, the Sand Hills, the Palmetto Flats, and the Long-leaf Pine Flats. Although such precision is important for understanding some agricultural practices, they do not necessarily clarify regional social and economic variations. Consequently, I have relied upon the simpler regional breakdown devised by the historian and economist Robert Preston Brooks: the Mountainous Region, the Upper Piedmont, the Black Belt, the Wiregrass, and the Coastal Region. For Brooks, regions were defined by both geographical traits and population characteristics and, consequently, he was as concerned with the ratio of blacks to whites across Georgia as he was with soil and geological features.

Among the merits of Brooks's approach is that each of the regions he describes did follow a distinctive historical development. In contrast, an overreliance upon soil types as the defining feature of the regions of Georgia may lead to the mistaken conclusion that, for example, the Sand Hills of central Georgia developed along lines quite distinct from the neighboring Cotton Belt. I have modified Brooks's regions in only a few regards. First, I have renamed the Black Belt the Cotton Belt. Second, I have relabeled the Wiregrass as Southern Georgia because the region included vast pine barrens as well as wiregrass plains. I have also expanded the boundaries of Brooks's Wiregrass region to include the southern oak and pine uplands of southwestern Georgia. The counties in the pine uplands, which Brooks placed in the Black Belt, seem to me to share as many traits with Southern Georgia as with the Black Belt. Although cotton cultivation and plantation agriculture had been established in the region before the Civil War, the region diverged from the Cotton Belt in various ways after the Civil War. The expansion of railroads into the region, which replaced the river-bound trade routes and stimulated growing trade and communication with the counties to the east in Southern Georgia, and the expansion of lumbering and turpentining from Southern Georgia into the extreme southwestern counties served at once to distinguish the region from the Cotton Belt and move it closer to Southern Georgia.

As these comments should indicate, precise regional boundaries are practically impossible to determine in Georgia, and to a lesser extent in Virginia. Seldom do regional boundaries follow county lines and therefore some counties that straddle regions must be arbitrarily assigned to a region. Despite these restrictions, the regional divisions in Georgia that I have drawn have the virtue of simplicity and yet allow for a degree of precision that is not possible by generalizing about the state as a whole.

For various approaches to the historical geography of Georgia, see Frederick A. Bode and Donald E. Ginter, *Farm Tenancy and the Census in Antebellum Georgia* (Athens: University of Georgia Press, 1986), chapter 4; Robert Preston Brooks, "The Agrarian Revolution in Georgia, 1865–1912," *Bulletin of the University of Wisconsin* 3 (1914): 393–524; Thomas W. Hodler and Howard A. Schretter, *The Atlas of Georgia* (Athens: Institute of Community and Area Development, 1986), 11–53; and Eugene W. Hilgard et al., *Report on Cotton Production in the United States also Embracing Agricultural and Physico-Geographical Descriptions of the Several Cotton States and California* (Washington, D.C.: U.S. Census Office, 1884), 277–424.

Population by Race by Region, Virginia, 1880–1930
(Based on U.S. Census)

Year	Total Population	White	Black	Percent Black
Tidewater				
1880	443,905	212,693	231,212	52
1890	506,049	254,804	251,245	50
1900	603,435	313,739	289,696	48
1910	696,353	382,361	313,992	45
1920	842,164	495,283	346,881	41
1930	852,792	528,938	323,854	38
Piedmont				
1880	305,356	164,724	140,632	46
1890	295,473	171,086	124,387	42
1900	305,376	187,569	117,807	39
1910	314,713	204,484	110,229	35
1920	326,140	223,653	102,487	31
1930	338,164	245,922	92,242	27
Southside				
1880	367,126	170,508	196,618	53
1890	382,416	189,797	192,619	50
1900	398,603	212,113	186,490	47
1910	427,569	244,683	182,886	43
1920	463,815	282,151	181,664	39
1930	475,946	299,269	176,677	37
Shenandoah Valley				
1880	160,892	129,497	31,395	19
1890	173,214	144,570	28,644	16
1900	183,745	157,573	26,172	14
1910	189,892	166,679	23,213	12
1920	193,249	173,865	19,384	10
1930	202,491	185,475	17,016	8
Southwestern Virginia				
1880	235,286	203,527	31,759	13
1890	298,828	260,285	38,543	13
1900	363,025	322,468	40,557	11
1910	433,085	392,309	40,776	9
1920	483,819	444,218	39,601	8
1930	552,458	512,612	39,846	7

Population by Race by Region, Georgia, 1880–1930
(Based on U.S. Census)

Year	Total Population	White	Black	Percent Black
Mountain Region				
1880	125,027	111,219	13,808	11
1890	143,359	129,700	13,659	9
1900	158,223	144,412	13,811	9
1910	167,097	153,238	13,859	8
1920	174,763	161,989	12,774	7
1930	188,013	175,744	12,269	6
Upper Piedmont				
1880	356,102	253,645	102,457	29
1890	436,456	309,996	126,460	29
1900	523,900	372,673	151,227	29
1910	644,343	469,819	174,524	27
1920	745,358	557,969	187,389	25
1930	844,199	648,413	195,786	23
Cotton Belt				
1880	757,549	291,709	465,840	61
1890	841,192	320,641	520,551	62
1900	941,477	352,670	588,807	62
1910	1,021,018	391,618	629,400	62
1920	1,073,498	461,795	611,703	57
1930	962,536	465,466	497,070	52
Southern Georgia				
1880	223,980	131,176	92,804	41
1890	314,131	179,193	134,938	43
1900	473,754	265,241	208,513	44
1910	647,045	363,379	283,666	44
1920	751,673	434,842	316,831	42
1930	718,723	445,480	273,243	38
Coastal Region				
1880	79,522	29,298	50,224	63
1890	102,215	39,008	63,207	62
1900	118,977	46,522	72,455	61
1910	129,168	53,630	75,538	58
1920	150,540	72,863	77,677	52
1930	150,961	77,139	73,822	50

Appendix C
Sources Used in This Book

The reconstruction of the causes of, participants in, and aftereffects of each lynching is replete with difficulties. All scholarly attempts to understand and explain lynching in the South have had to contend with the inherent limitations of extant sources. In light of the methodological problems that confront any study of lynching, an explanation of the methods and sources I have used is necessary.

The first question that any scholar of lynching must address is what constitutes a lynching. As I explain in chapter 1, the problem of defining lynching is a vexing one. As a general rule, I have followed the definition agreed upon by antilynching activists in 1940: "there must be legal evidence that a person has been killed, and that he met his death illegally at the hands of a group acting under the pretext of service to justice, race, or tradition."

To a considerable extent, by distinguishing the various mob types as I do in chapter 1, some of the problems of defining lynching are alleviated. For example, the acts of mob violence that fit my definition of private and mass mobs (chapter 1) probably satisfy virtually any definition of lynching. However, other acts of violence defy easy classification. Southern posses, for instance, frequently gunned down fleeing black suspects in circumstances that seem far closer to mob violence than to the preservation of law and order. And yet, there were instances when posses did not intentionally kill suspects. In an attempt to distinguish between posses that committed a form of mob violence from posses that unintentionally killed a suspect, I have defined as lynchings any deaths that resulted from excessive violence by posses against unarmed, severely wounded, or surrendering suspects. I also have included a few instances in which posses resorted to extraordinarily violent measures—dynamite and fire—to overcome and kill armed black suspects before less lethal measures were attempted. Similarly, the actions of terrorist mobs sometimes straddle the line between mob violence and simple murder. I have counted an act of terrorist violence as a lynching when evidence exists that the murder was carried out by a group rather than one or two people, that the group intended to inflict bodily harm on its victim, and that race or tradition (which applies both to prevailing traditions of labor and race relations) provided the motive for the murder.

As should be clear, all definitions of lynching, to varying degrees, are arbitrary. Any record of lynchings will be compromised by the unavoidable imprecision of the term, and these inherent ambiguities make it impossible to compile a definitive list of all lynchings. And yet, the difficulties of defining lynching should not be exaggerated. After all, both blacks and whites relied upon common sense to differentiate acts of mob violence from the abundant violence that pervaded southern life. Unlike antilynching activists, for whom a precise definition of lynching was vital for effective antilynching laws, historians should seek a convenient definition of lynching that is both broad enough to capture the full range of mob violence and yet narrow enough to winnow out acts that did not fall within southern traditions of mob violence. In short, the historian's task is less to provide a precise definition of lynching than to explain the phenomenon.

In addition to the problem of defining lynching, scholars of mob violence face a variety of difficulties in gathering information on lynching in the South. The starting point for this study, as well as most others on the topic, is the lists of lynchings compiled during the early twentieth century by the Tuskegee Institute, the National Association for the Advancement of Colored People, the Commission on Interracial Cooperation, and the Association of Southern Women for the Prevention of Lynching. Unfortunately, each of these lists, including even the frequently cited *Thirty Years of Lynching* by the NAACP or the annual lists of the Tuskegee Institute, contain numerous errors, many of which can substantially affect interpretations. For example, *Thirty Years of Lynchings* records that three blacks were lynched in Lynchburg, Virginia, on November 4, 1893, when, in fact, the three had actually been lynched near the small country town of Lynchburg, Tennessee. The list also records the lynching of four blacks in Richmond, Virginia, on February 1, 1893, although they actually were lynched near the southwestern Virginia town of Richlands. Numerous errors of equal magnitude occur in the listing of lynchings in Georgia. Only by methodically corroborating each lynching on the various lists with contemporary newspaper accounts will it be possible to determine with any accuracy the location, cause, and number of lynchings.

It should come as no surprise that many of the extant accounts of lynchings must be used with great caution. Because lynchings were extralegal acts and lynchers were punished only in exceptional instances, state and local officials left few records that shed light on individual lynchings. County coroner's reports of the proceedings of coroner's courts held after lynchings are among the few official sources that reveal considerable detail about the circumstances surrounding each event. They also often demonstrate the willful complicity of local authorities, who often ignored testimony that strongly implicated local residents as mob members. Unfortunately, in Georgia before 1932, no state law required that coroner's reports be saved, and Virginia coroner's reports also were routinely discarded. Consequently, reports were saved in some counties but not in others, and even when saved, they are seldom cataloged. In a search in nearly thirty lynching-prone counties in southern Georgia, I found only five reports. I was unable to locate a single coroner's report in Virginia. For all of these reasons the records of state and local authorities in Virginia and Georgia manifestly are a flimsy foundation for any study of lynching.

The richest sources for information are contemporary newspapers. Stories about lynching were a staple of journalism between 1880 and 1930, and newspapers routinely devoted columns and, in a few exceptional instances, even pages to accounts of lynchings. From at least the 1890s, when black antilynching activist Ida Wells-Barnett used newspaper accounts of lynchings to compile a record of mob violence, newspapers have been the principal source for the study of mob violence. In later years, the Tuskegee Institute, the NAACP, the CIC, and the ASWPL all relied upon newspaper accounts when collecting information on lynchings. Newspapers typically provide a wealth of information on the events that precipitated each lynching, the size and actions of the mob, the manner of execution, and the community response to the lynching.

For all of the information that newspaper accounts provide, their serious limitations also must be recognized. Because the majority of extant newspapers from the period are white newspapers, they reflect the harsh racial attitudes of the day, and their accounts of lynchings, the alleged crimes that prompted lynchings, and the portrayals of mob victims must be treated with great caution. For example, white descriptions of both the alleged offenses and the character of lynching victims cannot be accepted without question. And yet, the unquestioned conventions of white racism sometimes did not prevent newspapers from publishing what seem to be frank discussions of the alleged offenses of mob victims. For example in 1885, Georgia newspapers carried extensive coverage of the lynching that ended the love affair between Peter Stamps, a black farmhand, and the daughter of his white employer. Although we might be surprised that white newspapers would admit such a relationship, the explanation may be that the conventional white wisdom was that Stamps's seduction of his employer's daughter only proved how debased and threatening he was. In the eyes of white readers, the combination of Stamps's treachery and his victim's teenage innocence explained the tragic relationship. We will never be able to determine the depth of affection that existed between the two lovers on the basis of newspaper accounts, but the bare outlines of the events that preceded the lynching are clear. Moreover, white news accounts almost certainly can be trusted to provide with a measure of accuracy details about the location of the lynching, the number of lynchers, and even some vague sense of the local response to the event. Despite the serious limitations of white accounts, there simply is no other foundation upon which to base a comprehensive study of lynching.

By collecting accounts from as many different newspapers as possible, I have attempted to compare news reports and reach a more accurate composite account of each lynching. Too often, studies of lynchings have relied on major urban dailies such as the *New York Times* or the *Chicago Tribune* for news accounts of southern lynchings. Scholars have also drawn upon the news clipping files of the Tuskegee Institute. Unfortunately, the Tuskegee files consist largely of accounts published in the larger southern and northern daily newspapers, which often published reports of lynchings taken from the news wires, many of which were marred by inaccurate details. Sometimes they even published descriptions of lynchings that did not happen or were prevented. While the major dailies and the Tuskegee clipping files are convenient resources, they are only the starting points for research into lynching.

My general strategy when compiling information on lynchings was to use the list of lynchings compiled by the Tuskegee Institute, the NAACP, and the ASWPL and then search the major dailies in Georgia and Virginia for information on each lynching. Local news accounts provide a valuable corrective to the frequent errors to be found in the major regional and national dailies. By combining research in both the rural weeklies and the urban dailies, it is possible to go far beyond the rudimentary portrait of lynchings provided by lists derived from daily newspapers, such as *Thirty Years of Lynching*. In addition, local white newspapers reported lynchings in a direct and detailed fashion, free from the moralizing and the flowery prose that characterized wire-service accounts. In sum, local newspapers provide a wealth of information that is unavailable anywhere else.

After completing a search of the major urban dailies, I searched rural newspapers. First I looked at issues of the county newspapers both several weeks before and several weeks after each lynching that occurred in each county. I then searched the columns of newspapers in neighboring counties for accounts of the lynching. By this method, I collected at least three and sometimes as many as ten different white accounts of each lynching. Usually the accounts differed only in minor details, but in several instances the local newspapers provided either greater detail or apparently more accurate stories than did the urban dailies. Moreover, a reading of every extant issue of several south Georgia newspapers between 1890 and 1910 revealed several lynchings that were not reported in urban dailies.

Although white accounts of lynchings are readily accessible, black versions are rare. Whenever possible I have compared white reports of lynchings with accounts in black newspapers. Unfortunately, very few of the numerous black newspapers in Georgia and Virginia are extant.

Newspaper accounts have been supplemented whenever possible with information from the files of the various antilynching organizations. The investigations of lynchings in Georgia and Virginia carried out by both branch members and officials of the national NAACP, beginning around 1916, reveal in great detail the pervasiveness of racial violence and the attitudes of local whites and blacks toward the practice. Similarly, beginning in 1920, the Georgia CIC gathered detailed information about lynchings in the state, as did the ASWPL after 1930. Because of these organizations, a wealth of detailed information exists about many lynchings after 1915 that is largely free from the worst distortions of contemporary racism.

By drawing upon these varied sources, I have compiled lists of lynching in Georgia and Virginia (Tables 22 and 23) which, at the very least, are more accurate than any currently available lists. The list of lynchings in Virginia, I believe, is a virtually complete record of this form of mob violence in the state between 1880 and 1930. I make no such claim for the list of Georgia lynchings. A tedious search, issue by issue, of county newspapers in Georgia, I suspect, would turn up previously uncounted lynchings as well as numerous instances of violence that arguably might be defined as mob violence. My lists are not definitive; they simply are as close to definitive as is feasible.

Applying quantitative methods to the lists of lynching victims is difficult. Since the 1920s, sociologists have employed a variety of statistical devices to the study of lynching and have drawn conclusions about the relationship between the frequency of lynchings and such variables as population density, illiteracy, levels of church attendance, and support for the Populist party. There can be little question that much has been and can be learned from these studies. But it is also important to recognize the obstacles that seriously compromise quantitative approaches to lynching. For example, it would be a mistake to assume that just because a lynching took place in a certain county assumptions can be made about the composition of the mob. For example, in 1922 two blacks were lynched in Liberty County, Georgia. The small mob responsible for the murders was comprised not of locals, but of men who had traveled nearly fifty miles from nearby Wayne County. While the Liberty County lynching is recorded as having occurred in Liberty County, the roots of the event had nothing whatsoever to do with race relations in Liberty County. Furthermore, unless the complexities of the lynching are recognized, it cannot easily be fit into quantitative calculations without producing distortions. For example, important differences will result if, in calculations about the relationship between the ratio of blacks and whites to lynching, the Liberty County lynching is traced to Wayne County, which had a substantially smaller black population than did Liberty County. The point is, that county boundaries, which mark the fundamental unit for population and socioeconomic data in the federal census, meant nothing to lynch mobs. Given that the precise composition of mobs is usually impossible to determine and that mobs often captured and executed their victims outside of the counties in which their victims' alleged offenses occurred, I doubt whether there is any easy way to apply quantitative methods without simplifying an inescapably complex phenomenon.

For these reasons, I have preferred to concentrate upon regional variations in mob violence. Although such generalizations may lack the apparent exactitude of results derived from county-by-county studies, they seem to me to avoid many of the methodological hurdles imposed by the inconvenient behavior of mobs. Finally, an exaggerated concern for detail may lead to a myopic approach to the topic. It is more important, for example, to know why mob violence was prevalent throughout the Cotton Belt as a whole than to know why Spalding County had seven lynchings and neighboring Henry County had only one. In light of all of these methodological challenges, the test of any study of lynching should be its ability to provide a *plausible* explanation for the phenomenon of southern mob violence. Any greater expectations will almost certainly remain unsatisfied.

Primary Sources

Newspapers

As I have explained, black and white newspapers are the essential source for my study. The late nineteenth and early twentieth centuries may well have been the golden age of southern journalism. Virtually every city had several newspapers, and even rural county seats had at least one. The best holdings of newspapers published in Virginia are at the Virginia State Library and can be supplemented by the collection at Alderman Library at the University of Virginia. The collection of Georgia newspapers at the University of Georgia is remarkably extensive and includes runs of most of the important urban dailies and county weeklies.

Georgia boasted numerous urban daily papers, several of which had national reputations. The *Atlanta Constitution* had the most extensive coverage of lynchings of any paper in the state, and its editorial treatment of racial violence reflected its political conservatism and paternalistic racism. The *Atlanta Journal,* which bore the imprint of its owner and sometimes editor Hoke Smith, seldom matched the coverage of lynchings carried in the *Constitution,* but its editorials on racial violence were filled with some of the most strident justifications of lynching to be found in the state. Although neither the *Atlanta Georgian* nor the *Atlanta News* published extensive accounts of racial violence, the two papers were noteworthy for their reactionary editorials. Elsewhere in the state, the *Augusta Chronicle,* the *Columbus Enquirer,* and the *Macon Telegraph* carried full accounts of lynchings in the immediate vicinity of their respective cities. The *Savannah Morning News,* a consistent opponent of lynching, mirrored the polite paternalistic racism of many whites in coastal Georgia.

Among the Georgia county newspapers that had the most extensive coverage of lynchings are the *Thomasville Times-Enterprise, Eastman Times Journal Spotlight, Americus Times-Recorder, Greenville Merriwether Vindicator, Griffin Daily News, Carrollton Carroll Free Press,* and the *Dalton Citizen.* The *Valdosta Daily Times,* which published in the heart of mob-prone southern Georgia, deserves special mention. Its columns are filled with stories of vigilantism against alleged white and black moral reprobates, lynchings, and mob violence of all kinds. The combination of the newspaper's area of coverage and daily publication make it a particularly rich source for information on lynching in Georgia. A study of the postwar history of journalism in Georgia is badly needed. The only survey of Georgia journalism is Louis T. Griffith and John E. Talmadge, *Georgia Journalism, 1763–1950* (Athens: University of Georgia Press, 1953).

The major urban dailies in Virginia, reflecting the more urbanized character of the state, extended their reach much further into the countryside than did their Georgia counterparts. In particular, several of Richmond's newspapers carried extensive regional coverage of race relations and racial violence. The *Richmond Times* was conservative politically and a confirmed opponent of mob violence. The *Richmond Dispatch* spoke for the mainstream Democratic party and often strongly condemned lynching in theory while offering complex sophistries defending specific lynchings. When the two papers consolidated in 1903 as the *Times-Dispatch,* the *Times*'s position on lynchings became ascendent. In Norfolk, the *Virginian* (later the *Virginian-Pilot*) published full accounts of lynchings in the Tidewater region and, like the *Dispatch,* maintained an ambivalent editorial stance toward mob violence. The *Petersburg Index-Appeal* covered lynchings in the Southside, while the *Lynchburg News,* the *Lynchburg Advance,* and the *Roanoke Times* published accounts of racial violence in western portions of the state. Finally, the *Baltimore Sun,* while published outside of the state, often carried extensive coverage of lynchings in Virginia, especially incidents of mob violence in northern Virginia. The best introduction to Virginia newspapers remains Lester J. Cappon, *Virginia Newspapers, 1821–1935* (New York: D. Appleton-Century, 1936).

Because of the comparative infrequency of lynchings in most Virginia counties and the inferior quality of most county weeklies, at least compared to Georgia, there are no rural papers in Virginia comparable to the best newspapers in rural Georgia. However, rural papers in Virginia can be relied upon to provide detailed accounts of local lynchings.

The best black weekly in Georgia, the *Savannah Tribune,* was published throughout the period and is widely available on microfilm. On several occasions, the *Tribune* carried lynching accounts written by black witnesses. More often, the newspaper provided blacks with both vigorous editorial denunciations of lynching and news of efforts to protest against mob violence. The *Atlanta Independent* seldom carried extensive news coverage of lynchings, but lynching did receive notice in its editorial page. The *Augusta Georgia Baptist,* edited by William Jefferson White, attracted the unwelcome attention of local whites on several occasions by publishing bold editorials against lynchings and racial violence in Augusta and elsewhere in the state. But the *Georgia Baptist* was a denominational journal rather than a traditional newspaper and made no effort to publish firsthand accounts of lynchings. A valuable survey of black newspapers is John M. Matthews, "Black Newspapermen and the Black Community in Georgia, 1890–1930," *Georgia Historical Quarterly* 68 (Fall 1984): 356–81.

Although Virginia boasted numerous black newspapers, very few are extant. Fortunately, full runs of the *Richmond Planet* and the *Norfolk Journal and Guide* are readily available on microfilm. The *Planet,* edited by John Mitchell, Jr., is the best single source for the study of lynching in Virginia. It carried extensive reprints of accounts of lynchings in white papers, as well as firsthand accounts from black witnesses. The *Planet* also published letters from readers who had been subjected to various forms of racial violence and intimidation. Despite Mitchell's tendency toward self-promotion, the *Planet* between 1890 and 1900 was one of the most effective black voices of protest in the South. Mitchell's increasing conservatism after 1900 remains puzzling, but the voice of black protest endured in

P. B. Young and the *Norfolk Journal and Guide*. Within a decade of acquiring the *Journal and Guide* in 1910, Young had made the newspaper into the preeminent black newspaper in the state. His thoughtful and gracefully written editorials were widely read and attracted favorable comment from liberal whites. A survey of black newspapers in Virginia that centers on the *Planet* and the *Journal and Guide* is Henry Lewis Suggs, ed., "Virginia," in *The Black Press in the South, 1865–1979* (Westport, Conn.: Greenwood Press, 1983).

Antilynching Organization Collections

The files of the National Association for the Advancement of Colored People (Manuscript Division, Library of Congress), now available on microfilm, are the richest single source for information on lynching in the South after 1915. The reports from local Georgia branches and investigations by the national office provide the most detailed and unbiased accounts of mob violence available. In addition, the various tactics of the lengthy crusade to end mob violence can be traced in the files of both the branches and the national organization.

The Commission on Interracial Cooperation Collection (Atlanta University Library) contains extensive files on investigations of lynching in Georgia, in addition to correspondence and documents relating to the campaign to end lynching. The CIC Papers are the starting point for the study of the white antilynching movement. The Association of Southern Women for the Prevention of Lynching Papers (Atlanta University Library) are an equally rich resource. Although the ASWPL was active after the period that is the focus of this study, the ASWPL collection is a rich resource for tracing the gradual demise of the tradition of lynching. Although the ASWPL papers are not heavily cited in this book, they have helped me form many of my conclusions about mob violence.

Manuscript Collections

The papers of prominent white Georgian politicians, on the whole, offer only spotty discussions of racial violence. The official papers of the various governors (Georgia Department of Archives and History) are largely devoted to patronage, political maneuvers, and the minutiae of the daily operations of state government. The gubernatorial papers of Hugh M. Dorsey contain a file on lynchings and the governor's efforts to suppress the practice. The Joseph M. Brown Papers (Atlanta Historical Society) contain many of his speeches on law and order and letters of strong praise for his handling of labor unrest. The Hoke Smith Collection (University of Georgia Library) contains little mention of Smith's attitudes toward racial violence. In contrast, the William J. Northen Papers (AC 00–74, Georgia

Department of Archives and History) demonstrates Northen's paternalistic attitudes toward blacks, his sincere opposition to lynching, and his failed efforts to organize a Law and Order League in 1907.

The Rebecca Lattimer Felton Papers (Hargrett Rare Book and Manuscript Library, University of Georgia Library) should be consulted for the attitudes of one of Georgia's most outspoken defenders of lynchings. The Felton Papers also include many letters from Georgians who supported her editorial polemics on lynching and race relations. For the attitudes of a white liberal, the Julian L. Harris Papers (Special Collection, Robert W. Woodruff Library, Emory University) are excellent, especially for the 1920s. The papers of Alexander R. Lawton (Georgia Historical Society, Savannah) offer only a few glimpses of the interracial reform efforts of a Savannah patrician active in the local CIC. The Robert Preston Brooks Papers (University of Georgia Library) contain valuable surveys of Georgia plantations which, along with the census, are among the most valuable sources on regional variation in labor relations and agricultural practices in the state.

The collections of Virginia governors' papers at the Virginia State Archives in Richmond contain considerable information on their efforts to combat lynching. The Charles O'Ferrall Papers include the forty-one-page report on the Alexandria lynching of 1897, a document of surprising candor. The Andrew J. Montague Papers contain the governor's private thoughts on lynchings as well as his official efforts to aid local authorities who were intent on preventing lynchings. Similarly, the papers of Claude A. Swanson, William H. Mann, Henry C. Stuart, Westmoreland Davis, and E. Lee Trinkle show the various steps that each governor took to prevent lynchings. Information on the last lynchings in the state and official investigations that followed are detailed in the Harry F. Byrd Papers. The Byrd Papers also include correspondence outlining the motives behind the Virginia antilynching law passed in 1928. The J. Hoge Tyler Collection (Special Collections Department, University Library, Virginia Polytechnic Institute and State University, Blacksburg) are an especially rich source for contemporary attitudes toward lynching in Virginia. Governor Tyler's handling of the Emporia affair provoked prominent lawyers, judges, and private citizens to write letters on lynchings and the governor's obligation to stop mob violence. There is perhaps no more revealing contrast between attitudes toward lynching in Virginia and in Georgia than the letters in the J. Hoge Tyler Collection and the letters in the Rebecca Lattimer Felton Collection.

Other manuscript collections in Virginia contain little mention of racial violence or race relations. The Louis Jaffé Papers (Alderman Library, University of Virginia) include information on the awarding of the 1928 Pulitzer Prize to Jaffé for his antilynching editorials, but otherwise are disappointing. Similarly, the Douglas S. Freeman Papers (Alderman Library, University of Virginia) are of little help. The Sively Family Papers (Alderman Library, University of Virginia) contain a brief discussion of a lynching near the Sively family home in Hot Springs, Virginia, in 1893.

State and Federal Government Documents and Publications

The reports of the Virginia adjutant general and the Georgia adjutant general are valuable sources for information on the use of militia to prevent lynchings. Militia commanders were required to file reports each time they were called out to aid civil authorities, and the reports were gathered and published annually. The papers of the Georgia Adjutant General (Georgia Department of Archives and History) contain detailed files relating to the Statesboro lynching of 1904, demonstrating conclusively the ineptitude of local authorities and the commanding officer who failed to prevent the lynching.

The General Records of the Department of Justice, Record Group 60 (National Archives) contain several files relating to lynching in Georgia, including the unsuccessful efforts of the assistant federal attorney in Savannah to seek convictions of mob members involved in the Statesboro lynching of 1904. The collection reveals the failure to use federal police powers to interfere in racial violence in Georgia and elsewhere.

For both Georgia and Virginia, the *Senate Journal* and *House Journal* are convenient sources for the annual messages of the governors. The annual messages, although often ponderous and wildly optimistic, contain a variety of proposals to combat lynching.

A revealing source of information on mob members is the Pardon Files at the Georgia Department of Archives and History. Three files of convicted lynchers, listed by the name of the principal mob leader and county, are J. A. Cochran (Fulton County), Bennie Devanne (Schley County), and Gaines Lastinger (Coffee County). The Clemency Request of Richard Knight and Welcome Golding (Ware County), two blacks who killed a white man in self-defense but pleaded guilty to murder charges to escape a lynch mob, is a harrowing account of a "legal" lynching.

I made an effort to use the extant county tax digests at the Georgia Department of Archives and History to determine the wealth of Georgia lynching victims. Unfortunately, the names of blacks were seldom recorded with the care devoted to the names of whites, making it difficult to trace blacks in the tax digests. Moreover, the majority of blacks were taxed at the lowest rate, and the value and nature of their property was not recorded.

Notes

Abbreviations Used in the Notes

ASWPL	Association of Southern Women for the Prevention of Lynching, Atlanta University Library
AC	*Atlanta Constitution*
AJ	*Atlanta Journal*
AN	*Atlanta News*
AUL	Atlanta University Library
BS	*Baltimore Sun*
CES	*Columbus Enquirer-Sun*
CIC	Commission on Interracial Cooperation, Atlanta University Library
GDAH	Georgia Department of Archives and History
LC	Library of Congress
MT	*Macon Telegraph*
NYT	*New York Times*
NV	*Norfolk Virginian*
NVP	*Norfolk Virginian Pilot*
RD	*Richmond Dispatch*
RNL	*Richmond News Leader*
RP	*Richmond Planet*
RS	*Richmond State*
RT	*Richmond Times*
RTD	*Richmond Times-Dispatch*
SMN	*Savannah Morning News*
SP	*Savannah Press*
ST	*Savannah Tribune*
VT	*Valdosta Times*
VSL	Virginia State Library, Richmond
WP	*Washington Post*
WH	*Waycross Herald*

Introduction

1. James E. Cutler, *Lynch Law: An Investigation into the History of Lynching in the United States* (New York: Longmans, Green, 1905), 1.

2. *RP,* March 30, 31, 1900.

3. W. E. B. Du Bois, *The Souls of Black Folk* (New York: 1903; repr. New York: New American Library, 1982), 141.

4. On the early forms of mob violence, see Richard Maxwell Brown, *The South Carolina Regulators* (Cambridge: Harvard University Press, 1963); Cutler, *Lynch Law,* 13–89; Alfred Percy, *Origin of Lynch Law, 1780* (Madison Heights, Va.: Percy Press, 1959); and John Raymond Ross, "At the Bar of Judge Lynch: Lynching and Lynch Mobs in America," Ph.D. diss., Texas Tech University, 1983, 55–75.

5. On antebellum mob violence, see Richard Maxwell Brown, *Strain of Violence: Historical Studies of American Violence and Vigilantism* (New York: Oxford University Press, 1975), esp. 91–180; Cutler, *Lynch Law,* 90–136; Paul A. Gilje, *The Road to Mobocracy: Popular Disorder in New York City, 1763–1834* (Chapel Hill: University of North Carolina Press, 1987); and Leonard L. Richards, *"Gentlemen of Property and Standing": Anti-Abolition Mobs in Jacksonian America* (New York: Oxford University Press, 1970).

6. Clement Eaton, "Mob Violence in the Old South," *Mississippi Valley Historical Review* 29 (Dec. 1942): 351–70; and Ulrich B. Phillips, *American Negro Slavery* (New York, 1918; repr., Baton Rouge: Louisiana State University Press, 1966), 460–63, 511–12; Bertram Wyatt-Brown, *Southern Honor: Ethics and Behavior in the Old South* (New York: Oxford University Press, 1982), passim.

7. Edward L. Ayers, *Vengeance and Justice: Crime and Punishment in the Nineteenth Century South* (New York: Oxford University Press, 1984), 132–37; Dickson D. Bruce, Jr., *Violence and Culture in the Antebellum South* (Austin: University of Texas Press, 1979), 114–60; and John Hope Franklin, *The Militant South, 1800–1861* (Cambridge: Harvard University Press, 1970), 66–72.

8. W. J. Cash, *The Mind of the South* (New York: Knopf, 1941), 35; Lawrence M. Friedman, "The Law Between the States: Some Thoughts on Southern Legal History," in *Ambivalent Legacy: A Legal History of the South,* ed. David J. Bodenhamer and James W. Ely, Jr. (Jackson: University Press of Mississippi, 1984), 30–46; and Michael S. Hindus, *Prison and Plantation: Crime, Justice, and Authority in Massachusetts and South Carolina, 1767–1878* (Chapel Hill: University of North Carolina Press, 1980).

9. Ayers, *Vengeance and Justice,* 9–33; Cash, *Mind of the South,* 87–89; Elliot J. Gorn, "Gouge and Bite, Pull Hair and Scratch": The Social Significance of Fighting in the Southern Backcountry," *American Historical Review* 90 (Feb. 1985): 18–43; and Wyatt-Brown, *Southern Honor,* passim.

10. George Frederickson, *The Black Image in the White Mind: The Debate on Afro-American Character and Destiny, 1817–1914* (New York: Harper & Row, 1971), esp. 71–96; and Orlando Patterson, *Slavery and Social Death: A Comparative Study* (Cambridge: Harvard University Press, 1982), 94–97.

11. Wyatt-Brown, *Southern Honor*, 425–93.

12. Eugene D. Genovese, *Roll, Jordan, Roll: The World the Slaves Made* (New York: Vintage, 1976), 33; Philip J. Schwarz, *Twice Condemned: Slaves and the Criminal Laws of Virginia, 1705–1865* (Baton Rouge: Louisiana State University Press, 1985), esp. 291–95; and Wyatt-Brown, *Southern Honor*, 402–34.

13. Michael Fellman, *Inside War: The Guerilla Conflict in Missouri during the American Civil War* (New York: Oxford University Press, 1989); Clarence L. Mohr, *On the Threshold of Freedom: Masters and Slaves in the Civil War* (Athens: University of Georgia Press, 1986), 32–36, 219–20; Phillip S. Paludan, *Victims: A True Story of the Civil War* (Knoxville: University of Tennessee Press, 1981); James Smallwood, "Disaffection in Confederate Texas: The Great Hanging at Gainesville," *Civil War History* 22 (Dec. 1976): 349–60; and William W. White, "The Texas Slave Insurrection of 1860," *Southwestern Historical Quarterly* 52 (Jan. 1949): 259–85.

14. Barry A. Crouch, "A Spirit of Lawlessness: White Violence, Texas Blacks, 1865–1868," *Journal of Social History* 18 (Winter 1984): 217–26; Eric Foner, *Reconstruction: America's Unfinished Revolution, 1863–1877* (New York: Harper & Row, 1988), 119–23; and J. C. A. Stagg, "The Problem of Klan Violence: The South Carolina Upcountry, 1868–1871," *Journal of American Studies* 8 (Dec. 1974): 303–18.

15. Foner, *Reconstruction*, 425–44; William Gillette, *Retreat from Reconstruction, 1869–1879* (Baton Rouge: Louisiana State University Press, 1979), 42–45; and Allen W. Trelease, *White Terror: The Ku Klux Klan Conspiracy and Southern Reconstruction* (New York: Harper & Row, 1979).

16. Ray Granade, "Violence: An Instrument of Policy in Reconstruction Alabama," *Alabama Historical Quarterly* 30 (Fall-Winter 1968): 181–202; Ralph L. Peek, "Lawlessness in Florida, 1868–1871," *Florida Historical Quarterly* 40 (Oct. 1961): 164–85; George C. Rable, *But There Was No Peace: The Role of Violence in the Politics of Reconstruction* (Athens: University of Georgia Press, 1984); and George C. Wright, *Racial Violence in Kentucky, 1865–1940: Lynchings, Mob Rule, and "Legal Lynchings"* (Baton Rouge: Louisiana State University Press, 1990), chapter 1.

17. Foner, *Reconstruction*, 454–59; Trelease, *White Terror*, 385–409; and Gillette, *Retreat From Reconstruction*, 42–55.

18. Foner, *Reconstruction*, 587–97; Jack P. Maddex, *The Virginia Conservatives, 1867–1879: A Study in Reconstruction Politics* (Chapel Hill: University of North Carolina Press, 1970), 184–203; and Judson C. Ward, "Georgia under the Bourbon Democrats, 1872–1890," Ph.D. diss., University of North Carolina, 1947.

19. Atticus G. Haygood, "The Black Shadow in the South," *Forum* 16 (Oct. 1893): 167.

20. For lynching totals, see Monroe Work, ed., *The Negro Yearbook: An Annual En-*

cyclopedia of the Negro, 1931–1932 (Tuskegee: Negro Year Book Publishing, 1931), 293. The totals for Virginia and Georgia, which are lower than those recorded in the *Negro Year Book,* are derived from my research. The totals for Kentucky are from Wright, *Racial Violence in Kentucky,* 71.

21. Richard Hofstader and Michael Wallace, *American Violence: A Documentary History* (New York: Vintage Press, 1971), 4.

22. Arthur F. Raper, *The Tragedy of Lynching* (Chapel Hill: University of North Carolina Press, 1933), esp. 41–43, 51–54. See also, Earl Fiske Young, "The Relations of Lynching to the Size of Population Areas," *Sociology and Social Research* 12 (March-April, 1928): 348–53; and W. E. Wimpy, "Lynchings: An Evil of County Government," *Manufacturers' Record* 76 (Dec. 25, 1919): 49–50.

23. John Dollard, *Caste and Class in a Small Southern Town* (New Haven: Yale University Press, 1937), passim; and John Dollard et al., *Frustration and Aggression* (New Haven: Yale University Press, 1939).

24. The correlation between cotton prices and lynchings is described in Carl Iver Hovland and Robert R. Sears, "Minor Studies of Aggression: VI. Correlation of Lynchings with Economic Indices," *Journal of Psychology* 9 (April 1940): 301–10; and Raper, *Tragedy of Lynching,* 30–31. For a methodological critique of Hovland and Sears, see Alexander Mintz, "A Re-Examination of Correlations Between Lynchings and Economic Indices," *Journal of Abnormal and Social Psychology* 41 (1946): 154–65.

25. James R. McGovern, *Anatomy of a Lynching: The Killing of Claude Neal* (Baton Rouge: Louisiana State University Press, 1982), 151; and Dollard, *Caste and Class in a Southern Town,* esp. chapter 15.

26. For a discussion of the refinements of the "frustration-aggression" theory, see Albert Bandura, *Aggression: A Social Learning Analysis* (Englewood Cliffs, N.J.: Prentice-Hall, 1973), passim; David D. Gilmore, *Aggression and Community: Paradoxes of Andalusian Culture* (New Haven: Yale University Press, 1987), 16–17; and Clayton A. Robarchek, "Frustration, Aggression, and the Nonviolent Semai," *American Ethnologist* 4 (Nov. 1977): 762–69.

27. Joel Williamson, *The Crucible of Race: Black-White Relations in the American South since Emancipation* (New York: Oxford University Press, 1984), 308. For similar conclusions, see Trudier Harris, *Exorcising Blackness: Historical and Literary Lynching and Burning Rituals* (Bloomington: Indiana University Press, 1984), 19–24; and Philip Resnikoff, "A Psychoanalytic Study of Lynching," *Psychoanalytic Review* 20 (Oct. 1933): 421–27.

28. Ayers, *Vengeance and Justice,* chapter 7; Jacquelyn Dowd Hall, *Revolt against Chivalry: Jesse Daniel Ames and the Women's Campaign against Lynching* (New York: Columbia University Press, 1979), chapter 5; and Wyatt-Brown, *Southern Honor,* chapter 16.

29. One illustration may reveal the difficulties that plague many psychohistorical explanations of racism and racist behavior. Peter Loewenberg argues that racism is a "psychological function of the personality related to character structure, patterns of society, and adaptation to personal and social change." Prejudice, he explains, is learned behavior, and

children learn stereotypes of racial inferiority as a matter of course. This line of reasoning can hardly be challenged. But then he concludes that "prejudiced behavior is, in a real sense, contagious and continuous, constantly reproducing itself." A more convincing argument would be that racist stereotypes persist as long as the social patterns that gave birth to those attitudes persist. See Peter Loewenberg, "The Psychology of Racism," in *The Great Fear: Race in the Mind of America*, ed. Gary B. Nash and Richard Weiss (New York: Holt, Rinehart, and Winston, 1970), 186, 188. Jonathan M. Wiener has dismissed the racial attitudes of southern whites as of "secondary significance" in explaining the evolution of the southern race relations. The key to black-white relations, he emphatically states, is to be found in "social and economic institutions and processes." See Jonathan M. Wiener, "The 'Black Beast Rapist': White Racial Attitudes in the Postwar South," *Reviews in American History* 13 (June 1985): 226.

30. David E. Stannard, *Shrinking History: On Freud and the Failure of Psychohistory* (New York: Oxford University Press, 1980), passim. See also, David Hackett Fischer, *Historians' Fallacies: Toward a Logic of Historical Thought* (New York: Harper, 1970), 193.

31. Oliver C. Cox, *Caste, Class and Race: A Study in Social Dynamics* (New York: Doubleday, 1948), 321–22.

32. The historian Barbara Fields has pointed out that too often historians of American race relations implicitly have reified race as a constant, primordial force. George Frederickson concurs and complains that many historians have failed to emphasize that racism is the product of specific social and historical circumstances. See Barbara J. Fields, "Ideology and Race in American History," in *Region, Race, and Reconstruction: Essays in Honor of C. Vann Woodward*, ed. J. Morgan Kousser and James M. McPherson (New York: Oxford University Press, 1982), 143–78; and George Frederickson, *The Arrogance of Race: Historical Perspectives on Slavery, Racism, and Social Inequality* (Middletown, Conn.: Wesleyan University Press, 1988), passim.

33. One study that is sensitive to regional variations is Lester C. Lamon, *Black Tennesseans, 1900–1930* (Knoxville: University of Tennessee Press, 1977). Despite the wealth of evidence in the book, Lamon concludes by emphasizing the static quality of race relations. Similarly, Neil R. McMillen reveals temporal change in race relations in Mississippi while shedding little light on the regional variations in racial contact. See Neil R. McMillen, *Dark Journey: Black Mississippians in the Age of Jim Crow* (Urbana: University of Illinois Press, 1989), passim. For evidence of significant regional and temporal changes in race relations, see Eric Arnesen, *Waterfront Workers of New Orleans: Race, Class, and Politics, 1863–1923* (New York: Oxford University Press, 1991); Elizabeth R. Bethel, *Promiseland: A Century of Life in a Negro Community* (Philadelphia: Temple University Press, 1981); Earl Lewis, *In Their Own Interests: Race, Class, and Power in Twentieth-Century Norfolk, Virginia* (Berkeley: University of California Press, 1991); Ronald L. Lewis, *Black Coal Miners in America: Race, Class, and Community Conflict, 1780–1980* (Lexington: University Press of Kentucky, 1987); William Lynwood Montell, *The Saga of Coe Ridge: A Study in Oral History* (Knoxville: University of Tennessee Press, 1970); Howard N. Rabino-

witz, *Race Relations in the Urban South, 1865–1890* (New York: Oxford University Press, 1978); Daniel Rosenberg, *New Orleans Dockworkers: Race, Labor, and Unionism 1892–1923* (Albany: State University of New York Press, 1988); and George C. Wright, *Life Behind the Veil: Blacks in Louisville, Kentucky, 1865–1930* (Baton Rouge: Louisiana State University Press, 1985).

34. Howard N. Rabinowitz, "More Than the Woodward Thesis: Assessing the Strange Career of Jim Crow," *Journal of American History* 75 (Dec. 1988): 848.

35. For discussions of the continuity-change debate in southern history, see Rabinowitz, "More Than the Woodward Thesis," 842–56; and John Herbert Roper, *C. Vann Woodward, Southerner* (Athens: University of Georgia Press, 1987), esp. 146–67.

36. Juanita W. Crudele, "A Lynching Bee: Butler County Style," *Alabama Historical Quarterly* 42 (Spring-Summer 1980): 59–71; Jack E. David, " 'Whitewash' in Florida: The Lynching of Jesse James Payne and Its Aftermath," *Florida Historical Quarterly* 68 (Jan. 1990): 277–98; Leonard Dinnerstein, *The Leo Frank Case* (New York: Columbia University Press, 1968); Dennis B. Downey and Raymond M. Hyser, *No Crooked Death: Coatesville, Pennsylvania, and the Lynching of Zachariah Walker* (Urbana: University of Illinois Press, 1990); McGovern, *Anatomy of a Lynching;* Howard Smead, *Blood Justice: The Lynching of Charles Mack Parker* (New York: Oxford University Press, 1986); James M. SoRelle, "The 'Waco Horror': The Lynching of Jesse Washington," *Southwestern Historical Quarterly* 86 (April 1983): 517–36; Stephen J. Whitfield, *A Death in the Delta: The Story of Emmett Till* (New York: Free Press, 1988); Edward C. Williamson, "Black Belt Political Crisis: The Savage-James Lynching, 1882," *Florida Historical Quarterly* 45 (April 1967): 402–9; and Jon L. Wilson, "Days of Fear: A Lynching in St. Petersburg," *Tampa Bay History* 5 (Fall-Winter 1983): 4–26.

37. Du Bois, *Souls of Black Folk,* 141.

1   Mobs and Ritual

1. Jesse Daniel Ames, *The Changing Character of Lynching* (Atlanta: Commission on Interracial Cooperation, 1942), 29. On the 1940 meeting and the struggle to define lynching, see "Definition of Lynching," Jan. 17, 1931-Nov. 6, 1941, file 9, reel 2, ASWPL Papers, AUL; and Linda O. McMurray, *Recorder of Black Experience: A Biography of Monroe Nathan Work* (Baton Rouge: Louisiana State University Press, 1985), 124–27.

2. See Jacquelyn Dowd Hall, *Revolt against Chivalry: Jesse Daniel Ames and the Women's Campaign against Lynching* (New York: Columbia University Press, 1979), 139, 141; Trudier Harris, *Exorcising Blackness: Historical and Literary Lynching and Burning Rituals* (Bloomington: Indiana University Press, 1984), 12. Bertram Wyatt-Brown refers to lynchings as ceremonies of "moral purification" in *Southern Honor: Ethics and Behavior in the Old South* (New York: Oxford University Press, 1982), 437.

3. Hall, *Revolt against Chivalry,* esp. 149–51. For similar interpretations, see Dennis B.

Downey and Raymond M. Hyser, *No Crooked Death: Coatesville, Pennsylvania, and the Lynching of Zachariah Walker* (Urbana: University of Illinois Press, 1991); Harris, *Exorcising Blackness*, esp. chapter 1; Joel Williamson, *The Crucible of Race: Black-White Relations in the American South since Emancipation* (New York: Oxford University Press, 1984), 183–89; and Wyatt-Brown, *Southern Honor*, esp. chapter 13. James M. Inverarity offers the most explicit functional model, derived from Durkheim, in "The Relationship of Social Solidarity to the Incidence and Form of Adjudication: A Sociological Investigation of Lynching in the American South," Ph.D. diss., Stanford University, 1976.

4. Clifford Geertz, *The Interpretations of Cultures: Selected Essays by Clifford Geertz* (New York: Basic Books, 1973), 448.

5. Two studies of mob actions that offer thoughtful approaches to the complexities of interpreting mob behavior are Suzanne Desan, "Crowds, Community, and Ritual in the Work of E. P. Thompson and Natalie Davis," in *The New Cultural History,* ed. Lynn Hunt (Berkeley: University of California Press, 1989), 47–71; and Paul A. Gilje, *The Road to Mobocracy: Popular Disorder in New York City, 1763–1834* (Chapel Hill: University of North Carolina Press, 1987).

6. See Appendix A, Table 1, "Mob Victims, 1880–1930."

7. See Madeleine M. Noble, "The White Caps of Harrison and Crawford County, Indiana: A Study in the Violent Enforcement of Morality," Ph.D. diss., University of Michigan, 1973; David Thelen, *Paths of Resistance: Tradition and Dignity in Industrializing Missouri* (New York: Oxford University Press, 1986), 86–100; George C. Wright, *Racial Violence in Kentucky, 1865–1940: Lynchings, Mob Rule, and "Legal Lynchings"* (Baton Rouge: Louisiana State University Press, 1990), 127–54; and Irvin G. Wyllie, "Race and Class Conflict on Missouri's Cotton Frontier," *Journal of Southern History* 20 (May 1954): 183–96.

8. *Augusta Chronicle,* May 22, 1907; *Swainsboro Forest-Blade,* May 30, 1907; *Bainbridge Democrat,* Sept. 13, 1883. See Appendix A, Table 3, "Lynchings of Blacks, 1880–1930."

9. *VT,* Jan. 28, 1899.

10. For an overview of the Klan's activities in Georgia, see Roger Kent Hux, "The Ku Klux Klan in Macon, 1922–1925," M.A. thesis, University of Georgia, 1972, and Clement C. Moseley, "Invisible Empire: A History of the Ku Klux Klan in Twentieth Century Georgia, 1915–1965," Ph.D. diss., University of Georgia, 1968, 1–108.

11. *RNL,* Nov. 12, 1920; *Augusta Chronicle,* Dec. 29–30, 1926, March 8, 21–22, June 14, 1927; *Atlanta Georgian,* Dec. 31, 1926; *CES,* Jan. 6, Feb. 27, 1927; *NYT,* March 14, 1927; *New York Sun,* June 13, 1927; *New York World,* July 19, 1927. For accounts of Klan violence in Virginia, see *NVP,* Sept. 2, 1926; *Norfolk Journal and Guide,* Sept. 11, 1926; and David M. Chalmers, *Hooded Americanism: The First Century of the Ku Klux Klan* (New York: Doubleday, 1965), 230–36.

12. Edward L. Ayers, *Vengeance and Justice: Crime and Punishment in the Nineteenth Century South* (New York: Oxford University Press, 1984), 255–64; William F. Holmes,

"Moonshining and Collective Violence: Georgia, 1889–1895," *Journal of American History* 67 (Dec. 1980): 589–611; William F. Holmes, "Whitecapping in Late Nineteenth-Century Georgia," in *From the Old South to the New: Essays on the Transitional South*, ed. Walter J. Fraser, Jr., and Winfred B. Moore, Jr. (Westport, Conn.: Greenwood Press, 1981), 121–32; and Wright, *Racial Violence in Kentucky*, 127–54.

13. For a detailed description of the membership and organization of the North Georgia whitecappers, see *AC*, Dec. 23, 1894. See also, Holmes, "Moonshining and Collective Violence," 596–98; and Holmes, "Whitecapping in Late Nineteenth-Century Georgia," 123–24.

14. The four lynchings are described in *AC*, Aug. 30, 1891; *VT*, Dec. 23, 1893; *SMN*, April 28, 1899; and *MT*, July 1, 1911.

15. For one example of an economically motivated whitecapping, see the lynching of Will Atwater on December 14, 1910 in Milner, Georgia, in *CES*, Dec. 15, 1910. For discussions of the motivations of whitecappers in Mississippi, see William F. Holmes, "Whitecapping: Agrarian Violence in Mississippi, 1902–1906," *Journal of Southern History* 35 (May 1969): 165–85; William F. Holmes, "Whitecapping in Mississippi: Agrarian Violence in the Populist Era," *Mid-America* 55 (April 1973): 134–48; and William F. Holmes, "Whitecapping: Anti-Semitism in the Populist Era," *American Jewish Historical Quarterly* 63 (March 1974): 244–61.

16. Thompson was listed in the 1901 tax records with one acre of land of $10 value, $50 in household furniture, $75 in horses and stock, $7 in tools, and $2 in other property, for an aggregate value of $144. Campbell County Tax Records, 1901, GDAH.

17. *Campbell News* (Fairburn), Jan. 4, 1901; *AC*, Jan. 5, 1901; *ST*, Feb. 16, 1901; *MT*, Aug. 10, 1901. The requests for pardons for several of the whites convicted of Thompson's murder provide many details lacking in the newspaper accounts. See Governor's Executive Correspondence, Pardons, Pegram Cochran File, GDAH.

18. Robert P. Ingalls has described a tradition of elite vigilantism in Birmingham, Alabama, and Tampa, Florida, directed against immigrants, blacks, radicals, and union organizers in "Antiradical Violence in Birmingham During the 1930s," *Journal of Southern History* 47 (Nov. 1981): 521–44 and *Urban Vigilantes in the New South: Tampa, 1882–1936* (Knoxville: University of Tennessee Press, 1988). While no cities in either Georgia or Virginia appear to have had equally virulent traditions of "establishment" vigilantism, urban vigilantism in Birmingham and Tampa points to the willingness of elites to participate in mob violence, including terrorist violence.

19. For examples, see accounts of the lynching of Henry Etheridge for advocating African colonization, *AC*, April 27, 1912; *MT*, April 27, 1912; *Monroe Advertiser* (Forsyth), May 3, 1912; and *ST*, May 4, 1912. An example of lynching for demanding higher wages is the murder of John Grant discussed in *Chicago Defender*, Aug. 14, 1920. For a description of the lynching of Bud Collins for enticing away farm tenants, see *AC*, Feb. 11, 1894 and Governor's Executive Minutes, reel 50–61, frame 314, GDAH. For an example of mob

violence for leaving an employer, see the lynching of John Moody, *AC*, March 1, 1901; *SMN*, March 1, 1901; and *Athens Banner*, March 2, 1901.

20. For one account of planter violence against blacks, see chapter 4 (111–13) of this volume.

21. Bryan Palmer, "Discordant Music: Charavaris and Whitecapping in Nineteenth-Century North America," *Labour/Le Travailleur* 3 (1978): 49–60.

22. *VT*, Feb. 28, 1899; *CES*, June 23, 24, 1909; *AC*, June 24, 1909; *ST*, June 26, 1909.

23. On the alleged crimes that provoked terrorist mobs, see Appendix A, Table 22, "Lynching Victims in Georgia, 1880–1930," and Table 23, "Lynching Victims in Virginia, 1880–1930."

24. *SMN*, Oct. 22, 1908. For similar sentiments, see *SMN*, March 28, 1893, April 15, 1893, Sept. 20, 1893, and Nov. 13, 1893.

25. *VT*, April 1, 1893.

26. *AC*, April 2–17, 1895; see also, Holmes, "Moonshining and Collective Violence," 605–6; and Wilbur R. Miller, *Revenuers and Moonshiners: Enforcing Federal Liquor Law in the Mountain South, 1865–1900* (Chapel Hill: University of North Carolina Press, 1990), 140–42, 167–68.

27. The restrained response of the federal government to whitecapping unrelated to moonshining was revealed in Attorney General William H. H. Miller's response to a plea from F. B. Carter, a black man in Washington County, Georgia, for protection. Miller, in a letter to the U.S. attorney in the district, explained, "I do not know that you can do anything to protect these colored men, who it seems are being threatened by white men. I wish, however, you would inquire into the matter and show that the government does not look with indifference at such proceedings." In fact, the U.S. attorney did look with indifference upon the whitecapping. Department of Justice Papers, RG60, Letters Sent to U. S. Marshals, 14701-30, National Archives.

28. *SMN*, Nov. 13, 1893.

29. Governor's Executive Minutes, reel 50–61, frame 14, GDAH; *Houston Home Journal*, Feb. 2, 1893; *SMN*, April 15, 1893.

30. *SMN*, April 16, 1893. For other examples of attempts by planters to protect their tenants from whitecappers, see *AC*, Feb. 25, 1903; *SMN*, Feb. 25, 1903; *Griffin Daily News*, Feb. 25, March 3, 1903; and *CES*, Dec. 15, 1910.

31. Unfortunately, virtually nothing of the trial record of the case of Thompson's murderers is extant, and as a result it is impossible to determine the details of the prosecution.

32. Examples of successful prosecutions of whitecappers include: *VT*, Feb. 12, 1901; *AC*, Jan. 17, 1915, Feb. 14, 15, 24, March 3, 1922; *Schley County News* (Ellaville), Feb. 17, 1922; *Americus Times-Recorder*, Feb. 17, 1922; *CES*, Feb. 18, April 15, 1922; *MT*, Feb. 23, 1922; and *Thomasville Enterprise*, April 15, 1922. For examples of attempted prosecution that was either unsuccessful or the outcome is unknown, see *AC*, March 27, 1893, June 27, 1894, Aug. 30, 1899, Aug. 13, 1902, Sept. 22, 1904, Aug. 28, 1919; *ST*,

April 8, 1893; *Eastman Times-Journal,* Aug. 21, 28, Sept. 4, Oct. 30, 1919; *Atlanta Georgian,* June 25, 1924, Dec. 31, 1926; *Griffin Daily News,* June 24–27, July 1, Aug. 7–8, 1924; and *Sylvester Local,* Dec. 9, 1926.

33. *VT,* Dec. 19, 1891, May 2, 1896, April 10, 1897, June 11, 1898, Sept. 6, 1902, Oct. 15, 1904, Jan. 3, 1899.

34. Marcel Mauss, *The Gift: Forms and Function of Exchange in Archaic Societies,* trans. I. Cunnison (New York: 1925, repr. New York: Free Press, 1954).

35. On the alleged crimes that provoked private mobs, see Appendix A, Tables 22 and 23.

36. *AC,* Nov. 19, 1890; *Thomasville Times-Enterprise,* Nov. 20, 1890; *RTD,* Oct. 14, 15, 18, 1923.

37. *Columbus Ledger,* Aug. 13, 1912; *AC,* Aug. 14, 31, 1912; *CES,* Aug. 14, 17, 1912; *MT,* Aug. 14–17, 1912; *ST,* Aug. 22, 1912; *AC,* Oct. 20, 1911; *MT,* Oct. 20, 1911; *Manchester Mercury,* Oct. 20, 1911; *Merriwether Vindicator* (Greenville), Oct. 20, 1911; *Merriwether Assault,* Oct. 20, 1911.

38. *BS,* Jan. 15, 1904; *WP,* Jan. 15, 1904; *NVP,* Jan. 15, 1904; *Eastman Times-Journal,* Nov. 19, 1897. For examples of blacks in other states participating in lynchings, see Jack S. Mullins, "Lynching in South Carolina, 1900–1914," M.A. thesis, University of South Carolina, 1961, 96–97; George B. Tindall, *South Carolina Negroes, 1877–1900* (Columbia: University of South Carolina Press, 1952), 245; and Wright, *Racial Violence in Kentucky,* 102–3.

39. *MT,* Aug. 16, 1913; *Dawson News,* Aug. 19, 1913; *Dade County Weekly Times* (Trenton), March 16, 1888; *AC,* Aug. 21–22, 1884; *Carroll Free Press,* Aug. 22, 1884.

40. *Waynesboro True Citizen,* Oct. 25, 1890; *SMN,* Oct. 25, 1890; *Augusta Chronicle,* Oct. 25, 1890; *AC,* Oct. 31, 1890. For an equally obvious instance of official complicity in Virginia, see *WP,* Aug. 6, 1904; *BS,* Aug. 6, 1904; *RTD,* Aug. 5, 1904; and *Charlottesville Daily Progress,* Aug. 6, 8, 10, 1904.

41. For examples of subterfuge in Virginia, see *NV,* Dec. 8, 1881; *BS,* Nov. 9, 1889; *Loudoun Mirror,* Nov. 14, 1889; and *Loudon Telephone,* Nov. 15, 1889. For examples in Georgia, see *AC,* June 28–30, 1905; *Athens Banner,* June 30, 1905; *Augusta Chronicle,* Aug. 26, 1908; and *MT,* Aug. 26, 1908.

42. *RD,* Feb. 6, 1884.

43. Arthur Raper, *The Tragedy of Lynching* (Chapel Hill: University of North Carolina, 1933), 247–49.

44. *WP,* Nov. 2, 1893; *RD,* Nov. 2, 1893; *NV,* Nov. 2, 1893; *RD,* Sept. 7, 1897; *BS,* July 2, 1901; *NVP,* July 2–7, 1901; *Portsmouth Star,* July 1, 1901; *RD,* July 2, 1901; *RP,* July 6, 1901; *WP,* July 2, 1901.

45. *RP,* July 8, 1899; *RD,* Aug. 10, 1902.

46. For a discussion of the first conviction of lynchers for murder in Georgia, see chapter 8 (241–42).

47. The most completely described protest meeting occurred in Talbot County, Geor-

gia, following the murder of two blacks in September 1904. See *CES*, Sept. 21–22, 1904; *MT*, Sept. 22, 1904; and *AC*, Sept. 22, 25, 1904.

48. *Atlanta Daily Worker*, July 30, 1946, Tuskegee Institute News Clipping File, reel 233, frame 336.

49. *AC*, April 16, 1899.

50. *Danville Register*, Aug. 18, 1917; *RTD*, Aug. 18, 1917.

51. Raper, *The Tragedy of Lynching*, 9–10. For another account of torture during a man-hunt, see Beulah Amidon Ratliff, "In the Delta: The True Story of a Manhunt," *Atlantic Monthly* 125 (April 1920): 456–61.

52. *AC*, June 19, 1918.

53. *AC*, May 19, 1918; *Report of the Acting Adjutant-General, State of Georgia, January 1, 1918 to February 28, 1919* (Atlanta: Byrd Printing, 1919), 9–13; Memorandum for Governor Dorsey from Walter F. White, July 10, 1918, and Memo from Walter White, Nov. 12, 1918, both in Group I, series C, box C-353, Brooks County File, NAACP Papers, LC.

54. On the alleged crimes that provoked posses, see Appendix A, Tables 22 and 23.

55. *AC*, Feb. 19, 1918; *Griffin Daily News*, Feb. 19, 1918; *NYT*, Feb. 19, 1918; *AC*, May 21, 1918.

56. Eugene Genovese, *Roll, Jordan, Roll: The World the Slaves Made* (New York: Vintage, 1976), 618–19; and Kenneth Stampp, *The Peculiar Institution: Slavery in the Antebellum South* (New York: Vintage Books, 1956), 214–15.

57. *AC*, Dec. 22–27, 1894; *MT*, Dec. 24–26, 1894; *NYT*, Dec. 24–26, 1894; *SMN*, Dec. 24–26, 1894; *VT*, Dec. 22, 29, 1894, Jan. 5, 1895; *RP*, Dec. 29, 1894. As one of Brice's neighbors explained, "[his blacks] are just as much his slaves as they were before the war. If one steals from him the old man will whip him just like he used to. He don't send them to the chain gang and the negroes are better pleased with the whipping than they would be if sent up." *AC*, Dec. 26, 1894.

58. *Albany Herald*, Jan. 3, 1921; *Bainbridge Post-Searchlight*, Jan. 6, 1921; *Cairo Messenger*, Jan. 7, 1921; *Savannah Journal*, Jan. 13, 1921; *Thomasville Times-Enterprise*, Jan. 3, 1921.

59. On the alleged crimes that provoked mass mobs, see Appendix A, Tables 22 and 23.

60. See Appendix A, Table 2, "Number of Lynching Victims, 1880–1930."

61. Pierre L. van den Berghe, *Race and Racism: A Comparative Perspective*, 2d ed. (New York: John Wiley & Sons, 1978), 90–91.

62. For descriptions of the participants in other mass mobs, see Dennis B. Downey and Raymond M. Hyser, *No Crooked Death: Coatesville, Pennsylvania, and the Lynching of Zachariah Walker* (Urbana: University of Illinois Press, 1991), esp. chapter 1; James McGovern, *Anatomy of a Lynching: The Killing of Claude Neal* (Baton Rouge: Louisiana State University Press, 1982), 76–82; Raper, *The Tragedy of Lynching*, 236; "The Burning at Dyersburg," *Crisis* 16 (Feb. 1918): 181; "The Burning of Jim McIlherron," *Crisis* 16 (May 1918): 16–17.

63. *AC*, July 27, 28, 1887; *Dekalb Chronicle* (Decatur), July 28, Aug. 4, 1887.

64. *RT*, March 28-April 5, 1900; *AC*, Aug.–Nov. 1904; *MT*, Aug.–Sept. 1922. For other lynchings during which participants in the mob were identified, see *DeKalb Chronicle*, July 28, Aug. 4, 1887; *RP*, July 23, 1893; and *WP*, July 31-Aug. 1, 1902.

65. For the details of the Alonzo Williams lynching, see *NYT*, July 30, 1908 and *AC*, July 30, 1908. On the Stephens lynching, see *AC*, June 15, 1915; *Clarkesville Advance*, June 15, 1915; and *Toccoa Record*, June 17, 1915.

66. *Lynchburg Virginian*, Feb. 13, 1892; *BS*, Feb. 13, 1892; *RT*, Feb. 10–20, 1892; *Lynchburg News*, Feb. 13, 16, 1892; *RP*, Feb. 20, 27, March 5, 1892.

67. *AC*, Aug. 23, 1904; *SMN*, Aug. 23, 1904, Aug. 1, 1906; *MT*, Aug. 1, 1906; *AC*, Aug. 1, 1906; *AN*, July 31, Aug. 1, 1906.

68. Wyatt-Brown, *Southern Honor*, 460. See also, Ayers, *Vengeance and Justice*, 247–48; and E. Merton Coulter, "Hanging as a Socio-Penal Institution in Georgia and Elsewhere," *Georgia Historical Quarterly* 57 (Spring 1973): 17–55.

69. Stanley J. Tambiah, *Culture, Thought and Social Action: An Anthropological Perspective* (Cambridge: Harvard University Press, 1985), 134.

70. Roy Rappaport, "Obvious Aspects of Rituals," *Cambridge Anthropology* 2 (Oct. 1974): 38. See also, René Girard, *Violence and the Sacred* (Baltimore: Johns Hopkins University Press, 1977), 124–25; Peter Shaw, *American Patriots and the Rituals of Revolution* (Cambridge: Harvard University Press, 1981), 227–28; and Victor Turner, "Social Dramas and Ritual Metaphors," in *Dramas, Fields, and Metaphors: Symbolic Action in Human Society*, ed. Victor Turner (Ithaca, N.Y.: Cornell University Press, 1985), 39–41.

71. *Augusta Chronicle*, May 25, 1909. For an example in Virginia, see *RTD*, Aug. 3, 4, 1921; and *NVP*, Aug. 3–6, 1921.

72. For examples, see *BS*, April 24, 1889; *RD*, April 24, 1889; *MT*, Aug. 9, 1898; *AC*, Aug. 9, 1898; *SMN*, Aug. 9, 1898; and *AC*, Aug. 18, 1923.

73. *AC*, June 4, 1888; *Augusta Chronicle*, June 4, 5, 1888; *AC*, July 28, 1913; *MT*, July 28, 1913; *RTD*, Aug. 17, 1917; *RP*, Aug. 25, 1917.

74. *AC*, Aug. 9, 10, Nov. 4, 1885; *MT*, Aug. 14, 1885; *Dawson Journal*, Aug. 13, 1885.

75. *Dade County Weekly Times* (Trenton), March 16, 1888. For another example of the ritual of confession, see *RD*, Nov. 17, 1885; *BS*, Nov. 17, 1885; *NV*, Nov. 17, 1885.

76. *Leesburg Mirror*, Feb. 5–19, 1880; *BS*, Feb. 18, 19, 1880; *Leesburg Washingtonian*, Feb. 21, 1880; *RS*, Feb. 19, 1880.

77. For one example, see *RT*, July 12, 13, 1898; *RD*, July 13, 1898; *WP*, July 12, 13, 1898; and *Cavalier Chronicle* (Charlottesville), July 12, 1898.

78. The statistics on the frequency of mutilation, of course, should be treated with caution. News accounts, however, almost certainly did not underreport occurrences of burnings or extended tortures.

79. Raper, *The Tragedy of Lynching*, 141–44.

80. *AC*, March 18, 19, 20, 1900; *MT*, March 18, 1900; *SMN*, March 19, 1900; *Marietta*

Journal, March 22, 1900; *ST,* March 24, 1900; *WP,* April 23–25, 1897; *BS,* April 23–25, 1897.

81. *NV,* March 15, 1889; *BS,* March 15, 1889; *AC,* Feb. 22, 23, 1891; *SMN,* Feb. 21, 22, 1891; *AC,* Oct. 7, 1886.

82. *AC,* June 16–20, 1921; *Moultrie Observer,* June 13–28, July 18, 1921; "A Friend to the NAACP," unsigned letter, July 14, 1921, Group I, series C, box C-353, Georgia General Lynching File 1919–22, NAACP Papers, LC.

83. *Lynchburg Virginian,* Oct. 3, 1882; *Charlottesville Chronicle,* Oct. 3, 1882; *RS,* Oct. 3, 1882; *RD,* Oct. 3, 1882.

84. For examples of macabre souvenir hunting after lynchings, see the lynching of Sam Hose, *AC,* April 24, 1899; *MT,* April 24, 1899; and the lynching of Thomas Smith, *RT,* Sept. 21, 1893; *RD,* Sept. 21, 1893.

85. *CD,* Feb. 17, 1923

86. For examples of prolonged racial violence following lynchings in Georgia, see *AC,* Dec. 22–27, 1894; *VT,* Dec. 22–29, 1894, Jan. 5, 1895; *MT,* March 16, 18, 1899; *Newman Herald and Advertiser,* March 17, 1899; *Eastman Times-Journal,* March 12–19, 1908; *MT,* Aug. 19, 20, 1911; *Montgomery Advertiser,* Aug. 27, 28, 1913; *AC,* Dec. 31, 1915, Jan. 1–3, 1916; *ST,* Jan. 1, Oct. 31, 1916.

87. *AC,* Oct. 13, 1912; *Georgia Senate Journal, 1913,* 30–31. The legacy of the campaign against the blacks provoked the racial hostilities that erupted in Forsyth County in January 1987. See *NYT,* Jan. 18, 1987; *Boston Globe,* Jan. 18, 1987; and *AC,* Jan. 18, 1987.

88. Ray Stannard Baker, *Following the Color Line* (New York: Doubleday, Page, 1908), 187.

89. For example, the testimony before the coroner's jury investigating the lynching of George Franklin on June 24, 1894 in Mitchell County, Georgia, not only makes it clear that the participants in the lynching were known to the jury but also that law officers allowed the mob to lynch the prisoner while they ate supper. See Coroner's Report on George Franklin, County Clerk's Office, Mitchell County Court House, Camilla, Georgia.

90. *Early County News* (Blakely), Aug. 7, 1884; *AC,* July 1, 1891.

91. Neither Georgia nor Virginia law required coroners' reports to be preserved at local courthouses. If a search of more than twenty counties in southern Georgia is an accurate measure, few coroners' reports of lynchings remain. However, the County Clerk's Office at the Mitchell County Court House in Camilla, Georgia, has on file the coroners' reports on several lynching victims in addition to George Franklin. See also the coroners' reports on Larkin Nix, Mark Johnson, and Collins Johnson. The County Clerk's Office in the Coffee County Court House in Douglas, Georgia, has the coroner's report on the lynching of Willie Ivory, Minnie Ivory, and Alex Byrd.

92. Jacquelyn Dowd Hall, " 'The Mind That Burns in Each Body': Women, Rape, and Racial Violence," in *Powers of Desire: The Politics of Sexuality,* ed. Ann Snitow, Christine Stansell, and Sharon Thompson (New York: Monthly Review Press, 1983), 331.

93. *WP,* Nov. 2, 1893; *RD,* Nov. 2, 1893; *NV,* Nov. 2, 1893; *RD,* March 25–27, 1900; *NVP,* March 25–27, 1900; *RP,* March 31, 1900; *Report of the Adjutant-General of the Commonwealth of Virginia for the Period Ended Oct. 20th, 1900* (Richmond, 1900), 29–33.

94. *SMN,* Aug. 30, 1904; *CES,* Dec. 15, 1910; *Montgomery Advertiser,* Aug. 27, 28, 1913; *AC,* May 19–28, 1918; Memorandum for Governor Dorsey from Walter F. White, July 10, 1918 and Memo from Walter White, Nov. 12, 1918, both in Antilynching Files, Group I, series C, box C-353, Georgia General Lynching File, May-Sept. 1918, NAACP Files, LC; Baker, *Following the Color Line,* 188–89; James R. Grossman, *Land of Hope: Chicago, Black Southerners, and the Great Migration* (Chicago: University of Chicago Press, 1989), 16–18.

95. For accounts of blacks attempting to protect themselves in the face of mob violence, see *SMN,* Dec. 26, 28, 31, 1890; *AC,* March 16–18, 1899; *Campbell News* (Fairburn), March 17, 1899; *Newman Herald and Advertiser,* March 17, 1899; *Eastman Times-Journal,* March 12, 19, 1908; *Washington Gazette-Chronicle,* May 26, 1909; *Washington Reporter,* May 27, 1909; *CES,* Dec. 15, 1910; *MT,* May 23, 1911; *ST,* Jan. 1, 1916, Oct. 31, 1916; *Bulloch Times* (Statesboro), April 17, 1919; and *Waynesboro True Citizen,* April 19, 1919. For examples in Kentucky, see Wright, *Racial Violence in Kentucky,* 162–72.

96. *WP,* April 25, 1897; *Alexandria Gazette,* April 26, 1897.

97. *Campbell News* (Fairburn), March 17, 1899; *ST,* March 18, 1899; *Newman Herald and Advertiser,* March 17, 1899; *RP,* March 25, 1899.

98. *VT,* Jan. 5, 1895. For examples of blacks lynched for protesting white violence, see *ST,* Aug. 20, 1892; Governor's Executive Minutes, reel 50–60, frame 203, GDAH; *SMN,* April 28, 1899; *MT,* June 28, 29, 1908; *AC,* June 28, 29, 1908; and *Waycross Herald,* July 4, 11, 1908.

99. *Eastman Times-Journal,* Sept. 9, 1892.

100. *AC,* Sept. 9, 1919; *NYT,* Sept. 11, 1919; *Oglethorpe Echo* (Lexington), Sept. 12, 1919; *Supreme Circle News* (Albany), Sept. 13, 1919; *Cordele Dispatch,* Sept. 24, 1919.

101. *CD,* Nov. 1, 1919.

102. *VT,* Sept. 4, 1897; *SMN,* Sept. 4, 1897.

2   "To Draw the Line"

1. *AC,* May 19, 1893.

2. On the alleged causes of lynchings, see Appendix A, Tables 22 anad 23.

3. Edward L. Ayers, *Vengeance and Justice: Crime and Punishment in the 19th-Century South* (New York: Oxford University Press, 1984), passim, esp. 9–33; Steven M. Stowe, *Intimacy and Power in the Old South: Ritual in the Lives of Planters* (Baltimore: Johns Hopkins University Press, 1987); Bertram Wyatt-Brown, *Southern Honor: Ethics and Behavior in the Old South* (New York: Oxford University Press, 1982).

4. Wyatt-Brown, *Southern Honor,* 117–25. For discussions of family honor in different historical settings, see Pierre Bourdieu, "The Sentiment of Honour in Kabyle Society," in

Honor and Shame: The Values of Mediterranean Society, ed. J. G. Peristiany (Chicago: University of Chicago Press, 1974), 201–2; and Julian Pitt-Rivers, "Honor and Social Status," in *Honor and Shame: The Values of Mediterranean Society,* ed. J. G. Peristiany (Chicago: University of Chicago Press, 1974), 35–36.

5. Pitt-Rivers, "Honor and Social Status," 55–57; Wyatt-Brown, *Southern Honor,* 362–401, 435–61.

6. Ayers, *Vengeance and Justice,* 27–33.

7. James Oakes, *Slavery and Freedom: An Interpretation of the Old South* (New York: Knopf, 1990), 14–24; Orlando Patterson, *Slavery and Social Death: A Comparative Study* (Cambridge: Harvard University Press, 1982), 77–101.

8. Ayers, *Vengeance and Justice,* 223, 250, 340; George M. Frederickson, *The Black Image in the White Mind: The Debate on the Afro-American Character and Destiny, 1817–1914* (New York: Harper & Row, 1972), 256–284; Joel Williamson, *The Crucible of Race: Black-White Relations in the American South since Emancipation* (New York: Oxford University Press, 1984), 111–23; and Monroe Work, "Negro Criminality in the South," *Annals* 41 (Sept. 1913): 75–76.

9. John Temple Graves, "The Mob Spirit in the South," *The Mob Spirit in America* (Chautauqua, N.Y.: Chautauqua Press, 1903), 12. See also, Thomas Nelson Page, "The Lynching of Negroes: Its Causes and Prevention," *North American Review* 178 (Jan. 1904): 46.

10. See Appendix A, Tables 22 and 23 and Figure 3.

11. The pardon papers of three of the white men who were charged with and convicted of the murder of Jones provide a wealth of detail. See Governor's Executive Correspondence, Pardons, Bennie DeVane et al. File, GDAH. See also, *AC,* Feb. 14, 15, 24, March 3, 1922; *Schley County News* (Ellaville), Feb. 17, 1922; *Americus Times-Recorder,* Feb. 17, 1922; *CES,* Feb. 18, April 15, 1922; *MT,* Feb. 23, 1922; *Thomasville Times-Enterprise,* April 15, 1922.

12. *SMN,* April 28, 1899; *MT,* April 28, 1899; *AC,* Oct. 4, 1919; *CD,* Oct. 11, 1919.

13. On arson as a means of black protest, Philip J. Schwarz, *Twice Condemned: Slaves and the Criminal Laws of Virginia, 1705–1865* (Baton Rouge: Louisiana State University Press, 1988), esp. 279–99; Albert C. Smith, "Southern Violence Reconsidered: Arson as Protest in Black-Belt Georgia, 1865–1910," *Journal of Southern History* 51 (Nov. 1985): 527–64.

14. *Dawson News,* May 31, June 28, Aug. 9, 1899.

15. For one example of the beating of a suspected arsonist, see *Dawson News,* Feb. 2–16, 1898.

16. *AC,* May 11, 1896; *MT,* May 11, 1896; *Dougls Breeze,* May 15, 1896.

17. *SMN,* Sept. 1, 1902; *AC,* Sept. 1, 1902; *MT,* Sept. 1, 1902; *Jasper County News* (Monticello), Sept. 4, 1902. For examples of insane or "half-wit" blacks being lynched, see *AC,* Nov. 27, 1885 and June 25, 1912; *Americus Times-Recorder,* June 25, 26, 1912; and *Milledgeville Union Recorder,* Sept. 17–Oct. 8, 1925. For examples of lynchings of

blacks for crimes committed while drunk, see *CD*, March 4, 1922; *MT*, June 22–23, 1913; and *Americus Times-Recorder*, June 22–July 8, 1913.

18. *AC*, Dec. 2, 1888; *Augusta Chronicle*, Dec. 3, 1888.

19. Thomas Nelson Page, *The Negro: The Southerner's Problem* (New York: Young People's Missionary Movement of the United States and Canada, 1904), 100.

20. Charles H. Poe, "Lynchings: A Southern View," *Atlantic Monthly* 93 (Feb. 1904): 156. See also, Edward Leigh Pell, "The Prevention of Lynch-Law Epidemics," *Review of Reviews* 17 (March 1898): 321–27.

21. Bishop Warren in *Forum* 76 (Dec. 1926): 813.

22. Ida Wells-Barnett, *On Lynchings: Southern Horrors; A Red Record; Mob Rule in New Orleans* (New York: Arno Press, 1969), 10.

23. Jane Addams, for example, sparked a protracted dispute with Wells-Barnett when she conceded that "a certain class of crimes," her polite euphemism for rape, led to lynchings. Frances Willard, president of the Women's Christian Temperance Union, also became locked in controversy with Wells-Barnett because of her statements that many lynchings were prompted by "unspeakable outrages." See Bettina Aptheker, ed., *Lynching and Rape: An Exchange of Views* (New York: American Institute for Marxist Studies, 1977); Ruth Bordin, *Frances Willard: A Biography* (Chapel Hill: University of North Carolina Press, 1986), 216–18, 221–22; and Ralph E. Luker, *The Social Gospel in Black and White: American Racial Reform 1885–1912* (Chapel Hill: University of North Carolina Press, 1991), 102–12.

24. Philip A. Bruce, *The Plantation Negro as Freeman* (New York: Putnam's, 1889), 83–85; Myrta Lockett Avary, *Dixie After the War: An Exposition of Social Conditions Existing in the South, during the Twelve Years Succeeding the Fall of Richmond* (Richmond, 1906; repr., New York: Books for Libraries Press, 1970), 381–84; Page, *The Negro*, 96; Willis B. Parks, "A Solution to the Negro Problem Psychologically Considered," *The Possibilities of the Negro in Symposium* (Atlanta: Franklin Printing and Publishing, 1900), 150–52.

25. Daniel J. Singal, *The War Within: From Victorian to Modernist Thought in the South, 1919–1945* (Chapel Hill: University of North Carolina Press, 1982), 8; see also, Jacquelyn Dowd Hall, *Revolt against Chivalry: Jesse Daniel Ames and the Women's Campaign against Lynching* (New York: Columbia University Press, 1979), 147–48; and Williamson, *Crucible of Race*, 115–17.

26. Bruce, *The Plantation Negro as a Freeman*, 83–84.

27. Valuable discussions of the interrelationship between racism, sex, and rape include Oliver C. Cox, *Caste, Class, and Race: A Study in Social Dynamics* (New York: Doubleday, 1948), 386–90; Allison Davis, Burleigh B. Gardner, and Mary R. Gardner, *Deep South: A Social Anthropological Study of Caste and Class* (Chicago: University of Chicago Press, 1965), 25–27; Jacquelyn Dowd Hall, " 'The Mind That Burns in Each Body': Women, Rape, and Racial Violence," in *Powers of Desire: The Politics of Sexuality*, ed. Anne Snitow, Christine Stansell, and Sharon Thompson (New York: Monthly Review Press, 1983).

28. Bruce, *The Plantation Negro as a Freeman*, 84.

29. Hall, *Revolt against Chivalry*, 150.

30. *RD*, July 12, 1888; *Wytheville Dispatch*, July 13, 1888; *AC*, July 12–18, 1884; *MT*, July 18, 1884; *Merriwether Vindicator* (Greenville), July 18, 1884.

31. *WP*, April 23, 24, 1897; *BS*, April 23, 24, 1897; *MT*, June 28, 29, 1908; *AC*, June 28, 29, 1908; *WH*, July 4–11, 1908. For a similar case, see the lynching of Peter Shaw, *AC*, May 29, 1897.

32. J. C. Reynolds, "If a Lady Was a Lady—Well, What?," *AN*, Aug. 14, 1903. For similar prescriptions, see Parks, "A Solution to the Negro Problem Psychologically Considered," 160–61; and Winfield P. Woolf, "What Shall We Do to Stop Lynchings," *AN*, Aug. 14, 1903.

33. In a letter prompted by news of the legal execution of a black for rape in 1884, Amelia A. Lines, a teacher in Macon, Georgia, spelled out to her daughter, a teacher in rural Irwin County, precautions that almost certainly were parroted by generations of white women: "my precious one let me caution you *never* take walks *alone, never,* even to & from your school-room. Never stay in the house or school house alone—no matter how much you may want to be alone." Amelia Akehurst Lines, *To Raise Myself a Little*, ed. Thomas Dyer (Athens: University of Georgia Press, 1982), 268.

34. "How Shall the Women and the Girls in the Country Districts Be Protected?" *AC*, April 23, 1899; and Ray Stannard Baker, *Following the Color Line* (New York: Doubleday and Page, 1908), 179–80.

35. *Oglethorpe Echo* (Lexington), July 9, 1887.

36. For other examples of blacks charged with crimes against their employers' wives or daughters, see *RD*, July 28, 1888; *BS*, July 28, 29, 1888, July 2, 1901; *Portsmouth Star*, July 1, 1901; *NVP*, July 2–7, 1901; and *RP*, July 6, 1901.

37. On the Loudoun lynching, see *Loudoun Telephone*, Nov. 1, 15, 1889; *WP*, Nov. 9, 1889; *RD*, Nov. 9, 1889; *BS*, Nov. 9, 1889; and *Loudoun Mirror* (Leesburg), Nov. 14, 1889; on the Swainsboro lynching, see *Swainsboro Forest Blade*, July 12, 1906; *SMN*, July 12, 1906; *MT*, July 12, 1906; and *AC*, July 12, 1906; and on the Thomas County lynching, see *AC*, March 3, 1917.

38. *RS*, Jan. 20, 1880; *BS*, Jan. 21, 22, 1880.

39. *AC*, July 25–29, 1885. In one instance in Virginia, a white woman publicly admitted during the trial of her black lover that she had initiated the romance. See *RP*, Jan. 16, 23, July 24, Oct. 30, Nov. 13, 1897.

40. *Turner County Banner* (Ashburn), April 15, 22, 1910; *MT*, April 16, 1910; *AC*, April 16, 1910; *Eastman Times-Journal*, April 21, 1910. For another example, see *AC*, Sept. 14, 1897 and *Griffin Morning Call*, Sept. 15, 1897.

41. *AC*, June 4, 7, 10, 1899.

42. On the attempted lynching of Drisdom, see *New York Globe*, March 18, 1922; *NYT*, March 19, 1922; *AC*, March 18, 1922; W. F. White to Monroe N. Work, April 14, 1922 and Monroe E. Work to W. F. White, April 17, 1922, both in Group I, series C, box C-338, NAACP Papers, LC. For one instance of a white planter defending his employees, see *AC*,

June 10–13, 1890; *MT*, June 10, 1890; and *Lawrenceville Herald*, June 10, 17, 1890. For an example of concerted efforts by relatives of the victim to prevent the lynching of alleged rapists, see *AC*, July 24, 1897, Nov. 10, 1905. The exemplary behavior of one planter in Georgia, who ensured that a mob did not lynch his daughter's alleged assailant, received editorial praise in the *NYT*, Aug. 20, 1897. For an account of a black man accused of rape who was protected against mob violence and then convicted of burglary, see Mary Louise Ellis, "A Lynching Arrested: The Ordeal of John Miller," *Georgia Historical Quarterly* 70 (Summer 1986): 306–16.

43. *AC*, Nov. 3, 4, 1919; *MT*, Nov. 3, 4, 1919; *CD*, Nov. 8, 1919.

44. Page, "The Lynching of Negroes," 39.

45. William Faulkner, *Light in August* (New York, 1932, repr. New York: Modern Library, 1959); James Baldwin, *Going to Meet the Man* (New York: Dell Publishing, 1965).

46. Lillian Smith, *Killers of the Dream* (New York: Norton, 1978), 162–63.

47. *RP*, Jan. 16, April 9, 1892.

48. For examples of lynchings of blacks by private mobs at a distance from the neighborhood of the crime, see *VT*, Nov. 9, 11, 1895; *MT*, Oct. 6, 1912; *AC*, Aug. 13, 1918; *MT*, Sept. 5, 1918; and *Atlanta Georgian*, Sept. 29, 1922.

49. Orville Vernon Burton, *In My Father's House Are Many Mansions: Family and Community in Edgefield, South Carolina* (Chapel Hill: University of North Carolina Press, 1985), 255–258, 284, 287.

50. For one example of an attempted lynching by a large mob of blacks and of the response of white officials, see the case of Will Harris, *AC*, Dec. 30, 1900 and *Athens Banner Herald*, Dec. 30, 1900.

51. *AC*, July 19, 1884; *Merriwether Vindicator* (Greenville), July 25, 1884.

52. See Appendix A, Table 3, "Lynchings of Blacks, 1880–1930" and Figure 2.

53. Hooper Alexander, "Race Riots and Lynch Law: A Southern Lawyer's View," *Outlook*, Feb. 2, 1907, 261.

54. On the ascendant values of the New South, see Don H. Doyle, *New Men, New Cities, New South: Atlanta, Nashville, Charleston, Mobile, 1860–1910* (Chapel Hill: University of North Carolina Press, 1990), passim, esp. 313–18; and Paul M. Gaston, *The New South Creed: A Study in Southern Mythmaking* (New York: Alfred A. Knopf, 1970).

55. Elizabeth Fox-Genovese, *Within the Plantation Household: Black and White Women of the Old South* (Chapel Hill: University of North Carolina Press, 1988), 38.

56. Jacquelyn Dowd Hall et al., *Like a Family: The Making of a Southern Cotton Mill World* (Chapel Hill: University of North Carolina Press, 1987), esp. 114–80; Steven Hahn, *The Roots of Southern Populism: Yeoman Farmers and the Transformation of the Georgia Upcountry, 1850–1890* (New York: Oxford University Press, 1983), 180–81, 201–2; Nancy MacLean, "The Leo Frank Case Reconsidered: Gender and Sexual Politics in the Making of Reactionary Populism," *Journal of American History* 78 (Dec. 1991), 917–48. Contrast with I. A. Newby, *Plain Folk in the New South: Social Change and Cultural Persistence, 1880–1915* (Baton Rouge: Louisiana State University Press, 1989), 258–86,

which unconvincingly portrays family life and gender roles in southern mill communities as perpetuations of rural patterns and values.

57. Dewey W. Grantham, *Southern Progressivism: The Reconciliation of Progress and Tradition* (Knoxville: University of Tennessee Press, 1983), 200–217; Hall, *Revolt against Chivalry,* 35–128; John P. McDowell, *The Social Gospel in the South: The Woman's Home Mission Movement of the Methodist Episcopal Church, South, 1886–1939* (Baton Rouge: Louisiana State University Press, 1982); Anne Firor Scott, "The 'New Women' in the New South," in *Making the Invisible Woman Visible* (Urbana: University of Illinois Press, 1984), 212–20.

58. Margaret Jarman Hagood, *Mothers of the South: Portraiture of the White Tenant Farm Woman* (Chapel Hill: University of North Carolina Press, 1939), 178. See also, Madelin J. Olds, "The Rape Complex in the Postbellum South," Ph.D. diss., Carnegie-Mellon University, 1989, 215–16; and Williamson, *Crucible of Race,* 457–63.

59. See Appendix A, Table 3 and Figure 2.

60. In the absence of any study of interracial homicide before the 1930s, general studies of southern violence must fill the void. On southern violence, see Raymond D. Gastil, "Homicide and a Regional Culture of Violence," *American Sociological Review* 36 (June 1971): 412–27; Sheldon Hackney, "Southern Violence," in *Violence in America: Historical and Comparative Perspectives,* ed. Hugh Davis Graham and Ted Robert Gurr (Beverly Hills: Sage Publications, 1979), 405–6; H. V. Redfield, *Homicide, North and South* (Philadelphia: J. B. Lippincot, 1880); and John Shelton Reed, "Below the Smith and Wesson Line," in *One South: An Ethnic Approach to Regional Culture* (Baton Rouge: Louisiana State University Press, 1982), 139–53.

61. Davis, Gardner, and Gardner, *Deep South,* 225. On Bennett's alleged crime and subsequent lynching, see *AC,* Oct. 23, 1893; on Earle's crime, see *AC,* July 26, 1901, *MT,* July 26, 1901, and *SMN,* July 26, 1901; and on Ware's crime, see *AC,* Sept. 19, 1904.

62. *NV,* Dec. 8, 1881; *RD,* April 8, 1902; *Lynchburg News,* April 8, 9, 1902; *NVP,* April 8, 1902; *Lexington Gazette,* April 11, 1902.

63. *AC,* June 9, 1903; *NYT,* June 9, 1903; *SMN,* June 9, 1903; *MT,* June 9, 1903; *NYT,* June 27, 1903; *SMN,* June 27, 1903; *Bainbridge Searchlight,* July 3, 1903.

64. *VDT,* Feb. 26, 1908; *MT,* Feb. 26, 1908; *AC,* Feb. 26, 1908.

65. For one example of an argument between planter and tenant that led to a lynching, see *AC,* Aug. 1, 1885. An account of a gambling dispute that concluded with mob violence is described in *RP,* Oct. 22, 1892; and for coverage of the lynching that resulted from a hunting controversy, see *Americus Times-Recorder,* Dec. 21, 22, 1919; *AC,* Dec. 22, 1919; and *NYT,* Dec. 22, 1919.

66. John Dittmer, *Black Georgia in the Progressive Era, 1900–1920* (Urbana: University of Illinois Press, 1977), 139. Although the role of law officers in the rural South has attracted little scholarly attention, valuable discussions of urban law enforcement include Howard N. Rabinowitz, "The Conflict Between Blacks and the Police in the Urban South, 1865–1900," *Historian* 39 (Nov. 1976): 62–76; Davis, Gardner, and Gardner, *Deep South,*

298–301; Gunnar Myrdal, *An American Dilemma: The Negro Problem and Modern Democracy* (New York: Pantheon Books, 1972), 2:535–46; and George C. Wright, *Life Behind the Veil: Blacks in Louisville, Kentucky, 1865–1930* (Baton Rouge: Louisiana State University Press, 1985), 71–76, 254–57.

67. *AC,* April 14, 1919; *Bulloch Times* (Statesboro), April 17, 1919; *Waynesboro True Citizen,* April 19, 1919; Harry H. Pace to Walter F. White, April 19, 1919 and Walter F. White to J. R. Shilladay, April 15, 1919, both in Group I, series C, box C-354, Millen File, NAACP Papers, LC. Ned Cobb, with characteristic eloquence, describes a confrontation with law officers that ended with bloodshed in Theodore Rosengarten, *All God's Dangers: The Life of Nate Shaw* (New York: Knopf, 1974), 323–28.

68. *AC,* Oct. 29, 1905; *MT,* Oct. 29, 1905.

69. Faulkner, *Light in August,* 322.

70. *SMN,* Feb. 28, 1890; *MT,* Feb. 28, 1890; *AC,* Feb. 28, 1890, March 1, 1890.

71. For sensational accounts of alleged murder plots by black criminals, see *AC,* Dec. 22–25, 1894; *MT,* Dec. 24, 25, 1894; *SMN,* Dec. 24–25, 1894; *VT,* Dec. 22, 29, 1894; *AC,* July 24, 26, 1899; *Augusta Chronicle,* July 24, 25, 1899; *MT,* July 24, 1899; *AC,* Aug. 17–20, 1904; and *SMN,* Aug. 15–20, 1904.

72. For a detailed description of a lynching in which the victim was dragged behind a car, see *AC,* May 2, 3, 1919; *Augusta Chronicle,* May 2, 3, 1919; and *CD,* May 10, 1919. For an example of a victim riddled beyond recognition with gunshot, see *Americus Times-Recorder,* June 22, 23, 1913; *MT,* June 22, 23, 1913; and *NYT,* June 22, 1913. For an example of decapitation, see *SMN,* Feb. 5, 12, 1903; and *Sandersville Progress,* Feb. 10, 1903. For examples of mobs burning victims alive, see *SMN,* April 15, 1893; *AC,* Aug. 17, 1904; *NYT,* Aug. 17, 1904; *AC,* Dec. 2, 1909; *MT,* Dec. 2, 1909; and *NYT,* Dec. 2 1909.

73. John Dollard, *Caste and Class in a Southern Town* (New Haven: Yale University Press, 1937), 292. Ned Cobb describes a violent argument he had with a white bully in which he astutely judged the degree of defiance that he could get away with. See Rosengarten, *All God's Dangers,* 170–79.

74. George Bernard Shaw, *Man and Superman: A Comedy and a Philosophy* (New York: Viking Penguin, 1987), 214. Frederick Douglass made much the same point. See Philip S. Foner, ed., *The Life and Writings of Frederick Douglass* (New York: International Publishers, 1955), 4:493.

75. Mobs in other states do not appear to have been any more likely to murder women. In North Carolina, no women appear to have been lynched, and in South Carolina mobs claimed only four female victims. See Walter S. Lockhardt III, "Lynching in North Carolina, 1888–1906," M.A. thesis, University of North Carolina, 1972, 18; Jack S. Mullins, "Lynching in South Carolina, 1900–1914," M.A. thesis, University of South Carolina, 1961, 129–31; and Susan P. Garris, "The Decline of Lynching in South Carolina, 1915–1947," M.A. thesis, University of South Carolina, 1973, 130–33.

76. See Appendix A, Table 4, "Lynchings of Black Women in Georgia, 1880–1930."

77. John Dollard provides an interesting discussion of the greater leeway given black

women in *Caste and Class in a Southern Town,* 289–90. For one instance when black women were particularly outspoken about threatened mob violence, see W. Fitzhugh Brundage, "The Darien 'Insurrection' of 1899: Black Protest during the Nadir of Race Relations, *Georgia Historical Quarterly* 74 (Summer 1990): 234–53.

78. *AC,* Aug. 14, 31, 1912; *CES,* Aug. 14, 17, 1912; *MT,* Aug. 14–17, 1912; "Sandy Ray, 17 Years of Age, Short-trousered, Lynched in Georgia," undated memo, Group I, series C, box C-355, Waycross File, NAACP Papers, LC; *AC,* Sept. 25, 1918; *MT,* Sept. 25, 1918. For other examples, see the lynching of fourteen-year-old Andrew Dudley: *RTD,* Aug. 5, 1904; *NVP,* Aug. 5, 1904; *WP,* Aug. 6, 1904; *BS,* Aug. 6, 1904; and *Charlottesville Daily Progress,* Aug. 6–10, 1904. For discussions of attitudes of black youths toward whites, see Charles S. Johnson, *Growing up in the Black Belt: Negro Youth in the Rural South* (Washington, D.C.: American Council on Education, 1941), 274–327; and I. A. Newby, *Jim Crow's Defense: Anti-Negro Thought in America, 1900–1930* (Baton Rouge: Louisiana State University Press, 1973), 39–40.

79. In many instances, newspapers describe a mob victim as a "floater" while offering evidence to the contrary. Therefore, only crude estimates can be made. For a few examples in which great emphasis is placed on the vagrant status of the mob victim, see the lynching of Warren Powers: *MT,* Sept. 5, 1889; *AC,* Sept. 5–6, 1889; and *ST,* Sept. 14, 1889; and the lynching of Henry White: *AC,* Sept. 21, 1916; and *Chicago Defender,* Sept. 30, 1916.

80. Ayers, *Vengeance and Justice,* 236. For contemporary attitudes toward vagrant blacks, see Baker, *Following the Color Line,* 56–57, 60–61, 178–79, and Steven W. Wrigley, "The Triumph of Provincialism: Public Life in Georgia, 1898–1917," Ph.D. diss., Northwestern University, 1986, 90–93.

81. *SMN,* June 13, 1893. Earlier in the year, the newspapers had described floaters as "the enemies of society and there ought to be no hesitation in making war upon them." *SMN,* Feb. 2, 1893. For similar attitudes, see *VT,* Aug. 1, 1899, and Aug. 18, 1903.

82. *AC,* July 27, 28, 1887; *DeKalb Chronicle* (Decatur), July 28, Aug. 4, 1887.

83. The term *social conterfeit* is borrowed from John F. Kasson, *Rudeness and Civility: Manners in Nineteenth-Century Urban America* (New York: Hill and Wang, 1990), 100–111. Although Kasson's concern is to describe the complex system of public and private etiquette of middle-class urban dwellers, many of his conclusions offer suggestive approaches to the equally complex codes of racial etiquette in the South.

84. A group of black antilynching activists in Chicago, led by the Reverend Reverdy C. Ranson, hired a private detective to investigate the circumstances surrounding Hose's alleged crimes. The detective's report was widely published in white newspapers in the North and black newspapers in the South. For two accounts of the detective's report, see *New York Age,* June 22, 1899, and the *RP,* Oct. 14, 1899. The campaign to challenge white accounts of Hose's crimes is discussed in Mary Church Terrell, "Lynching from a Negro's Point of View," *North American Review* 178 (June 1904): 859–60. For other examples of acts of self-defense being punished by lynching and similar distortions of the lynching victims' reputations, see the lynching of Mary Conley in *Southwest Georgian* (Fort Gaines),

Oct. 4, 1916; *Early County News* (Blakely), Oct. 5, 1916; and *Dawson News*, Oct. 11, 1916. The lynching of Banjo Peavy appears in *SMN*, June 9, 1903; and *MT*, June 9, 1903.

85. *AC*, April 13–16, 1899; *AJ*, April 13–25, 1899; *MT*, April 13–26, 1899; Wells B. Whitmore to Rebecca Lattimer Felton, April 25, 1900, Rebecca Lattimer Felton Papers, Special Collections, University of Georgia Library. Italics in original.

86. Cox, *Caste, Class and Race*, 564.

87. Jesse Daniel Ames, *The Changing Character of Lynching* (Atlanta: Commission on Interracial Cooperation, 1942), 54.

3   "When White Men Merit Lynching"

1. *Augusta News*, quoted in *AC*, July 22, 1897.

2. See Appendix A, Table 5, "Lynchings of Whites by Region, 1800–1930." See chapters 4 and 5 for a detailed discussion of the regions in Virginia and Georgia.

3. See Appendix A, Table 6, "Alleged Crimes of White Mob Victims, 1880–1930."

4. Horace V. Redfield, *Homicide: North and South* (Philadelphia: J. B. Lippincott, 1880), 189. This attitude persists in some areas of the South; see William Lynwood Montell, *Killings: Folk Justice in the Upper South* (Lexington: University Press of Kentucky, 1986), esp. 134–43.

5. Dickson D. Bruce, Jr., *Violence and Culture in the Antebellum South* (Austin: University of Texas Press, 1979), 7.

6. *The Nation*, Oct. 26, 1882, 349–59.

7. *AC*, Dec. 17–22, 1886; *Charlottesville Chronicle*, Sept. 29, Oct. 3, 6, 13, 20, Nov. 5, 1882; *Lynchburg Virginian*, Oct. 3, 1882; *NYT*, Oct. 3, 1882; *RS*, Oct. 3, 1882; *RD*, Oct. 3, 1882.

8. For one example of flogging, see *AC*, Aug. 10, 1897.

9. For two perceptive discussions of mob violence and moral crimes, see Bertram Wyatt-Brown, *Southern Honor: Ethics and Behavior in the Old South* (New York: Oxford University Press, 1982), esp. 435–93; and Charles L. Flynn, *White Land, Black Labor: Caste and Class in Late Nineteenth-Century Georgia* (Baton Rouge: Louisiana State University Press, 1983), 40–54.

10. *AC*, July 30, 1885; *Bainbridge Democrat*, July 30, 1885; *NYT*, July 30, 1885; *MT*, July 31, 1885.

11. *Bainbridge Democrat*, July 30, Aug. 6, 1885; *AC*, July 30, 1885.

12. *AC*, July 2, 1907; *MT*, July 2, 1907; *SMN*, July 2, 1907; *Dalton Citizen*, July 4, 1907; *ST*, July 5, 1907.

13. *Dalton Citizen*, July 4, 1907.

14. Quoted in the *Dalton Citizen*, July 4, 1907.

15. *SMN*, July 2, 1907. Lee Chitwood, a white farmer in southern Georgia, was lynched for the same alleged crime as Posey. Chitwood, a newcomer to the region, allegedly raped his fifteen-year-old stepdaughter. Seven men who claimed to be guarding him until officials

could arrive shot him to death. *AC,* April 18, 1912; *SMN,* April 18, 1912; *Vienna News,* April 19, 1912.

16. Edward L. Ayers, *Vengeance and Justice: Crime and Punishment in the Nineteenth Century South* (New York: Oxford University Press, 1984), 256.

17. On Rhodes, see *Charlottesville Chronicle,* Sept. 29, Oct. 3, 6, 13, 20, Nov. 5, 1882; *RS,* Oct. 3, 1882; *RD,* Oct. 3, 1882; and *Lynchburg Virginian,* Oct. 3, 1882; on Redmond, see *WP,* Nov. 2, 1893; *RD,* Nov. 2, 1893; and *NV,* Nov. 2, 1893; on Watts, see *RD,* Jan. 5, 6, 1900; *BS,* Jan. 6, 8, 1900; *NVP,* Jan. 6, 1900; and *RT,* Jan. 6, 1900.

18. Dock Posey and Thomas Brantly were both recent arrivals in the counties where they were lynched. Other examples in Georgia include Lee Chitwood (described as "a foreigner" and as having no relatives in the area where he was lynched), and Frank Sanders (an itinerant farmhand). Examples in Virginia include William W. Watts (described as a "travelling gambler") and Brandt O'Grady ("a tramp"). Newspaper accounts of the lynchings of whites refer to eight of the victims in Georgia and seven of the victims in Virginia as outsiders.

19. *AC,* Dec. 17–21, 1886.

20. Pete Daniel, *Standing at the Crossroads: Southern Life in the Twentieth Century* (New York: Hill and Wang, 1986), 66–68; Flynn, *White Land, Black Labor,* 48–50.

21. For just a sampling of such incidents, see Bess Beatty, "The Loo Chang Case in Waynesboro: A Case Study of Sinophobia in Georgia," *Georgia Historical Quarterly* 67 (Spring 1983): 35–48; Ken Driggs, " 'There Is No Law in Georgia for Mormons': The Joseph Standing Murder Case of 1879," *Georgia Historical Quarterly* 73 (Winter 1989): 745–72; Richard Gambino, *Vendetta* (Garden City, N.Y.: Doubleday, 1977); William F. Holmes, "Whitecapping: Anti-Semitism in the Populist Era" *American Jewish Historical Quarterly* 63 (March 1974): 244–61; William W. Hatch, *There Is No Law: A History of Mormon Civil Relations in the Southern States, 1865–1905* (New York: Vantage Press, 1969), 61–68; Robert P. Ingalls, *Urban Vigilantes in the New South: Tampa, 1882–1936* (Knoxville: University of Tennessee Press, 1988); John R. Ross, "At the Bar of Judge Lynch: Lynching and Lynch Mobs in America," Ph.D. diss., Texas Tech University, 1983, 134, 214–18; and Gene A. Sessions, "Myth, Mormonism, and Murder in the South," *South Atlantic Quarterly* 75 (Spring 1976): 212–25.

22. For a brief account of one lynching of a white man in which blacks participated, see chapter 6 (178–79).

23. See Appendix A, Table 7, "Lynchings of Whites, 1880–1930." The only cases in either state in which the mobs that killed whites exceeded a hundred members were the lynching of James Moore at Macon, Georgia, on August 13, 1886 and the lynching of Brandt O'Grady at Emporia, Virginia, on March 24, 1900.

24. *AC,* Aug. 15, 1886; *MT,* Aug. 15, 1886. For two excellent accounts of well-organized and small mobs that lynched white men, see Ross, "At the Bar of Judge Lynch," 204–5, 211–12.

25. The reputations of women victims of rape remains intricately involved in present-

day attitudes toward rape and rapists; see Susan Brownmiller *Against Our Will: Men, Women, and Rape* (New York: Bantam Books, 1981), esp. 410–20; and Susan Estrich, *Real Rape* (Cambridge: Harvard University Press, 1987), esp. chapters 3–4.

26. *RD*, Jan. 5, 6, 1900; *BS*, Jan. 6, 8, 1900; *NVP*, Jan. 6, 1900; *RT*, Jan. 5, 6, 13, 1900; *RP*, Jan. 13, 1900.

27. *RT*, Jan. 13, 1900. The *AC* had reached a similar conclusion five years earlier on Dec. 7, 1895. After detailing a case in New York of a white woman falsely charging a white man with rape, the newspaper concluded, "it must be apparent to any fair-minded man that the hasty and impromptu lynching of a person charged with assault is not always nor at any time the surest road to justice."

28. The many intricacies of the lynching of Moore and its aftermath may be traced in *AC*, Aug. 10–30, 1886; *MT*, Aug. 10–27, 1899; and *SMN*, Aug. 10–Aug. 24, 1899.

29. *RD*, July 2, 1899, Aug. 10, 1902; *RP*, July 8, 1899; *WP*, June 30, July 2, 1899; *Charlotte Daily Observer*, July 2, 1899; *BS*, July 3, 1899.

30. The first successful prosecution in North Carolina followed the lynching of a white man in 1906. See Walter S. Lockhardt, III, "Lynching in North Carolina, 1888–1906," M.A. thesis, University of North Carolina, 1972, 70–94.

31. *SMN*, Dec. 2, 1926; *Coffee County Progress* (Douglas), Aug. 26–Dec. 2, 1926; *Douglas Enterprise*, Aug. 27–Dec. 3, 1926; "Georgia's Body Blow to Mob Murder," *Literary Digest*, Dec. 4, 1926, 10.

32. *AC*, Nov. 24, 25, Dec. 3, 1895; *SMN*, Nov. 24, 1895; *MT*, Nov. 25, 1895; *NYT*, Nov. 25, 1895.

33. Thirty-five percent of all murders in one study of homicide in the South were ambushes. See Montell, *Killings*, 146–47.

34. *AC*, Sept. 27, 1897; Robert H. Jordan, *There Was a Land: A Story of Talbot County, Georgia and Its People* (Talbotton, Ga.: Published privately, 1971), 168–69.

35. *AC*, April 12, 1896.

36. *AC*, May 26, 27, 1896.

37. *AC*, Sept. 14–18, 26, 27, Oct. 10, Nov. 2, 3, 7, 1896.

38. *AC*, July 20, 1897; Jordan, *There Was a Land*, 176.

39. *AC*, July 21, 1897.

40. *AC*, July 23, 1897.

41. Quoted in *AC*, Aug. 3, 1897.

42. *AC*, Aug. 3, 1897. For a later editorial attack on the insanity plea, see the *Waynesboro True Citizen*, April 15, 1899. During the Ryder trial, the *AC* reported on several other trials of white men charged with murder and who plead insanity. In each case, the men had been threatened with lynchings. More important, the accounts led readers to believe that virtually every murderer would plead insanity in order to escape the death sentence. See *AC*, April 24, 1896, Sept. 18, 1896, Oct. 10, 1896, and March 12, 1897. The best discussion of late nineteenth century attitudes toward law and criminal responsibility is Charles E. Rosenberg, *The Trial of Assassin Guiteau: Psychiatry and Law in the Gilded Age* (Chicago: University of Chicago Press, 1968).

43. *AC*, Aug. 1, 2, 4, 1897.

44. Two studies that draw connections between legal attitudes and the threats to the established order during the late nineteenth century are Morton Keller, *Affairs of State: Public Life in Late Nineteenth Century America* (Cambridge: Harvard University Press, 1977), 343–70; and Arnold M. Paul, *Conservative Crisis and the Rule of Law: Attitudes of Bar and Bench, 1887–1895* (Ithaca: Cornell University Press, 1960). On the difficult process of raising professional standards of lawyers, see Samuel Haber, *The Quest for Authority and Honor in the American Professions, 1750–1900* (Chicago: University of Chicago Press, 1991); and Joseph Gordon Hylton, Jr., "The Virginia Lawyer from Reconstruction to the Great Depression," Ph.D. diss., Harvard University, 1986. The term *pre-professional* is borrowed from Lawrence M. Friedman, "The Law Between the States: Some Thoughts on Southern Legal History," in *Ambivalent Legacy: A Legal History of the South* (Jackson: University Press of Mississippi, 1984), 37.

45. In 1887, one editor complained that the Texas Court of Appeals "seems to have been organized to overrule and reverse. At least, since its organization that has been its chief employment." "Overruled Their Judicial Superiors," *American Law Review* 21 (1887): 610. For other complaints about legal procedure, see Seymour D. Thompson, "More Justice and Less Technicality," *Report of the Fifth Annual Meeting of the Georgia Bar Association* 5 (1888): 107–43; John J. Strickland, "Are the Courts Responsible for Lynchings, and if so, Why?" and J. F. DeLacy, "The Necessity of Reforms in the Criminal Law," both in *Report of the Sixteenth Annual Session of the Georgia Bar Association* 16 (1899): 184–90, 191–98; and Reuben R. Arnold, "Delays and Technicalities in the Administration of Justice," *Report of the Eighteenth Annual Session of the Georgia Bar Association* 18 (1901): 114–27.

46. For examples of the calls for reforms in the jury selection process, often marked by outspoken hostility to the "present class of jurors," see Thompson, "More Justice and Less Technicality," 114–16, 142–43; James H. Malone, "Judge Lynch and the Jury Laws," *The American Lawyer* 3 (Feb. 1895): 57–58; and "Lynch Law," *The American Lawyer* 6 (July 1896): 293. See also, Richard M. Brown, "Lawless Lawfulness: Legal and Behavioral Perspectives on American Vigilantism," in *Strain of Violence: Historical Studies of American Violence and Vigilantism,* ed. Richard M. Brown (New York: Oxford University Press, 1977); and Samuel Walker, *Popular Justice: A History of American Criminal Justice* (New York: Oxford University Press, 1980), 111–12.

47. For a sampling of contemporary newspaper commentary on pardoning, see *AC,* July 13, 1887, Oct. 4, 1897; and *SMN,* June 16, 1897, Oct. 23, 1897, and Jan. 15, 1903.

48. *WP,* March 18, 1892; *RD,* March 19, 1892; *BS,* March 19, 1892; *Fredericksburg Lance,* March 22, 1892. Resentment of Georgia's Governor Gordon's reprieve of Henry Pope in 1888 stirred a mob in Summerville to seize and lynch the alleged rapist. During the previous year, a mob burned the governor in effigy after he commuted another prisoner's sentence; *AC,* July 13, 1887, May 2, 4, 1888.

49. The Leo Frank case has received extensive treatment. Among the many works on the topic, see Leonard Dinnerstein, *The Leo Frank Case* (New York: Columbia University Press, 1967); and Harry Golden, *A Little Girl Is Dead* (New York: Avon, 1965). A valuable

corrective of many of the errors in earlier works is Clark J. Freshman, "Beyond Pontius Pilate and Judge Lynch: The Pardoning Power in Theory and Practice as Illustrated in the Leo Frank Case," honors' thesis, Harvard College, 1986.

50. *AC*, Aug. 7, 1897.

51. John L. Hopkins to *AC*, July 27, 1897.

52. For examples of contempt for any justifications of lynchings, see Judge John L. Hopkins to *AC*, July 21, 27, 1897; Colonel J. H. Worrill to *AC*, July 21, 1897; Hon. N. J. Hammond to *AC*, July 21, 1897; and Clyde Shropshire to *AC*, Aug. 7, 1897.

53. *MT*, July 21, 1897.

54. Richard E. Stevenson to Will Alexander, undated [1930]; Mrs. E. S. Cook to Frederick Sullens, May 25, 1937, reel 3, ASWPL Papers, AUL.

4   The Geography of Lynching in Georgia

1. Arthur Raper, *The Tragedy of Lynching* (Chapel Hill: University of North Carolina Press, 1933), 27.

2. Hubert Blalock, *Toward a Theory of Minority-Group Relations* (New York: Wiley, 1967), 157–159; Jay Corzine et al., "Black Concentration and Lynchings in the South: Testing Blalock's Power-Threat Hypothesis," *Social Forces* 61 (March 1983): 774–96; John Shelton Reed, "Percent Black and Lynching: A Test of Blalock's Theory," *Social Forces* 50 (March 1972): 356–60.

3. Richard M. Brown, "Vigilantism in America," in *Vigilante Politics,* ed. H. Jon Rosenbaum and Peter C. Sederberg (Philadelphia: University of Pennsylvania Press, 1976), 80–109; James R. McGovern, *Anatomy of a Lynching: The Killing of Claude Neal* (Baton Rouge: Louisiana State University Press, 1982), 3–4.

4. Raper, *The Tragedy of Lynching,* 5–6, 21–22, 40–51.

5. Earle F. Young, "The Relation of Lynching to the Size of Population Areas," *Sociology and Social Research* 12 (March-April 1928): 348–53; W. E. Wimpy, "Lynching: An Evil of County Government," *Manufacturers' Record,* Aug. 24, 1916, 49–50.

6. Reed, "Percent Black and Lynching": 356–57.

7. Some of the causes of urban lynching are discussed in Robert P. Ingalls, "Lynching and Establishment Violence in Tampa, 1858–1935," *Journal of Southern History* 53 (Nov. 1987): 613–44; Howard N. Rabinowitz, *Race Relations in the Urban South, 1865–1890* (New York: Oxford University Press, 1978), 52–54; and Jon L. Wilson, "Days of Fear: A Lynching in St. Petersburg," *Tampa Bay History* 5 (Fall–Winter 1983): 4–26.

8. Edgar T. Thompson, *Plantation Societies, Race Relations, and the South: The Regimentation of Populations* (Durham, N.C.: Duke University Press, 1975), 98–99.

9. For an attempt to trace lynchings to fluctuations in cotton prices, see Raper, *The Tragedy of Lynching,* 30–31; E. M. Beck and Stewart E. Tolnay, "The Killing Fields of the Deep South: The Market for Cotton and the Lynching of Blacks, 1882–1930," *American Sociological Review* 55 (1990): 525–53 and "A Season of Violence: The Lynching of Blacks

and Labor Demand in the Agricultural Production Cycle in the American South," *International Review of Social History* 36 (1992): 1–24; and C. J. Hovland and R. R. Sears, "Minor Studies in Aggression: Correlation of Lynchings with Economic Indices," *Journal of Psychology* 9 (May 1940): 301–10. In "Re-examination of Correlation between Lynchings and Economic Indices," *Journal of Abnormal and Social Psychology* 41 (April 1946): 154–65, Alexander Mintz dissects the methodological weaknesses of the Hovland and Sears article. For discussions of the links between economic upheaval and violence, see Edward Ayers, *Vengeance and Justice: Crime and Punishment in the Nineteenth Century South* (New York: Oxford University Press, 1984), 223–65; and Gordon B. McKinney, "Industrialization and Violence in Appalachia in the 1890s," in *An Appalachian Symposium,* ed. Joel Williamson (Boone, N.C.: Appalachian Consortium Press, 1977), 131–44.

10. Walter White, *Rope and Faggot* (New York: Knopf, 1929), 82.

11. Numan V. Bartley, *The Creation of Modern Georgia* (Athens: University of Georgia Press, 1983), 108.

12. Among the useful studies of Georgia agriculture are Steven W. Engerrand, " 'Now Scratch or Die': The Genesis of Capitalistic Agricultural Labor in Georgia, 1865–1880," Ph.D. diss., University of Georgia, 1981; Willard Range, *A Century of Georgia Agriculture, 1850–1950* (Athens: University of Georgia Press, 1954); Arthur F. Raper, *Preface to Peasantry: A Tale of Two Black Belt Counties* (Chapel Hill: University of North Carolina Press, 1936); and Joseph P. Reidy, "Masters and Slaves, Planters and Freedmen: The Transition from Slavery to Freedom in Central Georgia, 1820–1880," Ph.D. diss., Northern Illinois University, 1982.

13. For works that stress (convincingly, I believe) the coercive traits of southern labor laws and practices, see William Cohen, *At Freedom's Edge: Black Mobility and the Southern Quest for Racial Control, 1861–1915* (Baton Rouge: Louisiana State University Press, 1991); Pete Daniel, *The Shadow of Slavery: Peonage in the South 1901–1969* (Urbana: University of Illinois Press, 1972), 3–81; Harold Woodman, "Sequel to Slavery: The New History Views the Postbellum South," *Journal of Southern History* 43 (Nov. 1977): 523–44; and Harold Woodman, "Post-Civil War Southern Agriculture and Law," *Agricultural History* 53 (Jan. 1979): 319–37. For dissenting arguments, see Stephen J. DeCanio, *Agriculture in the Postbellum South: The Economics of Production and Supply* (Cambridge: Massachusetts Institute of Technology Press, 1974) and Robert Higgs, *Competition and Coercion: Blacks in the American Economy 1865–1914* (Chicago: University of Chicago Press, 1980).

14. Gavin Wright, *Old South, New South: Revolutions in the Southern Economy since the Civil War* (New York: Basic Books, 1986), 113. Jonathan Wiener has argued that the system of tenancy in the South perpetuated the "labor-repressive nature of [antebellum] southern production," which was "qualitatively different from the North's classic capitalism." See "Class Structure and Economic Development in the American South, 1865–1955," *American Historical Review* 84 (Oct. 1979): 970–92. Wright has challenged this argument by emphasizing the importance of the South's low-wage labor market within a national

high-wage labor market. The essential point remains that the urgency of white planters' complaints about laborers' mobility, the shrillness of calls for severe laws against vagrancy, and the simple fact that on average at least 15 percent of laborers were locked into debt peonage at the end of each year are evidence of a labor market distorted by restraints. As a system of "free labor" expanded in the North, rural labor practices in the South remained rife with broad planter prerogatives.

15. Thompson, *Plantation Societies, Race Relations, and the South*, 93; see also, Jay Mandle, *The Roots of Black Poverty: The Southern Plantation Economy after the Civil War* (Durham, N.C.: Duke University Press, 1978), 46–48.

16. Raper, *The Tragedy of Lynching*, 56. See also, Neil R. McMillen, *Dark Journey: Black Mississippians in the Age of Jim Crow* (Urbana: University of Illinois Press, 1989), 125–27.

17. Oliver C. Cox, *Caste, Class and Race: A Study in Social Dynamics* (New York: Doubleday, 1949), 561.

18. See Appendix A, Table 8, "Lynchings in Cotton Belt Georgia, 1880–1930."

19. See Appendix A, Table 8.

20. See Appendix A, Table 8.

21. For the details of the Leesburg lynching, see *AC*, Feb. 12, 1899; *MT*, Feb. 12, 1899; *SMN*, Feb. 12, 13, 1899; and *ST*, Feb. 18, 1899; and for the Taliaferro County lynching, see *AC*, May 23, 1911 and *MT*, May 23, 1911.

22. *AC*, June 24, 1909; *CES*, June 23, 24, 1909; *ST*, June 26, 1909; Robert H. Jordan, *There Was A Land: A Story of Talbot County, Georgia and Its People* (Talbotton, Ga.: Published privately, 1971), 180–82.

23. John H. Goff, "The Great Pine Barrens," *Emory University Quarterly* 5 (March 1949): 20–31; Ann Patton Malone, "Piney Woods Farmers of South Georgia, 1850–1900: Jeffersonian Yeomen in an Age of Expanding Commercialism," *Agricultural History* 60 (Fall 1986): 51–84; Mark V. Wetherington, "The New South Comes to Wiregrass Georgia, 1865–1910," Ph.D. diss., University of Tennessee, 1985, chapter 2. For an autobiography that traces the changes in the region, albeit with excruciating quaintness, see Willie P. Howell, *The Country Boy* (New York: Comet Press, 1958), esp. 1–70.

24. J. L. Herring, *Saturday Night Sketches: Stories of Old Wiregrass Georgia* (Tifton: Sunny South Press, 1978), 14.

25. Jefferson Max Dixon, "Georgia Railroad Growth and Consolidation, 1860–1917," M.A. thesis, Emory University, 1949, passim; U.S. Census, *Manufactures* (Washington D.C.: Government Printing Office, 1902): 1003–112; U.S. Census, *Manufactures* (Washington D.C.: Government Printing Office, 1919): 597–603; Mary Ellen Tripp, "Longleaf Pine Lumber Manufacturing in the Altamaha River Basin, 1865–1918," Ph.D. diss., Florida State University, 1983, 273–74, 377–400; Wetherington, "The New South Comes to Wiregrass Georgia," 177–243.

26. *Eastman Times*, March 20, 1879; *SMN*, May 9, 1893. See also, Thomas F. Armstrong, "Georgia Lumber Laborers, 1880–1917: The Social Implications of Work," *Geor-*

gia Historical Quarterly 67 (Winter 1983): 444–47; Thomas F. Armstrong, "The Transformation of Work: Turpentine Workers in Coastal Georgia, 1865–1901," *Labor History* 25 (Fall 1984): 530–31; Wetherington, "The New South Comes to Wiregrass Georgia," 213. For a harsh portrait of turpentine camp life, see Robert N. Lauriault, "From Can't to Can't: The North Florida Turpentine Camp, 1900–1950," *Florida Historical Quarterly* 67 (Jan. 1989): 310–28. A small number of black turpentine hands continue to be attracted to labor in the pine forests of southern Georgia; according to a conservation agent, "They're settled in on the quiet of working in the woods." *AC*, Nov. 23, 1989, E-2.

27. See Federal Census, *Agriculture, 1900* (Washington, D.C.: Government Printing Office, 1900), 68–71; and Federal Census, *Agriculture, 1920* (Washington, D.C.: Government Printing Office, 1920), 304–17.

28. See W. E. B. Du Bois, *The Negro Landholder in Georgia*, U.S. Department of Labor Bulletin no. 35 (Washington, 1901), 676–82; Raper, *The Tragedy of Lynching*, 171; and Wetherington, "The New South Comes to Wiregrass Georgia," 346–48.

29. Herring, *Saturday Night Sketches*, 14.

30. *VT*, Dec. 19, 1891. For similar sentiments, see also, issues of May 15, Dec. 4, 1897, Nov. 4, 1900, and Oct. 14, 1902. The columns of *VT* are filled with sensational accounts of violent crimes by itinerant blacks, especially turpentine hands. See, for example, issues of Sept. 23, 1893, Jan. 19, 1895, Sept. 14, 1897, Oct. 22, 1898, Feb. 18, 1899, Oct. 10, 1899, Aug. 7, 1900, Jan. 29, 1901, May 27, 1902, and Nov. 24, 1903. See also, Wetherington, "The New South Comes to Wiregrass Georgia," 379, 398, 411–23.

31. The details of the dispute between Sears and Varn and the subsequent violence at Lot 2 are described in the testimony at the trial of Welcome Golden and Robert Knight. The trial transcript is included in the Application for Executive Clemency of Golden and Knight, Governor's Executive Correspondence, Pardons, Golden and Knight File. GDAH.

32. *AC*, Dec. 14, 1891; *MT*, Dec. 14, 1891; *SMN*, Dec. 14, 1891; *ST*, Jan. 2, 1892; Executive Minutes, reel 50–60, frame 501, GDAH.

33. *AC*, Feb. 8, 1892; *ST*, Feb. 13, 1892.

34. *Message of the Governor of Georgia to the General Assembly, 1903* (Atlanta: George W. Harrison, 1903), 29.

35. For other violent confrontations over land and property claims that were strikingly similar to the Varn Mill affray, see *VT*, Feb. 17, 1894, May 19, 1894, Sept. 14, 1897, and Oct. 12, 1897; and *SMN*, Feb. 9, 14, 1903.

36. See Appendix A, Table 9, "Average Population Density in Southern Georgia, 1880–1930" and Table 10, "Average Population Growth in Southern Georgia, 1880–1930."

37. See Appendix A, Table 11, "Percent Black Population in Southern Georgia, 1880–1930."

38. See Appendix A, Table 12, "Lynchings in Southern Georgia, 1880–1930."

39. See Appendix A, Table 12.

40. See Appendix A, Table 12.

41. *SMN*, Oct. 3, 1903.

42. *ST,* July 16, 1892, March 17, 1894. For other scathing portraits of the "piney woods," black newspaper, see *ST,* Sept. 14, 1889, Aug. 12, 1893.

43. Ruth A. Allen, *East Texas Lumber Workers: An Economic and Social Picture, 1870–1950* (Austin: University of Texas Press, 1961); John F. H. Claiborne, "A Trip through the Piney Woods," *Publications of the Mississippi Historical Society* 9 (1906): 487–538; Nollie W. Hickman, *Mississippi Harvest: Lumbering in the Longleaf Pine Belt, 1840–1915* (Oxford: University of Mississippi Press, 1962), esp. 143–152; Nollie W. Hickman, "Black Labor in the Forest Industries of the Piney Woods, 1840–1933," in *Mississippi's Piney Woods: A Human Perspective,* ed. Noel Polk (Jackson: University Press of Mississippi, 1986), 79–91.

44. *ST,* Sept. 14, 1889.

45. Steven Hahn, *The Roots of Southern Populism: Yeoman Farmers and the Transformation of the Georgia Upcountry, 1850–1890* (New York: Oxford University Press, 1983), 15–49; Roland M. Harper, "Development of Agriculture in Upper Georgia from 1850 to 1880," *Georgia Historical Quarterly* 6 (March 1922): 3–27.

46. Charles L. Flynn, Jr., *White Land, Black Labor: Caste and Class in Late Nineteenth Century Georgia* (Baton Rouge: Louisiana State University Press, 1983), 136–49; Hahn, *The Roots of Southern Populism;* Thomas A. Scott, "Cobb County, Georgia, 1880–1900: A Socioeconomic Study of an Upper Piedmont County," Ph.D. diss., University of Tennessee, 1978.

47. The class tensions, which were played out in Populism, are treated by Flynn, *White Land, Black Labor;* Hahn, *The Roots of Southern Populism;* and Randolph D. Werner, "Hegemony and Conflict: The Political Economy of a Southern Region: Augusta, Georgia, 1865–1895," Ph.D. diss., University of Virginia, 1977. On levels of white tenancy, see, for example, Federal Census, *Agriculture, 1910,* 344–57.

48. Theodore Rosengarten, *All God's Dangers: The Life of Nate Shaw* (New York: Knopf, 1974), 511–12. While offering evidence to support Cobb's observation, Jack Temple Kirby describes a bitter dispute between a white planter and a white tenant in *Rural Worlds Lost: The American South, 1920–1960* (Baton Rouge: Louisiana State University Press, 1987), 147.

49. White planters could not intimidate white tenants to the same degree that they did black tenants, but they were often quite antagonistic. See Allison Davis, Burleigh B. Gardner, and Mary R. Gardner, *Deep South: A Social Anthropological Study of Class and Caste* (Chicago: University of Chicago Press, 1969), 266–69.

50. See Appendix A, Table 13, "Lynchings in Upper Piedmont Georgia, 1880–1930."

51. *AC,* Oct. 13, 1912; for other examples see issues of Jan. 8, 1900, Nov. 20, 1900, Jan. 13, 1916, and June 1, 1916; John M. Matthews, "Studies in Race Relations in Georgia, 1890–1930," Ph.D. diss., Duke University, 1970, 163; Royal Freeman Nash, "The Cherokee Fires," *Crisis* 11 (March 1916): 265–70; Robert Preston Brooks, "A Local Study of the Race Problem," *Political Science Quarterly* 26 (June 1911): 193–221.

52. See Appendix A, Table 22, "Lynching Victims in Georgia, 1880–1930."

53. Don Doyle, *New Men, New Cities, New South: Atlanta, Nashville, Charleston, Mobile, 1860–1910* (Chapel Hill: University of North Carolina Press, 1990), 262.

54. For examples of attempted lynchings or outbreaks of racial violence that were prevented or defused by law officers, see *AC*, July 27, 1883, Nov. 8, 1894, Dec. 3–4, 1895, Aug. 23, 1898, June 24, 1900, March 12, 1901, May 18–22, 1902, Sept. 19, 1903, Nov. 9–10, 1905, and Feb. 21, 1916; *AJ*, May 25, 1900.

55. Du Bois to Ray Stannard Baker, May 6, 1909, quoted in John Dittmer, *Black Georgia in the Progressive Era, 1900–1920* (Urbana: University of Illinois Press, 1977), 123–31, 172.

56. Charles Crowe, "Racial Violence and Social Reform: Origins of the Atlanta Race Riot of 1906," *Journal of Negro History* 53 (July 1968): 234–56; Charles Crowe, "Racial Massacre in Atlanta, September 22, 1906," *Journal of Negro History* 54 (April 1969): 150–173; Dittmer, *Black Georgia in the Progressive Era*, 123–131; Herbert Shapiro, *White Violence and Black Response: From Reconstruction to Montgomery* (Amherst: University of Massachusetts Press, 1988), 96–103.

57. *AC*, March 18–20, 1900; *MT*, March 18, 1900; *SMN*, March 19, 1900; *Marietta Journal*, March 22, 1900; *ST*, March 24, 1900.

58. For news accounts of mass lynchings in the region, see *AC*, Oct. 24, 1902, Aug. 23, 1904, Sept. 19, 1904, April 8, 1911, and June 28, 29, 30, 1911; *Gwinnett Herald News*, April 10, 1911; *Gwinnett Journal*, April 12, 15, 1911; *SMN*, May 29, 1911; *Covington News*, June 28, 1911; *Lawrenceville Progress*, June 28, 1911; and *Athens Banner*, June 28–30, 1911.

59. *AC*, April 2–3, 1902; *SMN*, April 2, 1902; *Cartersville Courant-American*, April 3, 1902; *ST*, April 5, 1902.

60. *AC*, Sept. 5, 1889; *MT*, Sept. 5, 1889.

61. *AC*, Sept. 6, 1889.

62. *AC*, Sept. 6, 1889; *ST*, Sept. 14, Oct. 5, 12, Nov. 23, 1889.

63. On race relations and the urban ethos of the New South, see John Cell, *The Highest Stage of White Supremacy: The Origins of Segregation in South Africa and the American South* (Cambridge: Cambridge University Press, 1982), esp. chapter 7; Doyle, *New Men, New Cities, New South*, 261–69; and John William Graves, "Jim Crow in Arkansas: A Reconsideration of Urban-Race Relations in the Post-Reconstruction South," *Journal of Southern History* 55 (Aug. 1989): 427, 435, 445–48; and John William Graves, *Town and Country: Race Relations in an Urban-Rural Context, Arkansas, 1865–1905* (Fayettville: University of Arkansas Press, 1991), 70–96, 226–29.

64. Frederick A. Bode, *Farm Tenancy and the Census of Antebellum Georgia* (Athens: University of Georgia Press, 1986), 77–78.

65. Ayers, *Vengeance and Justice*, 255–24; William F. Holmes, "Moonshining and Collective Violence: Georgia, 1889–1895," *Journal of American History* 67 (Dec. 1980): 589–611; Dale E. Soden, "Northern Georgia: Fertile Ground for the Urban Ministry of Mark Matthews," *Georgia Historical Quarterly* 69 (Spring 1985): 39–54.

66. Wilbur R. Miller, "The Revenue: Federal Law Enforcement in the Mountain South, 1870–1900," *Journal of Southern History* 55 (May 1989): 195–216.

67. See Appendix A, Table 14, "Lynchings in Northern Georgia, 1880–1930."

68. For examples of racial motivations in whitecapping, see the accounts of the lynching of John Duncan for miscegenation, *AC*, Oct. 1, 1889; the lynching of Hosea Jones, a black Populist, *Dalton Argus*, May 9, 1891; and the lynching of Jack Wilson, *North Georgia Citizen* (Dalton), Oct. 27, Nov. 3, 1893.

69. Holmes, "Moonshining and Collective Violence," 608–11. For similar conclusions about whitecappers in Missouri, see David Thelen, *Paths of Resistance: Tradition and Dignity in Industrializing Missouri* (New York: Oxford University Press, 1986), 88–99.

70. See Appendix A, Table 14.

71. Holmes, "Moonshining and Collective Violence," 604–7.

72. *Montgomery Advertiser*, March 1, 1913; *Toccoa Record*, March 6, 1913; *AC*, June 15, 1915; *Clarkesville Advance*, June 15, 1915; *Toccoa Record*, June 17, 1915; *AC*, Sept. 21, 1916; *Chicago Defender*, Sept. 30, 1916.

73. *SMN*, Oct. 3, 1903. Among the important works on coastal Georgia are Thomas F. Armstrong, "From Task Labor to Free Labor: The Transition along Georgia's Rice Coast, 1820–1880," *Georgia Historical Quarterly* 64 (Winter 1980): 432–47; James M. Clifton, "Twilight Comes to the Rice Kingdom: Postbellum Rice Culture on the South Atlantic Coast," *Georgia Historical Quarterly* 62 (Summer 1978): 146–54; George A. Rogers and R. Frank Saunders, Jr., *Swamp Water and Wire Grass: Historical Sketches of Coastal Georgia* (Macon: Mercer University Press, 1984); and Monroe N. Work, "The Negroes of Warsaw, Georgia," *Southern Workman* 37 (Jan. 1908): 29–40.

74. *SMN*, Oct. 12, 1906.

75. The richest source for expressions of white paternalism is found in the editorial pages of the *SMN*. See, for example, issues of Aug. 25, 1890, Dec. 8, 1890, June 22, 1893, Feb. 19, 1903, Nov. 25, 1903, Oct. 12, 1906, and Dec. 3, 1909. A concise survey of the failings and strengths of white paternalism in Savannah is provided in Linda O. McMurry, *Recorder of the Black Experience: A Biography of Monroe Nathan Work* (Baton Rouge; Louisiana State University Press, 1985), 31–47. For a form of paternalism in Charleston, see Doyle, *New Men, New Cities, New South*, 260–79.

76. *SMN*, Sept. 1, 1895.

77. *SMN*, Oct. 12, 1906.

78. The *SMN* steadfastly opposed lynching, regardless of the alleged cause, throughout the postbellum era. For a sampling of antilynching editorials see issues of May 9, 1890, April 21, 1892, June 22, 1893, Nov. 26, 1895, June 7, 1897, Aug. 13, 1901, June 28, 1903, April 27, 1905, June 29, 1908, and April 21, 1909.

79. *SMN*, Dec. 29, 1890, Sept. 16, 1895.

80. *SMN*, Sept. 15, 1903, Nov. 21, 1903, Oct. 12, 1906.

81. During Reconstruction, indignant coastal blacks turned to displays of force to intimidate whites and curb attacks, see Paul A. Cimbala, "The Freedmen's Bureau, the

Freedmen, and Sherman's Grant in Reconstruction Georgia, 1865–1867," *Journal of Southern History* 55 (Nov. 1989): 603; and Herbert Shapiro, "Afro-American Responses to Race Violence during Reconstruction," *Science and Society* 36 (Summer 1972): 158–70. On the communitarian traditions among coastal blacks, see Thomas A. Armstrong, "The Building of a Black Church: Community in Post Civil War Liberty County, Georgia," *Georgia Historical Quarterly* 66 (Fall 1982): 346–67; Gerald David Jaynes, *Branches without Roots: Genesis of the Black Working Class in the American South, 1862–1882* (New York: Oxford University Press, 1986), esp. 289–300; John Scott Strickland, " 'No More Mud Work': The Struggle for the Control of Labor and Production in Low Country South Carolina, 1863–1880," in *The Southern Enigma: Essays on Race, Class, and Folk Culture,* ed. Winfred B. Moore, Jr. (Westport, Conn.: Greenwood Press, 1983), 43–62; and John Scott Strickland, "Traditional Culture and Moral Economy: Social and Economic Change in the South Carolina Low Country, 1865–1910," in *The Countryside in the Age of Capitalist Transformation: Essays in the Social History of Rural America,* ed. Steven Hahn and Jonathan Prude (Chapel Hill: University of North Carolina Press, 1985), 141–78.

82. The extent of black landholding in the coastal region is vividly demonstrated in W. E. B. Du Bois, "The Negro Farmer" in *Contributions by W. E. B. Du Bois in Government Publications and Proceedings,* ed. Herbert Aptheker (Washington, D.C.: 1904, repr. Millwood, N.Y.: Kraus-Thomson Organization Ltd., 1980), 259–65, 290–95. See also, Du Bois, *The Negro Landholder in Georgia,* esp. 665–66, 739–41; and G. S. Dickerman, "Tenure of Farms in the South," *Southern Workman* 32 (Jan. 1903): 36–47.

83. *SMN,* Aug. 27, 1899. Neils Christensen, Jr., reached a similar conclusion about the typical black farmer in Beaufort County, South Carolina: "Fish and oysters are so plentiful that, with a few acres of corn, peas, rice and sugar-cane, little else is needed to satisfy his wants." See "The Negroes of Beaufort County, South Carolina," *Southern Workman* 32 (Oct. 1903): 481–85. Also see Du Bois, *The Negro Landholder of Georgia,* 739–40. It is also noteworthy that some areas of the coastal region, including McIntosh County, were open range and that farmers fenced their crops. Open range allowed small landholders, whose land might not be sufficient to support livestock, access to vast areas of land for their cattle and pigs to forage. See G. L. Fuller et al., *Soil Survey of McIntosh County, Georgia,* U. S. Department of Agriculture, Bureau of Chemistry and Soils, Bulletin no. 6 (Washington, D.C.: Government Printing Office, 1929), 9–12.

84. John W. Blassingame, "Before the Ghetto: The Making of the Black Community in Savannah, Georgia, 1865–1880," *Journal of Social History* 6 (Summer 1973): 463–88; Linda O. Hines and Allen W. Jones, "A Voice of Black Protest: The Savannah Men's Sunday Club, 1905–1911," *Phylon* 35 (June 1974): 193–202; McMurry, *Recorder of the Black Experience,* 31–47; and Robert E. Perdue, *The Negro in Savannah, 1865–1900* (New York: Exposition Press, 1973), 88–104.

85. In Georgia, at least one black representative from the coastal area served in the state legislature until the disfranchisement of blacks in 1908. The political history of postbellum coastal Georgia is traced in Russell Duncan, *Freedom's Shore: Tunis Campbell and the*

Georgia Freedmen (Athens: University of Georgia Press, 1987); Joseph P. Reidy, "Aaron A. Bradley: Voice of Black Labor in the Georgia Low Country," in *Southern Black Leaders of the Reconstruction Era*, ed. Howard Rabinowitz (Urbana: University of Illinois Press, 1982), 281–308; and Albert E. Smith, "Down Freedom's Road: The Contours of Race, Class, and Property Crime in Black-Belt Georgia, 1866–1910," Ph.D. diss., University of Georgia, 1982, 117–64.

86. See Appendix A, Table 22.

87. See Appendix A, Table 15, "Lynchings in Coastal Georgia, 1880–1930."

88. The most detailed coverage of the early events in Darien is in *AC*, Aug. 24–27, 1899; *SMN*, Aug. 24–27, 1899; and *SP*, Aug. 24–27, 1899.

89. *SP*, Aug. 25, 1899; *AC*, Aug. 26, 1899; *SMN*, Aug. 26, 1899.

90. *SP*, Aug. 26–27, 1899; *SMN*, Aug. 26–27, 1899.

91. The local white newspaper, for example, noted that Reverend Mifflin "is thought a heap of by the white people of Darien." *Darien Gazette*, April 29, 1899.

92. *AC*, Aug. 28, 1899; *Georgia Senate Journal, 1899*, 112–25, includes the militia commander's account as well as the proclamation issued by the committee of local blacks.

93. McIntosh County Superior Court Minutes, Book E, 1896–1905, 174–97, GDAH; *SP*, Sept. 1, 1899.

94. McIntosh County Superior Court Minutes, Book E, 1896–1905, 227–28, GDAH.

95. For an extended discussion of the Darien "Insurrection," see W. Fitzhugh Brundage, "The Darien 'Insurrection' of 1899: Black Protest during the Nadir of Race Relations," *Georgia Historical Quarterly* 74 (Summer 1990): 234–53. Contrast with Raper, *The Tragedy of Lynching*, 232.

96. For example, in Brooks County in December 1894, whites launched a campaign of terrorism against the black population after some blacks armed to protect themselves against a marauding mob of white lynchers. Militia failed to prevent the murder of five blacks and the beating of countless others. See *AC*, Dec. 22–27, 1894; *MT*, Dec. 24, 25, 1894; and *VT*, Dec. 22, 29, 1894, and Jan. 5, 1895.

97. As early as May 16, 1892, the *SMN* had warned of the dangerous consequences for whites and blacks alike of black retaliation for white lawlessness.

98. Two studies that provide discussions of black leaders in Norfolk and Louisville also shed light on attitudes that were similar to those of black leaders in coastal Georgia. See Earl Lewis, *In Their Own Interests: Race, Class, and Power in Twentieth-Century Norfolk, Virginia* (Berkeley: University of California Press, 1991), esp. chapter 3; and George C. Wright, *Life Behind the Veil: Blacks in Louisville, Kentucky, 1865–1930* (Baton Rouge: Louisiana State University Press, 1985), esp. 156–75.

99. *Darien Gazette*, Aug. 26, 1899, Sept. 2, 1899.

100. *Darien Gazette*, Sept. 2, 1899, emphasis added. .

101. For strident editorials, see *SMN*, Aug. 27, 1899; and *SP*, Aug. 28, 1899. Contrast with *SMN*, Aug. 29, 1899; and *SP*, Aug. 29, 1899.

102. *SP*, Aug. 29, 1899.

103. *SMN*, Aug. 29, 1899.

104. *SMN*, Oct. 3, 1903.

105. Among the many important discussions of coercion and plantation agriculture, see DeCanio, *Agriculture in the Postbellum South*, 16–50; Wiener, "Class Structure and Economic Development in the American South," 970–92; and Woodman, "Sequel to Slavery," 523–54.

106. In *Dusk of Dawn* (New York: Shocken Books, 1968), 67, W. E. B. Du Bois describes the trauma that the lynching of Sam Hose produced in him.

107. Richard Wright, *Black Boy: A Record of Childhood and Youth* (New York: Harper and Row, 1966), 190.

5   The Geography of Lynching in Virginia

1. Jonathan M. Wiener, "Class Structure and Economic Development in the American South, 1865–1955," *American Historical Review* 84 (Oct. 1979): 982. See also, William Cohen, *At Freedom's Edge: Black Mobility and the Southern White Quest for Racial Control, 1861–1915* (Baton Rouge: Louisiana State University Press, 1991), 232–33, 239.

2. Ronald D. Eller, *Miners, Millhands, and Mountaineers: Industrialization of the Appalachian South, 1880–1930* (Knoxville: University of Tennessee Press, 1982), 65–80; Joseph T. Lambie, "The Norfolk and Western Railroad, 1881–1896: A Study in Coal Transportation," Ph.D. diss., Harvard University, 1948, 54; Randall G. Lawrence, "Appalachian Metamorphosis: Industrializing Society on the Central Appalachian Plateau, 1860–1913," Ph.D. diss. Duke University, 1983, 28–47.

3. U.S. Census Bureau, *Twelfth Census of the United States, 1900* (Washington, D.C.: U.S. Census Office, 1901), 1:561–62.

4. *Weekly Virginian* (Abingdon), April 11, 1889. See also, Eller, *Miners, Millhands, and Mountaineers*, 170–72; and Lawrence, "Appalachian Metamorphosis," 48–122.

5. Gordon B. McKinney, "Industrialization and Violence in Appalachia in the 1890's," in *An Appalachian Symposium*, ed. Joel W. Williamson (Boone, N.C.: Appalachian Consortium Press, 1977), 131–44; Robert P. Stuckert, "Racial Violence in Southern Appalacia, 1880–1940," *Appalachian Heritage* 20 (Spring 1992): 35–41. Contrast McKinney with Altina L. Waller, *Feud: Hatfields, McCoys, and Social Change in Appalachia, 1860–1900* (Chapel Hill: University of North Carolina Press, 1988), 7–11, 235–49.

6. See Kenneth R. Bailey, "A Judicious Mixture: Negroes and Immigrants in the West Virginia Mines, 1880–1917," *West Virginia History* 34 (Jan. 1973): 141–61; Stephen Brier, "Interracial Organizing in the West Virginia Coal Industry: The Participation of Black Mine Workers in the Knights of Labor and United Mine Workers, 1880–1894," in *Essays in Southern Labor History*, ed. Gary M. Fink and Merl E. Reed. (Westport, Conn.: Greenwood Press, 1977), 18–43; David A. Corbin, *Life, Work, and Rebellion in the Coal Fields:*

The Southern West Virginia Miners, 1880–1922 (Urbana: University of Illinois Press, 1981), chapter 3; and Ronald L. Lewis, *Black Coal Miners in America: Race, Class, and Community Conflict, 1780–1980* (Lexington: University Press of Kentucky, 1987), passim.

7. See Appendix A, Table 16, "Average Population Growth in Southwestern Virginia, 1880–1930"; and Table 17, "Percent Black Population in Southwestern Virginia, 1880–1930."

8. See Appendix A, Table 18, "Lynchings in Southwestern Virginia, 1880–1930."

9. See Appendix A, Table 23, "Lynching Victims in Virginia, 1880–1930."

10. *RP*, July 23 and Feb. 11, 1893. See also, *RD*, Feb. 2–3, 1893; *RS*, Feb. 2, 1893; and *WP*, Feb. 2, 1893.

11. *Valley Virginian* (Clifton Forge), Oct. 22, 1891.

12. *RP*, Oct. 31, 1891

13. *Valley Virginian*, Oct. 22, 1891. The events at Clifton Forge can be reconstructed from *RD*, Oct. 17, 1891; *NYT*, Oct. 18, 1891; *Lynchburg Virginian*, Oct. 18, 20, 1891; *Lynchburg News*, Oct. 20, 1891; *Augusta County Argus* (Lexington), Oct. 20, 1891; and *Lexington Gazette*, Oct. 22, 1891.

14. *RP*, Oct. 31, 1891; *Valley Virginian*, Oct. 22, 1891.

15. *Valley Virginian*, Oct. 22, 1891.

16. *RP*, Oct. 31, 1891.

17. *Valley Virginian*, Oct. 22, 1891.

18. Ibid.

19. Charles Tilly argues that communities undergoing rapid urbanization and industrialization have often endured *less* violence than stable communities. Cited in James B. Rule, *Theories of Civil Violence* (Berkeley: University of California Press, 1988), 173. In contrast, Howard Zehr contends that crime peaked in Germany and France at the outset of modernization. See "The Modernization of Crime in Germany and France, 1830–1913," in *Readings in Comparative Criminology*, ed. Louise I. Shelley (Carbondale: Southern Illinois University Press, 1981), 120–40.

20. The absence of the harshest manifestations of racism and discrimination in West Virginia undoubtedly attracted blacks. Blacks in West Virginia also resisted white violence, whether from mobs or hired thugs from mining companies. See Corbin, *Life, Work, and Rebellion in the Coal Fields*, chapter 3; Lewis, *Black Coal Miners in America*, chapters 7–8; and especially, Joe William Trotter, Jr., *Coal, Class, and Color: Blacks in Southern West Virginia, 1915–132* (Urbana: University of Illinois Press, 1990), chapters 5, 9.

21. Valuable discussions of the region's economy include "The Fishing Industry of Chesapeake Bay," *Southern Workman* 29 (Dec. 1900): 716–20; S. Walker Blanton, Jr., "An Economic and Social Profile: Virginia in the 1920s," Ph.D. diss., University of Virginia, 1969, passim; J. E. Davis, "Oystering in Hampton Roads," *Southern Workman* 32 (March 1903): 156–63; J. E. Davis, "The Peanut Industry in Virginia," *Southern Workman* 32 (Nov. 1903): 536–42; and Joseph P. Harahan, "Politics, Political Parties, and Voter Partici-

pation in Tidewater Virginia during Reconstruction, 1865–1900," Ph.D. diss., Michigan State University, 1973, 31–71.

22. Jack Temple Kirby, *Rural Worlds Lost: The American South, 1920–1960* (Baton Rouge: Louisiana State University Press, 1987), 40.

23. Among the few extant discussions of the postbellum Piedmont, see S. T. Bitting, "Classes Among Albemarle Negroes," *Southern Workman* 46 (Jan. 1916): 42–48; Ruth C. Fitzgerald, *A Different Story: A Black History of Fredericksburg, Stafford, and Spotsylvania, Virginia* (n.p.: Unicorn, 1979); Charles P. Poland, Jr., *From Frontier to Suburbia* (Marceline, Mo.: Walsworth Publishing, 1976); and Crandall A. Shifflett, *Poverty and Patronage in the Tobacco South: Louisa County, Virginia, 1860–1900* (Knoxville: University of Tennessee Press, 1982).

24. See Pete Daniel, *Breaking the Land: The Transformation of Cotton, Tobacco, and Rice Cultures since 1880* (Urbana: University of Illinois Press, 1985), esp. 23–38; Katherine S. Perry, "A History of Farm Tenancy in the Tobacco Region of Virginia," Ph.D. diss., Radcliffe College, 1956, esp. 107–264; Shifflett, *Poverty and Patronage;* and Nannie May Tilley, *The Bright Tobacco Industry 1860–1929* (Chapel Hill: University of North Carolina Press, 1948).

25. Perry, "A History of Farm Tenancy in the Tobacco Region of Virginia," esp. 198–201, 227–35; *Federal Census, Agriculture, 1900,* 5:132–35.

26. Shifflett, *Poverty and Patronage,* 25–38.

27. Ibid., 48–56; Tilley, *The Bright Tobacco Industry,* 93–102.

28. Tilley, *The Bright Tobacco Industry,* 23, 52, 59–61.

29. For the extent of black landholding in the coastal region, see W. E. B. Du Bois, "The Negro Farmer" in *Contributions by W. E. B. Du Bois in Government Publications and Proceedings,* ed. Herbert Aptheker (Washington, D.C.: 1904, repr. Millwood, N.Y.: Kraus-Thomson Organization Ltd., 1980), 259–65, 290–95. See also, Samuel T. Bitting, *Rural Landownership among the Negroes of Virginia with Special Reference to Albemarle County* (Charlottesville: Phelps-Stokes Fellowship Papers no. 2, 1915); G. S. Dickeman, "Tenure of Farms in the South," *Southern Workman* 32 (Jan. 1903): 36–47; William E. Garnett and John M. Ellison, *Negro Life in Rural Virginia, 1865–1934* (Blacksburg: Virginia Polytechnic Institute, 1934), 9–15; Sarah S. Hughes, "Farming in Lower Tidewater," in *Readings in Black and White: Lower Tidewater Virginia,* ed. Jane H. Kobelski (Portsmouth: Portsmouth Public Library, 1982), 27–34; Loren Schweninger, *Black Property Owners in the South, 1790–1915* (Urbana: University of Illinois Press, 1990), 173–75, 236; and T. C. Walker, "Development in the Tidewater Counties of Virginia," *Annals of the American Academy of Political and Social Science* 48 (July 1913): 28–31. The origins of Tidewater black landholding are described in Ira Berlin, *Slaves without Masters: The Free Negro in the Antebellum South* (New York: Pantheon, 1974), 244–45; and Luther P. Jackson, "The Virginia Free Negro Farmer and Property Owner, 1830–1860," *Journal of Negro History* 24 (Oct. 1939): 405–9.

30. Crandall Shifflett argues that there is evidence of class conflict in Louisa County, Virginia, but his evidence is unconvincing. The weakness of Populism in Virginia suggests that farm laborers in the state lagged behind their southern counterparts in developing an understanding of their exploitation. Contrast Shifflett, *Patronage and Poverty*, 51–56; with Lawrence Goodwyn, *The Populist Moment: A Short History of the Agrarian Revolt in America* (New York: Oxford University Press, 1981), 182, 198; Allen W. Moger, *Virginia: Bourbonism to Byrd, 1870–1925* (Charlottesville: University Press of Virginia, 1968), 110–11; and William D. Sheldon, *Populism in the Old Dominion: Virginia Farm Politics, 1885–1900* (Princeton: Princeton University Press, 1935), passim.

31. See Appendix A, Table 19, "Lynchings by Race in Eastern Virginia, 1880–1930."

32. See Appendix A, Table 23.

33. See Appendix A, Table 20, "Lynchings by Mob Type in Eastern Virginia, 1880–1930."

34. For news accounts of the four lynchings in which the victim's corpse was mutilated, see *RD*, April 20, 1886; *NV*, March 15, 1889; *Charlotte Gazette* (Drake's Branch), Dec. 11, 1890; and *RTD*, March 21, 1925.

35. *BS*, July 2, 1901; *WP*, July 2, 1901; *RD*, July 2, 1901; *Portsmouth Star*, July 1, 1901; *NVP*, July 2–7, 1901; *RP*, July 6, 1901.

36. *WP*, April 23, 24, 1897; *BS*, April 23, 24, 1897; *NVP*, Aug. 8, 9, 1908; *Portsmouth Star*, Aug. 8–10, 1908; *RTD*, Aug. 8, 9, 1908.

37. For accounts of lynchings or attempted lynchings in Alexandria, see *WP*, April 23, 24, 1897, Aug. 10, 1898 and *NYT*, May 24, 1900; in Charlottesville, see *Charlottesville Chronicle*, Sept. 29-Nov. 5, 1882 and *RD*, Aug. 6, 1884; in Danville, see *WP*, Nov. 8, 1889, *Report of the Adjutant-General of Virginia, 1893, RD*, July 19, 1904, and *Danville Register*, Aug. 18, 1917; in Fredericksburg, see *WP*, May 19, 1904; in Manchester, see *RD*, May 8, 1901; in Newport News, see *NVP*, Jan. 6, 1900; in Petersburg, see *RP*, April 8, 1916; in Portsmouth, see *Report of the Adjutant-General of Virginia, 1888* and *Portsmouth Star*, Aug. 6, 1908; in Richmond, see *RP*, Oct. 4, 1902.

38. For examples, see *Report of the Adjutant-General of Virginia, 1888; RP*, Oct. 4, 1902 and April 8, 1916; *WP*, May 19, 1904; *RD*, July 19, 1904; and *Portsmouth Star*, Aug. 6, 1908.

39. Although the antebellum history of the Shenandoah has attracted considerable attention, the postwar history of the region remains virtually uncharted. One contemporary discussion that sheds light on the status of blacks in the region is M. J. Sherman, "Trips A-Field: Among the Virginia Mountains," *Southern Workman* 31 (April 1902): 223–28.

40. *Richmond News Leader*, Feb. 28, 1905; *RP*, March 4, 1905.

41. Dennis B. Downey and Raymond M. Hyser, *No Crooked Death: Coatesville, Pennsylvania and the Lynching of Zachariah Walker* (Urbana: University of Illinois Press, 1991); Elliot Rudwick, *Race Riot at East St. Louis, July 2, 1917* (Carbondale: Southern Illinois University Press, 1964); Roberta Senechal, *The Sociogenesis of a Race Riot: Springfield,*

Illinois in 1908 (Urbana: University of Illinois Press, 1990); William M. Tuttle, Jr., *Race Riot: Chicago in the Red Summer of 1919* (New York: Antheneum, 1970).

42. *AC,* May 24–27, 1899; *Griffin News,* May 23, 25, 26, 29, 31, June 2, 5, 13, 14. See also, Melton A. McLaurin, *Paternalism and Protest: Southern Cotton Mill Workers and Organized Labor, 1875–1905* (Westport, Conn.: Greenwood Press, 1971), 65; and Mercer G. Evans, "The History of the Organized Labor Movement in Georgia," Ph.D. diss., University of Chicago, 1929, 89.

43. Robert P. Ingalls has described the prevalence of "establishment"-sanctioned mob violence, especially against labor activists, in "Lynching and Establishment Violence in Tampa, 1858–1935," *Journal of Southern History* 53 (Nov. 1987): 613–44 and *Urban Vigilantism in the New South: Tampa, 1882–1936* (Knoxville: University of Tennessee Press, 1988). For a provocative portrait of southern businessmen's social vision, see James C. Cobb, *Industrialization and Southern Society, 1877–1984* (Lexington: University Press of Kentucky, 1984), 156–58.

6   The Response to Lynching in Virginia

1. *Clinch Valley News* (Tazewell), July 2, 1897.

2. On Tidewater politics, see Michael B. Chesson, "Richmond's Black Councilmen, 1871–96," in *Southern Black Leaders of the Reconstruction Era,* ed. Howard N. Rabinowitz (Urbana: University of Illinois Press, 1982), 191–222; and Joseph P. Harahan, "Politics, Political Parties, and Voter Participation in Tidewater Virginia during Reconstruction, 1865–1900," Ph.D. diss., Michigan State University, 1973.

3. *NYT,* May 20, 21, 1879; *RD,* Jan. 22, 1880; Herbert Shapiro, *White Violence and Black Response: From Reconstruction to Montgomery* (Amherst: University of Massachusetts Press, 1988), 20; Luther P. Jackson, *Negro Officeholders in Virginia, 1865–1895* (Norfolk: Guide Quality Press, 1945), 7.

4. For examples of black church conventions in Virginia condemning mob violence, see *NYT,* May 28, 1892; *RT,* July 27, 29, 1897; and *RD,* July 28, 1897.

5. Raymond Gavins, *The Perils and Prospects of Southern Black Leadership: Gordon Blaine Hancock, 1884–1970* (Durham: Duke University Press, 1977), chapters 1–4; Earl Lewis, *In Their Own Interests: Race, Class, and Power in Twentieth-Century Norfolk, Virginia* (Berkeley: University of California Press, 1991), esp. chapter 3; Cynthia Neverdon-Morton, *Afro-American Women of the South and the Advancement of the Race, 1895–1925* (Knoxville: University of Tennessee Press, 1989), 104–21.

6. Unfortunately, little is known about most black editors in Virginia, and, with the exception of the *Richmond Planet,* virtually no files of Virginia black newspapers remain. On Mitchell, see Ann F. Alexander, "Black Protest in the New South: John Mitchell, Jr. and the *Richmond Planet,*" Ph.D. diss., Duke University, 1973; and W. Fitzhugh Brundage,

"To Howl Loudly: John Mitchell and the Campaign against Lynching," *Canadian Journal of American Studies,* 22 (Winter 1991): 325–42.

7. Gunnar Myrdal, *An American Dilemma: The Negro Problem and Modern Democracy* (New York: Harper & Row, 1944), 2:910.

8. For examples of accounts of lynchings in the *Planet* that are far superior to white news accounts (if white newspapers even mentioned the lynchings), see issues of June 6, 1891, Jan. 16, April 9, April 16, 23, May 7, July 23, Oct. 22, 1892, February 11, March 4, 1893, and July 23, 1893.

9. *RP,* Jan. 3, 1891.

10. *RP,* June 11, 1891.

11. *RP,* Sept. 6, 1890, Aug. 10, 1901.

12. *New York Freeman,* May 26, 1886; Alexander, "Black Protest in the New South," 151–52; *RP,* Jan. 3, 1891.

13. *RP,* July 22, 29, Aug. 5, 12, Sept. 30, Oct. 14, Nov. 4, 18, 28, 1893; *NYT,* July 19, 1893.

14. Henry Warren Readnour, "Fitzhugh Lee, Confederate Calvaryman of the New South," in *The Governors of Virginia, 1868–1978,* ed. Edward Younger and James T. Moore (Charlottesville: University Press of Virginia, 1982), 115.

15. The election of 1883 marked the turning point in Democratic prospects after a decade of frustration. See Charmoin Higgenbotham, "The Danville Riot of 1883," M.A. thesis, Virginia State College, 1955; John T. Melzer, "The Danville Riot, November 3, 1883," M.A. thesis, University of Virginia, 1963; and James T. Moore, *Two Paths to the New South: The Virginia Debt Controversy, 1870–1883* (Lexington: University Press of Kentucky, 1974), 115–17.

16. The various elements of the heightened tensions in the South are discussed in Joel Williamson, *The Crucible of Race: Black-White Relations in the American South since Emancipation* (New York: Oxford University Press, 1984), 112–13. Governor McKinney earned the enduring enmity of blacks by recommending segregation in railroad coaches and by his pronouncements and actions on education, criminal justice, and black holiday celebrations. See Bernice B. Zuckerman, "Phillip Watkins McKinney, Governor of Virginia, 1890–1894," M.A. thesis, University of Virginia, 1967, 60–64, 67.

17. *RP,* April 9, 16, 1892, May 20, 1893. For other attacks by Mitchell on McKinney, see issues of Feb. 21, 28, March 28, April 11, Nov. 21, 1891, and July 22, 1893.

18. *Roanoke Times,* Sept. 29, 1893.

19. The best discussions of the Roanoke riot are in the *Roanoke Times,* Sept. 21–27, 1893, and *NV,* Sept. 21–23, 1893. Three scholarly accounts are Ann Alexander, "Like an Evil Wind: The Roanoke Riot of 1893 and the Lynching of Thomas Smith," *Virginia Magazine of History and Biography* 100 (April 1992): 173–206; John A. Waits, "Roanoke's Tragedy: The Lynch Riot of 1893," M.A. thesis, University of Virginia, 1972; and Gordon McKinney, "Industrialization and Violence in the 1890's" in *An Appalachian Symposium,* ed. J. W. Williamson (Boone, N.C.: Appalachian State University Press, 1977), 131–44.

20. *Roanoke Times,* Sept. 22–24, 1893; Waits, "Roanoke's Tragedy," 45–54.

21. For examples of the outpouring of editorial support for the local authorities of Roanoke and calls for aggressive steps to crush mob violence, see *RT,* Sept. 22, 1893; *RS,* Sept. 22, 1892; *RD,* Sept. 24, 1893; and *Staunton Daily News,* Sept. 24, 27, 1893.

22. *RD,* Sept. 24, 1893; *Roanoke Times,* Sept. 27, 1893.

23. On Sept. 30, 1893, the *Richmond Planet* complained, "Incompetency and cowardice is thoroughly exemplified in our present chief executive."

24. *Journal of the Senate of the Commonwealth of Virginia, 1893–1894* (Richmond: Superintendent of Public Printing, 1894): Message of the Governor, 45–46.

25. *RP,* Dec. 16, 1893.

26. *RS,* Sept. 24, 1893. For similar conclusions about the significance of the Roanoke lynching, see Raymond Pulley, *Old Virginia Restored: An Interpretation of the Progressive Impulse, 1870–1930* (Charlottesville: University Press of Virginia, 1968), 52–53; and Zuckerman, "Phillip Watkins McKinney," 54–57.

27. Carlos A. Schwantes, *Coxey's Army: An American Odyssey* (Lincoln: University of Nebraska Press, 1985), 248–54; C. Vann Woodward, *Origins of the New South, 1877–1913* (Baton Rouge: Louisiana State University Press, 1980), 267–68; *Journal of the Senate of the Commonwealth of Virginia, 1895* (Richmond: Superintendent of Public Printing, 1895), 34–37. O'Ferrall's paternalistic racism was most explicit in his response to the antilynching agitator Ida Wells-Barnett's speaking tour of Britain in 1894. See *RD,* Sept. 12, 13, 1894; and Governor Charles T. O'Ferrall to Afro-American Press Association, Sept. 12, 1894, O'Ferrall Papers, VSL. Also see Mildred Thompson, "Ida B. Wells-Barnett: An Exploratory Study of an American Black Woman, 1893–1930," Ph.D. diss., George Washington University, 1979, 119–20.

28. Charles T. O'Ferrall, *Forty Years of Active Service* (New York: Neale Publishing, 1904), 234; *Journal of the Senate of the Commonwealth of Virginia, 1894–1895,* Message of the Governor, 33.

29. For surveys of postwar political developments, see Jack P. Maddex, Jr., *The Virginia Conservatives, 1867–1979: A Study in Reconstruction Politics* (Chapel Hill: University of North Carolina Press, 1970); and Catherine S. Silverman, " 'Of Wealth, Virtue, and Intelligence': The Redeemers and Their Triumph in Virginia and North Carolina, 1865–1877," Ph.D. diss., City University of New York, 1972. Contrast with Paul D. Escott, *Many Excellent People: Power and Privilege in North Carolina, 1850–1900* (Chapel Hill: University of North Carolina Press, 1985), 159.

30. For surveys of the political fortunes of the Democratic party, see Allen W. Moger, *Virginia: Bourbonism to Byrd, 1870–1925* (Charlottesville: University Press of Virginia, 1968), 95–121; and Pulley, *Old Virginia Restored,* 48–66.

31. V. O. Key, Jr., *Southern Politics* (New York: Knopf, 1949), 19. See also, Herman L. Horn, "The Growth and Development of the Democratic Party in Virginia since 1890," Ph.D. diss., Duke University, 1949; and Allen W. Moger, "The Origin of the Democratic Machine in Virginia," *Journal of Southern History* 8 (May 1942): 183–209.

32. Moger, "Origin of the Democratic Machine," esp. 111–39, 259–84. There were prominent racial "radicals" in Virginia, including the author Phillip Alexander Bruce; Paul B. Barringer, a college professor and president; and the author Myrta Lockett Avary. They exerted hardly more influence than did such racial liberals as Lewis Harvey Blair, Orra Langhorne, and Samuel C. Mitchell.

33. A succinct discussion of the character of the Democratic party in Virginia is found in Allen W. Moger, "Virginia's Conservative Political Heritage," *South Atlantic Quarterly* 50 (July, 1951): 318–29. The best extended treatment of the Democratic party during the period remains Horn, "The Growth and Development of the Democratic Party in Virginia since 1890."

34. *Petersburg Index-Appeal*, Feb. 17, July 7, 1890. The newspaper complained on Feb. 19, 1896, that "much vicious legislation, [was] done ostensibly in the name of civilization and white supremacy, but in reality to promote partisan or factional advantage." See also, Dewey Grantham, *Southern Progressivism: The Reconciliation of Progress and Tradition* (Knoxville: University of Tennessee Press, 1983), 65–74; and Williamson, *Crucible of Race*, 234–41.

35. *RT*, Nov. 3, 1891, June 6, 1894; *RD*, May 15, 1895. For similar sentiments, see *RT*, Aug. 18, 1892, Jan. 24, 1895; *RD*, May 5, 7, 10, 15, 18, 21, 1895; and *Clinch Valley News* (Tazewell) June 22, 1891, July 2, 1897.

36. *RD*, Aug. 12, 1894, May 21, 1895; *RT*, June 26, 1897.

37. *RE*, April 14, 21, 1871.

38. The report, comprised of forty-one pages of interviews with local authorities in Alexandria, is a testament to O'Ferrall's determination to squelch mob violence. The investigation outraged many whites in Alexandria and provoked sharp criticism of the governor for meddling in county affairs. See Special Report on the Joseph McCoy Lynching, O'Ferrall Papers, VSL. The investigation is discussed in *BS*, April 26, 28, 1897; and *WP*, April 27, 1897. Predictably, the harshest criticism of the governor was in the local *Alexandria Gazette*, April 28, 29, 1897.

39. *BS*, April 26–28, 1897; *WP*, April 27, 1897; *RD*, April 26–28, 1897. In his annual address he censured Alexandria authorities and concluded that "there can be no possible excuse for the success of the mob." *Journal of the Senate of the Commonwealth of Virginia, 1897–1898* (Richmond: Superintendent of Public Printing, 1898), 15.

40. *BS*, April 28, 1897; *Alexandria Gazette*, April 29, 1897; *RP*, May 1, 8, 1897.

41. *RP*, July 20, 27, Aug. 3, 1895; *RD*, Sept. 13, 1895; *Annual Report of the Attorney General of the Commonwealth of Virginia, 1895*, 5; *Annual Report of the Adjutant General of the Commonwealth of Virginia, 1895*, 64–65.

42. *Journal of the Senate of the Commonwealth of Virginia, 1895–1896* (Richmond: Superintendent of Public Printing, 1896), 119.

43. According to Mitchell, Wise "was highly indignant over the alleged trial and declared their [the women's] treatment to be an outrage," *RP*, July 27, 1895. For biographical

detail on the three white lawyers, see Lyon G. Tyler, ed., *Men of Mark in Virginia* (Washington D.C.: Men of Mark Publishing Co., 1909), 5:189–94; and Lyon G. Tyler, ed., *Encyclopedia of Virginia Biography* (New York: Lewis Historical Publishing Co., 1915), 3:133, 264. The *RT* sent the attorney William M. Justis to Lunenburg to investigate the case against the women. His reports in the *Times* substantiated the charges that Mitchell had already made in the *Planet*. See *RP*, Aug. 10, 24, 1895.

44. *RP*, Aug. 24, 1895.

45. *RP*, Sept. 21, 1895.

46. *RP*, July 27, Aug. 10, 24, 1895; *RT*, July 23, 1895; *RD*, Sept. 13–19, 1895. The most lucid summary of the complex legal battles of the case is Samuel N. Pincus, *The Virginia Supreme Court, Blacks and the Law, 1870–1902* (New York: Garland, 1990), chapter 11.

47. Governor Charles T. O'Ferrall to Judge George C. Orgain, Nov. 11, 1895, reprinted in *Annual Report of the Attorney General of the Commonwealth of Virginia, 1895* (Richmond: Superintendent of Public Printing, 1895), 70; *Barnes v. Commonwealth*, 92 Va. 794 (1895); *RP*, Nov. 16-Dec. 13, 1895.

48. *Journal of the Senate of the Commonwealth of Virginia, 1895–1896*, 115–21.

49. *RP*, Jan.–Sept. 1896, Sept. 26, 1896; *Journal of the House of Delegates of the Commonwealth of Virginia, 1897–1898*, Communication from the Governor Transmitting List of Pardons, House Document 3, 4–5.

50. *RP*, Nov. 14, 1896.

51. *Journal of the Senate of the Commonwealth of Virginia, 1897–1898*, 16.

52. *Journal of the Senate of the Commonwealth of Virginia, 1895–1896*, 32–34; *Journal of the Senate of the Commonwealth of Virginia, 1897–1898*, 15–17. During the 1901–2 constitutional convention, various reforms similar to O'Ferrall's were suggested, but none was enacted. See Albert O. Porter, *County Government in Virginia: A Legislative History* (New York: Columbia University Press, 1947), 317.

53. *RD*, July 25, 1897.

54. O'Ferrall, *Forty Years of Service*, 235–37. O'Ferrall's strong stand against lynching won him widespread praise; for example, see Edward L. Pell, "The Prevention of Lynchings," *Review of Reviews* 17 (March 1898): 321–23. At least one Virginia newspaper was skeptical of O'Ferrall's claims. The *Winchester Times* complained, "The Governor, of course, claims all the credit for the suppression of lynching in recent years, but to well-informed people his claim is ridiculous." Quoted in *RT*, Dec. 9, 1897.

55. The number of lynchings between 1894 and 1897 is impossible to determine with precision. The NAACP recorded fourteen in *Thirty Years of Lynching in the United States, 1889–1918* (New York: Arno Press, 1969), 100. The NAACP list incorrectly includes several legal executions and several prevented lynchings in the total of actual lynchings, however. O'Ferrall claimed that only three lynchings occurred during his term; see *Journal of the Senate of the Commonwealth of Virginia, 1897*, 47.

56. J. Hoge Tyler to Waitman Stigleman, May 8, 1899, box 14, Tyler Papers, VSL.

57. Charles E. Wynes, *Race Relations in Virginia, 1870–1902* (Charlottesville: University of Virginia Press, 1961), 54–66. The tensions arising from the mobilization of black troops are treated in Willard B. Gatewood, Jr., "Virginia's Negro Regiment in the Spanish-American War," *Virginia Magazine of History and Biography* 80 (April 1971): 193–209; and Willard B. Gatewood, Jr., *Black Americans and the White Man's Burden, 1898–1903* (Urbana: University of Illinois Press, 1975), 82–83, 96–98.

58. *Roanoke Times*, Jan. 24–Feb. 17, 1904; *RTD*, Jan. 25–Feb. 18, 1904; Andrew J. Montague to W. F. Battel, Jr., March 8, 1905, Montague Papers, VSL; William Larsen, *Montague of Virginia: The Making of a Southern Progressive* (Baton Rouge: Louisiana State University Press, 1965), 122.

59. Swanson's visit is described in Brooks Miles Barnes, "The Onancock Race Riot of 1907," *Virginia Magazine of History and Biography* 92 (July 1984): 336–50; and Henry C. Ferrell, Jr., *Claude A. Swanson of Virginia: A Political Biography* (Lexington: University Press of Kentucky, 1985), 178. In 1925, Governor E. Lee Trinkle visited the scene of a lynching in Sussex County and strongly urged local authorities to take every possible action to punish the lynchers. He offered the state's aid in prosecuting the lynchers. See *Petersburg Progress-Index*, March 22, 23, 1925; and *RTD*, March 23, 1925.

60. For examples, see G. W. Smith to A. J. Montague, Jan. 20, 1902, Montague Papers, VSL; Henry C. Stuart to Judge George J. Hundley, July 21, 1917, Stuart to Hundley, July 27, 1917, and Stuart to Vernon Ford, Sept. 7, 1917, all in Stuart Papers, VSL.

61. *RD*, March 25, 1900; *NVP*, March 25, 1900; *RP*, March 31, 1900; *Report of the Adjutant-General of the Commonwealth of Virginia, 1900*, 29–33.

62. *Report of the Adjutant-General of the Commonwealth of Virginia, 1900*, 29–33.

63. *RT*, March 25, 27, 1900; *Portsmouth Star*, March 27, 1900. For similar conclusions, see *Alexandria Gazette*, March 27, 1900; *Norfolk Landmark*, March 27, 1900; and Letters to the Editor, *RT*, May 1, 4, 1900.

64. Phillip V. Cogbill to J. Hoge Tyler, March 27, 1900, Isaac B. Bell to Tyler, March 28, 1900, and George J. Hundley to Tyler, March 28, 1900, all in box 16, Tyler Papers, VSL.

65. Camm Patteson to Tyler, March 28, 1900. For similar denunciations of the lynching, see Rev. J. William Jones to Tyler, March 29, 1900, and George E. Smith to Tyler, April 5, 1900, both in box 16, Tyler Papers, VSL.

66. For valuable discussions of the attitudes of officials, see Richard M. Brown, *Strain of Violence: Historical Studies of American Violence and Vigilantism* (New York: Oxford University Press, 1977), 146–52; and Myrdal, *An American Dilemma*, 1:523–26.

67. *Staunton Post*, Sept. 9, 1895; *Shenandoah Valley* (New Market), June 10, 1897; *RD*, Feb. 7, 1886; *Augusta County Argus* (Staunton), Sept. 29, 1891; *RP*, April 2, 1916; *NYT*, July 22, 1922.

68. For example, authorities in Augusta County promised a mob that a black man charged with murder would receive a prompt trial. True to their words, he was tried, con-

victed, and sentenced to death within three days of the crime. *RP*, May 5, 1894; *Augusta County Argus* May 8, 15, 1894.

69. Richard W. Hale, "Lynching Unnecessary: A Report on Commonwealth v. Christian," *American Law Review* 45 (Nov.–Dec. 1911): 878–79. For other examples of authorities striking bargains with mobs, see *Charlottesville Chronicle*, March 21, 1889; *Charlottesville Cavalier Daily*, March 26, April 2, 1889; *Muscoe v. Commonwealth*, 87 Va. 460, 461 (1891); and *RP*, Feb. 10, 1894, Aug. 12, 1899, Feb. 16, 1901.

70. *Augusta County Argus*, July 2, 16, 1895; *Staunton Post*, July 9, 1895; *NVP*, April 25, 1900; *RD*, April 25, 1900; *RP*, May 5, 1900; *NYT*, Dec. 6, 1920; *Bluefield Daily Telegraph*, Dec. 7, 1920; *Lynchburg News*, Dec. 7, 1920.

71. *Report of the Adjutant-General of the Commonwealth of Virginia, 1888*, 60–62.

72. See Appendix A, Table 21, "Number of Times Militia Aid given to Civil Authorities to Prevent Lynchings, 1886–1908." There are no comparable records for the years after 1908 with which to compare the use of the militia in Virginia and other southern states.

73. On Fredericksburg, see *WP*, May 18, 1904; on Danville, see *RTD*, July 20–26, 1904; *NYT*, July 21, 1904; and *Norfolk Landmark*, July 26, 1904; on Portsmouth, see *Portsmouth Star*, Aug. 12–Sept. 24, 1908; and *NVP*, Sept. 23–26, 1908. In 1920, two leaders of an unsuccessful mob in Lynchburg were sentenced to ten days in jail and $25 fines; see *WP*, Aug. 16, 19, 1920, and *BS*, Aug. 19, 1920. Similarly, in 1921, fifteen members of a mob that attempted to lynch a black in Danville were convicted: the leader received a fine of $500 and a one-year jail sentence; see *RTD*, March 29–April 4, 1921, and *New York Globe*, March 29, April 4, 8, 1921.

74. On Roanoke, see *Roanoke Times*, Nov. 16–26, and Dec. 2, 1893. On Loudoun County, see *WP*, Aug. 2–Sept. 16, 1902; *NVP*, Aug. 6, 7, 1902; *Leesburg Washingtonian*, Aug. 2, 9, 1902; and *Loudoun Mirror* (Leesburg), Aug. 7, 1902. The harshest local criticism was in the *Hamilton Weekly Enterprise*, Aug. 8, 15, Sept. 12, 19, 1902. On Patrick County, see *RP*, July 8, 1899; *RT*, March 29, 1900; *Baltimore American*, March 31, 1900; and *RD*, Aug. 10, 1902. On Wise County, see C. R. McCorkle to Governor Westmoreland Davis, Nov. 16, 1920, and C. R. McCorkle to Westmoreland Davis, Aug. 16, 1921, both in Westmoreland Davis Papers, VSL. See also, *RTD*, Jan. 5, 1923; *Richmond Leader*, Jan. 31, 1923; and *Norfolk Journal and Guide*, March 17, 1923.

75. Other examples of attempts—all unsuccessful—to prosecute lynchers include two white men and a black man who allegedly had led the mob that lynched a white in Charlotte County in 1893; see *WP*, Nov. 2–5, 1893, and *NV*, Nov. 2–6, 1893. In 1895, several whites involved in a lynching in Tazewell County were prosecuted (*RP*, Aug. 8, 1895), and a white man who had led a mob that wounded but failed to kill a black in Campbell County was tried in 1898; see *RP*, March 30, May 29, Sept. 18, 1897, and Jan. 15, 1898.

76. Hale, "Lynching Unnecessary," 875–83; *Hampton Monitor*, March 26, 1909.

77. *Norfolk Journal and Guide*, Oct. 6, 1917; Robert F. Engs, *Freedom's First Generation: Black Hampton, Virginia, 1861–1890* (Philadelphia: University of Pennsylvania Press, 1979), 195; *RD*, May 8, 1901; *RP*, May 11, 1901.

78. *Portsmouth Star,* Oct. 24–27, 1904; *NVP,* Oct. 25–28, 1904; *RTD,* Oct. 25–28, 1904; *WP,* Oct. 24–28, 1904; *BS,* Oct. 25–26, 1904; *Richmond News Leader,* Oct. 24–31, 1904; *RP,* Oct. 29, 1904.

79. James Weldon Johnson, *Along This Way: The Autobiography of James Weldon Johnson* (New York: Viking, 1933), 315.

80. There is no adequate history of the origins or early history of the NAACP in Virginia. The expansion of the NAACP in the state can be traced in the Virginia Branch Files, Group I, series G, boxes G-206–212, NAACP Papers, LC. Scattered details of the founding of various branches can be gleaned from *Norfolk Journal and Guide,* Jan. 27, 1917, July 31, 1921; *RP,* July 31, 1921; Gavins, *Perils and Prospects of Southern Black Leadership,* 47; Lewis, *In Their Own Interests,* 72–74; *Crisis* 17 (1919): 285; Robert W. Bagnall, "Lights and Shadows in the South," *Crisis* 41 (April 1932): 125; and Andrew Buni, *The Negro in Virginia Politics, 1902–1965* (Charlottesville: University Press of Virginia, 1967), 127–28.

81. Norfolk Branch Files, Group I, series G, box G-208, NAACP Papers, LC.

82. Portsmouth Branch Files, Group I, series G, boxes G-209, G-210, NAACP Papers, LC.

83. For the campaigns of branches against segregation, see correspondence in Danville Branch Files, Group I, series G, box G-206; Falls Church Branch, Group I, series G, box G-207; Lynchburg Branch Files, Group I, series G, box G-207; and especially the Norfolk Branch Files, Group I, series G, box G-208; and the Richmond Branch Files, Group I, series G, box G-209, all in NAACP Papers, LC.

84. Thomas L. Dabney to Roy Nash, March 26, 1917, Richmond Branch Files, Group I, series G, box G-210, NAACP Papers, LC.

85. For examples, see James W. Johnson to Governor H. C. Stuart, Dec. 3, 1918, Group I, series C, box C-370, Virginia General Lynching File, 1914–23; Rev. C. B. Holloway to J. E. Springarn, Sept. 7, 20, 1926, Group I, series C, box C-370, Wytheville File; Royal L. Hurtt to Robert W. Bagnall, Nov. [?], 1927, Petersburg Branch Files, Group I, series G, box G-209; and P. B. Young to James Weldon Johnson, May 20, May 24, 1929, Norfolk Branch Files, Group I, series G, box G-208, all in NAACP Papers, LC.

86. *Norfolk Journal and Guide,* Aug. 9, 1917.

87. *Norfolk Journal and Guide,* Feb. 6, 1926. For examples of Young's denunciations of mob violence, see the issues of March 31, April 12, Oct. 27, 1923, Jan. 9, 16, 23, 1928; and Henry Lewis Suggs, *P. B. Young, Newspaperman: Race, Politics, and Journalism in the New South, 1910–1962* (Charlottesville: University Press of Virginia, 1988), 36–38, 41, 58–60, 61–62. On Jaffé's antilynching stance, see pages 189–90 of this volume.

88. *Virginia Baptist Annual, 1904* (Richmond: n.p.: 1904), 59–63, 67. The lack of concern of Virginia churches on all issues relating to race is discussed in F. Joseph Mitchell, "The Virginia Methodist Conference and Social Issues in the Twentieth Century," Ph.D. diss., Duke University, 1961, 294–334; and Samuel C. Shepherd, "Churches at Work: Richmond, Virginia, White Protestant Leaders and Social Change in a Southern City, 1900–1929," Ph.D. diss., University of Wisconsin, 1980, 191–218.

89. "Interracial Committee Meeting," February 17, 1920; and "Conference of Interracial Secretaries," June 25, 1920, 10. Both in Series II, File 3, CIC Papers, AUL.

90. Quoted in Lenoir Chambers and Joseph E. Shank, *Salt Water and Printer's Ink: Norfolk and Its Newspapers, 1865–1965* (Chapel Hill: University of North Carolina Press, 1967), 315.

91. Quoted in John Hohenberg, *The Pulitzer Prize Story* (New York: Columbia University Press, 1959), 78–79. See also, Louis I. Jaffé to Governor Harry F. Byrd, Jan. 12, 1929, Lynching File, Byrd Papers, VSL. For an account of southern journalists that places Jaffé in his milieu, see John T. Kneebone, *Southern Liberal Journalists and the Issue of Race, 1920–1944* (Chapel Hill: University of North Carolina Press, 1985), passim.

92. Robert T. Hawkes, Jr., "Harry F. Byrd: Leadership and Reform," in *The Governors of Virginia, 1860–1978,* ed. Younger and Moore, 233–46. See also, Robert T. Hawkes, Jr., "The Career of Harry Flood Byrd, Sr., to 1933," Ph.D. diss., University of Virginia, 1975, passim; and George B. Tindall, "Business Progressivism: Southern Politics in the Twenties," *South Atlantic Quarterly* 62 (Winter 1963): 92–106.

7   The Struggle against Lynching in Georgia, 1880–1910

1. Henry Grady's Speech at Dallas, Texas, State Fair, Oct. 27, 1888, quoted in *The Possibilities of the Negro in Symposium,* ed. Willis B. Parks (Atlanta: Franklin Printing and Publishing, 1904), 61; Alfred H. Colquitt, "Is the Negro Vote Suppressed," *Forum* 4 (Feb. 1888): 268. On Bourbon attitude towards blacks, see George M. Frederickson, *The Black Image in the White Mind: The Debate on Afro-American Character and Destiny, 1817–1914* (New York: Harper & Row, 1971), 198–227; John M. Matthews, "Studies in Race Relations in Georgia," Ph.D. diss., Duke University, 1970, 42–46; and Joel Williamson, *The Crucible of Race: Black-White Relations in the American South since Emancipation* (New York: Oxford University Press, 1984), 79–107. For contrasting portraits of Grady, see Raymond B. Nixon, *Henry W. Grady: Spokesman of the New South* (New York: Knopf, 1943), 315–23 and Harold E. Davis, *Henry Grady's New South: Atlanta, a Brave and Beautiful City* (Tuscaloosa: University of Alabama Press, 1990), esp. chapter 5.

2. *SMN,* Dec. 28, 1889. For similar statements, see issues of Aug. 17, 1886 and April 16, 1893; *Augusta Chronicle,* June 5, 1888; *AC,* July 21, 1892, Sept. 8, 1889.

3. For a study questioning the Bourbon's woeful neglect of social responsibilities, see Peter Wallenstein, *From Slave South to New South: Public Policy in Nineteenth-Century Georgia* (Chapel Hill: University of North Carolina, 1987), esp. 196–214. For an older and much less charitable account of the Bourbons, see Judson C. Ward, Jr., "The New Departure Democrats of Georgia: An Interpretation," *Georgia Historical Quarterly* 41 (Sept. 1957): 227–36.

4. *AC,* July 12, 13, 1884; *MT,* July 13, 1884; Columbus *Times,* July 13, 1884; *Merriwether Vindicator,* (Greenwood), July 18, 1884. For examples of proclamations offering re-

wards, see Executives Minutes, Microfilm reel 50–57, 732; reel 50–58, 527; reel 50–59, 201; reel 50–60, 17, GDAH.

5. Judson C. Ward, Jr., "The Republican Party in Bourbon Georgia, 1872–1890," *Journal of Southern History* 9 (May 1943): 209.

6. Quoted in Lawrence Grossman, *The Democratic Party and the Negro: Northern and National Politics, 1868–92* (Urbana: University of Illinois Press, 1976), 167–68.

7. See Michael L. Thurmond, "Black Journalists: Current Events and Controversies," *Papers of the Athens Historical Society* 2 (1979): 90; *MT*, June 6, 1892.

8. *AC*, Aug. 2–6, 1880, Jan. 3, 1890; *New York Freeman*, June 27, 1885.

9. *New York Age*, Feb. 4, 1888; August Meier, *Negro Thought in America, 1880–1915* (Ann Arbor: Ann Arbor Paperbacks, 1983), 70. The resolutions of the meeting are conveniently available in Herbert Aptheker, ed., *A Documentary History of the Negro People in the United States: From the Colonial Period to the Establishment of the N.A.A.C.P.* (New York: Citadel Press, 1951), 697–703.

10. Barton C. Shaw, *The Wool Hat Boys: Georgia's Populist Party* (Baton Rouge: Louisiana State University Press, 1984), 119–20.

11. Numan V. Bartley, *The Creation of Modern Georgia* (Athens; University of Georgia Press, 1983), 94–98; James C. Bonner, "The Gubernatorial Career of W. J. Northen," M.A. thesis, University of Georgia, 1936, passim; Shaw, *Wool Hat Boys*, 22–26, passim; Williamson, *Crucible of Race*, 288–91.

12. *Georgia Senate Journal, 1892*, 51–52; *Georgia Laws, 1893*, 128–29. See Appendix A, Table 21, "Number of Times Militia Aid Given to Civil Authorities to Prevent Lynchings, 1886–1908," for Northen's use of militia to disperse mobs. For Northen's opposition to mob violence, see *AC*, May 22, 1892; and *AJ*, Oct. 27, 1892.

13. *AC*, Dec. 8, 1895; *Georgia House Journal, 1895*, 688–90; *ST*, Aug. 13, 1892. Northen's stance on lynching won the praise and support of many blacks. In 1892, William A. Pledger, the state's most prominent black politician, along with the black editor of the *Macon People's Choice* urged blacks to back Governor Northen because of his opposition to mob violence. Bishop Henry McNeal Turner also praised Northen. *AJ*, Dec. 23, 1893.

14. *AC*, Aug. 21, 1899, May 18–21, 1902; Charles Crowe, "Racial Massacre in Atlanta, September 22, 1906," *Journal of Negro History* 54 (April 1969): 150–73; John Dittmer, *Black Georgia in the Progressive Era, 1900–1920* (Urbana: University of Illinois Press, 1977), 123–31.

15. John W. Cell, *The Highest Stage of White Supremacy: The Origins of Segregation in South Africa and the American South* (New York: Cambridge University Press, 1982), 123. Both presidents McKinley and Roosevelt angered southern whites by appointing blacks to choice patronage positions in the South. See *AIJ*, Sept. 6–20, 1897, and Feb. 4, 1898; and Clarence A. Bacote, "Negro Officeholders in Georgia under President McKinley," *Journal of Negro History* 44 (1959): 230–33. For a discussion of the racial tensions during the Spanish-American War, see Willard B. Gatewood, Jr., *Black Americans and the White Man's Burden, 1898–1903* (Urbana: University of Illinois Press, 1975), 139–44.

16. Quoted in C. Vann Woodward, *Tom Watson: Agrarian Rebel* (New York: Oxford University Press, 1978), 228.

17. *AC,* Oct. 3, 1896; Shaw, *The Wool Hat Boys,* 156.

18. Williamson, *Crucible of Race,* 108–39.

19. George M. Frederickson, *The Arrogance of Race: Historical Perspectives on Slavery, Racism, and Social Inequality* (Middletown, Conn.: Wesleyan University Press, 1988), 176.

20. Leonidas F. Scott to Rebecca Lattimer Felton, May 30, 1894, Felton Papers, University of Georgia Library.

21. *AJ,* Aug. 12, 1897; *AC,* April 23, 1899; John E. Talmadge, *Rebecca Lattimer Felton: Nine Stormy Decades* (Athens: University of Georgia Press, 1960), 113–18.

22. *AJ,* Aug. 12, 1897.

23. *AC,* Nov. 2, 1902. For other examples of Arp's praise for lynching, see issues of July 16, 1893, July 4, 1897, May 20, 1900, and Dec. 1, 1901. See also, David B. Parker, "Bill Arp and Blacks: The Forgotten Letters," *Georgia Historical Quarterly* 67 (Fall 1983): 336–49; and David B. Parker, *Alias Bill Arp: Charles Henry Smith and the South's "Goodly Heritage"* (Athens: Uiversity of Georgia Press, 1991), passim.

24. Wilbur Cash, *The Mind of the South* (New York: Knopf, 1941), 93–94. For a corrective of Cash's overdrawn argument, see Mark K. Bauman, "Race and Mastery: The Debate of 1903," in *From the Old South to the New: Essays on the Transitional South,* ed. Walter J. Fraser, Jr., and Winfred B. Moore, Jr. (Westport, Conn.: Greenwood Press, 1981), 181–94.

25. *AC,* Dec. 19, 22, 1898; Henry Y. Warnock, "Andrew Sledd, Southern Methodists, and the Negro: A Case History," *Journal of Southern History* 31 (Aug. 1965): 251–71; Talmadge, *Rebecca Lattimer Felton,* 113–25.

26. *Crawfordville Advocate-Democrat,* Aug. 28, 1903. See also, *AN,* Sept. 14, 15, 1903. For similar opinions, see Charles D. Toney to *AN,* Sept. 12, 1903; and Thomas D. Clark, *The Southern Country Editor* (New York: Bobbs-Merrill, 1948), chapter 14.

27. Bartley, *The Creation of Modern Georgia,* 110–26; Don H. Doyle, *New Men, New Cities, New South: Atlanta, Nashville, Charleston, Mobile, 1860–1910* (Chapel Hill: University of North Carolina Press, 1990), esp. chapters 8, 10; and Steven W. Wrigley, "The Triumph of Provincialism: Public Life in Georgia, 1898–1917," Ph.D. diss., Northwestern University, 1986, passim.

28. For examples, see *AC,* Nov. 10, 1894, Nov. 6, 1895, July 23, 1897, Jan. 8, 1900, and Sept. 9, 1903; *MT,* July 24, 1897 and March 19, 1901; and *SMN,* Nov. 25, 1895.

29. *AC,* Oct. 13, Nov. 1, 1904. Following a lynching in September 1904, in Huntsville, Alabama, federal indictments were brought against several mob members for burning the jail and threatening the lives of prisoners. Two years later, the sheriff of Hamilton County, Tennessee, and five other Chattanoogans were ruled in contempt of court for failing to protect the life of a black who had appealed to the Supreme Court. See File no. 41710, 77461, Department of Justice, Record Group 60, National Archives; Mary Frances Berry, *Black Resistance, White Law: A History of Constitutional Racism in America* (New York:

Appleton-Century-Crofts, 1971), 126–27; Pete Daniel, *The Shadow of Slavery: Peonage in the South, 1901–1969* (Urbana: University of Illinois Press, 1972), chapters 2–4; and Lester C. Lamon, *Black Tennesseans, 1900–1930* (Knoxville: University of Tennessee Press, 1977), 10, 232.

30. *Augusta Chronicle,* May 14–June 4, 1900.

31. *Special Message of the Governor of Georgia on Enforcement of Law* (Atlanta, 1895), 2–5; *Georgia Senate Journal, 1895,* 35–37; *Georgia Senate Journal, 1896,* 19–22; *Georgia Senate Journal, 1897,* 27–39; *Georgia Senate Journal, 1898,* 39; Shaw, *Wool Hat Boys,* 137.

32. *AN,* Aug. 14, 1903; *MT,* Aug. 19, 1904; *AC,* Oct. 17, 1904.

33. See chapter 8 (201, 211–15) for a discussion of the responses to the Atlanta race riot and the Christian League in Atlanta.

34. Typescript, [1907?], Northen Papers, GDAH. Northen's scrapbooks contain numerous clippings from county weeklies and urban dailies, chronicling and commenting on his campaign.

35. *AC,* Jan. 4, 1907; Henry Hugh Proctor, "The Atlanta Race Riot: Fundamental Causes and Reactionary Results," *Southern Workman* 36 (Aug. 1907): 425–26; Henry Hugh Proctor, "A Southerner of the New School: William J. Northen," *Southern Workman* 42 (July 1913): 403–4; Matthews, "Studies in Race Relations," 354–56.

36. For Governor Candler's protests, see *AJ,* April 24, 1899; and *Augusta Chronicle,* April 24, 1899. For examples of Georgians who mistook Northen's position on lynching, see *Sparta Ishmaelite* clipping, Scrapbook 3; John Hall to W. J. Northen, May 23, 1899; and Clyde Givens to W. J. Northen, May 29, 1899, both in Northen Papers, GDHA.

37. See *Augusta Chronicle,* Aug. 1, 1902; *SP,* Aug. 20, 1904; *AC,* Aug. 24, 1904.

38. See *Message of Governor Allen D. Candler to the General Assembly, October 25, 1899,* 6–10; *Message of Governor Joseph M. Brown to the General Assembly, June 28, 1911,* 3–7; and Wrigley, "The Triumph of Provincialism," 42–45. One example of the attacks on governors by defenders of lynching occurred in 1899, when Governor Allen D. Candler remarked that mob members were as guilty as black rapists in the eyes of God. Dr. William H. Felton, Rebecca Lattimer Felton's husband, denounced the governor and his unwarranted attack on white men. See William H. Felton to Editor of *AC,* Aug. 2, 1899, Felton Papers, University of Georgia Library.

39. *AC,* Aug. 16–31, 1904; *SMN,* Aug. 16–20, 1904; Charlton Moseley and Frederick Brogdon, "A Lynching at Statesboro: The Story of Paul Reed and Will Cato," *Georgia Historical Quarterly* 65 (Summer 1981): 104–18.

40. *SMN,* Aug. 15, 1904; *SP,* Aug. 18, 19, Sept. 15, 17, 1904; *AC,* Aug. 25, 1904; *MT,* Sept. 21, 1904. The Statesboro incident is described in *AC,* Sept.–Dec. 1904, and *SMN,* Sept.–Dec. 1904.

41. *Gwinnett News-Herald* (Lawrenceville), Oct. 5–8, 1897; *AC,* April 22, 1902. The sheriff of Carroll County attracted national attention by opening fire on a mob that attacked the county jail in June 1901. When his brave stand later led to his defeat for reelection,

President Theodore Roosevelt gave him a federal job. See *AJ*, June 8–9, 1901; *NYT*, June 8, 1901, Dec. 20, 1906.

42. *AJ*, April 24 1899; *AC*, April 25 1899.

43. For examples of blacks lynched for criticizing lynching and "wild talk" leading to violence against blacks, see *ST*, Aug. 20, 1892; *MT*, June 28, 29, 1908; *AC*, June 28, 29, 1908; *Waycross Herald*, July 4, 11, 1908; *AC*, April 27, 1912; *MT*, April 27, 1912; *ST*, May 4, 1912; *Monroe Advertiser* (Forsyth), May 3, 1912; and N. B. Young to Dr. W. E. B. Du Bois, Nov. 14, 1916, Group I, series C, box C-336, General Lynching File, Oct.–Nov. 1916, NAACP Papers, LC.

44. Whites argued that black fraternal organizations were centers of subversive activities and should be banned. In 1907, a bill to eliminate black fraternal organizations narrowly failed to pass the legislature. See Charles A. Bacote, "Some Aspects of Negro Life in Georgia, 1880–1908," *Journal of Negro History* 43 (July 1958): 186–213.

45. *SMN*, Aug. 30, 1904; *CES*, Dec. 15, 1910; *Montgomery Advertiser*, Aug. 27, 28, 1913; *AC*, May 19–28, 1918; NAACP Memo, "Memorandum for Governor Dorsey from Walter F. White," July 10, 1918, and "Memo from Walter White, Nov. 12, 1918," both in Group I, series C, box C-353, Brooks County File, NAACP Files, LC; Ray Stannard Baker, *Following the Color Line* (New York: Doubleday, Page, 1908), 188–89; James R. Grossman, *Land of Hope: Chicago, Black Southerners, and the Great Migration* (Chicago: University of Chicago Press, 1989), 16–18.

46. *Augusta Chronicle*, June 3–5, 1900, Sept. 22–29, 1906; *AC*, Sept. 26, 1906; Dittmer, *Black Georgia in the Progressive Era*, 164–65; "Why Mr. Barber Left Atlanta," *Voice of the Negro* 3 (Nov. 1906): 470–72; Penelope L. Bullock, *The Afro-American Periodical Press, 1838–1909* (Baton Rouge: Louisiana State University Press, 1981), 118–34.

47. *Americus Times-Recorder*, Feb. 1, 1912.

8   Opposition to Lynching in Georgia, 1910–1930

1. Ray Stannard Baker, *Following the Color Line* (New York: Doubleday, Page, 1908), 271.

2. Dewey W. Grantham, *Southern Progressivism: The Reconciliation of Progress and Tradition* (Knoxville: University of Tennessee Press, 1983), esp. chapter 1; Joel Williamson, *The Crucible of Race: Black-White Relations in the American South Since Emancipation* (New York: Oxford University Press, 1984), chapter 15; C. Vann Woodward, *Origins of the New South, 1877–1913* (Baton Rouge: Louisiana State University Press, 1951), chapters 14–15.

3. Numan V. Bartley, *The Creation of Modern Georgia* (Athens: University of Georgia Press, 1983), 112; George M. Frederickson, *The Arrogance of Race: Historical Perspectives on Slavery, Racism, and Social Inequality* (Middletown, Conn.: Wesleyan University Press, 1988), 180; David R. Goldfield, *Cotton Fields and Skyscrapers: Southern City*

and Region, 1607–1980 (Baton Rouge: Louisiana State University Press, 1982), 101–03; Howard L. Preston, *Automobile Age Atlanta: The Making of a Southern Metropolis, 1900–1935* (Athens: University of Georgia Press, 1979), esp. chapter 4.

4. Oscar Handlin, "The Social System," in *The Future Metropolis*, ed. Lloyd Rodwin (New York: G. Braziller, 1961), 22.

5. Blaine A. Brownell, *The Urban Ethos in the South, 1920–1930* (Baton Rouge: Louisiana State University Press, 1975), 47. The contradictory consequences of modernization are traced in James C. Cobb, *Industrialization and Southern Society, 1877–1984* (Lexington: University Press of Kentucky, 1984); Winfred B. Moore, Jr. et al., eds., *Developing Dixie: Modernization in a Traditional Society* (Westport, Conn.: Greenwood Press, 1988); and Daniel Joseph Singal, *The War Within: From Victorian to Modernist Thought in the South, 1919–1945* (Chapel Hill: University of North Carolina Press, 1982).

6. Bartley, *The Creation of Modern Georgia*, 110–26, 154–55; Brownell, *Urban Ethos in the South*, chapter 2; Grantham, *Southern Progressivism*, 5–9.

7. William Preston Few, "Southern Public Opinion," *South Atlantic Quarterly* 4 (Jan. 1905): 5.

8. *AC*, Sept. 26, 1906; *AJ*, Sept. 26, 1906; Baker, *Following the Color Line*, 15–16.

9. *AC*, Sept. 26-Oct. 6, 1906; "Results in Atlanta," *Independent* 20 (Dec. 1906): 51–52; Alexander J. McKelway, "The Atlanta Race Riots I.—A Southern White Point of View," *Outlook*, Nov. 3, 1906, 557–62; Booker T. Washington, "Golden Rule in Atlanta," *Outlook*, Dec. 15, 1906, 913–16. See also, Charles Crowe, "Racial Violence and Social Reform—Origins of the Atlanta Race Riot of 1906," *Journal of Negro History* 53 (July 1968): 234–56; and Ralph E. Luker, *The Social Gospel in Black and White: American Racial Reform, 1885–1912* (Chapel Hill: University of North Carolina Press, 1991), 187–90.

10. John E. White, "The Need of a Southern Program on the Negro Problem," *South Atlantic Quarterly* 6 (April 1907): 186.

11. Henry Hugh Proctor to Booker T. Washington, Oct. 1, 1906, in *Booker T. Washington Papers*, ed. Louis R. Harlan and Raymond W. Smock (Urbana: University of Illinois Press, 1980), 9:83–84; Baker, *Following the Color Line*, 20–21; Louis R. Harlan, *Booker T. Washington: The Wizard of Tuskegee, 1901–1915* (New York: Oxford University Press, 1983), 300–301. For background on the members of the upper-class black community in Atlanta that participated in the meetings, see August Meier and David Lewis, "History of the Negro Upper Class in Atlanta, Georgia, 1890–1958," *Journal of Negro Education* 28 (Spring 1959): 128–39.

12. Booker T. Washington to Wallace Buttrick, Sept. 30, 1906, in *Booker T. Washington Papers*, ed. Harlan and Smock, 9:78–80.

13. Baker, *Following the Color Line*, 20–21. For background on the Atlanta police force before the riot, see Eugene J. Watts, "The Police of Atlanta, 1890–1905," *Journal of Southern History* 39 (May 1973): 165–82.

14. *Atlanta Independent*, Jan. 19, 1907; "Results in Atlanta," *Independent*, Jan. 3, 1907, 51; "For Law and Order," *Independent*, July 11, 1907, 106–7; Baker, *Following the Color*

Line, 21; Anne E. S. Beard, "Solving the Race Problem in Atlanta," *World Today* 12 (Feb. 1907): 214–15; Henry Hugh Proctor, "The Atlanta Race Riot: Fundamental Causes and Reactionary Results," *Southern Workman* 36 (Aug. 1907): 425–26. See also, Thomas M. Deaton, "Atlanta during the Progressive Era," Ph.D. diss., University of Georgia, 1969, 200–201.

15. Baker, *Following the Color Line,* 24–25; Harlan, *Booker T. Washington,* 301–2. Excerpts of Washington's Atlanta Address can be found in *Booker T. Washington Papers,* ed. Harlan and Smock, 9:158–61.

16. Booker T. Washington, "The Golden Rule in Atlanta," *Outlook,* Dec. 15, 1906, 913.

17. Franklin Clarkin to Oswald Garrison Villard, Dec. 10, 1906, quoted in Harlan, *Booker T. Washington,* 304.

18. W. E. B. Du Bois, "Tragedy of Atlanta," *World Today* 11 (Oct. 1906): 1173–75; John Dittmer, *Black Georgia in the Progressive Era, 1900–1920* (Urbana: University of Illinois Press, 1977), 172; Herbert Shapiro, *White Violence and Black Response: From Reconstruction to Montgomery* (Amherst: University of Massachusetts Press, 1988), 129–30.

19. Quoted in Baker, *Following the Color Line,* 21.

20. Grantham, *Southern Progressivism,* 28–32; Singal, *The War Within,* esp. chapter 5.

21. For accounts of some of the educational innovations, see G. R. Mathis, "Walter B. Hill, Chancellor, the University of Georgia, 1899–1905," Ph.D. diss., University of Georgia, 1967, and Thomas G. Dyer, *The University of Georgia: A Bicentennial History, 1785–1985* (Athens: University of Georgia Press, 1985), chapter 7. On new campus attitudes toward race relations, see "The Phelps-Stokes Lectures," *Southern Workman* 42 (Feb. 1913): 65–66; and John J. Culley, "Muted Trumpets: Four Efforts to Better Southern Race Relations, 1900–1919," Ph.D. diss., University of Virginia, 1967, 194–95. Staunch conservatives in the Methodist church did attack the Candler School of Theology at Emory for its "liberalism," but such charges were easily dismissed by Bishop Candler, an archconservative who lacked any trait that might have been mistaken for tolerance. On the sedate atmosphere at Emory, see Thomas H. English, *Emory University, 1915–1965: A Semicentenial History* (Atlanta: Emory University, 1966), 8–32, 139; and John Herbert Roper, *C. Vann Woodward, Southerner* (Athens: University of Georgia Press, 1987), 32–38.

22. Ray Stannard Baker, "Gathering Clouds Along the Color Line," *World's Work* 32 (June 1916): 235.

23. E. Charles Chatfield, "The Southern Sociological Congress: Organization for Uplift," *Tennessee Historical Quarterly* 19 (Dec. 1960): 329–33; Paul K. Conkin, *Gone with the Ivy: A Biography of Vanderbilt University* (Knoxville: University of Tennessee Press, 1985), chapters 8–9; Don H. Doyle, *Nashville in the New South, 1880–1930* (Knoxville: University of Tennessee Press, 1985), chapter 7; Wilma Dykeman, *Prophet of Plenty: The First Ninety Years of W. D. Weatherford* (Knoxville: University of Tennessee Press, 1966), 72–78.

24. James E. McCulloch, *The Call of the New South* (Nashville: Southern Sociologi-

cal Conference, 1912); James E. McCulloch, *The South Mobilizing for Social Service* (Nashville: Southern Sociological Conference, 1913), passim; "The Southern Sociological Congress," *Southern Workman* 42 (June 1913): 323; Philip Weltner, "Southern Sociological Congress," *Survey,* May 17, 1913, 244; "Resolution on Lynching" and "Program of the Southern Sociological Congress for the Improvement of Race Relations," both in *Distinguished Service Citizenship,* ed. James E. McCulloch (Washington D.C.: Southern Sociological Congress, 1919), 106, 107–8. See also, Culley, "Muted Trumpets," 124–25.

25. "The University Commission on Race Relations," *Southern Workman* 42 (March 1913): 131; Luther J. Bernard, "The Southern Sociological Congress," *American Journal of Sociology* 19 (July 1913): 92; Chatfield, "The Southern Sociological Congress: Organization of Uplift," 328–47; E. Charles Chatfield, "The Southern Sociological Congress: Rationale of Uplift," *Tennessee Historical Quarterly* 20 (March 1961): 51–64; Culley, "Muted Trumpets," chapters 4–6.

26. "Lynching," *Five Letters of the University Commission on Southern Race Questions,* Occasional Papers of the John F. Slater Fund, no. 24 (n.p.: Trustees of the John F. Slater Fund, 1927), 5–7.

27. Josiah Morse, "The University Commission on Southern Race Relations," *South Atlantic Quarterly* 19 (Oct. 1920): 310; Culley, "Muted Trumpets," 137–68; Howard W. Odum, *Southern Regions* (Chapel Hill: University of North Carolina Press, 1936), 137.

28. Timothy L. Smith, *Revivalism and Social Reform in the Mid-Nineteenth Century* (New York: Abingdon Press, 1957), 8.

29. Wayne Flynt, "Dissent in Zion: Alabama Baptists and Social Issues, 1900–1914," *Journal of Social History* 35 (Nov. 1969): 539. See also, John O. Fish, "Southern Methodism and Accommodation of the Negro, 1902–1915," *Journal of Negro History* 55 (July 1970): 200–214, and Luker, *The Social Gospel in Black and White,* passim. On the conservatism of southern churches, see Samuel S. Hill, Jr., "South's Two Cultures," in *Religion and the Solid South,* ed. Hill (Nashville: Abingdon Press, 1972), 24–56; Kenneth K. Bailey, *Southern White Protestantism in the Twentieth Century* (New York: Harper and Row, 1964), passim; Rufus B. Spain, *At Ease in Zion: Social History of Southern Baptists, 1865–1900* (Nashville: Vanderbilt University Press, 1967), 213–14; and John L. Eighmy, *Churches in Captivity: A History of Social Attitudes of Southern Baptists* (Knoxville: University of Tennessee Press, 1987), esp. chapters 4–5.

30. Anne Firor Scott, *Making the Invisible Woman Visible* (Urbana: University of Illinois Press, 1984), 201–2; Jacquelyn Dowd Hall, *Revolt against Chivalry: Jesse Daniel Ames and the Women's Campaign Against Lynching* (New York: Columbia University Press, 1979), 73–74; John P. McDowell, *The Social Gospel Movement in the South: The Woman's Home Mission Movement in the Methodist Episcopal Church, South, 1886–1939* (Baton Rouge: Louisiana State University Press, 1982), passim.

31. Lily H. Hammond, *In Black and White: An Interpretation of Southern Life* (New York: Fleming H. Revell, 1914). See also, Culley, "Muted Trumpets," 211–23; Henry Y.

Warnock, "Moderate Racial Thought and the Attitudes of Southern Baptists and Methodists, 1900–1921," Ph.D. diss., Northwestern University, 1963, 69–73, 107, 207–8.

32. John E. White, "The True and the False in Southern Life," *South Atlantic Quarterly* 5 (April 1906): 97–113; White, "The Need of a Southern Program on the Negro Problem"; John E. White, "Securing Negro Advancement in the South," *Southern Workman* 39 (April 1910): 233–37; John E. White, "Thinking White Down South," *Southern Workman* 45 (Jan. 1916): 57–62; John E. White, "The Next Move for Southern Baptists in Education," *Baptist Education Bulletin* 2 (Sept. 1920): 9–13. On White's thought, see Warnock, "Moderate Racial Thought and the Attitudes of Southern Baptists and Methodists," 65–68, 86, 103, 110, 116, 267.

33. Peter W. Agnew, "The Social Vision of Atlanta's Baptist Leaders, 1918–1928," Ph.D. diss., Emory University, 1978, 87; Joseph H. Cosby, *Virginia Baptist Ministers, 1935–1950* (n.p.: Virginia Baptist Historical Society, 1977); Wilma Dykeman and James Stokely, *Seeds of Southern Change: The Life of Will Alexander* (Chicago: University of Chicago Press, 1962), 63; *Leigh Street Baptist Church, 1854–1954: A Brief History of Its First One Hundred Years in the Service of Christ* (Richmond: Whittet and Shepperson, 1954), 45–48; *Virginia Baptist Annual, 1904* (Petersburg: n.p., 1904), 59–63.

34. M. Ashby Jones, "Counting the Cost," *Southern Workman* 49 (Jan. 1920): 12–14; M. Ashby Jones, "The Approach to the South's Race Question," *Journal of Social Forces* 1 (Nov. 1922): 40–41; M. Ashby Jones, "The Negro and the South," *Virginia Quarterly Review* 3 (Jan. 1927): 1–12. Following a particularly savage lynching in Athens, Jones wrote a stinging letter of protest to *AC* (Feb. 27, 1921). For brief discussions of Jones, see Agnew, "The Social Vision of Atlanta's Baptist Ministers," 87–88; Morton Sosna, *In Search of the Silent South: Southern Liberals and the Race Issue* (New York: Columbia University Press, 1977), 28–29; and Warnock, "Moderate Racial Thought and the Attitudes of Southern Baptists and Methodists," 76, 267.

35. Katherine DuPre Lumpkin, quoted in Frances S. Taylor, " 'On the Edge of Tomorrow': Southern Women, the Student YWCA, and Race, 1920–1944," Ph.D. diss., Stanford University, 1984, 65 (Augusta Roberts quoted on 200). On the YMCA and race relations before World War I, see Dykeman, *Prophet of Plenty*, chapters 12–13; Grantham, *Southern Progressivism*, 236; and Hall, *Revolt against Chivalry*, 82–86.

36. Hammond, *In Black and White*, 210. See also, Willis D. Weatherford, *Negro Life in the South: Present Conditions and Needs* (New York: Young Men's Christian Association, 1910); Willis D. Weatherford, *Present Forces in Negro Progress* (New York: Young Men's Christian Association, 1912); Willis D. Weatherford, "Race Relationship in the South," *Annals of the American Academy of Political and Social Science* 49 (Sept. 1913): 164–72; and Dykeman and Stokely, *Seeds of Southern Change*, passim.

37. John M. Matthews, "The Georgia 'Race Strike' of 1909," *Journal of Southern History* 40 (Nov. 1974): 613–30; Woodward, *Origins of the New South*, 416–23.

38. Bartley, *The Creation of Modern Georgia*, 166.

39. William M. Gabard, "Joseph Mackey Brown: A Study in Conservatism," Ph.D. diss., Tulane University, 1963, 131, 136, 144–45, 216–20.

40. Victor H. Kreigshaber, quoted in Charles Garofalo, "The Atlanta Spirit: A Study of Urban Ideology," *South Atlantic Quarterly* 74 (Winter 1974): 35.

41. Quoted in Garofalo, "The Atlanta Spirit," 38–39. On the Atlanta Spirit, see Brownell, *Urban Ethos in the South,* 137–38; and George B. Tindall, *The Emergence of the New South, 1913–1945* (Baton Rouge: Louisiana State University Press, 1967), chapter 3.

42. Garofalo, "The Atlanta Spirit," 39–40; Charles Garofalo, "The Sons of Henry Grady: Atlanta Boosters in the 1920s," *Journal of Southern History* 42 (May 1976): 200; Helen B. Pendleton, "Hiking while They Pray," *Survey,* Feb. 15, 1924, 515–16.

43. *Dublin Courier Herald,* undated clipping [Aug. 1919?], Group I, series C, box C-354, Dublin File, NAACP Papers, LC; *Eastman Times-Journal,* Aug. 21, 28, Sept. 4, Oct. 30, 1919; *AC,* Aug. 28, Oct. 19, 1919; *NYT,* Aug. 29, 1919; *CD,* Sept. 6, 1919; *Butler Herald,* Oct. 23, 1919; *MT,* Aug. 5, 1922; *Athens News,* April 21, 1922; *Worth County Local* (Sylvester), Feb. 11, 1916. For other examples, see *Eastman Times-Journal,* Sept. 4, 1919; *Worth County Local,* Dec. 10, 1920; *Rome Herald,* July 6, 1921; *Winder News,* Dec. 14, 21, 1922; and *Milledgeville Union-Recorder,* Oct. 1, 1925.

44. The extent to which the attitudes of the Atlanta business community were suffused with heavy doses of racism and paternalism is made clear in Charles P. Garofalo, "Business Ideas in Atlanta, 1916–1935," Ph.D. diss., Emory University, 1972, 104–12. For a portrait of boosterism and race relations in general, see Brownell, *Urban Ethos in the South,* passim.

45. *MT,* Sept. 21, 1916.

46. Leonard Dinnerstein, *The Leo Frank Case* (New York: Columbia University Press, 1968).

47. *Outlook,* Aug. 25, 1915, 946; "Lynching and Illiteracy," *World's Work,* Oct. 1915, 637; *AC,* Jan. 23, 1916. See also, *Independent,* Aug. 30, 1915, 280–81; *Literary Digest,* Feb. 5, 1916, 274; *MT,* Jan. 22, 1916, and *SMN,* Jan. 30, 1916. The editorial tone also reflected the concern of Georgia's elite over the "populism" unleashed by the Frank affair. See Nancy MacLean, "The Leo Frank Case Reconsidered: Gender and Sexual Politics in the Making of Reactionary Populism," *Journal of American History* 78 (Dec. 1991): 917–48.

48. *Athens Banner,* Feb. 21, 1921; *AC,* May 6, Aug. 1–8, 1916, Jan. 17, 1917, July 25, 1921, July 30, 1925; *Atlanta Georgian,* Jan. 8, 1923; *Augusta Chronicle,* Feb. 18–20, 1921; *SMN,* Jan. 26, Feb. 18, 1922.

49. Quoted in *ST,* March 8, 1902.

50. *MT,* Feb. 14, 15, 1906; *ST,* Feb. 24, 1906, Jan. 26, 1907; *New York Age,* Feb. 22, 1906; *Voice of the Negro* 3 (March 1906): 163–66, 175–77; *Atlanta Independent,* Feb. 8, 1908; F. R. Torrence, *The Story of John Hope* (New York: Macmillan, 1948), 134–35.

51. Dittmer, *Black Georgia in the Progressive Era,* 174–75; Charles Flint Kellogg,

NAACP: A History 1909–1920 (Baltimore: Johns Hopkins University Press, 1967), 215, 245–46; Shapiro, *White Violence and Black Response*, 142–44.

52. W. E. B. Du Bois, ed., *Efforts for Social Betterment among Negro Americans* (Atlanta University Publications, no. 14 (Atlanta, 1910), 81–96, 126–27; Dittmer, *Black Georgia in the Progressive Era*, 62–63; Linda O. Hines and Allen W. Jones, "A Voice of Black Protest: The Savannah Men's Sunday Club, 1905–1911," *Phylon* 35 (June 1974): 193–202; Linda O. McMurry, *Recorder of the Black Experience: A Biography of Monroe Nathan Work* (Baton Rouge: Louisiana State University Press, 1985), chapter 2.

53. Tulia Hamilton, "The National Association of Colored Women, 1890–1920," Ph.D. diss., Emory University, 1978, passim; Maude Thomas Jenkins, "The History of the Black Woman's Club Movement in America," Ed.D. diss., Columbia University Teachers College, 1984, 80–94; Matthews, "Studies in Race Relations in Georgia," 266–69; Cynthia Neverdon-Morton, *Afro-American Women of the South and the Advancement of the Race, 1895–1925* (Knoxville: University of Tennessee Press, 1989), 139–63; Jacqueline Anne Rouse, *Lugenia Burns Hope: Black Southern Reformer* (Athens: University of Georgia Press, 1989), chapter 4; Jacqueline Anne Rouse, "Atlanta's African-American Women's Attack on Segregation, 1900–1920," and Rosalyn Terborg-Penn, "African American Women's Networks in the Anti-Lynching Crusade," both in *Gender, Class, Race, and Reform in the Progressive Era*, ed. Noralee Frankel and Nancy S. Dye (Lexington: University Press of Kentucky, 1991), 10–23, 148–61.

54. Quoted in Dittmer, *Black Georgia in the Progressive Era*, 174.

55. Tindall, *Emergence of the New South*, 53.

56. Dittmer, *Black Georgia in the Progressive Era*, 203–5.

57. William Cohen, "The Great Migration as a Lever for Social Change," in *Black Exodus: The Great Migration from the American South*, ed. Alferdteen Harrison (Jackson: University Press of Mississippi, 1991), 72–82; Matthews, "Studies in Race Relations in Georgia," 247–50; Tindall, *Emergence of the New South*, chapter 3.

58. Charles S. Johnson, "How Much of the Migration Was a Flight from Persecution," *Opportunity* 1 (Sept. 1923): 272.

59. Quotes in James R. Grossman, *Land of Hope: Chicago, Black Southerners, and the Great Migration* (Chicago: University of Chicago Press, 1989), 3, 17. See also, Carole Marks, *Farewell—We're Good and Gone: The Great Black Migration* (Bloomington: Indiana University Press, 1989), esp. chapter 2; and Peter Gottlieb, *Making Their Own Way: Southern Blacks' Migration to Pittsburgh, 1916–30* (Urbana: University of Illinois Press, 1987), chapters 1–2.

60. Stewart E. Tolnay and E. M. Beck, "Black Flight: Lethal Violence and the Great Migration, 1900–1930," *Social Science History* 14 (Fall 1990): 347–70; Stewart E. Tolnay and E. M. Beck, "Rethinking the Role of Racial Violence in the Great Migration," in *Black Exodus: The Great Migration from the American South*, ed. Alferdteen Harrison (Jackson: University Press of Mississippi, 1991), 20–35.

61. Dittmer, *Black Georgia in the Progressive Era,* 188–91; and Matthews, "Studies in Race Relations," 247–51.

62. Gavin Wright, *Old South, New South: Revolutions in the Southern Economy since the Civil War* (New York: Basic Books, 1986), 54, 56.

63. Grossman, *Land of Hope,* 41.

64. *Negro Migration in 1916–1917,* U.S. Department of Labor, Division of Negro Economics (Washington D.C.: U. S. Government Printing Office, 1919), 32.

65. Jack Temple Kirby, "Black and White in the Rural South, 1915–1954," *Agricultural History* 58 (July 1984): 421. See also, Matthews, "Studies in Race Relations," 256–57. For a nuanced discussion of the Great Migration and Mississippi, see Neil R. McMillen, *Dark Journey: Black Mississippians in the Age of Jim Crow* (Urbana: University of Illinois Press, 1989), chapter 8.

66. Minutes of Annual Meeting of the NAACP, Jan. 6, 1919, 13–14, Group I, series A, box A-1; and Georgia Branch File Records, Group I, series G, boxes G-43–46, both in NAACP Papers, LC; *Crisis* 20 (May 1920): 39; *Crisis* 21 (Dec. 1920): 68; James Weldon Johnson, *Along the Way: The Autobiography of James Weldon Johnson* (New York: Viking, 1933), 315–16; Kellogg, *NAACP: A History,* 215, 245–46; Shapiro, *White Violence and Black Response,* 142–44; Edgar A. Toppin, "Walter White and the Atlanta NAACP's Fight for Equal Schools, 1916–1917," *History of Education Quarterly* 7 (Spring 1967): 3–21; Walter White, *A Man Called White: The Autobiography of Walter White* (New York: Viking Press, 1933), 28–38.

67. See Augusta Branch Files, Group I, series G, box G-45, NAACP Papers, LC.

68. George A. Towns to John A. Shillady, May 22, 1919, Group I, series C, box C-354; and Minutes of the Board of Directors, Jan. 14, 1924, 1–2, both in Group I, series A, box A-9, NAACP Papers, LC; Paul D. Bolster, "Civil Rights Movements in Twentieth Century Georgia," Ph.D. diss., University of Georgia, 1972, 32–34, 61–65; Matthews, "Studies in Race Relations," 366–70.

69. See Atlanta Branch Files, Group I, series G, box G-43; Rome Branch Files, Group I, series G, box G-46; and Savannah Branch Files, Group I, series G, box G-46, all in NAACP Papers, LC.

70. For a detailed account of the NAACP's national campaign against lynching, see Robert L. Zangrando, *The NAACP Crusade against Lynching* (Philadelphia: Temple University Press, 1980).

71. "Memo from Walter F. White to John R. Shillady," undated [Nov. 1919?], Quitman File, Group I, series C, box C-355; "Memorandum for Mr. Dam RE Georgia Lynchings," Nov. 19, 1918, Quitman File, Group I, series C, box C-355; and Athens N. Grant to Walter White, Nov. 20, 1918, Quitman File, Group I, series C, box C-355, all in NAACP Papers, LC. In another case, A. L. McDonald, editor of the *Albany Supreme Circle News,* the newspaper of the black fraternal organization, and a member of the Albany branch, alerted the national office of the NAACP of the particularly brutal treatment of a family

of tenant farmers in Worth County. McDonald helped the victims initiate an unsuccessful criminal suit against their landlord. See Worth County, 1920 File, Group I, series C, box C-355, NAACP Papers, LC.

72. For two particularly plaintive letters from rural blacks to the president, see Emma Murry to Mr. McKinley, Oct. 6, 1899, Record Group 60, #17743-1898, 237–38; and L. Keleogg [sic] to Pres. Wm. McKenley [sic], July 12, 1900, Record Group 60, #17743-1898, 73–75, both in Department of Justice Papers, National Archives.

For just a few examples—all from the NAACP Papers, LC—from Georgia of accounts of mob lawlessness by blacks, see N. B. Young to W. E. B. Du Bois, Nov. 14, 1916, Group I, series C, box C-336, General Lynching File, Oct.–Nov. 1916; H. H. Thweat to Walter F. White, Oct. 26, 1918, Group I, series C, box C-354, Millen File; Unsigned to NAACP, Nov. 19, 1919, Group I, series C, box C-338, General Lynching File, Nov. 1919; H. S. Martin to John A. Shillady, Feb. 23, 1920, Group I, series C, box C-338, General Lynching File, Feb. 1920; A. L. McDonald to John A. Shillady, April 30, 1920, Group I, series C, box C-355, Worth County File; C. P. Waddell to James W. Johnson, April 27, 1921, Group I, series C, box C-353, General Georgia Lynching File, 1919–22; and "A Friend" to N.A.A.C.P., July 14, 1921, Group I, series C, box C-353, General Georgia Lynching File, 1919–22. In some cases, descriptions of lynchings by blacks were published verbatim in *Crisis*. For example, see letter from "Oblige" to N.A.A.C.P., Aug. 11, 1919, Group I, series C, box C-354, Dublin File, NAACP Papers, LC; and "The End of Jim Waters," *Crisis* 20 (Aug. 1920): 183–84.

73. Rev. Judson Dinkins to the Tuskegee Institute, May 26, 1919, reel 221, Microfilm Tuskegee Lynching Records; "A Lynching Uncovered," Group I, series C, box C-354, Milan File, NAACP Papers, LC.

74. *AC,* July 25, 29, Aug. 27, Sept. 7, 1919; *MT,* Aug. 11, 1919; *Eastman Times-Journal,* May 29, Sept. 11, Oct. 30, 1919.

75. See correspondence in Group I, series C, box C-355, "Wayne County—1921–22," NAACP Papers, LC.

76. James W. Johnson to Harry E. Davis, July 5, 1922; Walter F. White to Marion E. Anther, July 5, 1922; L. E. Williams to John E. Nail, July 21, 1922; and "The Petition of Joe Jordan & James Harvey," undated [June 1922?], all in Group I, series C, box C-355, Wayne County File, NAACP Papers, LC.

77. *SP,* July 1, 4, 1922, Feb. 24, 1923; *SMN,* July 2, 4, 1922; *NYT,* July 14, 1922; *CD,* July 15, 1922; Report of the Secretary, July 8, 1922, July 31, 1922, Group I, series A, box A-15, NAACP Papers, LC.

78. After the NAACP investigated a lynching in neighboring Dodge County in 1919, the *Dublin Courier Herald* erupted furiously: "The best thing. . . [the NAACP] can do for the betterment of negroes of the country is to shut its filthy mouthpiece and organs of racial equality and die in a grave filled with hog slops. . . . If the nigger lovers want to make an official investigation of the affair let them send Shillady [the NAACP president] or some

other representative to this county, and, . . . we will venture that the investigator will reach Hell before his scheduled time" (undated clipping, Group I, series C, box C-354, Dublin File, LC).

At a time when black schools, churches, and fraternal organizations were regular targets of arsonists, NAACP activists were well-advised to take such threats seriously. Some NAACP members even chose to communicate furtively with regional and national NAACP officers. For example, a member of the Hawkinsville branch in November 1919 informed Harry H. Pace of the Atlanta branch of a lynching in Dodge County. The letter concluded, "Will not give my name for reasons, but if you want any information, write P. O. box #521, Hawkinsville and [I] will furnish names of several if you will not make them public . . . Do not even make known box number." (Unsigned letter to N.A.A. of C.P., Nov. 19, 1919, Group I, series C, box C-338, General Lynching File, Nov. 6–26, 1919.) Similarly, in 1921 C. P. Waddell of Douglas offered information about the lynching of three blacks in Coffee County, but he stressed that "I would have to be careful about my name being connected with this information." C. P. Waddell to James W. Johnson, April 27, 1921, Group I, series C, box C-353, General Georgia Lynching File, 1919–22, NAACP Papers, LC.

79. Charles Sherrod quoted in Clayborne Carson, *In Struggle: SNCC and the Black Awakening of the 1960s* (Cambridge: Harvard University Press, 1981), 57.

80. Two able discussions of the origins of the CIC are Ann Wells Ellis, "The Commission on Interracial Cooperation: Its Activities and Results," Ph.D. diss., Georgia State University, 1975; and Sosna, *In Search of the Silent South*, 40–41.

81. Matthews, "Studies in Race Relations in Georgia," 357; Ellis, "Commission on Interracial Cooperation," 7–11.

82. Thomas Jesse Jones to Robert R. Moton, March 12, 1919, quoted in Ellis, "Commission on Interracial Cooperation," 11; Dykeman and Stokely, *Seeds of Southern Change,* 63–68.

83. Dykeman and Stokely, *Seeds of Southern Change,* chapters 6–7; Ann Wells Ellis, " 'A Crusade against Wretched Attitudes': The Commission on Interracial Cooperation's Activities in Atlanta," *Atlanta Historical Review* 23 (Spring 1979): 21–24; and August Meier and Elliot Rudwick, *Black History and the Historical Profession, 1915–1980* (Urbana: University of Illinois Press, 1986), 17.

84. Dykeman and Stokely, *Seeds of Southern Change,* 112–13, 114–15, 157–59. The vitality of the CIC in Georgia is attested to by the large number of chapters that remained active throughout the 1920s. In 1928, for example, local CIC chapters were active in Albany, Americus, Athens, Atlanta, Augusta, Bainbridge, Brunswick, Columbus, Cordele, Ft. Valley, Greensboro, LaGrange, Macon, Madison, Milledgeville, Montezuma, Newnan, Savannah, Statesboro, Swainsboro, Thomasville, Tifton, Valdosta, and Waycross. See Annual Meeting, Georgia CIC, May 8–11, 1928, reel 45, file 41, CIC Papers, AUL.

85. See, for example, CIC *Annual Minutes,* Jan. 15, 1930, Microfilm reel 45, file 42.

86. "Statement of October 1 of the Work for 1922 of the Commission on Interracial

Cooperation," reel 4, CIC Papers, AUL; Commission on Interracial Cooperation, *Progress in Race Relations, 1924–1925* (Atlanta: n.d.), 5–13; *Progress in Race Relations: A Survey of the Work of the Commission on Interracial Cooperation for the Year 1926* (Atlanta: n.d.), 9–15.

87. Report of the Secretary of the Georgia Committee on Race Relations, *Progress in Race Relations in Georgia, 1922* (Atlanta: n.d.), 2–15; Commission on Interracial Cooperation, *Progress in Race Relations: A Survey of the Work of the Commission on Interracial Cooperation for the Year 1923–1924* (Atlanta: n.d.), 6–17.

88. Hugh M. Dorsey, *A Statement from Governor Hugh M. Dorsey as to the Negro in Georgia* (Atlanta: n.p., 1921); Ellis, "Commission on Interracial Cooperation," 65–66.

89. "Georgia's Indictment," *Survey,* May 7, 1921, 183, 190–91; "Governor Dorsey Stirs up Georgia," *Literary Digest,* June 4, 1921, 19; "The Negro in Georgia," *Southern Workman* 50 (June 1921): 243–45; "Georgia Sees Need of State Police," *The State Trooper* [1921]: 9–10, in Falls Church Branch Files, Group I, series G, box G-207, NAACP Papers, LC.

90. W. E. B. Du Bois expressed the skepticism of many black activists toward the CIC in a biting editorial in *Crisis.* See "Inter-racial Comity," *Crisis* 22 (May 1921): 6–7; and Dykeman and Stokely, *Seeds of Southern Change,* 131. For a more charitable response to the CIC, see "Out of the South," *Crisis* 24 (Aug. 1922): 179–80.

91. See Report of the Secretary, Dec. 8, 1931, 6, Group I, series A, box A-17; and correspondence in Group II, series L, box L-13, General Office File, Commission on Interracial Cooperation, both in NAACP Papers, LC; series I, reel 9, NAACP Correspondence File, CIC Papers, AUL. See also, Dykeman and Stokely, *Seeds of Southern Change,* 123–24.

92. T. J. Woofter to Roger N. Baldwin, June 30, 1922, Group II, series L, box L-13, General Office File, Commission on Interracial Cooperation, NAACP Papers, LC.

93. T. J. Woofter to Walter F. White, July 14, 1922, Group II, series L, box L-13, General Office File, Commission on Interracial Cooperation, NAACP Papers, LC. For two perspectives on the case and its significance, see Dykeman and Stokely, *Seeds of Southern Change,* 104–8; and Benjamin E. Mays, *Born to Rebel: An Autobiography,* 2d ed. (Athens: University of Georgia Press, 1987), 71–75.

94. Will Alexander, quoted in Dykeman and Stokely, *Seeds of Southern Change,* 107.

95. Howard Odum to Forester Washington, April 21, 1936, box 74, folder 86, CIC Papers, AUL.

96. For a richly detailed discussion of the attitudes of southern journalists, including several Georgians, toward lynching and race relations, see John T. Kneebone, *Southern Liberal Journalists and the Issue of Race, 1920–1944* (Chapel Hill: University of North Carolina Press, 1985), esp. 74–97.

97. *Atlanta Independent,* Jan. 12, 1922. For examples of mass meetings to denounce lynchings, see *Eastman Times-Journal,* Aug. 21, 28, Sept. 4, 1919; *Athens Banner,* Feb. 17–21, 1921; *Monroe Advertiser* (Forsyth), Aug. 1922; and *Millegeville Union Recorder,* Oct. 1, 1925.

98. Numerous church bodies endorsed the CIC and its antilynching campaign. Endorsements came from the Southern Baptist Convention in 1920, and in 1921 from the Church Assembly of the Georgia Presbyterian church, the Annual Missionary Conference of the Methodist Episcopal Church South, the Sewanee Provincial Synod, Episcopal church, the Episcopal Diocese of Georgia, and from the Georgia Federation of Women's Clubs. See "Endorsements, May 1918-October 1942," reel 3, file 38, CIC Papers, AUL.

99. Walter White, *Rope and Faggot: A Biography of Judge Lynch* (New York: Knopf, 1929), 49.

100. *AC*, Oct. 3, 1920; *Athens Banner*, Feb. 19, 1921; *MT*, Aug. 7, 1922.

101. *SMN*, July 6, 1922.

102. There are no existing statistics of prevented lynchings in Georgia. The statistics for lynchings and prevented lynchings for the entire South between 1914 and 1924 suggest that law officers throughout the region were increasingly less inclined to allow lynchings. See Monroe N. Work, "The Law vs. the Mob," Pamphlet no. 4, Commission on Church and Race Relations, 1930.

103. For examples of the successful movement of prisoners to safe jails, see *AC*, February 12, 1919, February 16, May 15, 1920, and May 23, 1922.

104. *SP*, June 20–24, 1923; *SMN*, June 20–25, 1923, Jan. 9, 1924; *AC*, June 21–23, 1923; *MT*, June 20–24, 1923; *The Nation*, July 4, 1923, 2. For other examples of the use of militia, see *Report of the Adjutant-General of Georgia, 1919*, 32–35; and *Report of the Adjutant-General of Georgia, 1920*, 12–15. Unfortunately, because of the lack of adjutants general reports for many years between 1915 and 1930, it is not possible to compile full statistics on the use of militia.

105. For examples of lynchings followed by indictments, see *AC*, Nov. 25, 30, Dec. 2, 1920; *Worth County Local* (Sylvester), Nov. 26, Dec. 3, 1920; *MT*, Aug. 3–Sept. 12, 1922; *SMN*, July 2–14, 1922; and *Griffin Daily News*, June 24–July 1, Aug. 7, 8, 1924. In 1922, the deputy sheriff of Wilkinson County sued fourteen mob members whom he charged with wounding him when he prevented them from seizing an alleged black criminal. The outcome of the case is unknown. See *New York Call*, July 24, 1922.

106. *AC*, May 20, Feb. 15, 1922; *Schley County News* (Ellaville), Feb. 17, 24, March 3, 1922; *Americus Times-Recorder*, Feb. 17, April 19, 1922; *CES*, Feb. 18, April 15, 1922; *MT*, Feb. 23, 1922; *AC*, Jan. 10, 1924.

107. "Georgia's Body Blow to Mob Murder," *Literary Digest*, Dec. 4, 1926, 10; *Coffee County Progress* (Douglas), Aug. 26–Dec. 2, 1926; *Douglas Enterprise*, Aug. 27–Dec. 3, 1926.

108. *Douglas Enterprise*, Nov. 19, 1926; *Augusta Herald*, Nov. 20, 1926.

109. *Cordele Dispatch*, March 1, 1916.

110. "Governor Dorsey Stirs up Georgia," *Literary Digest*, June 4, 1921, 19: Ellis, "Commission on Interracial Cooperation," 64–65.

111. The Klan used violence against opponents of lynching in several instances. For

example, in 1922, a group of Klansmen in Lyons County severely whipped the attorney who was prosecuting members of a mob that had murdered a black man. *AC*, Jan. 7, 1926.

Epilogue   The Passing of a Tradition

1. *AC*, Feb. 3, 1930; *MT*, Feb. 3–5, 1930; *SMN*, Feb. 3–5, 1930; Arthur Raper, *The Tragedy of Lynching* (Chapel Hill: University of North Carolina Press, 1933), 143–44; and correspondence in Group I, series C, box C-355, Ocilla File, NAACP Papers, LC.

2. Ann Wells Ellis, "The Commission on Interracial Cooperation, 1919–1944: Its Activities and Results," Ph.D. diss., Georgia State University, 1975, 69–72; Jacquelyn Dowd Hall, *Revolt against Chivalry: Jesse Daniel Ames and the Southern Women's Campaign against Lynching* (New York: Columbia University Press, 1979), 160–71; John T. Kneebone, *Southern Liberal Journalists and the Issue of Race, 1920–1944* (Chapel Hill: University of North Carolina Press, 1985), 77–80.

3. *Chattanooga News*, Nov. 12, 1931, quoted in Kneebone, *Southern Liberal Journalists and the Issue of Race*, 83.

4. *Lynchings and What They Mean: General Findings of the Southern Commission on the Study of Lynching* (Atlanta: Commission on Interracial Cooperation, 1931), 53.

5. Jesse Daniel Ames, *The Changing Character of Lynching* (Atlanta: Commission on Interracial Cooperation, 1942), 60. The founding of the ASWPL is described in detail in Hall, *Revolt against Chivalry,* chapter 6.

6. Hall, *Revolt against Chivalry,* 173–74, 178, 183, 186, 195, 188, 204–5, 215–16, 228–29.

7. Wilma Dykeman and James Stokely, *Seeds of Southern Change: The Life of Will Alexander* (Chicago: University of Chicago Press, 1962), 147; Lewis T. Nordyke, "Ladies and Lynchings," *Survey Graphic* 27 (Nov. 1939): 685. For broad discussions of ASWPL methods, see Hall, *Revolt against Chivalry,* chapter 8; and John Shelton Reed, "An Evaluation of an Anti-Lynching Organization," *Social Problems* 16 (Fall 1968): 172–81.

8. For evidence of the rebirth and activities of branches in Georgia and Virginia, see Albany Branch Files, Group I, series G, box G-43; Augusta Branch Files, Group I, series G, box G-45; Brunswick Branch Files, Group I, series G, box G-45; Petersburg Branch Files, Group I, series G, box G-209; and Portsmouth Branch Files, Group I, series G, box G-209, all in NAACP Papers, LC.

9. James R. McGovern, *Anatomy of a Lynching: The Killing of Claude Neal* (Baton Rouge: Louisiana State University Press, 1982), chapter 6; and Robert L. Zangrando, *The NAACP Crusade Against Lynching, 1909–1950* (Philadelphia: Temple University Press, 1980), esp. chapters 5 and 6.

10. Among the most helpful studies of the New Deal and southern agriculture are Pete Daniel, *Breaking the Land: The Transformation of Cotton, Tobacco, and Rice Cultures since 1880* (Urbana: University of Illinois Press, 1985), esp. chapter 11; Gilbert C. Fite, *Cotton*

Fields No More: Southern Agriculture, 1865–1980 (Lexington: University Press of Kentucky, 1984), esp. chapters 6–7; and Jack Temple Kirby, *Rural Worlds Lost: The American South, 1920–1960* (Baton Rouge: Louisiana State University Press, 1987), esp. chapter 2.

11. Kirby, *Rural Worlds Lost*, 60–63; Arthur W. Raper, *Preface to Peasantry: A Tale of Two Black Belt Counties* (Chapel Hill: University of North Carolina Press, 1936), passim; Theodore Saloutous, *The American Farmer and the New Deal* (Ames: University of Iowa Press, 1982), 100–104; and Raymond Wolters, *Negroes and the Great Depression: The Problem of Economic Recovery* (Westport, Conn.: Greenwood Press, 1970), part 1.

12. Wolters, *Negroes and the Great Depression*, 153.

13. Gavin Wright, *Old South, New South: Revolutions in the Southern Economy since the Civil War* (New York: Basic Books, 1986), 236.

14. Dominic J. Capeci, Jr, "The Lynching of Cleo Wright: Federal Protection of Constitutional Rights during World War II," *Journal of American History* 72 (March 1986): 886.

15. Robert K. Carr, *Federal Protection of Civil Rights: Quest for a Sword* (Ithaca: Cornell University Press, 1947), 70–77, 163–76; Capeci, "The Lynching of Cleo Wright," 882–87; McGovern, *Anatomy of a Lynching*, 144–47.

16. *Walton Tribune*, July 19, 1946.

17. *NYT*, July 27, 1946.

18. "Georgia: The Best Men Won't Talk," *Time*, Aug. 5, 1946, 25. See also, *Atlanta Daily World*, July 27, 1946; H. William Fitelson, "The Murders at Monroe," *New Republic*, Sept. 2, 1946, 258–60; and Walton County File, Group II, series A, box A-400, NAACP Papers, LC. In 1992, a witness to the lyching came forward; see *AC*, May 31, 1992, 1, 8–10.

19. *Atlanta Daily World*, July 28, Aug. 25, 1946; *Walton Tribune*, Aug. 2, 1946; *Baltimore Afro-American*, Aug. 3, 1946; *NYT*, July 27, Dec. 3, 20, 21, 1946, Jan. 5, 1947; "The Shape of Things," *The Nation*, Aug. 3, 1946, 220.

20. Ames, *The Changing Character of Lynching*, 16; David L. Lewis, "The Origins and Causes of the Civil Rights Movement" in *The Civil Rights Movement in America*, ed. Charles W. Eagles (Jackson: University Press of Mississippi, 1986), 12–13; August Meier and Elliot Rudwick, *Black Detroit and the Rise of the UAW* (New York: Oxford University Press, 1979), esp. chapter 4; Sitkoff, *A New Deal For Blacks*, chapter 7. For a discussion of lynching in Florida in 1945 that provoked similar local and national condemnation, see Jack E. Davis, " 'Whitewash' in Florida: The Lynching of Jesse James Payne and its Aftermath," *Florida Historical Quarterly* 68 (Jan. 1990): 277–98.

21. *Brunswick News*, July 12, 1947; "Flaws Revealed in Massacre Reports," NAACP Press Release; J. M. Atkinson to Walter White, July 15, 1947; and Walter White to Governor M. E. Thompson, July 17, 1947; all in Group II, series A, box A-393, Anguilla Prison Camp File, NAACP Papers, LC.

22. Gloster Current to LeRoy E. Carter, July 31, 1947, Group II, series A, box A-393, Anguilla Prison Camp File, NAACP Papers, LC.

23. *AC*, Oct. 9, 1947.

24. For a recent account that argues that "the decline of lynching throughout the nation was due in part to the states taking the role of the mob," see George C. Wright, *Racial Violence in Kentucky, 1865–1940: Lynchings, Mob Rule, and "Legal Lynchings"* (Baton Rouge: Louisiana State University Press, 1990), chapters 7–8.

25. Dan T. Carter, *Scottsboro: A Tragedy in the American South* (Baton Rouge: Louisiana University Press, 1969).

26. James L. Massey and Martha A. Myers, "Patterns of Repressive Social Control in Post-Reconstruction Georgia, 1882–1935," *Social Forces* 68 (Dec. 1989): 474–87.

27. Louis P. Masur, *Rites of Execution: Capital Punishment and the Transformation of American Culture, 1776–1865* (New York: Oxford University Press, 1989), 116. See also, Michael S. Hindus, *Prison and Plantation; Crime, Justice, and Authority in Massachusetts and South Carolina, 1767–1878* (Chapel Hill: University of North Carolina Press, 1980), 195–202; and Michael Ignatieff, *A Just Measure of Pain: The Penitentiary in the Industrial Revolution, 1750–1850* (New York: Pantheon, 1978), 21–24, 88–89.

28. *AN*, Oct. 21, 1903. For similar sentiments, see Edward L. Ayers, *Vengeance and Justice: Crime and Punishment in the Nineteenth Century South* (New York: Oxford University Press, 1984), 247–48.

29. Quoted in Richard Kluger, *Simple Justice: The History of* Brown v. Board of Education *and Black America's Struggle for Equality* (New York: Knopf, 1975), 1:191.

30. Among the valuable discussions of the maturing legal attack on segregation during the 1920s by the NAACP, Houston, and others, see Richard C. Cortner, *A Mob Intent on Death: The NAACP and the Arkansas Riot Cases* (Middletown, Conn.: Wesleyan University Press, 1988); Kluger, *Simple Justice*, part 1; Genna Rae McNeil, "Charles Hamilton Houston: Social Engineer for Civil Rights," in *Black Leaders of the Twentieth Century*, ed. John Hope Franklin and August Meier (Urbana: University of Illinois Press, 1982), 221–40; August Meier and Elliot Rudwick, "Attorneys Black and White: A Case Study of Race Relations within the NAACP," *Journal of American History* 41 (March 1976): 913–46; and Mark V. Tushnet, *The NAACP and the Strategy against Segregated Education, 1925–1950* (Chapel Hill: University of North Carolina Press, 1987), 21–48.

31. *NYT*, Dec. 31, 1953.

32. These cases continue to attract attention from historians and journalists. See Seth Cagin and Philip Dray, *We Are Not Afraid: The Story of Goodman, Schwerner, and Chaney and the Civil Rights Campaign in Mississippi* (New York: Macmillan, 1988); Howard Smead, *Blood Justice: The Lynching of Mack Charles Parker* (New York: Oxford University Press, 1986); and Stephen J. Whitfield, *A Death in the Delta: The Story of Emmet Till* (New York: Free Press, 1988).

33. For a comprehensive examination of the intertwined racial and political motives in Reconstruction violence, see George Rable, *But There Was No Peace: The Role of Violence in the Politics of Reconstruction* (Athens: University of Georgia Press, 1984).

34. The scale and effects of extralegal terrorist violence during the early years of the civil rights struggle are eloquently described in Taylor Branch, *Parting the Waters: America in the King Years, 1954–63* (New York: Simon and Schuster, 1988), passim.

35. Numan V. Bartley, "In Search of the New South: Southern Politics After Reconstruction," in *The Promise of American History*, ed. Stanley T. Kutler and Stanley N. Katz (Baltimore: Johns Hopkins University Press, 1982), 160.

36. For a discussion of the role of southern business elites during the racial and social tumult of the civil rights era, see James C. Cobb, *The Selling of the South: The Southern Crusade for Industrial Development, 1936–1980* (Baton Rouge: Louisiana State University Press, 1982), chapter 5; Elizabeth Jacoway and David R. Colburn, eds., *Southern Businessmen and Desegregation* (Baton Rouge: Louisiana State University Press, 1982); and Wright, *Old South, New South*, 264–69.

37. Jesse Kornbluth, "The Woman Who Beat the Klan," *New York Times Magazine*, Nov. 1, 1987, 26–39.

38. Leslie Fielder, "Afterthoughts on the Rosenbergs," in *An End to Innocence* (Boston: Beacon Press, 1955), 25–45.

Index

W. FITZHUGH BRUNDAGE is an assistant professor of history at Queen's University, Kingston, Ontario. He received his B.A. at the University of Chicago and Ph.D. at Harvard University.

Keeping the Faith: A. Philip Randolph, Milton P. Webster, and the
Brotherhood of Sleeping Car Porters, 1925–37
William H. Harris

Abolitionism: The Brazilian Antislavery Struggle
Joaquim Nabuco; translated and edited by Robert Conrad

Black Georgia in the Progressive Era, 1900–1920
John Dittmer

Medicine and Slavery: Health Care of Blacks in Antebellum Virginia
Todd L. Savitt

Alley Life in Washington: Family, Community, Religion, and
Folklife in the City, 1850–1970
James Borchert

Human Cargoes: The British Slave Trade to Spanish America, 1700–1739
Colin A. Palmer

Southern Black Leaders of the Reconstruction Era
Edited by Howard N. Rabinowitz

Black Leaders of the Twentieth Century
Edited by John Hope Franklin and August Meier

Slaves and Missionaries: The Disintegration of Jamaican
Slave Society, 1787–1834
Mary Turner

Father Divine and the Struggle for Racial Equality
Robert Weisbrot

Communists in Harlem during the Depression
Mark Naison

Down from Equality: Black Chicagoans and the Public Schools, 1920–41
Michael W. Homel

Race and Kinship in a Midwestern Town: The Black Experience in
Monroe, Michigan, 1900–1915
James E. DeVries

Coal, Class, and Color: Blacks in Southern West Virginia, 1915–32
Joe William Trotter, Jr.

No Crooked Death: Coatesville, Pennsylvania, and the
Lynching of Zachariah Walker
Dennis B. Downey and Raymond M. Hyser

Black Towns and Profit: Promotion and Development in the
Trans-Appalachian West, 1877–1915
Kenneth Marvin Hamilton

Slaves, Peasants, and Rebels: Reconsidering Brazilian Slavery
Stuart B. Schwartz

Africa in America: Slave Acculturation and Resistance in the
American South and the British Caribbean, 1736–1831
Michael Mullin

The Creation of Jazz: Music, Race, and Culture in Urban America
Burton W. Peretti

Kenneth and John B. Rayner and the Limits of Southern Dissent
Gregg Cantrell

Lynching in the New South: Georgia and Virginia, 1880–1930
W. Fitzhugh Brundage

REPRINT EDITIONS

King: A Biography
Second Edition
David Levering Lewis

The Death and Life of Malcolm X
Second Edition
Peter Goldman

Race Relations in the Urban South, 1865–1890
Howard N. Rabinowitz; foreword by C. Vann Woodward

Race Riot at East St. Louis, July 2, 1917
Elliott Rudwick

W. E. B. Du Bois: Voice of the Black Protest Movement
Elliott Rudwick

The Negro's Civil War: How American Negroes Felt and Acted
during the War for the Union
James M. McPherson

Lincoln and Black Freedom: A Study in Presidential Leadership
LaWanda Cox

Slavery and Freedom in the Age of the American Revolution
Edited by Ira Berlin and Ronald Hoffman

Diary of a Sit-In
Second Edition
Merrill Proudfoot; introduction by Michael S. Mayer

They Who Would Be Free: Blacks' Search for Freedom, 1830–61
Jane H. Pease and William H. Pease

The Reshaping of Plantation Society: The Natchez District, 1860–80
Michael Wayne

Rice and Slaves: Ethnicity and the Slave Trade in Colonial South Carolina
Daniel C. Littlefield

University of Illinois Press
1325 South Oak Street
Champaign, Illinois 61820-6903
www.press.uillinois.edu